MIGRATION AND MOBILITY
IN THE MODERN AGE

Migration *and* Mobility
in the
MODERN AGE

❖

*Refugees, Travelers, and Traffickers
in Europe and Eurasia*

Edited by
ANIKA WALKE, JAN MUSEKAMP, and NICOLE SVOBODNY

INDIANA UNIVERSITY PRESS
Bloomington & Indianapolis

This book is a publication of

Indiana University Press
Office of Scholarly Publishing
Herman B Wells Library 350
1320 East 10th Street
Bloomington, Indiana 47405 USA

iupress.indiana.edu

© 2017 by Indiana University Press

All rights reserved

No part of this book may be reproduced or utilized in any form or by any means, electronic or mechanical, including photocopying and recording, or by any information storage and retrieval system, without permission in writing from the publisher. The Association of American University Presses' Resolution on Permissions constitutes the only exception to this prohibition.

The paper used in this publication meets the minimum requirements of the American National Standard for Information Sciences—Permanence of Paper for Printed Library Materials, ANSI Z39.48–1992.

Manufactured in the United States of America

Cataloging information is available from the Library of Congress.

ISBN 978-0-253-02476-3 (cloth)
ISBN 978-0-253-02490-9 (pbk.)
ISBN 978-0-253-02508-1 (e-bk.)

1 2 3 4 5 22 21 20 19 18 17

Anika Walke would like to dedicate this book to the memory of Ingrid Oswald.

Jan Musekamp dedicates this book to the memory of Helga Schultz.

Nicole Svobodny would like to dedicate this book to the memory of Virgil Svobodny.

CONTENTS

Acknowledgments ix

Introduction. Anika Walke 1

Part I. Locomotions: Ways of Moving

1 Paris—St. Petersburg: Shrinking Spaces in the Nineteenth Century. Jan Musekamp 35

2 "A Main Station at One's Front Door": Bicycles, Automobiles, and Early Adopters' Dreams of Personal Mobility in Poland, 1885–1939. Nathaniel D. Wood 55

3 Walking with a Tolstoyan Dancer: Physical and Psychic Mobility in Vaslav Nijinsky's Diary. Nicole Svobodny 80

4 Russian Resorts and European Leisure: Railroad Vacations, "Native" Sites, and the Making of a Russian (Post)Colonial Identity in Manchuria, 1920s–1930s. Chia Yin Hsu 108

Part II. Migrations: People in Motion

5 Dynamic Bohemians: The *Russian Artistic Circle in Paris (Russkii Artisticheskii Kruzhok v Parizhe)*. Anna Winestein 139

6 Sex at the Border: Trafficking as a Migration Problem in Partitioned Poland. Keely Stauter-Halsted 164

7   Evacuation as Migration: The Soviet Experience during the Great Patriotic War. Lewis H. Siegelbaum and Leslie Page Moch   188

8   Far from Home: Soviet and Non-Soviet Railway Workers' Experiences during the Construction of the Baikal-Amur Mainline Railway (BAM), 1974–1984. Christopher J. Ward   209

Part III. Narrations: Literatures of Migration and Mobility

9   Traumatic Mobility: Motivating Collective Authorship in Siberian Narratives of Polish Exiles from the Inter-revolutionary Epoch (1832–1862). Elizabeth Blake   235

10 Technology, the City, and the Body: Bergelson and Shklovsky in Berlin. Harriet Murav   260

11 Andrzej Stasiuk and the Myth of the Literary *Gastarbajter*. George Gasyna   276

12 Journeys of Identity: From Soviet Jew to German Writer. Adrian Wanner   301

Contributors   321
Index   327

ACKNOWLEDGMENTS

THE EDITORS WOULD like to thank the authors for their excellent work and steadfast commitment to this publication. We are grateful for your generosity, encouragement, and patience as we completed the book.

The International and Area Studies program at Washington University in St. Louis, in particular the Migration, Identity, and State research collective and the Eurasian Studies concentration provided crucial financial support. We owe heartfelt thanks to Timothy Parsons, Kathy Daniel, and Toni Loomis of IAS who, each in their own way, made possible what seemed impossible at times.

We express our gratitude to the Volkswagen Foundation (Hannover, Germany), which supported this project from its very inception till the very end.

Two anonymous reviewers offered helpful critique in bringing the volume to completion, and we thank them for their time and effort.

Raina Polivka, Janice Frisch, and Daniel Miller at Indiana University Press were a pleasure to work with, and we are grateful for their unwavering support. Charlie Clark deserves a big thank-you for shepherding the book through the final production stage. We are indebted to our copy editor, Amy Schneider, for her excellent work.

MIGRATION AND MOBILITY
IN THE MODERN AGE

Introduction

Anika Walke

SINCE THE FALL of the Iron Curtain in the late 1980s, the movement of people is a central topic of concern, among the citizenry, among politicians, and among scholars in Central and Eastern Europe (CEE) and the former Soviet Union. The intense debate about people's ability to move and the transfer of goods and ideas and about ways to deal with unregulated migration reflects a complex web of movements and their assigned meanings. Recent scholarship on the movement of people in this region largely uses and expands on sociological and political science frameworks, focusing on pressing problems of integration and security, and striving to provide background for strategic policy making.[1] But there is a lack of historical depth to these accounts, as a scholar recently noted: "migration is presented as something new and unprecedented."[2] A look into the past reveals both continuous and changing patterns of migration and can thereby help alleviate the panic at supposedly threatening waves of migration that, in fact, only continue a regular pattern of human behavior.[3] Migration is at the center of cultural and social developments and representations and has helped forge global and local interaction and interrelations over long periods.[4] Imaginations of sedentism as the norm, either in the past or in the present, are seriously flawed; as Leslie Page Moch writes, "People were on the move, and where and why they traveled tells us a good bit about the past and about the pressures and processes that produced the world with which we are familiar."[5] What Moch powerfully demonstrates for Western Europe is true for the central and eastern parts of the continent and Russia as well. The historical and cultural analyses presented in this volume show that realities and imaginations of movement have determined the lives of individuals and communities in the region in complex and highly instructive ways for centuries.

This volume provides a fresh look at the landmass of and people originating from the area between the westernmost borders of present-day Poland; the former Hapsburg Lands, including the current Czech Republic, Slovakia, Austria, and Slovenia; the Balkan Peninsula; and the territory that once constituted the Russian Empire and, later, the Soviet Union. Studying the mobility and migrations of people, including train passengers, bicyclists, tourists, worker delegates, exiles and deportees, female sex workers, writers, dancers, artists, and others, chapters turn their gaze toward France, Germany, Switzerland, China, and North America as well. The focus of all studies, however, remains the impact of migration and mobility on the societies in CEE and Russia.

Many studies exist on the mutual relationship between population movements and social, political, economic, and cultural processes, yet this region is largely absent in these studies; only a few recent volumes are beginning to fill the gap.[6] The regional and temporal focus of this collection thus expands the reach of migration and mobility studies that, for a long time, have not taken full advantage of examining the rich historical and cultural dynamics of this region. Tracing the development of means of transportation and the relationships they facilitated, or artists' work as a result of human movement, helps us better understand modernization, state formation, and individual and popular imaginations of self and other in a part of the world that has repeatedly been at the center of globally significant developments. Analyzing how workers experienced encounters with representatives of the Western world, or how exiles described unfamiliar landscapes, one learns how identities and aspirations were defined in an area that has likely seen more border redrawings and state formations in the past two hundred years than any other region of the world.

Why distinguish *migration* and *mobility*, two concepts that are seemingly synonymous? Migration is typically understood to mean a move across a specified border or boundary from one location to another, usually with the aim of redefining one's main place of residence. Borders include those between urban and rural spaces, states, countries, or continents;

thus, some migrations are internal (i.e., the migrant remains within the confines of a state), while others have an international dimension. Within these movements, scholars distinguish between unidirectional and multidirectional, temporary and long-term, labor and educational, voluntary and forced, and settlement and return migrations—accounts of nearly all of these appear in the chapters of this book.

We have specified mobility as a subject of interest in its own right, because the ability to move is a precondition for people's travels and cultural change, and it determines their scale and extent.[7] When Eastern European states closed their borders and thus restricted their citizens' physical movement to a closely monitored and circumscribed space, they also limited social and cultural interactions and hoped to prevent the free flow of people as much as of ideas and goods.[8] Expanding the view to mobility, thus, integrates analyses of "large-scale movements of people, objects, capital and information . . . as well as the more local processes of daily transportation, movement through public space and the travel of material things within everyday life."[9] Technology transfer, for instance, often relies on migrants who carry ideas, knowledge, and skills, and it also stimulates the mobility of others.[10] In sum, mobility and migration are closely intertwined but deserve to be named and explored separately as well.

As we attempt to link the study of mobility with migration studies, the nexus between spatial and social mobility comes into view as the principal connection between the two fields. Two central fields of inquiry—the study of daily mobility patterns and respective transportation means on the one hand, and analyses of residential mobility as an effect of career and life path changes on the other—showcase the dynamics of movement through time and space that are at the core of migration scholarship. The crucial distinction is that such mobility studies focus on available infrastructure and technology and often on limited spaces such as cities or countries, whereas migration studies typically grapple with larger frameworks and their impact on people's movement across distinct borders.

Mobility is determined by power relations. Depending on social status and income, people rely on motorized transportation or resort to walking; the ability and time needed to cross long distances thus often reflects inequalities and social structures. Internal hierarchies, for instance along the lines of gender, impact who gets or has to go and why; access to resources, passports, and mobility devices as well as role conceptions determine migrant populations.[11] State or urban planning may exacerbate social inequalities by favoring automobility over other less expensive means of transportation (think of Los Angeles's expansive network of highways and simultaneous absence of sidewalks).[12] As a result, and contrary to popular belief, it is rarely the poorest or the most marginalized who move or migrate.[13] By exploring the distribution of resources including technology and capital, scholars can better ascertain who can move and who cannot. The people who stay behind are therefore as much part of the story as those who move, a relationality requiring close attention as we grapple with complex dynamics and outcomes of people's movement. Nonmobility or nonmigration—staying home even though means of transportation are available—thereby may come into view as a privilege as well.[14] Not leaving or not being forced to move, because one is able to make a living beyond poverty or is not uprooted by violence in the form of war, genocide, or persecution, promises a stable life unperturbed by insecurity and uncertainty. Last but not least, immobility can also indicate a "positively charged, critical response to the worst excesses of 'modern' life" and thus reveal concepts of human life that favor deceleration over acceleration and constant, mechanized movement.[15] It is here, in the ways in which individuals and societies perceive, produce, or prevent movement, or the reasons why some people move and others don't, where we see important clues for understanding historical development and change over time.

This volume's chapters on expanding transportation networks, labor migrations, artists' cross-border productions, and evacuations and deportations, among others, place the impact of material and technological development or state rationale, and cultural mobility as a result of encounters thus produced at the center of Central and Eastern Europe and Russia's history. These analyses build on the work of migration scholars who have advocated for the exploration of people's movement to make sense of the relation between individuals and social structures, macro and micro levels of organization, freedom and force, and objective and subjective factors of decision making. Drawing on multiple disciplinary apparatuses to track the role of migration for major social, historical, and political trends, contributors to this volume analyze how people identify systems of belonging and their position within them.[16] Focusing on relationships and networks, their role for the many ways in which people move, and the idea of being mobile, such studies allow us to question the pervasive focus on national boundaries in historical studies, a focus that is misleading because of the relatively recent establishment of these demarcations in the late eighteenth century.[17]

The movement of people in Central and Eastern Europe and Russia has a long history, as do the ways by which people and goods move: on foot; by horse and coach; with kibitkas and troikas; on trains or bicycles; by car, bus, and airplane—all these modes of transportation mark specific steps of industrial development and of the prospects of interaction and encounter. Whereas previous migrants often never came back home once they had left because it took too much time and money, present-day migrations follow airplane schedules and special ticket sales, in many ways resembling regular commutes rather than resettlement.[18] In contrast, the formation of nation-states in the nineteenth and early twentieth centuries and the limitations it placed on people's ability to move is a rich field for investigation, teaching us much about the recent need for would-be refugees and immigrants to cross the borders to the United States or Greece on foot or in fragile boats while celebrities and academics regularly fly back and forth between North America and Europe. Paying attention to the voluntary and involuntary nature of movement and responses to these differently motivated mobilities is instrumental for a comprehensive investigation of the nexus between movement and distinct historical phenomena in Central and Eastern Europe and Russia.

FACETS OF MIGRATION AND MOBILITY IN CENTRAL AND EASTERN EUROPE AND RUSSIA

Any effort to account for the history of people's movement and various forms of mobility in Central and Eastern Europe and Russia runs up against several questions: How do frequent border redrawings affect the study? Do they invalidate distinctions between international and internal migrations? Do all time periods similarly reflect a unique history that, nonetheless, tells us something about the movement of individuals and communities in general? Which categories and concepts do scholars of migration and mobility employ when looking at the historical and cultural developments in the region? The chapters give different answers to these questions, reflecting the multiplicity of experience and development in the region. Tracing mobile lives and cultures, the chapters often traverse national boundaries and show that, in hindsight, internal movements often turn into international migrations, and vice versa. Scholarship on movement in the past thus asks the reader to consider the fluid and flexible nature of borders, notions of force and agency, or analytical categories such as national identities that may shift from imperial Russian to Polish or oscillate between Russian, Jewish, Soviet, and German. These processes are framed by characteristic forms and instances of movement in the nineteenth and twentieth centuries that deserve to be explained briefly.

The middle of the nineteenth century is our point of departure. At that time, crucial connections were forged and decisive lines were drawn: railroad networks expanded significantly and reached farther east than ever before, and nationalist movements gained momentum that would lay the ground for the foundation of modern nation-states in the early twentieth century. Some of these technological advances that enabled economic and cultural connections but also ideologies and forms of identification structure the lives of residents of Europe and Russia until today, including their ability to move and interact with each other.

The Russian and Austro-Hungarian Empires ruled over the region explored in the following chapters, side by side with the emerging German Empire and the Ottoman Empire. In the eighteenth century, imperial borders were quite stable, locking different ethno-religious groups in political spaces that allowed for some diversity: Hungarians and Jews were subjects of the House of Hapsburg, while Serbs, Greeks, and Turks lived under Ottoman rule, and rather than following the national principle, "faith and dynasty were held to be natural, adequate, and appropriate foundations of political order"—that is, loyalty.[19] This would change dramatically in the nineteenth century, as the European empires not only pursued agendas of modernization and increased bureaucratization but also saw a rise of national and nationalist sentiment.

The Russian Empire, for instance, increased efforts to position the Russian nationality as the official, or superior, nationality and to keep down, or keep out, un-Russian or unwanted populations.[20] The number of Russian border guard troops, for instance, quadrupled between 1827 and 1898, from 3,200 to 12,100.[21] These attempts to secure the Russian imperial space restricted unwanted immigration as much as emigration, limiting, among others, the interaction of Jews residing in different empires. At the same time, the Russian Empire saw the rise of a movement that turned against imperial powers and challenged its frontiers. Polish subjects of the Russian Empire, stripped of national sovereignty since the late eighteenth century and residing within and outside the tsarist empire, demanded independence from Russian rule based on their national identity. Border enforcement and control over travel was thus also a way to curtail contact and communication between Russian-subject Poles and Poles abroad.[22]

Other European empires were confronted with similar movements; Serbian, Romanian, Bulgarian, and Montenegrin nationalists were initially repressed but eventually succeeded in securing statehood and independence from the Ottoman Empire. The Polish movement, however, was crushed; thousands of Poles went into exile abroad or were punished. Five thousand Polish nationalists left for France and ended up in Paris, the French capital that, in the tradition of the 1789 French Revolution, offered asylum to those fighting for self-determination and liberation.[23] Many others were sent into exile or banishment to Siberia, a form of retaliation that the Russian tsar expanded after a second uprising in 1863.[24] During the uprising, ethnic Poles of the western regions of the Russian Empire had claimed national self-determination, a challenge that tsarist authorities answered with the banishment of more than 36,000 people; between 18,000 and 24,000 of them were sent to Siberia.[25] The banishment constitutes one of the largest waves of forced migration at the time. Lesser known than the emigration of radical and liberal opponents of tsarist authority such as Vladimir Lenin, Alexander Herzen, or Mikhail Bakunin, the Polish deportees represent a deeply communal experience that, like many other collective displacements, till today underwrites Polish-Russian relations.[26]

The mass deportation of Polish nationalists and other groups within the Russian Empire is not only significant in the history of forced migration; it was also embedded in the tsarist government's agenda of internal expansion, settling and productivizing parts of the empire far away from the seat of power, St. Petersburg, and of frontier development. In many cases, the colonization of Russian lands involved force—many of those who settled were banished by the tsarist regime to remote areas; others came on their own volition but appropriated land and other resources that had provided the livelihood for native tribes and non-Russian peoples.[27]

A central instrument of settling and incorporating Siberia and the Far East, among others, was the Siberian Railroad. This newly available infrastructure transported people and goods, but it was also conceived as a globally relevant connector between Europe and Asia.[28] The emerging railroad system thus not only was necessary to transport thousands of people; it also signaled the advent of a new era in terms of linking different places and cultures on a stable and mass basis.

The Russian Empire, in this sense, was very much part of a larger trend that encompassed the European continent as a whole but also, for instance, the United States, in the 1800s. The railroad replaced stagecoaches and allowed travel across greater distances in less time and with more comfort. The new technology not only produced more mobility and facilitated the exchange of goods, ideas, and services; it also changed concepts of space, distance, and self in dramatic ways.[29] What is more, the nineteenth-century traveler in Europe was able to move between places previously separated geographically or by borders and compare different lifestyles, cultures, and landscapes. Much of the scholarship of the nineteenth-century transport revolution focuses on Western Europe and the United States; this book offers glimpses into distinct experiences and effects of similar developments farther east.[30]

States increased their efforts to guard their borders in response to the growing mobility options. By midcentury, nearly all European states mandated that international travelers carry a passport, though it appears that the requirement was not widely enforced. In fact, it was abolished in the 1860s in most European countries, with the exception of the Russian and Ottoman Empires.[31] Nevertheless, it is clear that governments were increasingly concerned with preventing criminals, vagrants, politically suspicious foreigners, and laborers in search of employment that might not be available from entering state territory. The bureaucratization of travel was not merely an inconvenience, however. Costs for travel documents limited the ability to travel to those who had the means to do so, and having to interact with state institutions to obtain the document ingrained the relevance of national belonging in people's consciousness.[32] A familiar pattern emerges here, in which, on the one hand, we see increasing options for mobility, and many states' efforts to control, regulate, and even prevent people's movement on the other.

Trains and steamboats made travel more comfortable and efficient, and they allowed for leisurely exploration as well as more permanent changes of residence. Alongside the political activists and revolutionaries of the Spring of Nations, other groups sought to rebuild their lives outside their home countries. Artists restricted by authoritarian regimes and thirsting for inspiration gathered in Paris, Vienna, and Berlin and served as mediators between Western and Eastern European cultures.[33] Hundreds of them nurtured each other through critique, shared housing, and meals. Others, who found themselves in deep poverty or excluded from basic rights and discriminated against, packed up and embarked on an often transatlantic journey.

Thousands of Jews, Poles, Lithuanians, Belorussians, Ukrainians, and Russians saw no prospects for themselves in their home countries, either because increased proletarianization had set them free or because, for Russian Jews, antisemitic legislation and pogroms made their already precarious life unbearable.[34] Complemented by a rapidly expanding industrial economy in the United States that demanded thousands of new laborers, a wave of migration unfolded that was new in size, scope, and extent. Between 1880 and 1920, about four million people moved from Eastern Europe to North America.[35]

Many women were among them and, for instance, became the mainstay of New York's textile production in the 1910s. For decades, the experience of female migrants to North America at the dawn of the twentieth century was understudied, a gap that reflected scholarly bias toward women as historical subjects and requires more attention.[36] The mass emigration during this period was fueled not only by economic necessity and violence, however. New means of communication and travel such as the telegraph and oceangoing steamships allowed employers to recruit laborers and migrants to travel. Families who stayed behind, in turn, received remittances: between 1902 and 1906 alone, families in Austro-Hungary and Russia received money orders worth $70 million.[37] Technological development, thus, was crucial for movement and immense social and cultural change. Knowledge about immigrant success (even if minimal), adventurousness, and desires to join others who had gone before or to reinvent oneself further fueled a massive stream of emigration.[38]

Ethnic discrimination, which was one of the central triggers for the transatlantic migration especially of Jews, but also of Slovaks subject to Hungarian rule, was a widely shared experience and regularly the root cause for mass displacement by the early twentieth century. The national movements of Serbia, Poland, Italy, and others had all followed the same logic: they claimed sovereignty over historically significant, national territories to be inhabited by their respective ethnic or (more accurate for the time) ethno-religious group. The sovereign state, once established, would represent the ethnically homogenous population—Serbs would govern Serbs, Greeks would rule over Greeks, and so on; "power now flowed upward from the people constituted as a nation to its chosen rulers, and peoples of all sizes began to demand representation of their collective interests and rulers of the same nationality."[39] These movements inscribed themselves into a discourse rooted in the French Revolution, where basic human rights were to be enforced by one's own people: "the whole question of human rights was . . . blended with the question of national emancipation."[40] In other words, national self-determination, as aspired to by subjects of the empires, disavowed the possibility of multiethnic self-governance. Over the course of the nineteenth century, European diplomacy firmly established this principle, condoning or facilitating the compulsory resettlement of populations—that is, national minorities facing majorities that gained statehood.[41] Most notably, the formation of Serbian, Greek, Bulgarian, and Montenegrin states included the resettlement of national minority groups, and major parts of the Muslim populations were driven off the Balkan Peninsula during the nineteenth century. By the end of the Balkan Wars of 1912–1913, the final blow to the Ottoman Empire, only 38 percent of the population residing in the Ottoman-ruled Balkans were still in their homes; 62 percent had been forced to migrate or killed. Over four hundred thousand Muslims from the newly established Balkan states came to Anatolia.[42]

World War I showed a continuation of expulsions and forced resettlement based on the same logic of ethnic homogenization, alongside mass refugee movements. In the western parts of the Russian Empire, imperial subjects of Polish, German, Latvian, Lithuanian, Ukrainian, and Jewish nationality were told to move further inland; the tsarist government mistrusted these populations as potential fraternizers with German and Austrian adversaries. In addition, thousands of people in the war zone fled warfare and occupation; overall, up to seven million people were displaced within the Russian Empire. The state's failure to end the war and supply refugees and resident populations with enough food and the ensuing dissatisfaction was one of the major factors for the downfall of the regime by way of the revolutionary upheaval in 1917.[43] Other parts of Europe saw thousands of refugees too; more than a million Belgians and 1.53 million French fled the German invasion, five hundred thousand Serbs exited after the defeat by Austrian forces, more than seventy thousand Jews from Bukovina and Galicia arrived in Vienna, and so forth.[44]

The fate of Armenians under Ottoman rule like no other exemplifies the radicalization of nationalist movements that foregrounded ethnic belonging as a measure of loyalty and took on eliminationist positions.[45] One million Armenian Christians were killed, and about half a million fled across the Russian border or into Western Europe because they were perceived to undermine the foundation of the Ottoman state and its war effort.[46] Overall, World War I uprooted about 9.5 million people.[47] What is more, similarly to the way that passports reminded people of belonging to a particular national identity, mass displacement and ethnic cleansing "convinced many refugees that they were fundamentally unlike the group that had caused them to flee."[48] In a context where states came to be imagined as nation-states, both administrative practices and violence were driven by and reinforced the idea that national identity determines one's privileges and rights.

At the end of the war, the European Great Powers further implemented the nationality principle. The breakup of the German, Austro-Hungarian, and Ottoman Empires resulted in the establishment of a new European order consisting of nation-states that, for the most part, exists today. The system of Minority Treaties established in the aftermath of the 1919 Paris Peace Treaty sought to reconcile nationality-based citizenship principles with minorities' rights claims, though it failed in major parts. Population exchanges, such as those between Turkey and Greece, or Bulgaria and Greece, established a problematic precedent for future violent demographic engineering including during the Nazi regime.

The impact of World War I on human movement, however, goes far beyond the massive displacement of groups of people. The European train system, for instance, which originated in pre-1848 national railroad networks facilitating travel and trade, was extended according to economic and strategic needs of national militaries.[49] The passport became ubiquitous across the globe. During World War I even governments that had so far been lenient in enforcing border controls began to issue and demand passports and visas for and from people on the move.[50] Identity documents curtailed the departure of professionals or young men of draft age trying to evade military service and prevented the entry of foreign spies and politically undesired people.[51] Travel and movement were increasingly bureaucratized and regulated and became further determined by state or military rationale.

The Russian Empire, similarly shattered during World War I, experienced these developments in an exacerbated way. The revolution of 1917 set in motion an immense push to modernization on the one hand and state intervention in mobility on the other. The drive to industrialization in the 1920s and 1930s triggered an unprecedented migration from villages to cities, and from everywhere to large construction sites, which by far exceeded the earlier rural-to-urban moves directed at St. Petersburg or Moscow and a few other regional centers (or, for that matter, in other countries). In 1897, some 9.4 million people had left their home provinces, but in the new Soviet Union, enthusiasm or necessity brought at least 11.9 million people to urban centers between 1928 and 1932 alone.[52] For example, more than two hundred thousand people arrived at Magnitogorsk to build both a new metal production facility and a town housing employees and those who provided infrastructure for them.[53] The pressure on cities and newly industrializing areas was so big that the government reintroduced the internal passport, resembling an authoritarian instrument of population control of tsarist times. The document secured housing, food, and social services but, perhaps more importantly, closely tracked and limited migrations within the Soviet Union—a bureaucratic mechanism that would produce especially difficult situations in times of crisis such as during World War II.[54] Alongside these labor-driven migrations based on deliberation and recruitment, forced migrations in the form of deportations to labor camps and special settlements, as well as deportations of so-called suspicious nationalities (Germans, Poles, Koreans) from the borderlands uprooted thousands more—Soviet society was on the move.[55] The Moscow Metro, the subway that still runs and expands today, marked the young state's commitment to building public infrastructure. While eventually facilitating the mobility of residents, the construction, beginning in 1935, relied on internal labor migration, like so many other infrastructure projects in the USSR.[56]

The Russian Revolution and the ensuing civil war drove thousands of people who either disagreed with the state ideology or were identified as enemies of the new order, out of the country or away from the center. Some sought to remain in the country, yet under the new rulers' radar, and moved to the Far East, attempting to re-create a Russian civilization according to their own values.[57] This politically motivated migration also brought thousands of professionals, intellectuals, and artists to Paris and Berlin, where they connected with Russian and Jewish emigrants from the Pale of Settlement of the late tsarist period.[58] Existing networks of communication and support facilitated these moves but, as earlier, also enabled a substantial contingent of the émigrés to maintain close ties to their homeland and even support those at home.

In Paris and Berlin they joined the many who had been stranded without a home or even citizenship as a result of World War I and the new geopolitical architecture. National minorities, and primarily Jews who saw no future in countries such as Poland, Romania, and Hungary, struggled to make ends meet and claim basic human rights—yet in the aftermath of a devastating war and a context of national and antisemitic radicalization, one country after another declined to provide asylum to the thousands in search of shelter and legal security. Statelessness, the loss of citizenship and related access to basic human rights, excluded more and more individuals from the established politico-legal system and made them vulnerable to street and state violence.[59] The League of Nations' Commissariat for Refugees, the predecessor of the United Nations High Commissioner for Refugees (UNHCR), attempted to create an internationally funded and coordinated network of support yet eventually failed to challenge what had been established since the nineteenth century: a system of governance in which nation-states represent and protect national populations.[60]

The crisis intensified with the Nazi regime, when several hundred thousand German Jews were stripped of their citizenship and systematically humiliated and abused. When the Polish government denaturalized Polish Jews living abroad in March 1938, statelessness threatened the existence of thousands more. The European refugee crisis of the 1930s, when no country in the world was willing to admit Jewish refugees fleeing from the Nazi regime, encapsulates one of the central contradictions of modern European history: whereas modernization had offered previously unseen opportunities for connection, thinking in national categories—or, as in the case of Nazi Germany, defining national belonging in racial terms—created new separations, separations that in turn relied on new technologies of identification. When the exiled Stefan Zweig, perhaps somewhat nostalgically, remembered that "before 1914 I traveled from Europe to India and to America without passport and without ever having seen one," he juxtaposed this with his more recent experiences of having to apply for passports and visas and permits of all kinds that made him recognize "how much human dignity has been lost in this century which, in our youth, we had credulously dreamed of as one of freedom, as of the federation of the world."[61]

This vision came to a violent end when German administrators and troops executed a genocide by drawing on extremely modern technologies of registration, transportation, and extermination. The stateless Jews of the 1920s and 1930s, including the Austrian-born Jew Stefan Zweig, personify the destructive effects of mobilization, technologization, and categorization of modern societies: "On the day I lost my passport I discovered, at the age of fifty-eight, that losing one's native land implies more than parting with a circumscribed soil."[62] Stefan Zweig took his own life in exile in Brazil in 1942.

Zweig and many others despaired at the brutal assault on humanity unleashed by the Nazi regime, in the form of devastating warfare and systematic violation and extermination of distinct groups. After annexing and occupying several regions in the East and most of Western Europe between 1938 and 1940, German troops extended their reach into the East and beyond Poland by attacking Yugoslavia and the Soviet Union, in the spring and summer of 1941 respectively. The occupations relied on eliminationist terror against local leadership and civilians, exploitation of local resources, and the destruction of whole populations and their heritage. Thousands tried to flee, yet spaces of rescue were scarce: even the Poles of Jewish origin, who managed to escape the 1939 invasion and found shelter in Soviet territories, sooner or later were caught under German threat again. The Soviet government's attempt to evacuate workers and crucial production facilities thus stands out. While conceived primarily as a protection of industrial capacities, the efforts saved thousands of people's lives and ought to be written into the history of World War II and of state-induced migration.[63]

In Eastern Europe, German war planners and administrators pursued an agenda of exploitation and extermination, using the occupation of the continent to extract natural and production resources where possible and to force local populations to work for the German war economy. They thereby drew on previous instances of foreign workers' contribution, on their own volition and against their will. Since the late 1800s, Prussian Poles had come to help collect the harvest in eastern German territories; in the first two decades of the twentieth century, miners from present-day Poland arrived for work in the Ruhr region and Saxony. During World War I, the German occupation regime in Poland conscripted Poles and Polish prisoners of war into labor duty. Whereas Polish workers who came on their own were paid less than German workers and experienced other restrictions, wartime forced labor was accompanied by violent abuse and not remunerated.[64] The Nazi regime further radicalized this practice and deported thousands from German-occupied Polish territories, but also Soviet, Yugoslavian, French, Dutch, and Belgian territories, for forced labor in German enterprises, farms, private households, and public works. At the height of this practice in summer 1944, about six million foreign civilians were working for the German economy.[65] The *guest worker* (*Gastarbeiter*) of previous times was now reconfigured as a *forced laborer*, a continuity that presumably contributed to widespread acceptance of using foreign labor among the German population. The continuity was a broken one, however, because the foreign workers were brought against their will and, if they did not comply, were harshly punished or even killed.

Violence, force, and deportation were the defining features of the Nazi regime's attempts to reorder Europe according to its racist vision. Drawing on a notion similar to that of ethno-territorialists, the German occupation authorities began to resettle national groups as soon as possible; to make room for ethnic Germans from the Baltic republics that were to be brought "home into the Reich"—that is, resettled into territories newly under German rule—up to one million Poles and Jews were expelled from the so-called Warthegau and collected in the territory of the General Government. This forced migration and concentration cost thousands of people their lives, but it was also the first step toward the ghettoization of Jews and, eventually, their extermination.[66] These murderous policies were part and parcel of the Nazi genocide and, like previous wars and conflicts that had used and radically reframed ethnic difference, facilitated new forms of violence. Once Allied Forces—Soviet, US, or British—had liberated European countries from the German occupation, ethnic Germans were expelled, with many of them suffering injury or death.[67] Questions of individual responsibility for participation in the violent occupation regime, which had existed in many cases, retreated into the background and made room for imaginations of peace that relied on the ethnic homogenization of populations within national boundaries. The 1945 Potsdam Conference and other peace conferences in 1946 and 1947 followed this dictum and legalized the population transfers of Germans from Czechoslovakia, Poland, Hungary, and Romania to the occupied German zones, but also of Poles from the Soviet Union, Ukrainians from Poland, and Hungarians out of Czechoslovakia.[68]

The twenty-one million people who were displaced at the end of World War II—liberated prisoners of war, concentration camp inmates or forced laborers, and resettled populations, among others—are the largest group of forcibly uprooted people in Europe at any one given time. Once more, the nexus between ethnic (national) identity, territory, and rights, inscribed as a central tenet into international law with the Paris Peace Treaty of 1919, was the grounds for mass displacement and ensuing hardship. This unsettlement, alongside the Soviet wartime practice of deporting ethnic communities such as the Crimean Tatars or Chechens for allegedly supporting the German regime into remote areas, has lasting impacts on Eastern European and former Soviet societies. Personal distrust toward state agencies but also people of other identity, as much as individual and collective economic instability caused by disruptions of educational and professional careers, have regularly undermined international relations between emerging states and relationships within individual societies.[69] The breakup of the Socialist Federal Republic of Yugoslavia in the mid- to late 1990s displaced more than two million people and marked another instance in which the resettlement of populations according to their ethnic identity shook societies to the core.

While millions of displaced people attempted to return or find new homes after World War II—for some, especially Jews, it took well into the early 1950s to do so—Eastern European countries began to rebuild their countries after a devastating war. In many areas, especially formerly German-occupied Soviet territories, the public infrastructure was severely damaged, and functioning transportation systems took years to establish. Private car ownership was, in most countries, a privilege of a select few, which made the state's responsibility for buses, trams, and trains even more meaningful; routes and schedules determined the ways in which people planned their work day, their family life, and their vacations.[70] Yet major infrastructure projects such as the Soviet Baikal-Amur Mainline (BAM), a 2,697-mile-long railroad line through eastern Siberia and the Russian Far East, were not only designed to facilitate mobility; they were also thought to showcase state power and capability. In addition, they triggered new labor-oriented migrations within select countries. For many BAM workers, recruited from all over the Soviet Union, the Far East became a new home. They personify a modern iteration of settler migrants who came to largely undeveloped land, built houses and other infrastructure, and stayed on.[71]

Labor mobility across borders, however, was limited. Western European countries including France and Germany actively recruited workers from less economically successful countries, attracting millions of Turkish, Greek, and Portuguese workers.[72] Yugoslavs were the only contingent from Central and Eastern Europe—the Iron Curtain restricted emigration, even if temporary, from other socialist countries. Especially for those discontent with the socialist system, their national borders were barriers not only to physical mobility but also to self-aspirations.[73] Borders, however, are never completely sealed, especially not when they consist of natural elements: citizens of Hungary and other states along the Danube River benefited from the state government's inability to control the waters at all times and accessed Western goods or crossed into neighboring countries.[74]

The breakup of the socialist bloc in the late 1980s enabled new mobility and migrations and facilitated encounters between people that had been impossible for decades. The globalizing effects of railroad systems, so defining for the nineteenth century, have accelerated through aviation and computer technology, but personal experiences of enthusiasm and estrangement are experiences that migrants of the past share with those of the present. Many Poles regularly commute between Ireland, Sweden, Great Britain, Germany, and Poland. Coming to Germany, they have to contend with a history of fraught connections that include Polish guest workers as well as forced laborers and other victims of World War II.[75] Perhaps the transnational character of much of the Polish-German migration is partly a result of continued resentment.[76] In any case, facilitated by recent advancements in travel and communication technologies, the emerging networks are being woven ever more densely, allowing migrants to cross national borders and large distances regularly; to stay in touch with families and communities at home; and to transport goods, dreams, and lifestyles along the way.[77]

Recent studies of the nexus between globalization—the increased connections and dependencies between local and global economic structures—and migration that focus on the role of regional integration and large cities with their concentration of capital and a cumulative need of service and labor complement the studies of such systems, networks, and transnational spaces.[78] They show that every movement is impacted by small-scale, local, and current factors as well as larger ones—regional, global, and often long-term trends—and vice versa.[79]

The same is true for the way in which migrants perceive their own movement, development, and identity—a process that is especially momentous for recent immigrants from the former Soviet Union to Germany. Like many of the other recent intra-European movements, theirs crosses a border that once marked significant political and geopolitical divisions.[80] The division is layered, as one of the major groups among recent Russian-German immigrants is Jewish, and their resettlement symbolizes a rapprochement that goes far beyond a simple border crossing. The history of the Nazi genocide, the occupation of Soviet territories, the murder of 2.7 million Soviet Jews, and the death of 27 million Soviet citizens during World War II pose a challenging backdrop for the intercultural encounter: the ancestors of many recent immigrants or their friends were killed by Germans or their collaborators, so that resentment can have a powerful impact on individual interpretations and aspirations.[81] Immigrants and new hosts negotiate these historical (dis)connections in various ways and reveal that ideas of migration and migrants are often more impactful in determining how people see each other and structure their behavior than concrete, present actions or experiences.

Notions of identity and belonging are at the center of such (mis)recognition and have encouraged a vibrant field of scholarship on how individuals, groups, societies, and states incorporate diversity. In many instances, these studies are about the failure to deal productively with difference and about conflicts between groups that follow different customs, speak different languages, or pursue different value systems, often aiming to suggest policies on how to alleviate them. This book, however, develops a different take on the potential of human movement to challenge notions of identity and belonging. We foreground a view into the past that reveals how those who move themselves make sense of their experience, thereby often undermining state rationales or opening up possibilities of redefining well-established patterns of social organization and personal lives.

A cursory view on recent forms of movement and mobility in the region of interest reveals that this collection is timely and offers both the materials and tools to evaluate the role of individuals and institutions in ongoing processes of transfer, exchange, and relocation. Thousands of refugees left Ukraine in early 2014 when they were displaced by open military conflict or feared worsening interethnic relationships. Some chose to move to Russian or Ukrainian territory as a reflection of their political loyalty; they received shelter and were greeted with an outpouring of support that reflected ethnic bias, in favor of either supporters of Russian policy or Ukrainian co-nationals.[82] Simultaneously, Russian immigration officials have steadily intensified their efforts to curtail immigration by citizens of former Soviet republics—Tajikistan, Uzbekistan, Azerbaijan—who came to work and earn a living in areas that were the economic and political centers of a federation to which they or their ancestors once belonged.[83]

The European Union (EU), in turn, since the mid-1990s has allocated substantial resources, including money, technology, and training, to a number of Central, Eastern, and Southern European countries to secure the external borders of the Schengen Area.[84] The borders mark the EU's limits in the region and have been loaded with meaning beyond national security.[85] The EU supports countries like Ukraine in their efforts to improve border enforcement via the so-called European Neighborhood Policy, a program that provides funds to help regulate migration that may be directed at EU member states.[86] These eastern borders and border states are important barriers for both non-EU citizens from the former Soviet Union and citizens of other countries who cross these territories on their way to Western and Central Europe and are regularly perceived as threats to national and economic security.

As this book goes to press, European countries are facing an influx of refugees that exceeds the Balkan crisis of the 1990s, when hundreds of thousands of refugees escaped the breakup of Yugoslavia. In 2015 alone, more than one million women, men, and children fled Syria, Afghanistan, and other countries in the Middle and Near East and North Africa in search for shelter from war and persecution.[87] As borders in the refugees' home regions are contested and redrawn, they resort to precarious modes of transportation to save their lives. State rationales and public opinion in the countries of hoped-for asylum conflict with the appeals of a humanitarian crisis, oscillating between compassion and national security concerns as determinants of appropriate responses. The emerging tensions are yet another example of the contradictory nature of people's movement and its perception by those who are privileged to stay or move on their own volition.

For tourists and others who have EU citizenship or appropriate visas, airlines offer cheap and quick connections between cities whose residents were once divided by the so-called Iron Curtain; weekend trips from Düsseldorf to Cracow or Riga are as easy as a bus ride from Prague to Karlovy Vary. Newly sovereign countries, such as Croatia and Estonia, steadily increase their trade networks, in this case tripling the two countries' trade volume between 2009 and 2012, an exchange that is accompanied by business professionals', students', and tourists' travel.[88]

In sum, people, ideas, and goods are moved, boundaries reshaped, and new connections forged. Some of these transfers and transitions are new, but many of them follow in the footsteps of earlier migrations or emulate familiar processes of movement and exchange that are now simply redirected or draw on new carriers, literally and figuratively. Movement and mobility are thus constant factors of human development: the movement of people, things, or ideas through space facilitate, as well as result from, social, political, economic, or cultural change.

LOCOMOTIONS, MIGRATIONS, NARRATIONS

While historical in scope, the book is organized in three thematic sections. The various models for understanding the history of human movement—more precisely, how political, economic, and social change inform the movement of people, ideas, or things and their representation or vice versa—are grouped with a view on *Locomotions, Migrations,* and *Narrations*. Within these three parts, authors attend to recurring problems of migration and mobility studies, seeking to synthesize the tools, potential, and findings of studies based on both historical and present movements.

Chapters in Part I, "Locomotions: Ways of Moving," explore how technological development and technology transfer conjoined with visions of the future, of how traversing distance and indefinite movement have shaped societies and individual lives. In chapter 1, Jan Musekamp demonstrates that nineteenth-century transportation innovations, such as regular stagecoach connections, steamships, and the railroad, created new networks linking Eastern and Western Europe. These connections motivated more and more European citizens to think of themselves as agents of cultural and technological progress and produced an early form of globalization on a continental scale.

In the 1930s, Polish enthusiasts pitted bicycles and cars against each other, hoping to make good on these devices' promise to enable personal and national achievement. In chapter 2, Nathaniel Wood studies this little-known aspect of Polish history and reminds us that the automobile was not always the vehicle of choice to get around. The chapter is a meditation on the common yet often unacknowledged experience of falling behind and thus disrupts popular imaginations of continuous acceleration and movement.

A dancer's diary is at the center of chapter 3, by Nicole Svobodny, showcasing a trajectory between Vaslav Nijinsky's bodily movements; his deliberations on life, death, and the environment; and his revolutionary performances in the late 1910s. Experiences of displacement, literal and figurative, thereby emerge as the foundations of his movements, and Svobodny demonstrates the profound role of experimentation for individuals to make sense of modern life. The unsettlement evidenced here gives a rare glimpse into the reciprocity of psychic and physical mobility demanded from so many who travel, migrate, or flee and are asked to refashion themselves, and suggests that studies of movement ought to be at the center of cultural and intellectual history.

The departure of some profoundly affects communities, while imaginations of movement, and the movement to imagined places, have similar impact, as Stephen Greenblatt argues: "Cultures of mobility provoke both intense pleasure and intense anxiety."[89] In chapter 4, Chia Yin Hsu's work on railroad resorts in colonial Manchuria brings this home in a most unsettling way: refugees from the Russian Revolution transplanted ideas of French vacation destinations to reshape landscapes in the Far East of Russia in order to be able to feel "properly European." Transportation infrastructure, the Chinese Eastern Railway, here produces a cultural space that fuels the creation of an imagined community in the decade after the Russian Revolution.

Part II, "Migrations: People in Motion," takes a close look at how people who leave their home, forcibly or not, connect to others based on their experience and make sense of it. Authors scrutinize concepts of the self and images of migrants shared by onlookers and scholars as much as facilitators of human movement and reveal unexpected forms of agency. In chapter 5, Anna Winestein powerfully shows that female artists were at the center of a turn-of-the-century Russian émigré artist circle in Paris that enabled a transnational network of support for painters on either side of the continent. Her chapter proves that cross-border mobility of artists and creative minds is crucial for the exchange of ideas and resources and is by no means distinct for the age of high-speed travel.

At the dawn of the twentieth century, Polish women left home and migrated, often across the Atlantic Ocean, to gain financial and emotional independence from their homes. This migration is an often misperceived step, as it involved sex work and thus challenged traditional role models for reputable women in multiple ways, as Keely Stauter-Halsted shows. Chapter 6 teases out the fine differences between how women used emigration to claim independent lives on the one hand, and relatives who could see this departure only as the work of force on the other. Stauter-Halsted reveals how we can understand myths of oppression—here, that of the trafficked woman—and uncover agency within a context that involves exploitation, alienation, and marginalization.

In chapter 7, Lewis Siegelbaum and Leslie Page Moch trace the complex bureaucratic and geographical journeys of Soviet citizens who fled the German occupation during World War II. In many ways, the systematic and organized removal of civilians from the war zone failed and was marred by political and economic priorities, and the story Moch and Siegelbaum relate represents an important reminder that individual people's agency is always circumscribed by personal needs, state agendas, cultural values, and social dynamics. Understanding evacuation as a form of migration, the authors explicate the relationship between regimes and repertoires of migration—the institutional frameworks and infrastructure regulating human movement on the one hand, and migrants' practices and networks on the other.

Soviet railway workers, who were sent to meet workers in brotherly nations to promote the building of the Baikal-Amur Mainline (BAM), a major railroad line in the USSR, redefined the purpose of their trips to enjoy intercultural encounters and higher standards of living. Reminding us of an important attempt to increase mobility in the Soviet Union, Christopher Ward suggests in chapter 8 a number of ways in which Soviet citizens undermined state-sponsored campaigns and visions once they were liberated from travel restrictions and thus disassembles a Soviet display project from an unexpected viewpoint.

Part III, "Narrations: Literatures of Migration and Mobility," presents studies of how the exchange and representation of ideas of otherness facilitates the production of localized and distinct identities. In particular, the chapters explore writers' attempts to grapple with political and personal pressures on life in the context of exile and displacement that, among others, required adaptation to new languages and cultural norms. In chapter 9, Elizabeth Blake discusses how the nineteenth-century writings of exiled Poles have played a crucial role for portrayals of Russian imperial rule that reached far beyond Polish society. Reading against the grain accounts of Poles punished by the Russian tsar, Blake shows how collective accounts of forced migration and repression draw on established cultural traditions and work to claim the identity that is slated for destruction.[90] These writings, coauthored by those in exile and their free compatriots, are instructive for conceptualizing scholarship based on memoirs of repression. Polish accounts of Russian banishment emerge as well-traveled and hybrid texts rather than single-authored, local eyewitness accounts, as which they have been used previously, and give a powerful example for how physical and cultural mobility coincide.

Literary innovation that is informed by migration and encounters with new technologies signifies cultural mobility par excellence. In chapter 10, on the Yiddish writer David Bergelson and the Russian and Soviet writer and literary critic Viktor Shklovsky, Harriet Murav dissects a trajectory—the exchange of ideas and changing worldviews as a result of movement—that is so common for modern lives that one often forgets about it. New technologies of the early twentieth century redefined bodily capacities and movements in light of mass-based production and mass violence, a trend reflected in the works of two authors who found themselves in 1920s Berlin after escaping the former Russian Empire. Bergelson and Shklovsky caution their readers against the ability of mechanized movement—cars, clocks, machines—to overpower human agency and thus offer a stark reminder for the ambiguous nature of modernization.

In chapter 11, George Gasyna analyzes a writer's self-alienating ruminations on the hybridity of European cultures to develop a critical analysis of Polish emigration to the West. Despite recent rapprochement between Poland and Germany, the writer Andrzej Stasiuk's rejection of inclusion and hospitality, based on the strained historical relationship between the two countries, illustrates that the memory of past violence fortifies boundaries between people even though material barriers have been removed.

In chapter 12, Adrian Wanner taps the writings of several recent immigrants from the former Soviet Union to Germany and decodes the ways in which different practices of national or ethnic identification among authors reflect distinct personal and generational experiences. His analysis of an emerging literary tradition sits at the intersection of new opportunities for mobility, physical and cultural, and recent migratory trends in post-1989 Europe that are very much rooted in socialist times and imaginations. Generational differences among migrants mark shifts in the ways in which people negotiate questions of power and identity that emerge in the process of migration.

The collection's long and multifaceted view on migration and mobility in Central and Eastern Europe and Russia removes the region from its outsider status in the field of mobility and migration studies, and it shows the potential of the interdisciplinary apparatus of the field for a broad and comprehensive understanding of the history and culture of the region. Applying recent advances in understanding issues of movement, integration, and representation to gaze backward in time, the book shows that regionalization and connectivity—tropes so central for analyses of contemporary migrations—were already visible in in the nineteenth and early twentieth centuries and are thus part of what one may call a history of the present. While scholars of art and literature will benefit from placing transnational individual and collective artistic production in larger contexts, historians can appreciate how people perceived social and economic transformation by studying representations of transportation and movement in literature and art. This volume sketches out a path to establish scholarly connections that have existed in real life for centuries.

Further studies may use the case studies presented here as starting, middle, or end points of a *longue durée*, as particular moments of a longer trajectory of the movement of people and ideas, or complement them with comparative studies within and across multiple disciplines including history, literature, and art history. Assuming multiple points of vision, the book is thus an invitation to proceed along various analytical, temporal, and spatial routes to improve our understanding of migration, mobility, and Central and Eastern Europe and Russia.

NOTES

1. Recent examples include Frank Laczko, ed., *New Challenges for Migration Policy in Central and Eastern Europe* (Geneva: T.M.C. Asser Press, 2002); Oxana Shevel, *Migration, Refugee Policy, and State Building in Postcommunist Europe* (Cambridge: Cambridge University Press, 2011); and Umut Korkut, Gregg Bucken-Knapp, Adian McGarry, Jonas Hinnfors, and Helen Drake, eds., *The Discourses and Politics of Migration in Europe* (New York: Palgrave Macmillan, 2013).
2. Imke Sturm-Martin, "Migration: Europe's Absent History," *Eurozine*, April 30, 2012, http://www.eurozine.com/articles/2012-04-30-sturmmartin-en.html.
3. Christiane Harzig and Dirk Hoerder, *What Is Migration History?* (Cambridge: Polity Press, 2009), 7.
4. Dirk Hoerder, *Cultures in Contact: World Migrations in the Second Millennium* (Durham, NC: Duke University Press, 2002).
5. Leslie Page Moch, *Moving Europeans: Migration in Western Europe since 1650*, 2nd ed. (Bloomington: Indiana University Press, 2003), 1.
6. John Randolph and Eugene M. Avrutin, eds., *Russia in Motion: Cultures of Human Mobility since 1850* (Urbana: University of Illinois Press, 2012); Leslie Page Moch and Lewis H. Siegelbaum, *Broad Is My Native Land: Repertoires and Regimes of Migration in Russia's Twentieth Century* (Ithaca: Cornell University Press, 2014); Kathy Burrell and Kathrin Hörschelmann, eds., *Mobilities in Socialist and Post-Socialist States: Societies on the Move* (Basingstoke, UK: Palgrave Macmillan, 2014).
7. Mobility has recently gained momentum as a subject of academic inquiry, alongside an interest in the spatial dimensions of history; see Vincent Kaufmann, "Mobility: Trajectory of a Concept in the Social Sciences," in *Mobility in History: The State of the Art in the History of Transport, Traffic, and Mobility*, ed. Gijs Mom, Gordon Pirie, and Laurent Tissot (Neuchâtel, Switzerland: Editions Alphil, 2009), 41–60; Lauren Coats, review of "Cultural Mobility: A Manifesto," *Comparative Literature Studies* 50, no. 1 (2013): 178; and John Randolph and Eugene M. Avrutin, "Introduction," in Randolph and Avrutin, *Russia in Motion*, 1.
8. See also Burrell and Hörschelmann, *Mobilities*, 8.
9. Kevin Hannam, Mimi Sheller, and John Urry, "Editorial: Mobilities, Immobilities and Moorings," *Mobilities* 1, no. 1 (2006): 1.
10. Valentina Dillenseger, *Technologietransfer durch Migranten aus Entwicklungsländern*, UAMR Studies on Development and Global Governance No. 63 (Bochum, Germany: Logos, 2013).
11. Laura Velasco Ortiz, "Women, Migration, and Household Survival Strategies: Mixtec Women in Tijuana," in *Women and Migration in the U.S.-Mexico Borderlands: A Reader*, ed. Denise A. Segura and Patricia Zavella (Durham, NC: Duke University Press, 2007), 341–359; Patricia R. Pessar, "The Role of Gender, Households, and Social Networks in the Migration Process: A Review and Appraisal," in *The Handbook of International Migration*, ed. Charles Hirschmann, Philip Kasinitz, and Joshua DeWind (New York: Russell Sage, 1999), 53–70.
12. See also Tim Cresswell, "Towards a Politics of Mobility," *Environment and Planning D: Society and Space* 28 (2010): 21; and Burrell and Hörschelmann, *Mobilities*, 9, 14.
13. Michael Lipton, "Migration from the Rural Areas of Poor Countries: The Impact on Rural Productivity and Income Distribution," *World Development* 8, no. 1 (1980): 1–24;

Hein de Haas, "Remittances, Migration and Social Development: A Conceptual Review of the Literature," Social Policy and Development Programme Paper No. 34 (Geneva: United Nations Research Institute for Social Development, 2007), 10.

14. Moch, *Moving Europeans*, 2.

15. See Burrell and Hörschelmann, *Mobilities*, 14-15; and chapter 4 of this volume.

16. Robin Cohen, "Introduction," in *Cambridge Survey of World Migrations*, ed. Robin Cohen (Cambridge: Cambridge University Press, 1995), 8; Jan Lucassen and Leo Lucassen, "Introduction," in *Migration, Migration History, History: Old Paradigms and New Perspectives*, ed. Jan Lucassen and Leo Lucassen (Bern, Switzerland: Peter Lang, 1997), 31-32.

17. See John Torpey, *The Invention of the Passport: Surveillance, Citizenship, and the State* (New York: Cambridge University Press, 1999).

18. See Karl Schlögel, "Einen Karlspreis für Eurolines!," in *Grenzland Europa: Unterwegs auf einem neuen Kontinent* (Köln: Hanser Verlag, 2013), 31.

19. Ernest Gellner, "Nationalism and Politics in Eastern Europe," *New Left Review* 189 (1991): 127.

20. Ronald Grigor Suny, "Nationalities in the Russian Empire," *Russian Review* 59, no. 4 (2000): 488.

21. Eric Lohr, *Russian Citizenship: From Empire to Soviet Union* (Cambridge, MA: Harvard University Press, 2012), 25.

22. Ibid., 26.

23. Michael R. Marrus, "Toward a Mass Movement," in *The Unwanted: European Refugees from the First World War through the Cold War*, ed. Michael R. Marrus (Philadelphia: Temple University Press, 2002), 15–16, 24.

24. Andrew A. Gentes, "Siberian Exile and the 1863 Polish Insurrectionists According to Russian Sources," *Jahrbücher für Geschichte Osteuropas* 51, no. 2 (2003): 197.

25. Ibid, 197.

26. See chapter 10.

27. Dirk Hoerder, "The Russo-Siberian Migration System," in Hoerder, *Cultures in Contact*, 306–330; Alexander Etkind, *Internal Colonization: Russia's Imperial Experience* (Cambridge: Polity Press, 2011). Similar tendencies continued during the Soviet period; see Lynne Viola, *The Unknown Gulag: The Lost World of Stalin's Special Settlements* (New York: Oxford University Press, 2007).

28. Chia Yin Hsu, "Frontier Urban and Imperial Dreams: The Chinese Eastern Railroad and the Creation of a Russian Global City, 1890–1917," in Randolph and Avrutin, *Russia in Motion*, 43–62.

29. A classic on the impact of the railroad is Wolfgang Schivelbusch, *The Railway Journey: The Industrialization of Time and Space in the 19th Century*, 3rd ed. (Oakland: University of California Press, 2014).

30. In particular, see chapter 1.

31. Thomas Michell, ed., *Murray's Handbook for Travellers in Russia, Poland, and Finland*, 2nd ed. (London: Murray, 1868), 51.

32. Andreas Fahrmeir, "Passports and the Status of Aliens," in *The Mechanics of Internationalism: Culture, Society, and Politics from the 1840s to the First World War*, ed. Martin H. Geyer and Johannes Paulmann (Oxford: Oxford University Press, 2001), 96–101.

33. See chapters 3 and 5.

34. Ewa Morawska, "East Europeans on the Move," in Cohen, *Cambridge Survey of World Migrations*, 97.

35. Marrus, "Toward a Mass Movement."
36. Suzanne M. Sinke, "Gender and Migration: Historical Perspectives," *International Migration Review* 40, no. 1 (2006): 82–103.
37. Morawska, "East Europeans," 99.
38. See chapter 6.
39. Suny, "Nationalities in the Russian Empire," 488.
40. Hannah Arendt, "The Decline of the Nation-State and the End of the Rights of Man," in *The Origins of Totalitarianism* (San Diego, CA: Harcourt, 1976), 291.
41. Eric Weitz, "From the Vienna to the Paris System: International Politics and the Entangled Histories of Human Rights, Forced Deportations, and Civilizing Missions," *American Historical Review* 113, no. 5 (2008): 1313–1343.
42. Nedim Ipek, "The Balkans, War, and Migration," in *War and Nationalism: The Balkan Wars, 1912–1913, and Their Sociopolitical Implications*, ed. M. Hakan Yavuz and Isa Blumi (Salt Lake City: University of Utah Press, 2013), 649; Cathy Carmichael, *Genocide before the Holocaust* (New Haven, CT: Yale University Press, 2009), 10–13.
43. Peter Gatrell, "Refugees and Forced Migrants during the First World War," *Immigrants and Minorities* 26, no. 1/2 (2008): 86; Peter Gatrell, *A Whole Empire Walking: Refugees in Russia during World War I* (Bloomington: Indiana University Press, 1999).
44. Peter Gatrell, "Refugees and Forced Migrants," 83–86.
45. Carmichael, *Genocide*, 5.
46. Ibid., 17–18; Gatrell, "Refugees and Forced Migrants," 87; Gérard Noiriel, "Russians and Armenians in France," in Cohen, *Cambridge Survey of World Migrations*, 145–147.
47. Michael R. Marrus, "The Nansen Era," in Marrus, *The Unwanted*, 51.
48. Carmichael, *Genocide*, 16.
49. Jan Musekamp, *A Cultural History of Transnational Mobility in East Central Europe: How the Royal Prussian Eastern Railroad Connected Paris to St. Petersburg and Kovno to New York* (unpublished manuscript, forthcoming).
50. Marrus, "The Nansen Era," 92.
51. Andreas Fahrmeir, "Governments and Forgers: Passports in Nineteenth-Century Europe," in *Documenting Individual Identity: The Development of State Practices in the Modern World*, ed. Jane Caplan and John Torpey (Princeton, NJ: Princeton University Press, 2001), 218–234.
52. Hoerder, "The Russo-Siberian Migration System," 317; Sheila Fitzpatrick, "The Great Departure: Rural-Urban Migration in the Soviet Union, 1929–33," in *Social Dimensions of Soviet Industrialization*, ed. William G. Rosenberg and Lewis H. Siegelbaum (Bloomington: Indiana University Press, 1993), 21.
53. Stephen Kotkin, *Magnetic Mountain: Stalinism as a Civilization* (Berkeley: University of California Press, 1995), chap. 2, esp. 96.
54. Wendy Z. Goldman, "The Internal Soviet Passport: Workers and Free Movement," in *Extending the Borders of Russian History*, ed. Marsha Siefert (Budapest: CEU Press, 2003), 315–333.
55. See Viola, *Unknown Gulag*; Fitzpatrick, "The Great Departure," 24–25; Kate Brown, *A Biography of No Place: From Ethnic Borderland to Soviet Heartland* (Cambridge, MA: Harvard University Press, 2003); and Michael Gelb, "An Early Soviet Ethnic Deportation: The Far-Eastern Koreans," *Russian Review* 54, no. 3 (1995): 389–412.
56. See Irina Kokkinaki, "The Proletariat's Underground Paradise (2002)," in *The Russia Reader: History, Culture, Politics*, ed. Adele Barker and Bruce Grant (Durham, NC: Duke University Press, 2010), 437–440.

57. See chapter 4.
58. Noiriel, "Russians and Armenians in France." See also chapter 11 of this volume.
59. See Arendt, "The Decline of the Nation-State."
60. See Marrus, "The Nansen Era"; and ibid.
61. Stefan Zweig, *The World of Yesterday* (1943; repr., Lincoln: University of Nebraska Press, 1964), 410–411.
62. Ibid., 412.
63. See chapter 7.
64. On the history of Polish workers in Germany, see Ulrich Herbert, *Hitler's Foreign Workers: Enforced Foreign Labor in Germany under the Third Reich*, trans. William Templer (1999; repr., Cambridge: Cambridge University Press, 2006), chap. 2; and Norbert Cyrus, "'Wie vor Hundert Jahren?' Zirkuläre Arbeitsmigration aus Polen in der Bundesrepublik Deutschland," in *Die Migration von Polen nach Deutschland: Zu Geschichte und Gegenwart eines europäischen Migrationssystems*, ed. Christoph Pallaske (Baden-Baden, Germany: Nomos, 2001), 185–203.
65. For a comprehensive account of forced labor under the Nazi regime, see Herbert, *Hitler's Foreign Workers*.
66. See Christopher Browning, *Nazi Policy, Jewish Workers, German Killers* (Cambridge: Cambridge University Press, 2000), esp. chap. 1.
67. Rainer Schulze, "Forced Migration of German Populations during and after the Second World War: History and Memory," in *The Disentanglement of Populations: Migration, Expulsion and Displacement in Postwar Europe*, ed. Jessica Reinisch and Elizabeth White (Houndmills, UK: Palgrave Macmillan, 2011), 51–70.
68. Matthew Frank, "Reconstructing the Nation-State: Population Transfer in Central and Eastern Europe, 1944–8," in Reinisch and White, *The Disentanglement of Populations*, 27–49; Catherine Gousseff, "Evacuation versus Repatriation: The Polish-Ukrainian Population Exchange, 1944–6," in Reinisch and White, *The Disentanglement of Populations*, 91–113.
69. Ewa Morawska, "Intended and Unintended Consequences of Forced Migrations: A Neglected Aspect of East Europe's Twentieth Century History," *International Migration Review* 34, no. 4 (2000): 1049–1087.
70. See Burrell and Hörschelmann, *Mobilities*.
71. "People of the BAM," *Russia beyond the Headlines*, August 12, 2012, http://rbth.com/articles/2012/08/12/people_of_the_bam_17237.html. See also chapter 8.
72. For a succinct account of this labor migration, see Stephen Castles, Hein de Haas, and Mark J. Miller, *The Age of Migration: International Population Movements in the Modern World*, 5th ed. (New York: Guilford Press, 2014), 104–108.
73. See "Berlin Wall," "Cold War," Czechoslovakian Refugees," and "Hungarian Revolution," in *Immigration and Asylum: From 1900 to the Present*, ed. Matthew Gibney and Randall Hansen (Santa Barbara, CA: ABC-CLIO, 2005); and Heinz Fassmann and Rainer Münz, "European East-West Migration, 1945–1992," in Cohen, *The Cambridge Survey of World Migrations*, 470–481.
74. Nick Thorpe, *The Danube: A Journey Upriver from the Black Sea to the Black Forest* (New Haven, CT: Yale University Press, 2014).
75. See Pallaske, *Die Migration von Polen nach Deutschland*.
76. Birgit Glorius and Klaus Friedrich, "Transnational Social Spaces of Polish Migrants in Leipzig (Germany)," *Migracijske i etničke teme* 22 (2006): 163–180; Louise Ryan, Rosemary Sales, Mary Tilki, and Bernadetta Siara, "Family Strategies and Transnational

Migration: Recent Polish Migrants in London," *Journal of Ethnic and Migration Studies* 35, no. 1 (2009): 61–77. Foundational for the study of transnational migrations are Nina Glick-Schiller, Linda Basch, and Cristina Szanton Blanc, "From Immigrant to Transmigrant: Theorizing Transnational Migration," in *Transnationale Migration (Soziale Welt Sonderband No. 12)*, ed. Ludger Pries (Baden-Baden, Germany: Nomos, 1997), 121–140; and Peggy Levitt, Josh DeWind, and Steven Vertovec, "International Perspectives on Transnational Migration: An Introduction," *International Migration Review* 37, no. 3 (2003): 565–575. See also chapter 12.

77. Mirjana Morokvasic, "'Settled in Mobility': Engendering Post-Wall Migration in Europe," *Feminist Review* 77 (2004): 7–25.

78. Georges Photios Tapinos, "Globalisation, Regional Integration, International Migration," *International Social Science Journal* 52, no. 165 (2000): 297–306; Saskia Sassen, *Globalization and Its Discontents: Essays on the New Mobility of People and Money* (New York: New Press, 1998); Nikos Papastergiadis, *The Turbulence of Migration: Globalization, Deterritorialization and Hybridity* (Cambridge: Polity Press, 2000).

79. Stephen Castles, "International Migration at the Beginning of the Twenty-first Century: Global Trends and Issues," *International Social Science Journal* 52, no. 165 (2000): 269–281; Christiane Harzig, "Women Migrants as Global and Local Agents," in *Women, Gender and Labour Migration: Historical and Global Perspectives*, ed. Pamela Sharpe (London: Routledge, 2001), 15–28.

80. Marek Okolski, "Recent Trends in Major Issues in International Migration: Central and East European Perspectives," *International Social Science Journal* 52, no. 165 (2000): 329–341.

81. Judith Kessler, *Jüdische Migration aus der ehemaligen Sowjetunion seit 1990*, 2003, accessed December 27, 2015, http://www.berlin-judentum.de/gemeinde/migration.html; Yinon Cohen and Irena Kogan, "Jewish Immigration from the Former Soviet Union to Germany and Israel in the 1990s," *Leo Baeck Institute Year Book 2005* (London: LBI, 2005), 249–265. See chapter 13.

82. UNHCR Ukraine, UNHCR.ORG.UA, accessed July 10, 2014, http://unhcr.org.ua/en/2011-08-26-06-58-56/news-archive/1244-internal-displacement-map. See also *comments.ua*, May 8, 2014, http://comments.ua/life/467099-bezhentsi-krima-provedut-sezd-kieve.html; and Paul Sonne, "Thousands of Ukrainian Refugees Flee to Russia for an Uncertain Future," *Wall Street Journal*, online edition, July 2, 2014, http://online.wsj.com/articles/many-ukrainians-flee-to-russia-angry-afraid-determined-to-stay-1404333568.

83. Katarzyna Jarzynska, "Russia Tightens Up Residence Regulations for CIS Citizens," Centre for Eastern Studies, Warsaw, January 15, 2014, http://www.osw.waw.pl/en/publikacje/analyses/2014-01-15/russia-tightens-residence-regulations-cis-citizens.

84. The Schengen Area is the region comprising twenty-six European countries that have abolished passport controls and visa requirements for travel across their common borders, based on the Schengen Agreements of 1985 and the Schengen Convention of 1990.

85. Between 2007 and 2011, the EU External Border Fund provided funds in the amount of €15.5 million (Estonia), €9.4 million (Latvia), €18.1 million (Lithuania), and €41.4 million (Poland) to help secure "protection of the EU's external borders," an investment that "notably . . . for . . . those situated at the external frontiers of the Union . . . can be very large due to significant migratory pressure" (European Commission–Home Affairs, "External Borders Fund," accessed July 11, 2014, http://ec.europa.eu/dgs/home-affairs/financing/fundings/security-and-safeguarding-liberties/external-borders-fund/index_en.htm.

86. "Implementing Migration Control in Ukraine—A Brief History," in *Access to Protection Denied: Refoulement of Refugees and Minors at the Eastern Borders of the EU–The Case of Hungary, Slovakia and Ukraine. Report by Bordermonitoring Project Ukraine* (München: Bayerischer Flüchtlingsrat, 2010), 43.

87. UNHCR: The UN Refugee Agency, "Over One Million Sea Arrivals Reach Europe in 2015," December 30, 2015, http://www.unhcr.org/5683d0b56.html.

88. Estonian Ministry of Foreign Affairs, "Foreign Policy—Estonia and Croatia," accessed July 10, 2014, https://peaveeb.vm.ee/?q=en/node/107.

89. Stephen Greenblatt, "Cultural Mobility: An Introduction," in *Cultural Mobility: A Manifesto*, eds. Stephen Greenblatt, with Ines G. Županov, Reinhard Meyer-Kalkus, Heike Paul, Pál Nyíri, and Friederike Pannewick (New York: Cambridge University Press, 2009), 7.

90. See also Julia Creet and Andreas Kitzmann, eds., *Memory and Migration: Multidisciplinary Approaches to Memory Studies* (Toronto: University of Toronto Press, 2011).

PART I

Locomotions: Ways of Moving

CHAPTER 1

Paris—St. Petersburg
Shrinking Spaces in the Nineteenth Century

Jan Musekamp

> Travelers always speak with great indignation about the rudeness of the Prussian postilions... the impertinence of the postilions was insufferable. They stopped at every tavern for beer, and the unfortunate travelers had either to put up with this or bribe them to go on.... For example, less than a mile before Stolp we had to wait an hour while our postilions, despite our urgings, calmly ate and drank in a tavern.
> —Nikolai M. Karamzin[1]

IN 1789, THE AUTHOR of this account, famous Russian writer and historian Nikolai Mikhailovich Karamzin, went on an extended study tour of Western Europe.[2] Starting at Tver' in the Russian Empire, he traveled first to St. Petersburg, then to Königsberg (Kaliningrad) in East Prussia, then to Berlin and France, and, finally, to England. In 1791–1792, he published his *Letters of a Russian Traveler (Pis'ma russkogo puteshestvennika)*. Karamzin did not base his literary work on actual letters but rather on notes taken during his trip.[3] While scholars widely regard these "letters" as a model for contemporary Russian travel accounts that boosted "the confidence of a growing national literary tradition," it is equally illustrative to analyze Karamzin's observations in terms of travel at the time, 1789.[4] His account gives us an accurate description of European road conditions and stagecoach travel in the late eighteenth century. It took him thirty-five days to get from the Russian to the Prussian capital, a distance of 1,125 miles. When Karamzin continued his journey to the western part of Europe, he traveled twice as fast. As Karamzin did, travelers could cover the distance between Paris and Berlin (625 miles) in less than fourteen days, and this relatively high speed was the result of an already elaborate stagecoach system.[5] Of course, one could travel by ship to get from St. Petersburg to Western Europe, at least during the summer and fall, and this was indeed much quicker. However, because of unpredictable weather and the partly frozen Baltic Sea in the winter and spring, this was not the most reliable method to travel from Russia to France. As late as the mid-1850s, with steamboats already running from St. Petersburg to Baltic harbors farther west, and a fully fledged European railroad system west of Berlin, Eastern European winters still impacted travel times enormously. In 1856–1857, dispatches from the French embassy in St. Petersburg took twenty days longer in the winter to reach Paris than they did in the summer.[6] Today, more than 150 years later, airplanes cover the distance between St. Petersburg and Paris in about three hours.

In this chapter I focus on the impact of transportation and, to a lesser extent, communication innovations of the nineteenth century on mobility in Europe. The gradual implementation of better roads, railroads, and the telegraph had similarly dramatic effects to those that airplanes, cars, and communication innovations would have in the twentieth century. They changed not only mobility patterns but also the horizon and identity of Europeans who, by the end of the nineteenth century, could use a dense transportation network spanning all of Europe, regardless of weather conditions. Despite the tremendous importance these changes brought about for the European continent, previous research has either focused on a single country or a specific region within Europe, or analyzed the impact of the railroad and the stagecoach system separately.[7] A cultural history of cross-border mobility encompassing the nineteenth century as well as both Eastern and Western Europe has yet to be written.[8]

To grasp the aforementioned changes, it is worth focusing on several developments in cross-border mobility that occurred between the major European metropolises of St. Petersburg, Berlin, and Paris. Strong political, economic, and historical ties connected these cities since the eighteenth century. These bonds became even tighter when they were supported by new railroad connections in the early 1860s. The line between France and Russia thus serves as an example for dramatically changing mobility patterns in Western and Eastern Europe that showed an increase in cross-border trade, travel, and migration, among others. These developments are part of a new wave of economic and social globalization whose starting point historians set at about 1850.[9] I follow Antony G. Hopkins's idea of a critical new approach to globalization in world history in terms of a cultural history.[10] In the first part of this chapter I challenge the view that primarily the railroad facilitated important changes in transportation and highlight crucial developments in road building and stagecoach systems. In the second part, I show that the railroad accelerated a development of "shrinking spaces" between Paris and St. Petersburg.

SHRINKING SPACES BEFORE THE RAILROAD

For centuries, merchants and travelers crisscrossed the world. To give just one example, Europeans brought with them luxury goods and know-how from places as far as China, and Chinese merchants established a vast trade network in Africa and Asia. Beginning with the Renaissance, Northern European scholars traveled to Italy and Prague to attend universities and to meet and discuss contemporary issues related to technology and humanities, setting an example for today's worldwide movement of students that includes students from Asian countries coming to the United States as well as "Erasmus students" circulating within the European Union. The sixteenth and especially the seventeenth and eighteenth centuries saw the emergence of extensive trade networks between the Americas, Africa, Asia, and Europe.[11] Within European countries, far-reaching postal and carrier networks evolved. One example is England, where regular goods transportation across the country can be traced back to the fourteenth century, while scheduled stagecoach services appeared in the sixteenth century.[12] With regard to leisure or educational travel, the eighteenth century saw the heyday of the so-called *grand tour*, trips across and around the continent during which sons from wealthy, mostly noble families traveled to historically and culturally significant sites in Western and Southern Europe. However, what changed tremendously after the so-called *Sattelzeit* (saddle time) was the number of cross-border travelers and the amount of goods exchanged internationally.[13] International trade and knowledge exchange had an enormous impact on the lives of ever-increasing parts of the world's population, especially in the Northern Hemisphere.

As far as Europe is concerned, since the early 1800s, improved systems of canals, highways, stagecoaches, and steamboats facilitated the transport of people and goods and introduced organizational elements we usually associate with the railroad, such as schedules, fixed ticket prices, and rules of conduct. In France, a fairly advanced transportation system was already in operation at this time. Before the French Revolution, the French kings' mercantilist policies led to an improvement of both the canal and the road system. The postal system was well developed, too. However, cross-border trade and travel was limited. With an improving mail-coach system and better roads, travel times in France shrank decisively in the two hundred years before the introduction of the railroad. In 1650, when the French express post was established, it took fifteen days to cover the 540 miles between Paris and Marseille. This time was cut in half by 1732, and again by 1834. With the advent of the railroad between the two cities in 1855, the travel time was reduced drastically and averaged forty-eight hours.[14]

Since at least the Napoleonic Wars, private stagecoach connections existed between Prussia and France.[15] In the 1840s, an estimated seven hundred thousand people per year crossed the border between Germany, Belgium, and France.[16] This is an impressive number, given the fact that mail coaches accommodated a maximum of eighteen passengers. While most people still traveled on foot or rode their own horses, dozens of scheduled mail coaches crossed the borders daily.[17]

Development in the German lands was quite similar, even though substantial improvements occurred several decades later. Since the middle of the seventeenth century, a regular passenger transport service existed in southwest Germany. It quickly spread to northern Germany and Prussia. In the early eighteenth century, some southern German states started programs to improve road conditions, following the French model.[18] Several German states complemented their traditional ordinary mail delivery system that followed fixed schedules with a speedier extra post. This system allowed more affluent travelers to hire private coaches that made use of the existing relay stations of the ordinary post.[19] However, only after the

Napoleonic Wars did German states achieve far-reaching improvements in road conditions and stagecoach systems. At that time, governments focused on important improvements in the road system, neglected in the decades before. Ironically, Napoleon's army and its engineers started building new roads in the occupied territories—to benefit the movement of troops.[20] But Russian and Prussian engineers also learned from French achievements, either by getting in direct contact with French specialists during the occupation or after pushing Napoleon's armies back to France and exploring newly built infrastructure. Prussia forced the construction of macadamized roads (German: *Chaussee*), to diminish travel times, to knit its scattered territory together, and to enable an ever-faster mobilization of troops in case of war. The Prussian government began systematic improvements to the road network in the late eighteenth century and launched a new and far-reaching building effort in 1816.[21]

Transportation opportunities and networks in Eastern Europe were less developed. As the example of Nikolai Karamzin shows, covering the same distance in Russia and eastern Prussia took him twice the time the French mail-coach system would have required.[22] However, if one takes into account the difficult climatic and geographical situation in the sparsely populated Russian Empire, the picture is more nuanced. In Muscovy and later the Russian Empire, a system of post routes, the so-called *iams*, dated back to the sixteenth century. In a 1549 account of his missions to Muscovy, Hapsburg envoy Sigmund Freiherr von Herberstein reported on the elaborated *iam* system with relay stations where privileged travelers could change horses quickly and continue their travel.[23] Despite poor road conditions, this system knitted the country together and allowed for the transportation of official couriers and private travelers who had to obtain a permit. Traveling within the *iam* system, individual travelers paid for horses, drivers, and shelters at the relay stations. From the seventeenth century onward, it "became the backbone of the Russian letter-post system," extending out to all parts of the country.[24] When Russia introduced a regular, schedule-based stagecoach system in the early nineteenth century, alongside a major program to improve road conditions, this would revolutionize travel. In 1817, comparable to what happened in Prussia, the Russian Empire launched a program to improve the deteriorating roads and to build a network of new macadamized roads. This program came to a halt in 1864, when the government redirected the funds to railroad construction.[25] Also in the early nineteenth century, the government allowed for a regular Russian stagecoach system, when in the 1820s, and especially in the 1830s, private companies started operating a system that was accessible to the public and would soon become a huge success.[26] As a result, Prussia and Russia established regular cross-border connections in 1833, making individual travel between France and the Russian Empire much quicker, more predictable, and less expensive than before.[27] Roland Cvetkovski correctly assumed that the introduction of the scheduled stagecoach system in the Russian Empire was part of the "mechanization, geometrization, and rationalization of movement," directed at controlling subjects' mobility and thus stabilizing state power.[28] Still, only a privileged class could afford to travel: although in France the Revolution introduced freedom of movement, Prussia did not introduce it until 1810. Subsequently, it was money, not class, that decided on who would travel by stagecoach. On the contrary, for most of the Russian population, the Emancipation of the Serfs in 1861, at least theoretically, granted freedom of movement to most of the population. Until 1851, regulations that built on those for the stagecoach system stipulated that travelers needed special permits issued by the local police, even to buy a train ticket.[29]

Decreasing travel times, a higher frequency of stagecoach courses, and an increasing number of passengers required precise rules concerning schedules, travel fares, and luggage allowances. Where exact schedules were missing, passengers heavily relied on the goodwill of the postilions or on bribes to accelerate their travel. Describing his tour through Prussia, Karamzin informs us about the unreliability of the Prussian stagecoach system in 1789. However, also at this time, the Prussian ruler tried to improve the system when imposing stricter rules, though with limited success:

> The present king issued an order which obliges all postmasters to treat travelers with more respect and not to keep anyone more than an hour at each station. It also forbids postilions to stop at will on the road.... The order has produced some good results, but it is certainly not being carried out to the letter.[30]

Complaints like those mentioned at the beginning of this chapter were quite frequent, adding to objections against the poor conditions of many roads and carriages. Karamzin complained about the "cursed post coach" on the Prussian-Saxon border that "had so shaken" him: "the post-coach being very high and uncovered, the passengers [were] obliged incessantly to stoop down, that they may not have their brains knocked out against the branches of the tree."[31] Although an elaborate relay system was already in existence, it was only after the aforementioned extension of the network of macadamized roads and improvements of the carriages' suspension systems that travelers' speed and comfort improved decisively in the first half of the nineteenth century.

Important regulations concerned the passengers' luggage. On the Russian post, passengers were allowed one piece of luggage of 17.6 pounds free of charge; they had to pay a high fee for an additional 26.5 pounds.[32] The Prussian post, we learn from Karamzin, allowed passengers to bring along luggage of up to 60 pounds.[33] As Baedeker and Murray guidebooks reveal, this did not change in the age of steam and can even be traced until today, where railroad and airline passengers are usually allowed to check in luggage not exceeding 50 to 70 pounds, depending on carrier and class. And yet another institution that would be further developed in the railroad age dates back to the stagecoach system, namely postal stations as precursors of railroad stations that also functioned as modern city gates. Benjamin Schenk accurately called the latter "nucleus[es] of civilization," being part of a "reconfiguration of social spaces"—and the same is true for the age before the railroad.[34] At stagecoach stations, the postilions changed horses, exchanged mail from different directions, and admitted and released passengers. For those traveling onward, the stations served as inns offering meals and accommodation. The quality of inns varied, but because horses had to be changed frequently, they were situated at least every 10 to 15 miles and therefore heavily competed with each other, usually offering acceptable services.[35] As a result, with the introduction of exact timetables and fares, the postal service "created entirely new relationships between people's conceptions of space and time," which critics at the time called "tyrannical punctuality."[36] This seems odd, considering the travel times the railroad enabled later on. However, the French example shows that with regard to speed, stagecoaches had a huge impact indeed.

RAPID ACCELERATION: THE EMERGING EUROPEAN RAILROAD NET

Many believe that the introduction of the railroad closed the chapter of horse-powered mobility. A Belgian caricature of 1843 depicts former mail-coach horses' complaints about losing their job upon the opening of the railroad line between Antwerp in Belgium and Cologne in Prussia—the world's first cross-border railroad, linking Germany to Belgium and three years later to France.[37] (See figure 1.1.) However, the number of horses and other animals transporting goods and drawing carriages and stagecoaches increased until the end of the nineteenth century. Although more and more travelers used the railroad, and an increasing amount of goods was transported across the continent, many passengers still relied on horse-drawn transportation to reach their homes, and merchants transported goods and raw materials with carriages or coaches to production facilities.[38] What changed dramatically, though, was the amount of goods

Figure 1.1 *Post Horses Distresses. The Railroad from Anvers to Cologne.*
Source: Germanisches Nationalmuseum Nürnberg, Graphische Sammlung, Inventarnummer: HB14611, photography: M. Runge.

transported and the number of passengers traveling long distances or internationally.

The 1830s and 1840s saw a first wave of railroad construction in France, the German states, and, to a lesser extent, Russia. The construction of the Liverpool and Manchester Railway in 1830, the first fully functional railroad connection in Great Britain, reverberated throughout the whole European continent.[39] At the same time, North America saw the building of its first railroad lines. One of the witnesses of the American developments was Friedrich List, a southern German national economist and strong supporter of a unified German nation-state who, in 1825, was forced to emigrate to the United States. Here he became an entrepreneur in coal mining and an American railroad pioneer. When he returned to southern Germany in 1834, he developed a vision of a railroad network encompassing not only Germany but Europe as a whole.[40] The first French rail link had been established just two years earlier; Germany and Russia would follow in 1835 and 1836. At the time, few entrepreneurs and government officials embraced the idea of national or international networks. In this regard, List's thinking was revolutionary. In 1838, he compared the railroad to a "Hercules in his cradle who will deliver humankind from the evils of wars... and national hatred." The railroad, he thought, would make people visit foreign countries and thus raise their level of education.[41] Conversely, List's thinking reveals yet another dimension of railroad pioneers' argumentation: the railroad's strategic value. Indeed, European governments began to see how the emerging network of rail lines would satisfy their military interests.[42]

Using the example of two travel maps from 1849 and 1861, we can track the connections between stagecoach and railroad networks and the cross-border traffic they enabled.[43] The first map reveals an already impressively dense railroad network in the German states by the late 1840s. (See figure 1.2.) At the time, mostly private entrepreneurs invested in economically promising links in the German lands and Western Europe. In the 1840s, government-guaranteed interest rates and state funding became increasingly relevant for the expansion of the railroad network. Still, investments were mainly directed at internal connections, with the notable exception of the one between Cologne and Paris, via Antwerp, accomplished in 1843–1846, and the link between Warsaw, Berlin, and

Figure 1.2 *Railroad Map of Germany and its Neighbors, 1849.*
Source: Landesarchiv NRW, Abteilung Westfalen, Bestand Karten A, Signatur Nr. 11908.

Vienna, opened in 1848. The map also reveals that the eastern provinces of Prussia and the western parts of the Russian Empire lagged significantly with regard to existing rails. Interestingly, in the first years after the railroad was introduced, contemporaries continued to describe the distance between cities by the time it took to traverse the distance on foot. On the map, for instance, small cubes drawn along railroad lines signify approximately one hour of travel, with eight hours of movement on foot equaling one hour of railroad travel. The map reveals that it took 313 hours to walk from Paris to Berlin (650 miles) at an average speed of 2 miles per hour, equaling 39 hours on the train, averaging 15 to 20 miles per hour.[44]

Twelve years later, despite an increasingly dense net of railroad lines, stagecoaches remained important. As the 1861 travel map of Germany shows, there already was a dense railroad network with some cross-border connections. (See figure 1.3.) However, stagecoach services still covered the spaces between the lines, making use of macadamized roads

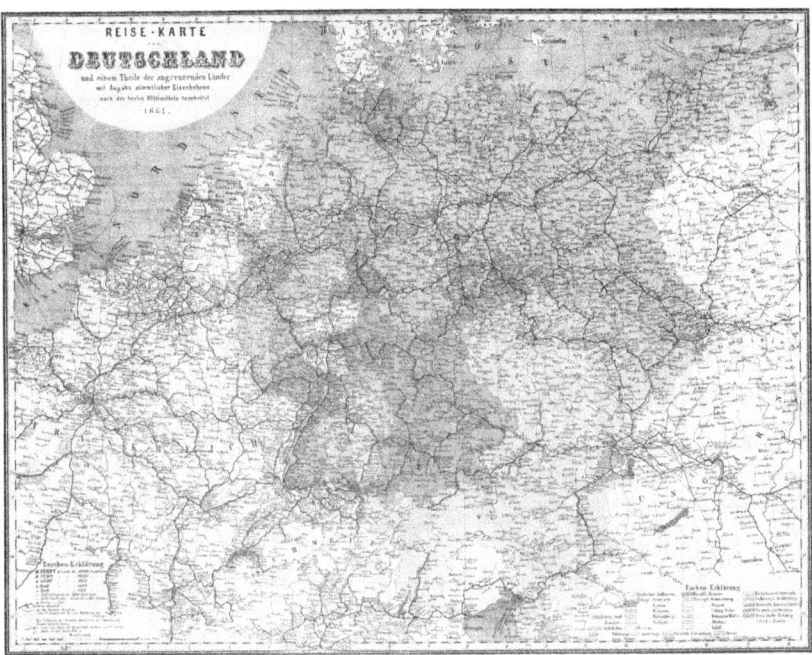

Figure 1.3 *Travel Map of Germany and Part of its Neighbors, 1861.*
Source: Landesarchiv NRW, Abteilung Westfalen, Bestand Karten A, Signatur Nr. 11907.

(*Chaussee*, continuous line) and ordinary roads (*Landstraße*, dotted line). Another important means of transportation that was also depicted on the map were steamships.

The map of 1849 indicates that railroad development in the Russian Empire lagged. Because of a reluctant tsar and opposition among ministers, who instead continued to support the road-building program, the first significant railroad line between Warsaw and Vienna, backed by a government-guaranteed interest rate, was not opened until 1848. Interestingly, it was not the Russian mainland that was connected to other parts of Europe through the railroad, but the peripheral Kingdom of Poland. The line connecting St. Petersburg and Moscow followed in 1851.

It is worth explaining why Russia did not adopt the same track gauge used in Western Europe. Although rumor was that it was for strategic reasons, John Westwood has shown that in 1842–1843, the American engineer George Washington Whistler, while planning the St. Petersburg–Moscow railroad, decided to introduce a 5-foot gauge as opposed to the 4 feet, 8.5 inches predominantly used in Western Europe.[45] At the time, few people took into account the future (international) connections between railroads, and construction plans focused on particular railroad lines and national networks. As a result, even the gauges in German states differed.[46] Engineers established the track gauge following local traditions in road vehicles, copying successful railroad lines in other parts of the world or simply arbitrarily. This explains why, in contrast, the link between Warsaw and Vienna and the subsequent link to Berlin were built with the Western European gauge.

As we have seen, the so-called transport revolution was not a revolution in the sense of an abrupt change.[47] Rather, it gradually altered mobility patterns of ever-wider population groups. The upper classes had traveled across Europe even before the "age of steam," and traveling and the exchange of goods between France, Prussia, and the Russian Empire had become more and more popular too. However, the connection of the Prussian railroad network to the French and the Russian networks in 1846 and 1861, respectively, enabled more people and ever-broader parts of society in these countries to travel more often, at a lower cost, and much faster than before.[48] Interestingly, as far as the Prussian-Russian border is concerned, Prussian government officials anticipated this development only with regard to passenger travel. They expected an ever-increasing "wanderlust" among Russian citizens, especially in the summer months. However, they did not consider a significant increase in goods transportation, which occurred quite surprisingly just months after the opening of the line. This was mainly a result of the traditional grain trade between East Prussia's capital, Königsberg, and Russia that had already developed over the previous centuries along sea and river routes, which the railroad would boost enormously.[49]

In 1861, railroad companies established regular passenger services between Paris, Berlin, and St. Petersburg. Inaugurating the link between the Russian Empire and Prussia, contemporaries were fully aware that now not only Berlin but also Paris "was getting closer" to St. Petersburg. As a matter of fact, the Russian trunk line leading to the border was planned by French engineers and financed mainly by French banks.[50] Consequently, the railroad locomotive that pulled the first train from Russia to the Prussian border station Eydtkuhnen was decorated not only with Prussian and Russian flags, but with a French one as well.[51] Travel times between the western and the eastern half of the continent decreased. An 1835 travel guide listed a land travel time of thirty-eight days between London and St. Petersburg, in case travelers would make use of privately hired carriages.[52] By the late 1840s, with steamboats between northern Germany and St. Petersburg in operation since 1839, the time shrank to six or seven days.[53] By 1868, this time was reduced further to three and a half days, and in 1914, the distance of 1,700 miles was covered in exactly forty-seven and a half hours.[54]

Not only did travel times shrink dramatically; transcontinental travel also became more and more comfortable. In the United States, sleeping cars had already been in use since the late 1830s, but after George M. Pullman developed more comfortable sleepers in 1864, they experienced widespread usage. In 1867, the Belgian entrepreneur Georges Nagelmackers went on a study trip to the United States and examined these wagons. Upon his return, he established the *Compagnie internationale des wagons-lits* (International Sleeping Car Company) in 1872. Backed by the Belgian king Leopold II, he began to negotiate with European railroad companies to obtain concessions for a network of luxury trains. As a result, a network between major European metropolises offered the quickest and most comfortable way to travel. After fierce negotiations with the Prussian government, which initially opposed the idea of allowing foreign companies to operate trains on their now state-owned railroads, Nagelmackers was able to establish the Nord-Express in 1896, allowing passengers to travel the 1,700 miles from the French to the Russian capital in forty-eight hours. Direct connections to Moscow and London via Oostende followed. In Paris, passengers could connect to trains to the French Riviera, Spain, and Portugal. In Russia, travelers could easily change to the Transsiberian Railroad and continue their voyage to the Pacific and to China. In sum, we observe here the emergence of a European "metropolitan corridor."[55]

Hand in hand with railroad construction went the introduction of electromagnetic telegraphy. Its precursor, the optical telegraphy system, established in France after 1793, was the first system to transmit information independently from physical means of transportation. While it was mainly the government and especially the military that made use of this early system, the electrical telegraph network in Great Britain, in use since 1837, became increasingly popular among commercial and private users. At first, it was used to control movements on the rail, ensuring efficiency and safety.[56] Soon it became a means to transmit information on a massive scale that would eventually revolutionize global communication and trade. As Roland Wenzlhuemer put it, "dematerialized information outpaced material transport and could, therefore, be used to efficiently co-ordinate, control and command such material movements."[57] Commodity markets became increasingly integrated, because information on price changes and other events in distant countries made their way to all parts of the connected world in a matter of hours.

To consider the impact of cross-border movement of information, goods, and people, it is instructive to have a closer look at border stations or relays between Prussia/the German Empire on the one side, and the Russian Empire on the other. One of these truly European places was Eydtkuhnen (Chernyshevskoe), a town that served as a "lock between two worlds," as Karl Schlögel has put it.[58] Eydtkuhnen, once a small village, became a major hub for travel and trade between Russia and Western Europe. Because of different railroad gauges in use on either side of the border, not only did freight trains have to be reloaded here, but also the European political, societal, and economic elite, traveling for business or leisure between Great Britain, France, Germany, and Russia, came to a forced halt. Eydtkuhnen exemplifies the international networks of the nineteenth century, with numerous shipping companies, customs and border control, and huge railroad facilities providing for smooth cross-border traffic of people and goods.

A comparison of Karamzin's travel account with the account of a traveler on the Nord-Express illuminates the difference in long-distance travel for an affluent passenger between the late eighteenth and early twentieth centuries. Famous Russian-American writer Vladimir Nabokov recalls his childhood travels as follows:

> In the early years of this century, a travel agency on Nevski Avenue displayed a three-foot long model of an oak-brown international sleeping car... One could make out the blue upholstery inside, the embossed leather lining of the compartment walls, their polished panels, inset

mirrors, tulip-shaped reading lamps, and other maddening details. Spacious windows alternated with narrower ones, single or geminate and some of these were of frosted glass. In a few compartments, the beds had been made....

In the far end of my mind I can unravel, I think, at least five ... journeys to Paris, with the Riviera or Biarritz as their ultimate destination. In 1909, the year I now single out, our party consisted of eleven people and one dachshund. Wearing gloves and a travel cap, my father sat reading a book in the compartment he shared with our tutor. My brother and I were separated from them by a washroom. My mother and her maid Natasha occupied a compartment adjacent to ours. Next came my two small sisters, their English governess, Miss Livingston, and a Russian nurse. The odd one of our party, my father's valet, Osip ... had a stranger for companion.[59]

GROWING SPACES: WORLD WAR I AND ITS AFTERMATH

As we all know, Friedrich List's optimistic vision of railroads' contribution to a more peaceful world did not materialize. However, the railroad (and telegraphy) was one of the most important elements of nineteenth-century globalization.[60] This globalization was quite impressive in the economic realm; between 1850 and 1913, the value of world trade increased tenfold.[61] Moreover, the growing mobility of ever-greater parts of the population boosted the exchange of ideas, novelties in culture, and technological knowledge. International long-distance travelers were important agents of this process. Comparing the European network of the International Sleeping Car Company at its heyday, right before World War I began, to today's network of airlines, it is no exaggeration to state that the density of these two nets, a hundred years apart, is similar. However, it would be misleading to only look at the bright side of international travel. On the one hand we observe the development of "international travel communities"; on the other, though, we witness the drawing of clear lines between the *Self* and the *Other*, holding the seeds of stereotypes and national antagonisms.[62] Similarly, the abovementioned innovations had a dramatic impact on workforce mobility of the poor and on mass emigration from Europe to the Americas, and, Wolfgang Kaschuba argues, were therefore part of a "fundamental experience of modernity."[63]

I close this chapter with the outbreak of World War I. Economic historians argue that the war did not fully interrupt most developments, even if it slowed them down. This is certainly true for the Western Hemisphere, where historians tend to set the approximate endpoint of this wave of globalization at 1950 or 1970.[64] Nevertheless, Central and Eastern Europe experienced a period of deglobalization starting in 1914, and the new borders and conflicts hindered international travel and trade. This was especially true for Germany, Poland, and the newly emerging Soviet Union. World War II and its aftermath severed these processes further, and not until 1989 did the region return to whole-scale global developments in travel and trade. This phenomenon of "growing spaces" is thus an example of the inversion of a development Wolfgang Schivelbusch called the "annihilation of space and time."[65]

NOTES

1. Nikolai M. Karamzin, "Letters of a Russian Traveler, 1789–1790, Part One: Moscow through Germany," in *Letters of a Russian Traveler, 1789–1790: An Account of a Young Russian Gentleman's Tour through Germany, Switzerland, France, and England by N. M. Karamzin*, ed. Florence Jonas (New York: Columbia University Press, 1957), 46.

2. On Karamzin in general, refer to Joseph L. Black, *Nicholas Karamzin and the Russian Society in the Nineteenth Century: A Study in Russian Political and Historical Thought* (Toronto: University of Toronto Press, 1975). On Karamzin's trip to Western Europe, refer to Hans Rothe, *N. M. Karamzins europäische Reise: Der Beginn des russischen Romans. Philologische Untersuchungen* (Bad Homburg v.d.H., Berlin: Verlag Gehlen, 1968).

3. Leon Stilman, "Introduction," in Jonas, *Letters of a Russian Traveler, 1789–1790*, 20.

4. Sara Dickinson, *Breaking Ground: Travel and National Culture in Russia from Peter I to the Era of Pushkin* (Amsterdam: Rodopi, 2006), 107.

5. For Karamzin's travel times in the German lands, see Karamzin, "Letters of a Russian Traveler, 1789–1790"; Klaus Beyrer, "The Mail-Coach Revolution: Landmarks in Travel in Germany between the Seventeenth and Nineteenth Centuries," *German History* 24, no. 3 (2006): 377–378.

6. "Archives du Ministère français des Affaires étrangères, Paris, Ambassade de France à St. Pétersbourg, Correspondance commerciale," fonds 282CCC, t. 30, f. 12, 90.

7. On stagecoach development in Russia and Germany, see Alexandra Bekasova, "The Making of Passengers in the Russian Empire: Coach-Transport Companies, Guidebooks, and National Identity in Russia, 1820–1860," in *Russia in Motion: Cultures of Human Mobility since 1850*, ed. John Randolph and Eugene M. Avrutin (Urbana: University of Illinois Press, 2012): 199–217.; Beyrer, "The Mail-Coach Revolution"; *Zeit der*

Postkutschen: Drei Jahrhunderte Reisen 1600–1900 (Karlsruhe: Braun, 1992); and John W. Randolph, "The Singing Coachman or, the Road and Russia's Ethnographic Invention in Early Modern Times," *Journal of Early Modern History* 11, no. 1–2 (2007): 33–61. For more details on railroad development, consult Ralf Roth, *Das Jahrhundert der Eisenbahn: Die Herrschaft über Raum und Zeit 1800–1914* (Ostfildern: Thorbecke, 2005); Frithjof Benjamin Schenk, *Russlands Fahrt in die Moderne: Mobilität und sozialer Raum im Eisenbahnzeitalter* (Stuttgart: Franz Steiner Verlag, 2014); John N. Westwood, *A History of Russian Railways* (London: Allen and Unwin, 1964); and Wolfgang Schivelbusch, *The Railway Journey: The Industrialization of Time and Space in the 19th Century* (Berkeley: University of California Press, 1986).

8. Florian Cebulla, "Grenzüberschreitender Schienenverkehr: Problemstellungen—Methoden—Forschungsüberblick," in *Die Internationalität der Eisenbahn 1850–1970*, ed. Monika Burri, Kilian T. Elsasser, and David Gugerli (Zürich: Chronos-Verlag, 2003): 21–35.

9. Antony G. Hopkins, "The History of Globalization—and the Globalization of History?," in *Globalization in World History*, ed. Antony G. Hopkins (New York: Norton, 2002), 25–41.

10. Ibid.

11. For an introduction into the topic, see Andreas Gestrich and Margrit Schulte Beerbühl, eds., *Cosmopolitan Networks in Commerce and Society 1660–1914*, German Historical Institute London Bulletin, Supplement No. 2 (London: German Historical Institute London, 2011).

12. Dorian Gerhold, *Carriers and Coachmasters: Trade and Travel before the Turnpikes* (Chichester, UK: Phillimore, 2005), 4, 79–150.

13. *Sattelzeit* is a term coined by Reinhart Koselleck, referring to the time period between 1770 and 1830. During this time, the ground for the following speedy industrialization was laid. Refer to Jürgen Osterhammel, *Die Verwandlung der Welt: Eine Geschichte des 19. Jahrhunderts* (München: Beck, 2009), 102–103.

14. Hans-Heinrich Nolte, "Eisenbahnen und Dampferlinien," in *Neue Wege in ein neues Europa: Geschichte und Verkehr im 20. Jahrhundert*, ed. Ralf Roth and Karl Schlögel (Frankfurt am Main: Campus Verlag, 2009), 134.

15. Heinrich von Stephan, *Geschichte der Preussischen Post von ihrem Ursprunge bis auf die Gegenwart* (Berlin: Decker, 1859), 606.

16. Louis-Maurice Jouffroy, *Une étape de la construction des Grandes Lignes de chemins de fer en France: La ligne de Paris à la frontière d'Allemagne (1825–1852)* (Paris: Dorbon-Ainé, 1932), 83.

17. Ibid., 70.

18. Beyrer, "The Mail-Coach Revolution," 378.

19. Ibid., 380.

20. Axel Heimsoth, "Chausseebau zwischen Brügge und St. Petersburg," in *Transit Brügge—Novgorod: Eine Straße durch die europäische Geschichte*, ed. Ferdinand Seibt, Ulrich Borsdorf, and Heinrich Theodor Grütter (Bottrop, Germany: Pomp Verlag, 1997), 475.

21. Uwe Müller, "Der Beitrag des Chausseebaus zum Modernisierungsprozess in Preußen," in *Die moderne Straße: Planung, Bau und Verkehr*, ed. Hans-Liudger Dienel and Hans-Ulrich Schiedt (Frankfurt am Main: Campus Verlag, 2010), 51–55.

22. Karamzin, "Letters of a Russian Traveler, 1789–1790."

23. Sigmund von Herberstein, *Das alte Rußland: In Anlehnung an die älteste deutsche Ausgabe aus dem Lateinischen übertragen von Wolfram von den Steinen* (1579; repr., Zürich: Manesse Verlag, 1984), 151–152. For a detailed description of Russian postal routes in the mideighteenth century, refer to M. Johann Joseph Haigold, *Beylagen zum Neuveränderten Russland: Erster Theil* (Riga: Johann Friedrich Hartknoch, 1769), 261–326.

24. Randolph, "The Singing Coachman," 39.

25. Roland Cvetkovski, *Modernisierung durch Beschleunigung: Raum und Mobilität im Zarenreich* (Frankfurt am Main: Campus Verlag, 2006), 161–164; Bekasova, "The Making of Passengers in the Russian Empire," 202.

26. Bekasova, "The Making of Passengers in the Russian Empire," 204.

27. Stephan, *Geschichte der Preussischen Post*, 561.

28. Cvetkovski, *Modernisierung durch Beschleunigung*, 170–171.

29. Frithjof Benjamin Schenk, "'This New Means of Transportation Will Make Unstable People Even More Unstable': Railways and Geographical Mobility in Tsarist Russia," in Randolph and Avrutin, *Russia in Motion*, 220.

30. Karamzin, "Letters of a Russian Traveler, 1789–1790," 46.

31. Nicolai Karamsin, *Travels from Moscow through Prussia, Germany, Switzerland and England, Vol. 1* (London: Sidney, 1803), 116. This passage is not part of the 1957 edition.

32. Bekasova, "The Making of Passengers in the Russian Empire," 205.

33. Karamzin, "Letters of a Russian Traveler, 1789–1790," 43.

34. Schenk, *Russlands Fahrt in die Moderne*, 189.

35. Wolfgang Behringer, "Eine neue Stufe der Verkehrsentwicklung: Das frühneuzeitliche Postsystem in Nordeuropa," in Seibt, Borsdorf, and Grütter, *Transit Brügge—Novgorod*, 365; Klaus Beyrer, "Aufbruch in die Moderne: Bürgerliches Reisen nach 1800," in *Zeit der Postkutschen: Drei Jahrhunderte Reisen 1600–1900*, ed. Klaus Beyrer, Wolfgang Behringer, and Deutsches Postmuseum (Karlsruhe: Braun, 1992), 223.

36. Beyrer, "The Mail-Coach Revolution," 379, 385; August Lewald, *Praktisches Reise-Handbuch nach und durch Italien: Mit Berücksichtigung aller dem Reisenden nothwendigen und wissenswerthen Angaben, auf Selbstanschauung begründet, und nach den neuesten und besten Quellen bearbeitet. Mit 2 Karten und 9 Plänen* (Stuttgart: Hoffmann, 1840), cf. Beyrer, "The Mail-Coach Revolution."

37. Julien Pecheux, *La naissance du rail européen 1800–1850* (Paris: Berger-Levrault, 1970), 113–115.

38. Klaus Beyrer, "Zeit der Postkutschen: Ein Überblick," in Beyrer, Behringer, and Deutsches Postmuseum, *Zeit der Postkutschen*, 20–23.

39. Philip Sidney Bagwell, *The Transport Revolution 1770–1985* (London: Batsford, 1974), 88–106.

40. Roth, *Das Jahrhundert der Eisenbahn*, 34–36.

41. Friedrich List, *Das deutsche National-Transport-System in volks- und staatswirthschaftlicher Beziehung.* (1838; repr. Berlin: Transpress, 1988), 6.

42. Jan Musekamp, "Friedrich List, die Eisenbahn, das Militär und Europa," *Themenportal Europäische Geschichte*, 2015, accessed November 24, 2015, http://www.europa.clio-online.de/2015/Article=735.

43. "Eisenbahn Karte von Deutschland und Nachbarländern" (Nürnberg: Sporer, 1849), accessed November 24, 2015, http://upload.wikimedia.org/wikipedia/commons/9/9f/Bahnkarte_Deutschland_1849.jpg; "Reise-Karte von Deutschland und einem Theile der angrenzenden Länder mit Angabe sämmtlicher Eisenbahnen nach den besten

Hülfmitteln bearbeitet," 1861, accessed November 24, 2015, http://upload.wikimedia.org /wikipedia/commons/5/54/Bahnkarte_Deutschland_1861.jpg.

44. Schivelbusch, *The Railway Journey*, 33–34; "Eisenbahn Karte von Deutschland und Nachbarländern."

45. Westwood, *A History of Russian Railways*, 30–31.

46. Bernt Mester, "Partikularismus der Schiene: Die Entwicklung einzelstaatlicher Eisenbahnsysteme bis 1870," in *Zug der Zeit—Zeit der Züge: Deutsche Eisenbahn 1835–1985. Das offizielle Werk zur gleichnamigen Ausstellung*, ed. Nürnberg Eisenbahnjahr Ausstellungsgesellschaft mbH (Berlin: Siedler, 1985), 204.

47. Bagwell, *The Transport Revolution 1770–1985.*

48. The construction of modern roads after 1815 and the development of a stagecoach network had already diminished the travel time between Berlin and Königsberg from twelve to three days; refer to N. N., "Wie man ehemals reiste," *Wanderer durch Ost- und Westpreußen* 2 (May 15, 1905), 36.

49. Geheimes Staatsarchiv Preußischer Kulturbesitz, Prussian Ministry of Finances, I. HA Rep. 151 III, Nr. 8127, Bl. 45–46; Friedrich Benecke, *Die Königsberger Börse* (Jena: Gustav Fischer, 1925), 79–81.

50. Juan Camilo Vergara, "La politique ferroviaire russe et les financiers étrangers: Les ambiguïtés d'un projet réformateur après la guerre de Crimée," *Cahiers du Monde russe* 55, no. 1–2 (2014).

51. "Eydtkuhnen, 23 kwietnia," *Dziennik Poznański* 99 (04/28/1861).

52. Augustus Bozzi Granville, *Guide to St. Petersburgh: A Journal of Travels to and from That Capital; Through Flanders, the Rhenish Provinces, Prussia, Russia, Poland, Silesia, Saxony, the Federated States of Germany, & France* (London: Henry Colburn, 1835), XXIII–XXXVI.

53. *Handbook for Northern Europe: Including Denmark, Norway, Sweden, Finland, and Russia; In Two Parts* (London: Murray, 1849), 438.

54. Thomas Michell, ed., *Murray's Handbook for Travellers in Russia, Poland, and Finland*, 2nd ed. (London: Murray, 1868), 65; Compagnie internationale des wagons-lits, *Guide officiel de la Compagnie internationale des wagons-lits* (1914).

55. John R. Stilgoe, *Metropolitan Corridor: Railroads and the American Scene* (New Haven, CT: Yale University Press, 1983).

56. Roland Wenzlhuemer, *Connecting the Nineteenth-Century World: The Telegraph and Globalization* (New York: Cambridge University Press, 2013), 31–32.

57. Ibid., 31.

58. Karl Schlegel [sic], "Europe a Country of Borders," *Herald of Europe*, no. 2 (2005), accessed November 24, 2015, http://www.heraldofeurope.co.uk/upload/iblock/405 /4058c6afd37b886b6bcb24934cd282da.pdf.

59. Vladimir Vladimirovich Nabokov, *Speak, Memory: An Autobiography Revisited* (New York: Knopf, 1999), 107–108.

60. Osterhammel, *Die Verwandlung der Welt*, 1018.

61. Ibid., 1033.

62. Barbara Schmucki, "'Nothing reminds you on the journey that England is an island...': Reiseerfahrungen, Verkehrsmittel und transnationale Mobilität in der ersten Hälfte des 20. Jahrhunderts," in *Verkehrsgeschichte: Histoire des transports*, ed. Hans-Ulrich Schiedt, Laurent Tissot, Christoph Maria Merki, and Rainer C. Schwinges (Zürich: Chronos Verlag, 2010), 310; Rudy Koshar, "'What ought to be seen': Tourists'

Guidebooks and National Identities in Modern Germany and Europe," *Journal of Contemporary History* 33, no. 3 (1998): 323–340.

63. Wolfgang Kaschuba, *Die Überwindung der Distanz: Zeit und Raum in der europäischen Moderne* (Frankfurt am Main: Gustav Fischer, 2004), 102.

64. Hopkins, "The History of Globalization," 25–41.

65. Schivelbusch, *The Railway Journey*, 38–40; Wenzlhuemer, *Connecting the Nineteenth-Century World*.

CHAPTER 2

"A Main Station at One's Front Door"
Bicycles, Automobiles, and Early Adopters' Dreams of Personal Mobility in Poland, 1885–1939

Nathaniel D. Wood

IN 1899, THE VARSOVIAN civil engineer Emil Sokal wrote, "In the West, they maintain that time is money; here it seems that time still has little value, yet there will come a time of change when rapid locomotion will prove extremely valuable, just as it allegedly already is abroad, except that the automobile will become an extraordinary advantage for us by replacing in many instances the railway with a main station at one's front door."[1] Sokal's enthusiasm for the automobile was much like the famed writer Bolesław Prus's fervor for the bicycle eight years earlier, when he gushed that the bicycle was a "miracle in an age that [did] not believe in miracles," a literal vehicle for personal and national regeneration.[2] In their enthusiasm for the new superlative machines of the age, Sokal and Prus were not that different from educated observers elsewhere, though both of them sensed that their society was somehow behind and they therefore placed greater hopes in the power of these new machines to help propel them forward. When, after a period of initial enthusiasm neither machine enjoyed as widespread adoption as in much of France, Germany, Great Britain, or the United States, Polish cycling and automotive enthusiasts were likely to be disappointed.

Bicycles and automobiles began as commodities for the elite, though in areas with advanced markets, a healthy middle class, and good roads, the new transportation technologies rapidly became more widespread during the period from their introduction in 1885 to 1939. Once the machines were mass-produced and more of them were in circulation, their prices dropped dramatically.[3] Before World War I, bicycles had become nearly ubiquitous in many Western cities. By 1908 in Stockholm, for example, there was one bicycle for every 10 citizens. In Warsaw, meanwhile, the figure was closer to one bicycle per 4,000 inhabitants.[4] Less than two decades later, there was one car per 245 inhabitants in Warsaw, while in Paris the ratio was 1:25, and if statistics in the Polish automotive press are to be believed, 1:13 in the United States.[5] In independent Poland, where the government insisted on seeing cars as luxury items and taxed them accordingly, automobile ownership actually declined in the 1930s, and only in 1939 did it match levels from the beginning of the decade. While bicycles had become more widespread in Poland by 1939, automobiles remained strictly in the preserve of the elite.

As literate participants in Western civilization, Polish elites were well aware of the new technologies of the "age of speed," a period of acceleration in transportation and communication that began in the 1880s with the creation of electric streetcars, safety bicycles, and automobiles.[6] They read specialist publications from France, Germany, and England and created similar journals of their own. They joined cycling and motoring clubs and followed the development of new technologies with great interest. And, whether under the rule of the partitioning powers or under the auspices of the new Polish state, they sought to popularize the machines among the general public, particularly as construed along ethno-national lines. They hoped that bicycles and automobiles would enable Poles to join the ranks of civilized nations, and better still, that they might be able to use them to race ahead of their perceived national rivals. They had grand dreams for the future, but these dreams were largely unfulfilled. When the age of speed came tearing through on foreign-built machines and without much infrastructure to sustain it, Poles, like many others, had a hard time steering its course. The best they could do was to go along for the ride.

In this Poles were of course not alone. While the history of technology typically focuses on "firsts"—those lucky and talented individuals whose innovations made an immediate or lasting impact—the story of early bicycle and automobile adoption in the Polish lands offers another, much more common lesson about the age of speed: the sensation of rushing forward, yet feeling behind. When viewed in the aggregate, according to national categories, Poles rarely triumphed. But this does not mean that Polish speakers were not participants in the race for mechanized personal mobility at all. Early adopters, who are the principal focus of this study, participated more or less simultaneously in the age of speed but felt more acutely the contrasts of speed and sluggishness as they noted the gap between the modernity embodied in these swift new machines and the general lack of infrastructure that surrounded them. Thanks to the related new technologies of the age, including increased railway connections, more efficient postal services, telegraphs, telephones, and the mass-circulation press, educated elites and early adopters could see or read about the proliferation of bicycles and automobiles in the West almost instantaneously. As they tried to mimic, "catch up with," or even supersede their contemporaries abroad, they inevitably had to deal with the constraints of backwardness in their race to the fore. Many of the impediments were of their own making—elitism and gender bias among the affluent and often aristocratic elites who first bought bicycles and automobiles in the Polish lands naturally limited the spread of new technologies to a broader populace—but plenty, such as poor roads, were not. Early adopters' dreams of national parity with the nations of the West were generally dashed, even if on a personal level they managed to ride alongside, both metaphorically and at times literally, their foreign contemporaries. Caught in the grips of two powerful and frequently conflicting ideologies of the day, the gospel of speed and the religion of nationalism, early adopters sometimes struggled to reconcile their adherence to both. If we shift from the national framework, we begin to see these early adopters as part of an international community of enthusiasts—rarely its leaders, but participants nonetheless.

RUSHING FORWARD: DREAMS OF THE FUTURE

The year 1885 was a momentous one in the history of personal mechanized movement. In that year Carl Friedrich Benz (1844–1929), a gifted mechanic in Mannheim, Germany, built the first automobile, a tricycle with a three-horsepower internal combustion engine of his own design. That same year, in Stuttgart, only 120 kilometers away, and independently of Benz, Gottlieb Daimler (1834–1900) and Wilhelm Maybach (1846–1929) constructed their first automobile, a two-wheeled vehicle with a small, fast one-cylinder gasoline engine.[7] All three men had looked to the bicycle as a model for designing a self-propelled vehicle. Benz had brainstormed ideas about creating a motorized vehicle while riding his bicycle, and when he designed his first automobile, it used wire wheels like bicycles of the day, instead of the wooden ones used on carriages. Daimler and Maybach's first automobile, meanwhile, clearly resembled a bicycle, and in fact anticipated the motorcycle.

That same year in Coventry, England, John Kemp Starley (1854–1901) modified his Rover safety bicycle into the first embodiment of the bicycle as we know it today, with both wheels of more or less equal size and a chain between the pedals and rear wheel.[8] In Polish the current word for "bicycle," *rower*, derives directly from this proprietary name. One year later, Count Edward Chrapowiecki, who had been impressed with cycling clubs in Paris, founded the Warsaw Society of Cyclists, Warszawskie Towarzystwo Cyklistów or WTC, with the blessing of Tsar Alexander III, whose son, Nicholas II, was also a cyclist.[9]

Half a decade later, in August 1891, the popular Varsovian writer Bolesław Prus (pseud. Aleksander Głowacki, 1847–1912), whose novels and feuilletons were widely read in all three Polish partitions and who would soon be world renowned for his novel *Pharaoh* (1894–1895), learned to ride a bicycle in the spa town of Nałęczów. Shortly afterward, Prus published a rapturous five-part article in the popular daily *Kurjer Codzienny* about the velocipede, as human-propelled vehicles were still more frequently called. In it, Prus described his own often humorous experience of learning to ride while extolling the virtues of the new machine. "In the vicinity of Warsaw there is probably not a single hardworking yokel who has not nicked his ax on some velocipede, no peasant horse that has not been frightened by one, nor a village dog that has not tasted a cyclist's calves." Prus began hyperbolically, before suggesting that "before one generation passes," cycling would catch on so thoroughly that "every Varsovian will only use the narrow trousers, wear several honorary badges on his chest [like members of the WTC], and have a lot of blisters on the organs that directly communicate with that miraculous machine."[10] Fear of the new, he hopefully predicted, would shortly be replaced with widespread adoption.[11]

> The velocipede has obtained tremendous popularity among us, perhaps thanks to the fact that it only requires healthy legs—and not exceptionally healthy ones at that. Already a good number do not consider riding on a velocipede as something indecent, street urchins no longer run after a speeding biker, now the peasant no longer bids farewell when he sees one, searching for a rod.[12]

Continuing, Prus noted the bicycle's status as a commodity, repeatedly referring to it in terms of cost, credit, and consumption. "You can already buy a velocipede in installments; shortly it will be sold 'at half price because it's been ridden before,' and who knows if sometime on the street we won't see a vendor of used goods holding worn-out galoshes in one hand and in the other—a used bicycle. In a word," he attested, "the velocipede will become an article of everyday use, like a watch, a piano, or Swedish matches."[13] Prus next explained how the velocipede worked, extolling its miraculous magnification of energy, and then relayed his personal diary entries about learning to ride. He noted that he had since purchased one himself, paying for it "in installments."[14]

Prus added another justification for the bicycle's utility: namely, its "social and hygienic" benefit. Convinced of the deleterious effect of modern urban life on the "miserable . . . ill fed" youth of "the wealthy and educated classes," whose "lives pass by within the walls of an unhealthful city, without any physical labor, and even without movement," Prus saw the bicycle as the perfect antidote. Instead of allowing "drinking establishments, cards and debauchery" to "consume what little strength they [had] left," this dubious intelligentsia could find its strength, health, and purpose on long bicycle rides into the countryside! Thus Prus enlisted the bicycle, like "small-scale work," engineering, and industry into the repertoire of tools that could bring about the Positivists' aim of revitalizing the Polish nation from within. Significantly, the bicycle followed the same pattern of flowing from the city to the countryside, while presuming that each side of the exchange had something to gain from the other's presence there.

Returning to the language of money and credit in his conclusion, Prus pitched the bicycle as a commodity wholly worthy of investment:

> And so, my readers, men and women alike! If you have the money, buy a bicycle. Don't think that it is of the devil, don't be afraid of the rigors of learning to ride, don't underestimate it as just a toy, but rather learn to ride—and ride as often and as far from town as you can. In a very short time your muscles will get thicker, you'll sleep better, your appetite and good humor will return, you'll become a brave and courageous person and you'll thank the author of this text that he so enthusiastically recommended it to you.

"Believe me for now on credit," he concluded, "that you'll find greater pleasure than you ever imagined and energy that you never knew you had in you."[15]

The 1890s were an age of tremendous enthusiasm for the bicycle, particularly in the less-developed parts of Europe, where the bicycle could be seen as a vehicle for future development. Unsurprisingly, Prus was not the only Polish writer who connected the new machines with a brighter future. In late 1896, the editors of the Varsovian cycling magazine *Cyklista* sent out a survey to "50 of the greatest Polish writers" and, pleasantly surprised with the response rate, published approximately twenty replies in the first issue of the new year.[16] Respondents included such notables as Henryk Sienkiewicz (whose reply was full of nationalist and personal bravura) and Aleksander Świętochowski, as well as many other writers largely forgotten today to all but specialists. Most of the writers had been born in the middle of the century and none of them admitted to have actually ridden a bicycle, though Sienkiewicz had recently taken up the sport.[17] This, of course, did not prevent them from sharing their observations about the wondrous new machine. Świętochowski noted that he could not write from experience, having never ridden a bicycle, but permitted himself the following observations:

1.) The bicycle has had and continues to have a tremendous influence on human transportation, particularly for societies where the roads are good;
2.) It has consumed a significant portion of the unused or wasted strength of the youth;
3.) To a certain extent it has become a means for democratizing societies.

"If I'm right about this," he concluded, then the bicycle could be seen "as one of the greatest inventions for good." Esteja (Józefa ze Skórzewskich Kisielnicka) likewise saw the bicycle as a social leveler. Noting that everyone who rode them assumed the "same physiognomy" and that a postal carrier was just as likely to win "the victor's palm" in a race as a margrave, she concluded that on a bicycle "the popular slogan 'time is money' rushes, rushes along briskly, without asking who directs or rides it. Democracy should have a bicycle as its emblem."[18] In a period when most people walked to traverse most distances, and only the well-to-do could afford to travel on horseback or in carriages, the bicycle seemed to be a tremendous leveler of space and time, revolutionizing the way that people would conceive distance, both social and literal.[19]

Other survey writers noted the bicycle's beauty, though several, including Marian Gawalewicz, poked fun at how silly riders looked with their hunched backs "like a cat hunting rats" and their "legs churning like an overturned maybug." Gawalewicz was more enthusiastic about "the bicycles themselves," particularly in the future, "when they will cease to be just a privileged toy for sportsmen and become a practical source of locomotion for us, when [he would] begin to see people who are obligated by time and punctuality such as delivery people, postal carriers, shop workers with packages, office workers rushing to work, pupils speeding to school, and so forth."[20]

If Polish writers in 1896 tended to have never ridden a bicycle, and to associate the machines with the desired future, another writer cited in *Cyklista* just a few weeks later, Émile Zola, who rode one regularly, connected them with the present—and an imagined youthful past:

> My thoughts on cycling? They're quite limited, because I'm just an amateur.... [I ride 15 to 20 km after breakfast to get my body moving.] But I really regret that I'm not younger and less busy. I'm convinced that if I were 20 years younger and had more time, I would be a committed cyclist. To give in to rapture from all sides, rise with the wind, and chase the horizon before us—is a delightful daze. Particularly for us, paper pushers with heads full of phrases, there is nothing so beneficial as to forget for a moment our trade [and get out on a bicycle]. I return from my outings on a velocipede fully rested, with a clear head, all ready for tomorrow's labors. A velocipede gives satisfaction and works on the hygiene of our bodies and spirits. What more could one ask for?'[21]

I do not wish to make too much of this distinction between Zola's acceptance of the bicycle as something familiar and ensconced in the present, as opposed to his Polish contemporaries who tended to see it as less familiar and a source of future development, but I do think it is significant. At almost exactly the same time, bicycles were already more familiar to the famed Western European writer than to his Polish contemporaries, particularly those who still lived in the Polish lands. Expatriate writer Marjan Jasieńczyk (1855–1911) wrote from Geneva that on the shores of Lake Leman, "the question of cycling has long been a foregone conclusion. The bicycle has come to life, it has inserted itself into the needs of everyday life, and has ceased to be a toy or exclusively limited to sport ... such that in city literature it will assuredly take an equal place with horses, carriages, and automobiles."[22] Prus would insert bicycles into literature with his novel *Ze wspomnienia cyklisty* (From the recollections of a cyclist) in 1902 (published in 1904 as a book), and of course he had taken up cycling more than a half decade before, but one gets the sense that when it came to cycling, the Poles remained slightly behind. Sienkiewicz's injunction to Polish bicycle racers in his survey response "to try not only to match the English, French, or Germans, but to beat them utterly" conveys this desire to catch up and even overtake the powerful nations of the West.[23]

Some twenty-five years later the automotive enthusiast Henryk Czaplicki expressed a similar sentiment. In 1922, flush with optimism and in just the second issue of the new specialist magazine *Auto*, he stated: "I hope that in the field [of automobiles], we'll soon overtake America!"[24] (See figure 2.1.) Czaplicki's dream was less easily obtainable than Sienkiewicz's—winning a few cycling races required far less than building roads and an entire automobile industry—but the inspiration was similar. For many people, automobiles, like bicycles, seemed to be an ideal vehicle to propel them or their nation into the future: few things were more evocative of modernity and an escape from one's backward past than the sleek new machines. Whether in the 1880s and 1890s, when the first automobiles appeared in the Polish lands, or in the early 1920s, when Polish independence gave nationalists reason to hope that Poland could join the ranks of modern motorized nations, automobile enthusiasts dreamed of catching up or even superseding technologically advanced nations to the west.

Figure 2.1 *"Our automotive activists. H. Czaplicki: 'I hope that in this field, we'll soon overtake America!'"*
Source: *Auto. Ilustrowane czasopismo sportowo-techniczne* 2 (June 2, 1922), 2.

The earliest Polish dreams for automobiles were more circumspect. In 1885 Bolesław Prus described for his readers in *Kurjer Warszawski* a new-fangled machine that had just been invented in Germany. It was, he wrote, "an 'automobile' ('samochód') a tool that moves without the exertion of 'any of the known forces,' and thus without the muscles of horses, the descent of water, wind momentum, gravity, elasticity, heat, or electromagnetic currents. Under this influence I fell into a dream." In Prus's "dream" the inventor of the automobile, visiting Warsaw with his invention, arrived in a horseless carriage pushed from behind by an accomplice. When, after a time, the machine did not go anywhere of its own accord, the disappointed populace wanted to pummel the inventor. This compelled the police to get involved, and in order to remove the stationary vehicle from the middle of the street, one of the policemen was obliged to push it, while the inventor, hauled along by his collar, doffed his hat and bowed to the crowd. Such a motive power, Prus wryly acknowledged, was already well known.[25]

By 1896, when Stanisław Grodzki had imported the first automobiles to Warsaw, two Benzes and a Peugeot, working automobiles were no longer machines no one had ever seen. Grodzki soon demonstrated their capabilities for the police chief, and the latter granted permission for automobiles to drive on Varsovian streets. Automotive historians Aleksander Rostocki and Jan Tarczyński speculate that the police chief simply adapted the law for bicycles, which had been adopted earlier that year, to automobiles.[26] In an effort to promote his machines, Grodzki worked with *Cyklista* and the newspaper *Kurjer Warszawski* to organize a road rally in the vicinity of Warsaw and then to publicize his successful Warsaw-to-Paris drive in 1897.[27] While in Paris, Grodzki met the owners of the De Dion-Bouton automotive company and obtained the rights to sell De Dion-Boutons in Warsaw. Especially popular were their motorized tricycles, which were often purchased with a trailer in which to tow one's family. By the waning years of the nineteenth century, automobiles were still rare, but plenty of Varsovians had at least seen them.[28] In 1899, Krogulec (the sparrow hawk, pseud. Antoni Orłowski) published a humorous verse about automobiles in Warsaw, in which he claimed that young Varsovians had no need to be envious of people abroad, for cars had appeared on their streets, too. They would soon see clerks driving to their offices, elegant women passing through town in automobiles for their rendezvous, and boys calling out from cars, "'The *Kurjer*, four grosze apiece!'"

Today no young Varsovian envies Anyone abroad. For here on our streets Automobiles have appeared. ... The sport catches on with everyone; One glance and they're seeing stars. And this declining century soon gone Will give way to the age of cars.[29]	Nie zazdrości zagranicy Dziś warszawiak żaden młody, Bo i u nas na ulicy Zjawiły się samochody. ... Sport ten w każdym wzrośnie człeku Po złamaniu pierwszych lodów I ginący schyłek wieku Będzie—erą samochodów.

By the second decade of the twentieth century, when cars were more common in Polish-speaking lands, an engineer who signed his article *Inż L Sz* contributed a thoughtful essay on the need for speed and mobility in the modern age. "In perhaps no other branch of progress and perfection of material culture of the first decade of the twentieth century have we seen such lengths as in motorized transportation," he began. "Motorized transportation, which until recently had been a novelty, . . . has become today an ordinary component of the picture of a modern street." Arguing that "speed" was the byword of the era, L Sz observed that the "car [had] become . . . an expression of the accelerated pulse of modern life."

> If an ancestor of ours from the Stone Age managed to be faster than one of his compatriots and catch an animal more swiftly than him, it could only be because of the fleetness of his legs; for us, people of the XXth century, the speed of the electric tram has begun to seem insufficient, with its frequent necessitated stops. Bah, desiring to precede our fellow professional, or to be the complete master of our own will, we already grumble about express trains, which depart only at certain times and are compelled to stop in cities that are entirely meaningless to the purposes of our travel.
>
> [It's] nothing that the roar of the engine rattles the nerves that are already a bit too sensitive, that the smell of burning gasoline pollutes the air, that after several dozen [kilometers], which at times can take more than several hours for travel, that a person climbs out of the car unconscious from the shaking, noise, and chaos of images that flashed before his eyes—just to get to his destination quicker!

Clearly cautious about the costs of the age of speed, L Sz thought that the power of automobility could be put to better use than for joyriding in the countryside or shuttling the elite to their destinations. "Fortunately, perhaps for the health of society and protection from general nervousness—such methods of benefiting from the growth of automobilism are not yet available to everyone," he mused. The remainder of his article promoted public motorized transportation, which, he was convinced, would compensate for the gaps and delays in rail service whether by tram or train, and the increased use of automobiles for industry and trade. The democratization of automobility, he opined, would be best served in the proliferation of taxis, buses, and trucks.[30]

Cities like Warsaw had a long way to go, however, in catching up to big cities abroad in terms of automobile or taxi use. The first gasoline engine taxis appeared, with the support of their local magistrates, at the turn of the century: in 1898 in Paris; 1899 in Berlin, Stockholm, and Vienna; 1900 in London; and 1903 in Copenhagen. A variety of companies tried to set up taxi service in Warsaw, with the first officially registered company beginning in 1908. By 1912 there were approximately 80 taxis in Warsaw, a year later 90, and nearly 150 just before the war broke out.[31] This represented significant growth. Yet in the same period there were some 12,000 taxis in London, according to a contributor to *Lotnik i Automobilista* (Airman and Motorist). "This is a huge number," he observed, "even for the biggest city in the world, and thus it shows that it pays to have taxis. There are no speed limits; everyone goes as fast as he wishes, but because there are so many taxis, traffic never gets too fast."[32] Readers of the magazine could envision their future while marveling at London traffic.

In its inaugural issue in 1922, the magazine *Auto* noted Poland's backwardness in relation to its Western neighbors, stating that its fundamental goal would be for "Poland to equal, as quickly as possible, all other Western states" in terms of motoring and aviation.[33] The magazine was prepared to blame the Polish state for its failures in this regard. In just its fourth issue, in an article titled "Our Automotive Industry and the Politics of the Government," *Auto* noted that "in all cultured states of Western Europe as well as in America, the automobile has for some time now ceased to be considered a luxury item, but rather is one of the most important and most valuable means to maintaining their current civilizational standard and promoting their further progress in culture as well as industrial growth and national wealth. Thanks to the short-sighted politics of the government, our country is being prevented from adopting" the vitally important automobile.[34] In articulating this perspective, the editors of *Auto* made clear their concern about the Ministry of Military Affairs' failure to invest properly in making Poland a hospitable place for automotive growth. Grasping this, however, did not prevent *Auto*, which shortly became the organ of the Polish Automobile Club (Polski Automobilklub), from perpetuating the same state of affairs. The club donated some of its funds to help the state build better roads, but it also regularly took the side of owners over chauffeurs and remained an elitist organization. Neither the state nor the privileged few who owned automobiles succeeded in making them affordable or accessible to the masses.

FOR WHOM "THE MAIN STATION AT ONE'S FRONT DOOR"?

One of the major problems limiting the proliferation of bicycles and automobiles in Polish-speaking lands was the fact that it took so long for either machine to progress beyond the realm of sport, to acquire a mass base beyond the elites, who had first adopted them. The Warsaw Society of Cyclists, the Galician Automobile Club, the Warsaw Automotive Club, and other such organizations were elitist establishments, which, despite their stated goal of promoting the growth of their sport, consistently espoused programs and policies that inhibited broader adoption. Each organization was founded by noblemen and strove to maintain its exclusivity. The membership rules of the WTC, for example, explicitly prohibited women, teachers, and professional cyclists, including cycling teachers (!), from joining.[35] Membership rosters of the various automobile clubs, from the Galician Automobile Club of the prewar era, whose president was the viceroy of Galicia, to the Polish Automobile Club of the 1920s, were stacked with noblemen of the most prominent aristocratic families, including the Potockis, Lubomirskis, Czartoryskis, Sapiehas, and Radziwiłłs. Count Karol Raczyński, brother of the future ambassador to England, Edward Raczyński, was president of the club for much of the 1920s. Ambassadors, foreign dignitaries, industrialists, and other eminent automobile owners also joined the club, which required an exclusive voting system in order to determine membership.[36] Nine women total made it onto the 1924 and 1927 rosters of the Polish Automobile Club, but only two of them were not a titled noblewoman, countess, princess, or ambassador's wife.[37] As a writer in *Auto* candidly observed several months before it became the official organ of the Polish Automobile Club, "automobile clubs both here in Poland and the world over are institutions of a purely sporting nature, and so it follows that the overwhelming majority of their members consists not of specialists but rather of putatively sophisticated dilettantes [whose interests do not match the range and complexity] of the branch of human endeavor that is motoring."[38] In an effort to maintain exclusivity while spreading motoring, Raczyński and others helped found the Polish Touring Club (Polski Touring Klub, PTK) in 1925, to reach out to the *średnie klasy* (middle classes). According to its charter, anyone who had a car or motorcycle could join.[39]

Early automotive clubs sought to teach motoring skills by offering free chauffeur classes on evenings and weekends, in a deliberate attempt to train drivers.[40] Competence at driving, however, did not mean that chauffeurs were welcomed into the fold of automotive enthusiasts. Well into the 1920s and 1930s there was mutual mistrust between owners and hired drivers of cars, a distinct class prejudice that failed to abate as quickly as in Great Britain or especially in the United States, where more professionals, farmers, and eventually working-class citizens could afford cars, thus leveling the sense of social superiority wealthy drivers may have felt vis-à-vis other motorists.[41] In the eighth issue of *Auto* a contributor writing under the pen name of SZCZEBEL ("level" or "grade") observed that chauffeurs were "not the most 'solid' individuals," apt to abuse or take advantage of their "access to expensive machines" by hauling people or cargo in them for their own profit on the side or tricking their employers to buy often unnecessary parts from shops where they stood to gain from making the recommendations. The author concluded by belittling the nouveaux riches who bought cars, too, observing that not all chauffeurs were unprofessional, but "shopkeepers" and "businessmen" who hired "the cousin of a chauffeur because he's cheaper, rather than relying on professional, qualified drivers," were ensuring that there were more "bad seeds" in the lot.[42] Slightly more sensitive, but no less convinced of his moral superiority, Zygmunt Borawski observed in *Auto* that the relationship between automobile owner and driver should not merely be that of a master and servant, but rather more collegial, because they share the car between them. If an owner wishes to have a chauffeur who is "devoted to him," Borawski wrote, he must treat him appropriately. "His relationship should be full of solicitude and thoughtfulness without showing his superiority."[43] Chauffeurs, meanwhile, felt caught between a public that distrusted the fast machines on the streets and the owners of those machines, who doubted their drivers' fealty. The first issue of *Szofer Polski* (Polish chauffeur) proclaimed in its mission statement its desire "to oppose the vicious and superficial allegations and accusations, spread so often against chauffeurs, as reflected in the columns of the press and administration of our government."[44] As befitting such a beleaguered group, each issue had a section called "Troski i bolączki dnia powszedniego" (Everyday concerns and pains).[45]

DREAMS DASHED OR DELAYED

Specialist clubs and their publications tended to get off to a strong start, but over time, interest waned and they had to scramble to maintain interest. In 1889, according to cycling historian Bogdan Tuszyński, there were 600 cyclists in all of Poland, of whom 12 were women.[46] Clubs arose in Lemberg (Lwów), Cracow, Łódź, and numerous smaller towns and cities within years of the creation of the WTC, which by 1897 had 763 members. Yet as late as 1913 *Lotnik i Automobilista* complained that moderately small towns in England, France, and Germany had more cycling club members than the WTC in Warsaw—which had a population of eight hundred thousand.[47]

The cycling magazine *Cyklista*, the semiofficial organ of the WTC, offers a great pattern of auspicious beginnings, followed by the sensation of dreams dashed or delayed. From the outset *Cyklista* did a marvelous job of providing competent and varied coverage about cycling in Warsaw and throughout Polish-speaking lands. After several years, however, articles suggesting dissension in the ranks of the club made it clear that there was an increasing divide among those who had joined more for the social aspects of membership and those who sought to promote the sport more particularly.[48] In 1898, *Cyklista* changed its name to *Sport* and, overnight, the balance of articles in the journal shifted from coverage of cycling in the Polish-speaking territories and abroad to close coverage of the ancient sport of kings, horse racing. By the beginning of the twentieth century, there was more diversity in the kinds of sport covered in its pages, but the magazine had largely become a digest of the foreign press. On the one hand it showed how international and interconnected the world of sport was, but on the other hand, one doubts that the French or English were reading about sporting events by Poles in Warsaw, for example, in their specialized journals. The WTC and its journal were on the outside looking in. In the final issue of 1906, the editors finally threw in the towel: "[This] is also the last issue of 'Polish Sport' because, due to truly difficult times and the indifference of our society toward matters of public health generally and to specific sports in particular, we do not feel that we have the strength to haul the wheelbarrow any further."[49] The editors' metaphor of a wheelbarrow, a wheeled machine associated not with speed or progress but with the rusticated life of the countryside, was telling.

Like its antecedent, *Cyklista/Sport*, *Lotnik i Automobilista* (1911–1914) struggled throughout its existence with a desire to make aviation, automobilism, and sport fit the Polish context, while keeping track of innovations elsewhere. It did well in the latter, offering readers an impressive array of high-quality original articles and translations of articles from the foreign specialist press, but it was quite inconsistent in the former, at times insisting on Polish neologisms for words like *airplane, aviation, pilot*, and the like while at other times using homonyms directly adapted from English or French. From its inception, *Lotnik i Automobilista* was the official organ of Awiata, an aviation club and airplane factory created thanks to the initiative and deep pockets of Prince Stanisław Lubomirski. Built "on a European standard of modern technology, on a level that [could] rival factories abroad," Awiata manufactured all of its airplane parts on site in Mokotów, just south of Warsaw, except the motors, which were imported. Adjacent to the factory was an aviation school, "in which a host of pupils [studied] under the direction of the pilot-instructor Mr. Segno." For 450 rubles, pupils could enroll in a six- to eight-week course covering "both theory and practice," including takeoffs from the Mokotów racetrack.[50] The club hosted flights by foreign aviators. The chauffeur school mentioned earlier was also located at the Mokotów facilities. Much like Dynasy, the impressive clubhouse and velodrome of the WTC built in the 1890s, the Awiata facilities at Mokotów were of a high standard, but they failed to bring about the widespread acceptance and adoption of their respective sports.

Despite its auspicious beginnings, by 1913 Awiata had begun to falter. In March of that year, the editors of *Lotnik i Automobilista* complained bitterly about the immediate prospects for aviation in the Polish lands. "If cycling, automobilism, rowing, etc. are vegetating here, they are still far better than aviation, which is totally anemic," the magazine asserted. "Let's be honest, and admit that one cannot even talk about any wider involvement with aviation here at all. Certainly there are people who follow the developments of aviation, and there are even some, who in the silence of their offices and workshops even think up new plans and experiences, but no one knows anything about it, and nor do they even try."[51] Once Awiata collapsed, *Lotnik i Automobilista* still managed to keep aloft. Continuing a trend that was already quite apparent, the journal published a greater proportion of articles about motoring and sports like rowing and hunting. It remained the official organ of the Polish Automobile Club and in addition to advertising revenues from local and foreign businesses connected to motoring, the magazine won the support of another aviation club, the Student Aviation Union in Lemberg (Związek Awiatyczny Studentów), which had also been founded in 1909 and was connected to Edmund Libański and the Lemberg Polytechnic.[52] *Lotnik i Automobilista* was not yet "buried for the eternities," but it could no longer dream of being a fundamental member of a culture that was "on a European standard."[53]

Polish cyclists and motorists clearly dreamed of developing their sport on a European standard, and at times they succeeded, but successes were generally small or fleeting. Not until the 1920s did cycling really take off in Poland, despite inflation, the lingering effects of war, and general difficulty, while one could argue that mass automobility really arrived in Poland in the 1990s, after the collapse of communism. The Federation of Polish Cycling Associations began its application to the International Federation of Cycling in 1922 and was granted membership in full standing in 1923. This meant that Poles could now participate in international championship competitions. In 1924 the Polish four-thousand-meter relay team, composed of three members of the WTC and a cyclist from Cracow's club, won silver at the Olympics, the first Olympic medal for Polish athletes. A quarter of a century after Sienkiewicz called for it, Polish cyclists had finally fulfilled his injunction to beat the English, Germans, and French—only the Italians, who took gold, had surpassed them. By 1925 there were thirty-nine cycling clubs in Poland, though only Warsaw and Łódź had a velodrome.[54] An archival letter Tuszyński includes in his text shows that official membership in cycling clubs across Poland leapt from 848 in 1919 to 7,452 on January 1, 1929.[55]

Growth of cycling was not limited to clubs, however. By the end of the 1920s many more people had taken up cycling for reasons other than sport or club association. In 1930, the State Armament Factory (Państwowa Wytwórnia Uzbrojenia), which advertised its "Łucznik" (archer) bicycles as "a Polish bicycle—for Polish roads," was building five thousand of them a month, thus producing most of the eighty thousand bicycles manufactured in Poland that year.[56] Even if some of those bicycles were sold abroad, plenty of foreign bicycles would have been purchased in Poland, too. Bicycles had become a mass-market item. But their dissemination in Poland remained paltry by Western standards. While bicycle sales had plummeted in the United States in the 1920s because of the relatively inexpensive cost of automobiles, in Western Europe, the sturdy machines had become a nearly ubiquitous means of transportation. Germany, which had half the population of the United States, had nearly five times as many bicycles—fifteen million. "Great Britain and France each had seven million cycles, followed by Italy with four million," notes cycling historian David Herlihy. "Even the tiny Netherlands had three million: one for almost every other citizen."[57]

What could account for the Polish lag from 1885 to 1939? Perhaps the most fundamental reason, Tuszyński suggests, was the terrible state of the roads, particularly in Galicia and the Congress Kingdom, where, unlike in the Prussian territories, there was a greater desire to form clubs. Poverty and an underdeveloped middle class also clearly hampered the widespread proliferation of cycling. Bicycles produced in the Polish lands were not of the newest design and too expensive for the average rider, in large part because they were produced in smaller quantities. Foreign firms—there were eighteen in Warsaw by 1912—offered bicycles of the highest quality, but at 150 rubles apiece they remained far too expensive for most people.[58] The bachelor protagonist of Bolesław Prus's *From the Recollections of a Cyclist*, a bank clerk, made 180 rubles a month in 1902, of which 25 rubles went to rent for his modest two-room apartment and 50 or so went to savings.[59] For ordinary urbanites, rent was a much higher proportion of their monthly salary and bicycles remained out of reach. Prus's belief that "there [would] come a time when the velocipede [became] an article of daily use, like a watch, piano, or Swedish matches" proved to be wishful thinking—at least in the time frame in which he envisioned it.

Bicycles did not catch on as quickly in the Polish lands as in Great Britain or Germany because material and social conditions for their use were underdeveloped. The gender and class imbalances present upon their introduction were more pronounced in Polish-speaking lands, where the lack of a strong middle class meant that aristocrats still disproportionately dictated the terms of their adoption. Women, elementary school teachers, soldiers, Junkers (Prussian aristocrats), and convicts were forbidden from joining the WTC. And while *Cyklista* published plenty of encouraging articles about women and cycling, they tended to be patronizing and limiting. One article from 1895 explored the reasons why, given the "tremendous growth of our sport, particularly in the last three years," so few of "our women" rode bicycles:

> It's true that even though publications that cater to women take up the issue from time to time, give advice regarding appropriate outfits, and even speak of it encouragingly, among our women a certain unjustifiable restraint persists. For while women abroad who participate in our sport number in the thousands and ladies from the highest spheres of society cultivate this beautiful and healthful entertainment, here a woman riding on a bicycle remains a very pretty, but rare, sight.[60]

The author attested that "the widely held, but incorrect, idea that cycling is too physically demanding and even harmful for the fairer sex" was outdated and misguided. He called for removing the corset to ride and encouraged more women to take to the saddle, so long as they did not think to pursue racing, which was unbecoming for them. Similar articles could be found in specialist magazines across Europe at the time. An article in the premiere issue of *Cyklista*, citing a study by "the youngest member of the French Academy of Sciences" that affirmed the health benefits of cycling for women, quoted Dr. Just Championnière, who "rightly observe[d]," the translator affirmed, that "'a woman looks beautiful on a bicycle, so long as she is not dressed like a man.'" The French doctor pointed out that a woman could not compete with a man in endurance and speed, "'but she looks better on the saddle, just as pretty as she looks dancing.'"[61] Such patronizing remarks aside, in countries like Great Britain with a proportionately larger group of middle- and even working-class women who could both socially and financially afford to ride, the barriers to women riders collapsed sooner. The same was true of postal workers and delivery people, who were among the first to see the practical and material benefits of cycling. Early on, there was simply not a large enough group of people in the Polish lands who could afford to use bicycles for workforce mobility, or who would have grasped their clear benefit.

Tuszyński argues that people remained suspicious of the machines while "negative pronouncements from doctors and hygienists and press campaigns (particularly in the years 1895–97 and 1908), along with the protests of all sorts of cyclophobes, of which there was never any shortage in Poland" limited their rapid adoption.[62] Numerous newspaper accounts complained of cyclists tearing through city streets and parks, though this was not unique to the Polish lands.[63] Stories and notices in *Cyklista* help confirm Tuszyński's observation that doctors were slow to accept the machines. (In the United States, Canada, and Great Britain, meanwhile, many doctors were quick to see the value of bicycle and automobile adoption for making house calls, while demonstrating their status as "moderns".) In one humorous instance of a Polish doctor's intransigence, Krogulec recounted his recent marriage to a lovely young woman he met at the club's masquerade ball the previous winter and their conflict over cycling due to poor counsel from a doctor. After the couple's wedding, the bride gave her groom an ultimatum: choose her or the bike. Not wishing to jeopardize the honeymoon, Krogulec acceded to her confusing request. But a few months later he took his bicycle out while she was gone and had a wonderful ride. He returned home to a devastated spouse. "'You rode? Oh how unfortunate I am. Who will take me once I divorce you?'" Not knowing what else to do, he embraced and kissed his weeping wife. "The method worked." Befuddled, she asked, "'How is it that you're kissing me?' 'Why wouldn't I kiss you? After all, you know I love you.' 'Yes, but . . .' 'But what?'" And then she confessed that their "friend the doctor" told her that if her husband rode a bicycle he would not be able—or have the desire—to be intimate with her. 'Oh I wish a dog would bite him! That old brusher, flat tire, hack Asclepius!'" Krogulec spouted, using curses a cyclist would particularly relish.[64]

Prejudices borne of ignorance and lack of experience with the machines, the lack of a stratum of potential buyers who could afford them, poor roads, elitism among aficionados and the lack of state support, particularly during the partition era, delayed the spread of cycling in the Polish lands. Early adopters participated more or less simultaneously with their fellow sportsmen in the West, but any dreams of widespread personal mobility took much longer to come true.

Motoring naturally suffered from many of the same fundamental problems, but because automobiles required much more infrastructure and state support, their delayed adoption can also be blamed on the state. The new Polish state actively endorsed aviation clubs as a source of future spe-

Figure 2.2 *Contemporary advertising acknowledged the sorry state of Polish roads. Advertisement for Austro-Daimler 17/60 HP, "An ideal car for our roads."*
Source: *Auto. Ilustrowane czasopismo sportowo-techniczne* 9 (May 1, 1923), 8.

cialists, but automobiles were less obviously vital for military purposes, and the Ministry of Railways saw them as competition. In 1921 there were only 40,000 kilometers of surfaced roads in all of Poland, with the better roads concentrated in the formerly German territories, parts of Galicia, and the westernmost parts of Russian Poland. Northeastern and eastern Poland were almost entirely without roads (figure 2.2). During the interwar period, the total of surfaced roads increased to 63,000 kilometers, but many of these roads were cobblestone. In a country of nearly 33 million inhabitants, there were 38,760 registered automobiles in 1931, the year that a new tax caused their precipitous decline.[65] It was not until 1939 that their numbers returned to 1931 levels. In 1928 slightly more cars were sold in Poland (3,900) than in Austria (3,300), but many fewer than in Czechoslovakia, where 17,560 cars were purchased, or even in Romania, which sold some 6,000 of them.[66] It did not help that none of the territories from Russia, Prussia, and Austria that formed the new Polish state housed automotive factories.

Innovative Poles created original automobile designs, including the Ralf Stetysz, which the expatriate Count Stefan Tyszkiewicz designed particularly for Polish roads. The automobile found tremendous success at the 1928 Monte Carlo Grand Prix, before withdrawing in first place on the last stage because the navigator had contracted appendicitis.[67] Tyszkiewicz's string of bad luck continued, when the factory in Warsaw designed to produce the cars burned down the following year.[68] By the mid-1930s, the Polish automotive industry, as is the case again today, was generally the preserve of foreign companies, whose cars (Fiats and Chevrolets) were either imported or built under licensing agreements in Poland for the local market.

Viewed through the lens of the nation as a whole, rather than from a personal or even class-based perspective, Polish cycling and motoring may have often seemed second rate. Poland proved incapable of matching France, Germany, Great Britain, or the United States in overall adoption of cycling and motoring. But for those privileged early adopters, like Prus and members of the WTC, Warsaw Automotive Club, Cracovian Cycling Club, Łódź Cycling Club, and others who, forgetting for a moment the dour demands of the nation, rode or drove the new machines, read articles about them, and met together to promote their sport, cycling and motoring were no less thrilling than for anyone else taking up the sport anywhere else. In relative simultaneity, these specialists had joined another "imagined community," becoming rarefied adherents of the gospel of speed.[69] In national or collective terms, they were rarely able to race to the lead, but then again, most participants in a race don't win. Studying the spread of cycling and motoring in a place like the Polish lands compels us to reflect on our relationship with mechanized modernity in new ways. It reminds us that there is a place in the history of technology and culture not only for the firsts, but also for the "also rans." It helps us see that in the modern age of speed, perhaps the commonest sensation, ironically, is the fear of falling behind. For most of us, most of the time, the best we can do is simply go along for the ride.

NOTES

1. Aleksander Rostocki and Jan Tarczyński, *Automobilizm w Warszawie do roku 1939* (Warsaw: Państwowy Instytut Wydawniczy, 1988), 39.

2. Bolesław Prus, "Jeden z cudów epoki, która nie wierzy w cuda," published in *Kurjer Codzienny* 1891, nos. 263–265, and reprinted in B. Prus, *Wczoraj-dziś-jutro.Wybór felietonów*, ed. Z. Szweykowski (Warsaw: Państwowy Instytut Wydawniczy, 1973), 224–237.

3. The price of Columbia bicycles, the major US brand, dropped by half between 1896 and 1900; see Glen Norcliffe, *The Ride to Modernity: The Bicycle in Canada, 1869–1900* (Toronto: University of Toronto Press, 2001), 32.

4. Bogdan Tuszyński, *Złota księga kolarstwa polskiego* (Warsaw: Polska Oficyna Wydawnicza BGW, 1995), 35.

5. *Szofer Polski* 2, December 15, 1925, 3. The actual figure was probably half that. According to Stacy C. Davis, Susan W. Diegel, and Robert G. Boundy, the ratio of cars to people in 1925 would have been closer to 1:6 (173.26 cars per 1,000 people). The figure 1:13 was accurate in 1919. Davis et al., *Transportation Energy Data Book* 31 (2012), Table 3.6, 3–10, accessed 2 November 2015, http://cta.ornl.gov/data/chapter3.shtml.

6. Wider use of telephones, the spread of rotary presses, and improvements in steamship technology also contributed to the sensation of an acceleration of life during this period. For more on the "age of speed," see Stephen Kern, *The Culture of Time and Space, 1880–1918* (Cambridge, MA: Harvard University Press, 2003), 109–130.

7. Benz's patent application for his 1885 Motorwagen was submitted in 1886, the year of his first successful ride. Daimler and Maybach designed their Reitwagen in 1884 and built it in 1885.

8. For more on Starley and the invention of the Rover safety bicycle, see John Woodforde, *The Story of the Bicycle* (London: Routledge and Kegan Paul, 1970), 95; Frederick Alderson, *Bicycling: A History* (Devon, UK: David and Charles, 1972), 79–82; Pryor Dodge, *The Bicycle* (Paris: Flammarion, 1996), 99–102; and David V. Herlihy, *Bicycle: The History* (New Haven, CT: Yale University Press, 2004), 225–250.

9. Tuszyński, *Złota księga*, 14. For more on Tsar Nicholas II's interest in cycling, see Herlihy, *Bicycle*, 273; and Gyorgy Manaev, "The Sports of the Russian Tsars: Chess, Cycling and Tennis," *Russia beyond the Headlines*, January 16, 2014, http://rbth.com/sport/2014/01/16/the_sports_of_the_russian_tsars_chess_cycling_and_tennis_33305.html.

10. Prus, "Jeden z cudów epoki," 224.

11. For examples of fear of new transportation technologies, see Wolfgang Schivelbusch, *The Railway Journey: The Industrialization of Time and Space in the 19th Century* (Berkeley: University of California Press, 1986), 129–130; and Nathaniel D. Wood, *Becoming Metropolitan: Urban Selfhood and the Making of Modern Cracow* (DeKalb: University of Northern Illinois Press, 2010), 129–160.

12. Prus, "Jeden z cudów epoki," 224.

13. Ibid., 225.

14. Ibid., 235.

15. Ibid., 237.

16. *Cyklista* 1, December 21, 1896 (January 2, 1897), 20–26. (Like other publications in the Polish Kingdom, *Cyklista* published both the Julian and Gregorian calendar dates on the masthead of each issue. The Julian date, used by the Russian masters of the Polish Kingdom, appears first; the Gregorian date, used by Poles and most other Europeans, appears second.)

17. On Sienkiewicz's learning to ride, see *Koło* 2, April 1895, 13.

18. Ibid., 20, 25.

19. Kern, *The Culture of Time and Space*, 216–217.

20. *Cyklista*, 1, December 21, 1896 (January 2, 1897), 21.
21. *Cyklista* 33, 2 (14) August 1897, 3–4.
22. *Cyklista* 1, December 21, 1896 (January 2, 1897), 25.
23. Ibid., 20.
24. "Mam nadzieję, iż na tem polu wkrótce już prześcigniemy Amerykę," *Auto* 2, June 2, 1922, 2.
25. *Kurjer Warszawski* 1885, November 30, 324b and 331. Cited in Rostocki and Tarczyński, *Automobilizm w Warszawie*, 13–14. See also Bolesław Prus, *Kroniki*, VIII, ed. Zygmunt Szweykowski (Warsaw: Państwowy Instytut Wydawniczy, 1953), 230–231.
26. Rostocki and Tarczyński, *Automobilizm w Warszawie*, 22–23.
27. Ibid., 28–35.
28. Ibid., 36–41.
29. Ibid., 46.
30. *Lotnik i Automobilista* 2, August 1911, 2–4.
31. Rostocki and Tarczyński, *Automobilizm w Warszawie*, 117, 119. The dates for first taxi services in various European cities are according to Rostocki and Tarczyński.
32. *Lotnik i Automobilista* 3, March 1913, 4–6.
33. *Auto* 1, May 12, 1922, 1.
34. "Nasz przemysł samochodowy a polityka rządu," *Auto* 4, July 8, 1922, 1.
35. *Ustawa Warszawskiego Towarzystwa Cyklistów* (Warsaw: Druk. i Lit. Jana Cotty, 1900).
36. Members in the Polish Automotive Club were voted in with black and white cards. One black card in every twenty was enough to keep someone out. Rostocki and Tarczyński, *Automobilizm w Warszawie*, 324.
37. *Automobilklub Polski: Spis członków—Maj 1924* (Warsaw: Zakł. Graf. Straszewiczów, 1924); and *Automobilklub Polski: Spis członków—Marzec 1927* (Warsaw: Drukarnia Stołeczna G. Kryzel, 1927).
38. *Auto* 3, June 20, 1922, 1.
39. Rostocki and Tarczyński, *Automobilizm w Warszawie*, 326. See also "Jest nas za mało" (There are too few of us), *Auto i Turysta* 5, June 1930, 1.
40. *Lotnik i Automobilista* 2, August 1911, 11–12.
41. See James L. Flink, "Developing a Mass Market," in his *America Adopts the Automobile, 1895–1910* (Cambridge, MA: MIT Press, 1970), 63–86.
42. *Auto* 8, September 5, 1922, 3.
43. As cited in *Szofer Polski* 2, January 15, 1926, 11–12.
44. *Szofer Polski* 1, December 1, 1925, 1.
45. *Szofer Polski* 1, December 1, 1925.
46. Tuszyński, *Złota księga*, 35. Poland, of course, did not exist as a state at this time. One wonders what territories and ethnicities fit into Tuszyński's calculations.
47. *Lotnik i Automobilista* 3, March 1913, 13.
48. *Cyklista* 13, 9 (21) December 1895, 2; *Cyklista* 1, December 23, 1895 (January 4, 1896), 5.
49. *Sport* 52, December 31, 1906.
50. *Lotnik i Automobilista*, July 1911, 13. Pupils were responsible for damage to the aircraft.
51. *Lotnik i Automobilista*, March 1913, 13.
52. Agnieszka J. Cieślikowska, "Polska prasa lotnicza do 1939r.," *Rocznik Historii Prasy Polskiej*, no. 1 (2000), 61–85.
53. *Lotnik i Automobilista*, July 1911, 13, and March 1913, 13.

54. "Wored" Alamanach Polska Towarzyska 1926 (Warsaw: Drukarnia Rolnicza, 1926), 171–173, accessed November 2, 2015, http://www.sbc.katowice.pl/dlibra/docmetadata?id=12806, pp. 423–25.

55. Tuszyński, Złota księga, 40–41.

56. Joanna Łuba-Wróblewska, Cykliści: Sympatycy, pasjonacy, misztrzowie, 1886–1939 (Warsaw: Karta, 2010), 59; for production statistics, see "Historia roweru—rower w Polsce," accessed May 28, 2014, http://wrower.pl/historia/rower-w-polsce,5431.html.

57. Herlihy, Bicycle, 328.

58. Tuszyński, Złota księga, 40–41.

59. Bolesław Prus, Ze wspomnień cyklisty (Warsaw: Gebethner i Wolff, 1904), 6–8.

60. Cyklista, 2, 5 (17) October 1895, 1–2.

61. Cyklista 1, 3 (15) September 1895, 10–11.

62. Tuszyński, Złota księga, 35.

63. See, for example, Cyklista 29, 6 (18) July 1896, 2, which contains a response to an article in issue 185 of Gazeta Warszawska complaining about cyclists in Warsaw, or Nowa Reforma 178, August 5, 1901, 2, which complains of a "genuine plague" of cyclists in Cracow.

64. Cyklista 33, 2 (14) August 1897, 2–6.

65. Janusz Żarnowski, Polska 1918–1939: Praca, Technika, Społeczeństwo, 2nd ed. (Warsaw: Książka i Wiedza, 1999), 195–196.

66. Samochód 1, October 7, 1928.

67. The cover story in the Great Poland Automobile Club's publication was about Tyszkiewicz and his team upon their return to Poland. See Samochód 20, February 17, 1929, 1, 5–6, 9.

68. Rostocki and Tarczyński, Automobilizm w Warszawie, 186–188. "Ralf-Stetysz" was an abbreviation of the title of the factory where it was produced: Rolniczo Automobilowo-Lotnicza Fabryka Stefana Tyszkiewicza (Agricultural/Automotive/Aviation Factory of Stefan Tyszkiewicz).

69. While Benedict Anderson's well-known formulation referred to the growth of national consciousness, I have found that his focus on the communities created by "print capitalism" and the use of a "first-person plural" can also helpfully refer to urban or other communities. See Anderson, Imagined Communities: Reflections on the Origin and Spread of Nationalism (New York: Verso, 1991), 9–46; and Wood, Becoming Metropolitan, 202.

CHAPTER 3

Walking with a Tolstoyan Dancer
Physical and Psychic Mobility in Vaslav Nijinsky's Diary

Nicole Svobodny

ON JANUARY 19, 1919, Vaslav Nijinsky, the Polish-Russian internationally acclaimed dancer, gave a solo recital for about two hundred people at the Suvretta House Hotel in St. Moritz, Switzerland. His wife, Romola, recalls how Nijinsky came out in plain practice clothes, picked up a chair, and sat down in front of the audience. The audience waited, ill at ease but full of expectation, while Nijinsky sat perfectly still. Everyone waited like this for about half an hour. Eventually Nijinsky took out a few rolls of black and white velvet cloth and made a big cross the length of the room. He stood at the head of it and said, "Now I will dance you the war . . . The war that you did not prevent." Then he launched into a dance that, in Romola's words, "petrified" and "fascinated" the audience.[1] The guests had expected to be dazzled by the technique of the biggest star of the Ballets Russes, but instead of a ballet recital, what they got was a performance that transgressed the boundary between art and life—a forerunner of performance art or "body art" of the later part of the twentieth century.

A few hours before this performance, Nijinsky began writing in Russian in a leather-bound school exercise notebook.[2] In the following six weeks he continued writing every day, often staying up all night. He filled four notebooks until he abruptly stopped, practically midsentence, on March 4, 1919. On that day, his wife and her family took Nijinsky to Zurich, where a doctor diagnosed him as "a confused schizophrenic with mild manic excitement."[3] Nijinsky, who at the time was twenty-nine years old and the most famous dancer in the world, spent the next three decades of his life in and out of psychiatric institutions. He never went back to his writing and never performed publicly again. Much of that time Nijinsky lived in what has been described as a catatonic stupor—"a captive in his own mind," as Igor Stravinsky wrote years later, "his most perfect gift of expression in movement stricken, immobile."[4]

The dancer's St. Moritz writing is known in English translation as *The Diary of Vaslav Nijinsky*, but Nijinsky himself indicates in the text that he wants to title it "Feeling" (*chuvstvo*) and to divide it into two parts, the first called "Life" and the second "Death."[5] The work is not strictly speaking a diary: there are no dated entries, and Nijinsky never refers to it as a diary.[6] (Here I refer to it as such for the sake of convenience, since that is what it is usually called in English discussions of the text.) Repeatedly Nijinsky alerts the reader to the meta-literariness of his work and proclaims his intent to make his written text public.

Nijinsky's last performance and his diary can be seen as symptoms of a disease that eventually immobilized the man whose name has become synonymous with dance, with mobility-in-form. From this point of view, the Suvretta House performance and the diary have little or no relevance to an understanding of Nijinsky's art; they manifest some of the profundity and intensity of his earlier work but lack the discipline, rigor, and analytical quality of his genius. They are curiosities, fascinating studies for psychologists, but in the end, they are the products of a failing mind.

However, it is also possible to see the last performance and the diary as extensions of Nijinsky's radical experiments in movement. From Romola's remembrance of Nijinsky's Suvretta House recital (and from Maurice Sandoz's eyewitness account, too, although he remembered the specifics very differently), one notices, first of all, Nijinsky's provocative stillness.[7] An interest in stillness in movement informs Nijinsky's earlier choreography as well. His first choreographic creation, the 1912 ballet *Afternoon of a Faun*, for example, dispensed with virtuosic demonstration of technique and instead emphasized "displaced moments of stillness" in that the faun is lying down or sitting for about half the ballet's duration and the dancers move languorously, in profile, with unusual pauses, creating the impression of a scene on an ancient Greek vase.[8] Along the same lines, explaining his dance theory to an American journalist in 1917, Nijinsky invited the public to imagine "a ballet almost—to put an extreme case—without movement."[9] Even earlier, Nijinsky conceived of movement in terms of its opposite. When asked if it was difficult to perform his seemingly gravity-defying leap (a feat that he downplayed in his own choreography), he looked confused and then responded, "No! No! Not difficult. You just have to go up and then pause a little up there."[10] This productive tension between mobility and stillness and the correlating hesitation between speech and silence are central to the diary as well.

Another notable aspect of the Suvretta House dance is the way Nijinsky uses words as part of his performance. On the one hand, this use of words in performance is a departure from his ballets; on the other, it can be seen as part of the dancer's attempts to translate movement into other forms of expression and to expand the boundaries of the artistic medium. His project of devising his own dance notation system—of inscribing movement in symbols—as well as his drawings, many of which resemble the symbols he was using in his dance notation system, can be considered side by side with Nijinsky's experiments in writing. In fact, scraps of both can be seen in the original manuscript of the diary. (He was reusing a notebook to save paper.)

In this chapter I consider the concept of mobility in Nijinsky's diary—both in a literal sense of physical movement and in a figurative meaning of crossing conventional borders.[11] Through literary analysis of one extraordinary text, I hope to contribute to broader discussions of how ordinary "bodies sense and make sense of the world as they move in and through it."[12] My goal is to address larger questions that explore the connection of bodily experience and language. Nijinsky states in the diary, "Museums and history are the scraps from what has already been lived through."[13] Is the written text also a "scrap"—a waste product or leftover—of lived experience? Does autobiographical writing merely re-present a life? Or, does the text have a more active role and actually immobilize and deaden the flow of life? Conversely, can words "do something" to propel a life and a body *into* motion? These questions are addressed in Nijinsky's diary, less through discursive explanation and more through the creative writing process itself. Ultimately Nijinsky's diary reveals *both* the limits of language and its transformative potential.

WALKING AS PERFORMANCE

The diary begins as Nijinsky gets ready for his Suvretta House performance. Unlike Romola's blow-by-blow "objective" description, Nijinsky gives us only a sketch of what actually happened on stage. For him, the performance really begins *before* he goes onstage, as Nijinsky expresses his ambivalence about performing and then relates his visit to the dressmaker's shop where he picks up the cloth he will use for the recital ("She knows I'm an artist, and therefore she understands me"); the performance continues offstage when at the reception Nijinsky shows a woman his bleeding foot: "She doesn't like blood. I gave her to understand that blood was war and that I don't like war."[14] The performance in the diary thus emphasizes the artist's body and the creative process, much like the performance Romola describes, but here it is unframed, at least by the material stage.

For Nijinsky the Suvretta House recital has another purpose besides showing the audience his artistic process. He pronounces it his "marriage to God."[15] In this sense, his literary account of the recital is not just performance but "performative," even in the stricter sense of J. L. Austin's term.[16] Nijinsky's performative may be unconventional (or "unhappy" in Austin's wording), but with it he aims not merely to describe or represent reality but to present and change it.[17] This desire to "do things with words" becomes Nijinsky's major objective in the diary and is acted out in a series of walks he takes and records in writing. In this light, the walks can be seen as extensions of the Suvretta House performance, but instead of a house full of spectators, we the readers are Nijinsky's only audience.

The act of walking had enormous significance for Nijinsky as a dancer and choreographer. In fact, Nijinsky could be said to have reinvented walking in his ballets. As opposed to the turned-out position of the feet and graceful roundness of the arms of classical ballet, Nijinsky's turned-in, crossed-over feet and spasmodic movements in *Petrushka* electrified audiences with their pathos of the mad clown who rebels against the control of his puppet master. The pigeon-toed feet and stomping of the maidens in *Rite of Spring* connected the dancers to the earth with a movement that was so unlike the airiness of classical ballet (and Nijinsky's own training at the Russian Imperial Ballet School) that it caused a riot when it was first performed in Paris in 1913. To my mind, it is especially his ballet *Afternoon of a Faun* that serves as a fitting image for the walks Nijinsky takes, perhaps because it is the only one of his previous ballets that he stands by wholeheartedly in the diary, defending it against charges of obscenity.[18] This ballet created a scandal when it was first performed, a scandal caused, as several dance historians contend, less by the final masturbatory spasm of orgasmic release and more by Nijinsky's "novel way of interrelating movement and music."[19] The movement of the ballet consisted of "simple walking steps [mostly with an emphatic heel-toe action] and jumps stripped of every vestige of balletic style and performed with absorbed focus."[20]

One look at Nijinsky's dance notation for *Faun* shows that considerable conceptualizing was involved in these "simple" walking steps. Nijinsky laments in the diary that it took him two months of concentrated effort (while under house arrest in Hungary in 1914) to notate what took ten minutes to perform onstage.[21] As his sister Bronislava Nijinska (also an accomplished dancer and major choreographer) explains about her brother's choreography for the ballet: "Each position of the dance, each position of the body down to the gesture of each finger, was mounted according to a strict choreographic plan."[22] It had taken Nijinsky months to figure out each movement (on his sister's body); the ballet required more than ninety grueling rehearsals and was performed onstage several times.[23] (See figure 3.1.)

The diary, by contrast, was a onetime effort (there are no drafts and almost no cross-outs), but as I will show, the "simple" steps of his walks in the diary, on closer inspection, reveal a multilayered, complex literary performance, executed with absorbed focus. While Nijinsky relates the movement of his body through space, he attends to the movement of his mind—at times frightening to him and at times exhilarating—and to shifts from one state of consciousness to another. Nijinsky's diary is thus not a record of his life in dance, nor is it an explanation of his theory of movement; instead it is a sensory enactment of the concept of mobility. Through his written accounts of his walks, Nijinsky connects physical mobility and psychic mobility and explores the fluidity between life and art,

Figure 3.1 *Vaslav Nijinsky, Afternoon of a Faun.*
Source: Photograph by Baron Adolph de Meyer, 1912. Photo reproduction supplied courtesy of Jerome Robbins Dance Division, The New York Public Library for the Performing Arts, Astor, Lenox, and Tilden Foundations.

reason and madness, verbal and nonverbal communication, movement and stillness, speech and silence.

VERTICAL AND HORIZONTAL MOVEMENT

In addition to recording his individual bodily movement, Nijinsky structures his diary in a way that shows his consciousness of its narrative movement. As readers of the diary, we feel a tension between two narrative movements in counterpoint: (1) In the foreground, Nijinsky is writing freely (automatically) about his walks and feelings, thereby *taking us*, his readers, on his mind-expanding flights of fancy (vertical movement); and (2) all the while that Nijinsky is relating his vertical flights of fancy, he records mundane events happening in the background—knocks on the door, telegrams received, muffled phone conversations overheard, train trip arrangements made—in which he is *being taken* to clinical diagnosis and institutionalization. (Is it prison or the asylum? he wonders). This "plot"—I use the word both in the sense of "storyline" and in the sense of "secret scheme"—involves the members of Nijinsky's household, including his wife and her family—especially her mother and stepfather, who arrive from Budapest—and a certain Dr. Frenkel, the sports medicine doctor whom Romola has employed to watch and psychoanalyze her husband. This horizontal movement through time gives the effect of a novel. Nijinsky does not know that he is writing a novel, let alone how it will end. As in much performance art or "live art," the elements of chance and contingency shape Nijinsky's diary. Even the title ("Feeling") and the structure of two parts ("Life," "Death") are not preconceived; Nijinsky arrives at them in the process of writing. It is as if Nijinsky attempts to stave off this accidental novel (horizontal movement) through his bodily movement and language (vertical movement). The dancer famed for his soaring leaps (in which, according to eyewitness reports, he remained awesomely suspended in air) turned to writing and through this new medium shares his "feeling"—his awe-inspiring (or disturbing, for some readers) leaps of the imagination.

My terms *vertical* and *horizontal* to describe these two narrative movements are inspired by the scraps of Nijinsky's dance notation system that I saw in the same notebooks as the diary. Although this unpublished dance notation has not yet been decoded, one can see that Nijinsky has written out several times the phrases "vertical movement" (*dvizhenie po vertikal'nomu napravleniiu*) and "horizontal movement" (*dvizhenie po gorizontal'nomu napravleniiu*).[24] In what follows, I show how Nijinsky translates this contrapuntal movement into writing through an engagement with the later works of Leo Tolstoy.

NIJINSKY'S WALKS AS PERFORMANCE OF TOLSTOY'S *CONFESSION*

Nijinsky moved to St. Moritz, Switzerland, in the beginning of December 1917, mostly because his Hungarian-born wife wanted to separate him from his Tolstoyan friends, whom he had met while on tour in the United States.²⁵ However, even while separated from his Tolstoyan friends (and, it seems, from any Russian speakers), Nijinsky certainly did not lose interest in Tolstoy's teachings. Romola blamed her husband's erratic behavior on his "imitating... that old lunatic Tolstoi," and the diary is permeated with Tolstoyan concerns such as pacifism, vegetarianism, a return to the land, sexual abstinence, and the moral purpose of art.²⁶ As Nijinsky is writing about this critical juncture in his life (his "marriage to God"), it seems natural that he would look to how his teacher Tolstoy had recorded the story of his "conversion" and profession of faith in *Confession*.

Two passages from Tolstoy's *Confession* have significant bearing on the topic of mobility in Nijinsky's confessional work: (1) the dream that Tolstoy relates as a coda to *Confession* (written three years after the main text), and (2) the "Eastern fable" he recounts to illustrate the moment of conversion in his life's journey. I mention the dream first because it relates to the overall narrative movement of Nijinsky's work. In the dream, Tolstoy is lying in bed when he starts to wonder if he is comfortable. He then looks down to see that he is lying on rope supports attached to the bed; the more he thinks about it, the more he feels that his body is slipping down, and he becomes terrified by the "bottomless abyss" below. He shifts his body position several times, but nothing assuages his fear until, in despair, he looks upward and is reassured by the "infinity above." The dream teaches him that "if one lies with the middle of one's body on the rope and looks up there can be no question of falling."²⁷ As one commentator wryly observes, "Tolstoy offers us a yoga pose to stop us from focusing on our imminent annihilation."²⁸ In the diary, Nijinsky experiences and presents Tolstoy's "yoga pose" as movement.²⁹ Tolstoy's horizontal position on the ropes becomes the sequence of events that is taking Nijinsky to Zurich: Will he look down at this "bottomless abyss"? Tolstoy's vertical glance up at infinity becomes Nijinsky's verbal recording of his walks.

Through his writing about the walks, Nijinsky reenacts the "old Eastern fable," which Tolstoy tells in chapter 4 of *Confession*. Let me first put Tolstoy's fable into context. After telling of his "dissipated" preconversion life in the first three chapters of *Confession*, Tolstoy begins chapter 4 with a description of his inner turmoil before his turning point: "It was as if I had lived and lived, walked and walked, until I walked up to a precipice from which I could see clearly that there was nothing ahead of me other than destruction."[30] He continues with this analogy, comparing his simultaneous fear of life and fear of death with a man "having walked up to the summit of life from which everything is revealed."[31] Here Tolstoy tells the "old Eastern fable." We can separate Tolstoy's telling of the fable into three parts that progress logically and linearly. The first part is the tale itself: a man is traveling on the steppe when he is pursued by a ferocious animal, so the man hides in an empty well, but lo and behold, there is a dragon at the bottom of the well, ready to devour him. So the man holds on to a branch and clings to it, knowing that death awaits him on both sides. He notices that two mice are gnawing at the branch, but he also notices some honey on the branch that he begins to lick. The second part of the passage is the explicit explanation of the allegory. Here Tolstoy likens the story of the traveler to his own life in a one-to-one correspondence ("In the same way I am clinging to the tree of life").[32] In the third part, Tolstoy sums up the moral of the fable in an authoritative voice that is clearly situated at a distance from the inner turmoil he himself had experienced: "And this is no fable but the truth, the truth that is irrefutable and intelligible to everyone."[33] With these words, it is as if Tolstoy wants to dismantle the allegory that he had set up in the preceding lines: this is not a *mere* fable but the living truth.

In his St. Moritz writing, Nijinsky takes up Tolstoy's challenge. He performs the "old Eastern fable" as lived experience, so that the metaphor Tolstoy sets up becomes literal. Nijinsky is *literally* living and walking until he reaches a precipice—in this case, the mountaintops he reaches on his walks around St. Moritz. There is a certain metaphorical element in how Nijinsky uses the image of the precipice: "I am standing in front of a precipice into which I may fall, but I am not afraid to fall and therefore will not fall."[34] He is describing a moment of crisis in his life, although when he continues to say that "he will not fall," Nijinsky does not want merely to describe this crisis but also wants the act of writing to ward off a looming disaster. In this sense, Nijinsky's writing is not just descriptive but performative. Immediately following that statement, the precipice becomes concrete when Nijinsky describes his walk.

This will be the first of three walks that Nijinsky retells in the diary. The reader cannot easily discern if these walks actually took place: they seem so ordinary, and Nijinsky insists that they are real: "I know that everyone will think that everything I write is made up, but I must say that everything I write is the absolute truth, because I have experienced it all in practice."[35] In Tolstoy's case, we know that despite his words to the contrary, we have just read an allegory; with Nijinsky we are not so sure of the dividing line between metaphor and life. Each of the three walks, as Nijinsky retells them, has the symbolic feel of dreams, and each contains the following elements: (1) a vertical motion upward or downward; (2) an utterance set apart by quotation marks, which distills a specific theme or motif of the walk; and (3) a tree evoking Tolstoy's tree of the fable.

The account of the first walk opens midparagraph with the following sentence: "I went out for a walk once, and it seemed to me that there was blood on the snow, and so I ran, following the trail."[36] Nijinsky hesitates between following the trail of blood and running in the other direction. He feels that God is guiding him to go in the direction of a precipice to save a person who is hanging there.[37] So he walks up to the precipice and is saved from falling when he is caught by the branches of a tree that he had not noticed was there. Keeping in mind the "old Eastern fable," we can see this tree as "the tree of life," although Nijinsky does not *cling* to the tree, but *is caught* by its branches; rather than seeing the tree from Tolstoy's distant, judgmental perspective, Nijinsky has a reciprocal, immediate experience of the tree, in which being saved by the branches of the tree "amazes" him, and he feels the tree's very existence as a "miracle."[38] Moreover, Nijinsky participates in the fable from a perspective not presented in Tolstoy's version: he approaches the precipice to save *another* person who is falling and is then saved himself.

Next in Nijinsky's story of his first walk comes an utterance set apart with quotation marks—these are God's words to him: "Go home and tell your wife that you are crazy." (*Idi domoi i skazhi zhene, chto ty sumasshedshii.*)[39] The word *sumasshedshii* ("crazy," "insane," "mad") is common in Russian, but since Nijinsky uses it so often in the diary and almost never uses a synonym, the word carries enormous weight. This *particular* word suggests *spatiality* and *mobility*. It is a past active verbal adjective that derives from the verb of motion (*soiti*), literally meaning "to descend" or "to go down from," and the prepositional phrase *s uma*, meaning "from the mind." Thus, *soiti s uma* suggests a concrete sense of place, as if the mind were an elevated stage one could step down from. In his performance of jumping down from the precipice, Nijinsky literalizes this figurative downward motion. His story thus becomes more direct, more urgent, than mere allegory.

Throughout the diary, Nijinsky contrasts the word *um* as in *soiti s uma* with its prefixed form *razum*.[40] This dichotomy between *um*/*razum* is the most important concept for Nijinsky, and he comes back to it on almost every single page of the diary. *Um* ("mind" or "intellect") is completely negative for Nijinsky, and he characterizes it as cold, dry, inert. By contrast, *razum* ("mind" or "reason") is entirely positive in Nijinsky's world, and he associates it with life, energy, mobility, and feeling. Nijinsky is consistent with this binary, and he seems fascinated by the sounds of these words. (The consistency of this rhythm and rhyme is definitely lost in translation because the words can be—perhaps have to be—translated variously into English so that one misses both the repetition of the words and the sound similarity in the original.) At the end of his first walk, Nijinsky asserts that "God is movement and therefore death is necessary. The body dies, but the mind (*razum*) lives."[41] This is not a Descartian mind/body split but rather a distinction between *um* (the intellect divorced from the body) and *razum* (reason felt through the body). *Razum* is fluid, and thus Nijinsky's paradoxical assertion to be "a crazy person with reason" (*sumasshedshii s razumom*) is not a contradiction.[42] Toward the end of the diary, Nijinsky situates his own philosophical writing on *razum* within a philosophical tradition: "Tolstoy speaks a lot about *razum*, Schopenhauer also wrote about *razum*. I too write about *razum*. I am the philosophy of *razum*. I am the true, not invented, philosophy."[43]

In his second walk, as if attempting to conquer *um*, Nijinsky counters the downward movement of descending from the mind by going up to a mountaintop. This time, while he is out walking, he imagines that "everybody will say that person is crazy" but that he knows he's not crazy because he "feels."[44] He has the desire to shout out on the mountaintop, but he sees a tree that says to him that "one could not speak here because people would not understand feeling."[45] Here again, Tolstoy's "tree of life" saves Nijinsky but this time not by serving as physical support but through speech and understanding:

> I was sorry to part with the tree because it understood me. I walked up to a height of 2,000 meters. I stood for a long time. I felt a voice and shouted

in French, "Parole." I wanted to speak, but my voice was so strong that I could not speak, and I shouted. "I love everyone, and I want happiness!"[46]

It is fitting that Nijinsky shouts out *"parole,"* the French word for "speech," since he is struggling over whether to speak or to be silent— and finally shouts. It is as if Nijinsky anticipates the way the term *parole* became used in linguistics to refer to individual, contextual acts of language usage, as opposed to *langue*, the structure or system of language. As Nijinsky puts it elsewhere in the diary, "To understand does not mean to know all the words. Words are not speech."[47] The line between signifier and signified breaks down here: the speech he makes is "speech."[48]

The story of the second walk then digresses to a paean to the Russian land, Russian food, his mother and sister stranded in Bolshevik Russia, his friend Kostrovsky (had he returned to Russia to join a Tolstoyan commune?), whom he imagines taking over the important task of writing so he himself can sleep; he praises Russian speech and Russian writers, including Tolstoy: "I am Tolstoy since I love him."[49] In this second walk, it is as if Tolstoy's "tree of life" speaks to him in Russian, although it would not make much difference in which language, since Nijinsky says he understands "speech" (not words) "in all languages."[50]

A little later Nijinsky tells the story of another walk, the third and final walk in the diary. Here Nijinsky again goes uphill; he feels cold and is frightened by an "untwinkling" star that does not say "Hello" to him.[51] Now he screams at the top of his lungs, "Death!" The act of shouting this word warms Nijinsky's body and gives him the energy to run. Again he sees a tree:

> I went quickly, but was stopped by a tree, which was my salvation. I was in front of a precipice. I thanked the tree. It felt me because I had taken hold of it. The tree received my warmth, and I received the tree's warmth. I do not know whose warmth was more necessary.[52]

To sum up, in the first walk, Nijinsky's tree resembles Tolstoy's "tree of life," even though it is experienced from multiple perspectives; by the second and third walks, the tree speaks, feels, gives and receives warmth; it is no longer an inert metaphor but a living being. In this sense, Nijinsky does not cling to the tree, but merges with the tree; he is not clinging to life, but *is* life.

Elsewhere in the diary, at some point between the first and second walks, Nijinsky writes, "Tolstoy spoke of a tree that had roots and branches."[53] And, later: "I know that the whole world is infected with this sickness of putrefaction that does not let a tree live. Tolstoy's tree is life, and therefore one must read him."[54] In a series of "I am" sentences, only part of which I will quote here, he makes the connection again: "I am a seabird. I am a land bird. I am Tolstoy's tree. I am Tolstoy's roots. Tolstoy is mine. I am his."[55] Taken out of context, these lines seem illogical and random, but they make more sense when we consider them in the context of Nijinsky's reenacting of the "old Eastern fable" through his St. Moritz walks. Nijinsky never directly names Tolstoy's *Confession* in his diary, but he certainly read and understood Tolstoy's words—and also lived them.

It may be tempting to dismiss Nijinsky's confession as the product of a confused, schizophrenic mind. In his 1911 monograph on schizophrenia, Dr. Eugen Bleuler (who coined the term in 1909 and diagnosed Nijinsky ten years later), describes symptoms of the disease that correspond to Nijinsky's writing style. Schizophrenia (from the Greek *skhizein*, "split," and *phren*, "mind") is primarily a cognitive disorder in which, as Bleuler elaborates, "displacements" arise because in a chain of thoughts "one idea is suddenly substituted for another" and the patient "soon loses himself in secondary associations."[56] In one example, Bleuler relates how a patient wants to say that she would like to have the key because for her it is a symbol for passage into freedom, but she is just as likely to say she *is* the key or simply, "I am freedom." Bleuler explains: "The difference between the use of such phrases in the healthy and in the schizophrenic rests in the fact that for the former it is a mere metaphor, whereas for the patients the dividing line between direct and indirect representation has become obscured. The result is that they frequently think of these metaphors in a literal sense."[57]

This blurring of the dividing line between direct and indirect representation is also one of the hallmarks of modernist, avant-garde art. Nijinsky's ballet *The Rite of Spring*, for instance, can be seen in this light: to the audience, the ballet seemed to present, rather than merely represent, an ancient pagan rite. This directness (getting away from "secondary literary meaning"), as Nijinsky had correctly predicted, made it "new, beautiful, utterly different—but for the ordinary viewer a jolting and emotional experience."⁵⁸ What one eyewitness to the opening night said about Nijinsky's ballet holds true for his diary as well: it is both "art" and "un-art" at the same time.⁵⁹ The "art" lies in the fact that the diary is a multilayered and complex work that makes extended use of literary allusion. But the "un-art" gives Nijinsky's diary the elusive quality that classic confessional writing strives for above all else: authenticity.

PSYCHIC MOBILITY: EMPATHY, CLIMATE CHANGE AWARENESS, AND "FEELING"

Although Nijinsky's shift to writing was borne out of the necessity to find a solitary creative outlet (as he was no longer part of a ballet troupe), he may also have seen the shift from dancing to writing as an opportunity to create unprofessional—"authentic"—art. At one point he calls his past ballets "death," and he "wants to prove that all of Diaghilev's art is sheer nonsense."⁶⁰ As for his new medium, Nijinsky says he knows how to write prettily but he chooses not to because he does not want to be perfect/finished (*sovershennym*).⁶¹ He declares himself "a person with mistakes."⁶² He points out errors in spelling (although the manuscript shows that in many cases he did not make them) and he deliberates over whether he should capitalize certain words. All the time he is writing, he calls attention to his body, his hand (*ruka*), and its connection to his product, his manuscript (*rukopis'*). He says his handwriting "leaps" and his manuscript is "alive."⁶³ He wants his manuscript to be photographed, not printed, so that readers can experience his handwriting (which is actually very neat).

The diary, however, is not merely an exercise in writing badly (or naively, in a neoprimitive vein), but aimed at what lies at the heart of Tolstoy's *What Is Art?*—that is, the communication of feelings. Tolstoy's idea of the "contagion of feeling," in turn, derives in part from the concept of *Einfühlung*, or *feeling into*, a term used in German aesthetics in the late nineteenth century to explain how spectators project their own feelings onto an object and thus can come to appreciate and enjoy its beauty. Eventually the concept of *Einfühlung* reached beyond aesthetic categories to explain the psychological phenomenon by which a person enters into another's being and comes to know how he or she feels. The English word *empathy* was coined in 1908 as a translation of *Einfühlung* by using the Greek words *em*, "in," and *path*, "suffer, feel."[64]

It is no coincidence that Nijinsky intended to title his work "Feeling" for the experience of feeling *into*, and the communication of this feeling to others is the core of his artistic purpose. It could be called his profession of faith. While Nijinsky's "Feeling" has similarities with all three of the concepts previously discussed—Tolstoy's "contagion," the German aesthetic term *Einfühlung*, and the English word *empathy*—I propose to use a different term here, *psychic mobility*, to describe what Nijinsky achieves through the linking of his experience of physical mobility (his walks, his dance) with the mobility of his mind.

First, however, let me differentiate my use of *psychic mobility* from how others have used the term. In an influential 1958 essay, Daniel Lerner discusses the modernization process in terms of progressive stages of mobilities. First came physical mobility, in which "ordinary men found themselves unbound from their native soil and relatively free to move."[65] This physical mobility entrained social mobility. Personal mobility thus became a "high-order value," and with the twentieth-century international diffusion of mass media emerged a "mobility sensibility, so adaptive to change that rearrangement of the self-system is its distinctive mode."[66] Lerner refers to this capacity as "psychic mobility." In *Renaissance Self-Fashioning*, Stephen Greenblatt critiques Lerner's argument, not by disagreeing with the assumption that psychic mobility has shaped modern Western society, but in the neutrality that Lerner attributes to it. What Lerner sees essentially as a necessary capacity to become a functioning adult in modern society ("the high empathizer tends to become also the cash customer, the radio listener, the voter"), Greenblatt sees as form of manipulation ("a ruthless displacement and absorption") that Western societies have used to enter the psychic structures of the native populations they have colonized.[67] Greenblatt's critique, however, is not really that different from what Lerner himself states. Lerner's use of the term, he clearly explains, "does not denote sympathy or antipathy ('understanding' may breed dislike as well as affection)."[68] What both Lerner and Greenblatt see as psychic mobility is the ability to move into the other's space, to "read" the other for one's own advantage, whether to get by in society, or to exercise power.

This vicarious sharing and "reading" is not what I have in mind when using the term *psychic mobility* in relation to Nijinsky's diary. The psychic mobility evinced in the diary is not about assimilating to society (Lerner) or exercising authority (Greenblatt); it is anti-assimilating, anti-authoritarian, something more akin to the "deterritorialized flows of desire" that Gilles Deleuze and Felix Guattari describe in *Schizophrenia and Capitalism: The Anti-Oedipus*. Deleuze and Guattari intend their "schizoanalytic" approach as an alternative to the "psychic repression" of psychoanalysis, and (although they do not) we can use the term *psychic mobility* (or, more in tune with their lingo, *schizomobility*) to describe what they see possible in orphans, nomads, and "schizos": "The schizo has his own system of co-ordinates for situating himself at his disposal because, first of all, he has his very own recording code, which does not coincide with the social code, or coincides with it only in order to parody it. The code of delirium or of desire proves to have an extraordinary fluidity."[69] What Deleuze and Guattari do here is transvalue the pathology of schizophrenia. They want to leave the stuffy room in which the psychoanalyst attempts to "cure" (and subjugate) the neurotic; instead, they affirm the behavior of the "schizo" (alien from the world of psychoanalysis) as a model of mobility: "The schizophrenic out for a walk is a better model than the neurotic lying on the analyst's couch. A breath of fresh air, a relation with the outside world."[70]

Nijinsky is among the "schizos" Deleuze and Guattari use as a model:

Lenz's stroll, Nijinsky's stroll, the promenades of Beckett's creatures are effective realities, but where the reality of matter has abandoned all extension, just as the interior voyage has abandoned all form and quality, henceforth causing pure intensities—coupled together, almost unbearable—to radiate within and without, intensities through which a nomadic subject passes.[71]

Writing in 1972, Deleuze and Guattari were likely using the French translation of the expurgated version of Nijinsky's diary (originally published in English translation—not in the original Russian—in 1936 with heavy edits by Nijinsky's wife) in which the sequence of the walks was altered and one of the walks entirely missing. So it is all the more perceptive of them to grasp the importance of "Nijinsky's stroll."[72]

While Bleuler sees a problem in the schizophrenic "displacements" that blur boundaries between direct and indirect representation, Deleuze and

Guattari celebrate that "something is produced ... not mere metaphors."[73] While psychoanalysis fears "ego-loss" as a problem, "schizoanalysis" sees it as liberating. They continue by quoting "I am" passages from Nijinsky's diary in which "he can situate himself, record himself, and take his bearings in all the branches at once, on all sides."[74] In light of Nijinsky's reenacting of Tolstoy's "old Eastern fable," Deleuze and Guattari are even more correct than they might have known.

Compare this "nonrestrictive" approach with Bleuler's explanation of the schizophrenic tendency to "ambivalence" (another term he introduced into psychoanalysis), which he characterizes as the "tendency of the schizophrenic psyche to endow the most diverse psychisms with both a positive and negative indicator at one and the same time,"[75] further explaining:

> Even for the healthy everything has two sides. The rose has its thorns. But in ninety-nine out of a hundred instances, the normal person compares the two aspects, subtracts the negative from the positive values. He appreciates the rose despite its thorns. The schizophrenic, with his weakened associative linkings does not necessarily bring the different aspects of a problem together. He loves the rose because of its beauty and hates it because of its thorns.[76]

Bleuler saw Nijinsky's diary as a manifestation of this pathology, whereas Deleuze and Guattari see the same lack of synthesis as freeing, "a flux that overcomes barriers and codes."[77]

In his preface to the English translation of *Anti-Oedipus*, Michel Foucault sets up the sociohistorical context of post-1960s Europe and invites us to read Deleuze and Guattari not as philosophy but as "an art of living counter to all forms of fascism, whether already present or impending." In what he dubs this *Introduction to Non-Fascist Life*, Foucault urges us to learn to prefer "what is positive and multiple, difference over uniformity, flows over unities, mobile arrangements over systems. Believe that what is productive is not sedentary but nomadic."[78]

Nijinsky's project, too, is an experiment that prefers "flows" over "systems."[79] On the one hand, Nijinsky was deeply disturbed by the death, destruction, and displacements caused by world events (World War I, the Bolshevik Revolution, civil war); on the other, he just as often sees the displacements in his own life and mind as opportunities for renewal, connection, and calls for action. "I don't live on the Moika at house #__," he joyously declares, "I live in people."[80] Preferring "mobile arrangements," he is wary of closed systems, fixed ideologies, and political parties: "I want to love everyone. This is my aim in life. I know socialists will understand me better, but I am not a socialist. I am God. My party is God's."[81] He insists that he is a "person without a party" and does not like "a party attitude," but even that assertion is up for revision: "I know I will be told, 'You belong to the partyless party,' but I do not belong to that party."[82] He likewise does not belong to any organized religion. He says he is "what Christ felt," but he does not think of himself as Christian.[83] Christianity has "habits" (*privychki*).[84] But, like Deleuze and Guattari's nomad, Nijinsky sees himself as a man without habits and territories ("I have a home everywhere").[85] There is another key difference: Christ "has a serene expression, my expression runs around (*begaet*) . . . He liked to sit. I like to dance."[86]

Nijinsky envisions making new global connections through several inventions he has planned, many of which have to do with transportation and communication technology. For example, he "will build a bridge between Europe and America that will not cost much."[87] It will be a "bridge-railway, along a wire, that can destroy [i.e. abolish the need for] all steamboats."[88] As the ink spills down his hand while he writes, Nijinsky imagines a young girl using such a pen and getting in trouble with her parents for staining her new white dress. He wants to invent a new pen that will not spill ink.[89] He will call the pen "God."[90]

In an all-inclusive, forceful flow of psychic mobility, Nijinsky feels an urgent need to conserve the earth's resources. For him, life is energy, and he literally *feels* the movement of the natural elements with and *in* his entire body. "I live as long as I have a fire in my head. My pulse is an earthquake."[91] Like the earth, he "shakes" when he is not understood.[92] This is not only a "merging with the earth" (Stravinsky's description of *The Rite of Spring*) but also a call for action in everyday life; Nijinsky worries about wasting energy by using paper and electric lights to continue his writing: "I do not mind wasting money, but I do mind wasting energy. I have realized that without energy there will be no life."[93] In a particularly prescient warning, Nijinsky identifies coal production and "the pumping of oil and petroleum"[94] as the major reason for ecological destruction.

"Fuel (*toplivo*) is the source of life.... People waste fuel. People think that they need lots of things, that the more they have, the happier they are."[95] He has plans for alternative sources of energy, "a way to get physical power without coal."[96] He foresees climate change, attributed not to divine forces or natural causes but to man's consumption of fuel: "I know that people do not understand earthquakes and therefore they blame God. People do not understand that they themselves have started earthquakes."[97]

Nijinsky might be called an ecological visionary not so much for his focus on what today we call carbon footprint and sustainable energy (although I cannot find any source he could have been using with this particular insistence on replacing fossil fuels) but more for the way he places emphasis on *feeling* in this realization of "the meaning of the earth which is being extinguished."[98] Contemporary debates on climate-change denial focus precisely on this role of empathy in mobilizing people to change their lifestyle and consciousness. In a recent review in the *New Yorker*, Paul Bloom discusses several books that want us "to emotionally join a global family" and "make the leap to a 'global empathic consciousness' as "the last best hope for saving the world from environmental destruction."[99] In *The Empathic Civilization*, for example, Jeremy Rifkin asks: "Can we reach biosphere consciousness and global empathy in time to avoid planetary collapse?" Bloom criticizes this enthusiasm as "misplaced" and calls for "reason" as a better guide for planning for future generations than "the gut wrench of empathy."[100] In his diary, Nijinsky has anticipated these debates in his vision of universal love. For him it is easy to imagine future generations: "I know many people will tell me that it is not important to live for a long time, that they say, 'This century will be long enough for life.' But after all, this phrase speaks of death. People do not love their children."[101] Nijinsky is certainly no scientist (he is antiscience in the same way he is anti-art) and does not offer a logical analysis of climate change, but if combating climate-change denial requires a change in global consciousness of *all* people, not just scientists, Nijinsky's psychic mobility in regard to environmentalism is relevant: "People will probably tell me that I am mistaken, because I have not studied the earth. I will say that I have studied the earth because I feel and do not think. I know that the earth is a living thing."[102] In this way, Nijinsky does not see a disjunction between "reason" and "feeling" as Bloom does.

This expression and exercise of psychic mobility can be related to Nijinsky's uncanny ability to "enter into" his roles and to his awareness of the various perspectives of his audience. As Ramsay Burt points out, to dance onstage is "to have to take into consideration how one might appear from points of view other than one's own and experience one's being through others."[103] How much more so, one would think, for a dancer who thrilled audiences on three different continents and became "the first international superstar of the globalized media."[104] For Nijinsky, however, movement is not only an aesthetic performance, but a somatic experience in which "reason" (*razum*) is felt through the life-mobilizing movements his body makes—in this case, his walks around St. Moritz.

IMMOBILIZATION

All the while Nijinsky is writing in his notebook, we get hints of another drama unfurling in the background. Nijinsky worries that his food is being poisoned, that his act of writing is seen as a sign of madness, and that he will be taken away: "I am afraid that I will be taken to a madhouse and lose all my work. I hid my notebooks behind a cupboard. I love my notebooks too much to lose them. I have written necessary things. I do not want the death of feeling." He suspects that "they have already packed my bags." And Nijinsky is not being unduly paranoid: we the readers are beginning to suspect the very same thing.[105]

Not long after the third walk, the "plot" of the diary thickens when Nijinsky and his wife get into a fight over his refusal to eat meat. Nijinsky runs out of the house, but this time his walk is less performance and more escape. Before, he went up to the mountains; now he goes down the hill to town, and on his way down, he notices Dr. Frenkel going up. (Nijinsky guesses that he is on his way to see Romola because she has telephoned him.) In town Nijinsky desperately seeks out a room to rent, a refuge where he can write undisturbed ("since my wife didn't understand me").[106] The refrain "I walked and walked" (*ia shel i shel*) punctuates his visits to various places, and his desire to find a room of his own is countered by his equally urgent need to move on.[107] He considers lying down in the snow (which would be certain death as he is dressed lightly), going forward (but where?), or going back. He ends ups in St. Moritz-Dorf at the telegraph office: "Suddenly somebody grabbed me by the shoulder. I turned and saw Dr. Frenkel."[108]

The capture causes Nijinsky to write even more furiously in his notebook. When he returns, he ends Book I ("Life") and begins Book II ominously: "Death came unexpectedly since I wanted it."[109] Although Nijinsky's dark thoughts give way to a reprisal of themes from Book I, something has changed. Nijinsky never goes out for a walk. He wants to, but each attempt is thwarted. For example:

> I want to go for a walk since I'm tired of sitting, but I'll go out alone, if nobody notices me. Everyone will think that I'm working, but I'll go out the back way. I will go up high and look down, for I want to feel the height. I'm going.[110]

The diary resumes with Nijinsky's description of his "walk." But from his description it is impossible to tell how far he made it. He mentions the cold he felt when he went outside, but then, "I exited the dining room since I felt I was not loved."[111] He runs into Dr. Frenkel, shakes his hand, and then "walk[s] out of the room."[112] But Romola's stepfather calls after him and asks him to join them for tea. While it is difficult to picture the *mise-en-scène* here, one thing is obvious: Nijinsky is being watched. And without his solitary walks, his body begins to implode: He feels the hairs in his nose moving and the blood draining from his head.[113] Meanwhile, the maid has arranged for a cab to take Nijinsky, his wife, and her parents to the train station; Romola asks her husband to tell their little daughter that he won't be coming back. In a last-ditch effort to assert free bodily movement, Nijinsky decides to walk by foot (*poidu*) to the station but yields in the very next sentence: "If everyone is going in a cab, I will too (*poedu*). God wants to show people that I am the same kind of person as they are."[114] An expression of ambivalence turns on the subtlety of a Russian verb of motion; one letter (from *i* to *e*) changes the motion from walking (through his own agency) to going by vehicle (in this case, being driven).

Nijinsky never published "Feeling," but he did take it with him to Zurich. His psychiatrists used it as evidence of his pathology and cited it in diagnostic reports. The language in the diary was considered an example of "verbigeration" and thus a symptom of the patient's "catatonia."[115] (It is still a mystery to me how the psychiatrists understood the content of the diary since apparently none of them knew Russian.[116]) On the horizontal timeline of life, the diary certainly marks Nijinsky's final departure for psychological exile, from which, sadly, there would be no return.

CONCLUSION: TOLSTOY'S "WISE WORDS" IN MOTION

In counterpoint to this plotline taking him to clinical diagnosis, Nijinsky offers us experimental art, a harbinger of contemporary performance art, and an in-depth exploration of psychic mobility. His diary might be called a mindfully choreographed experimental performance in trance: "I want everyone to be in such a trance because Tolstoy was in such a trance," Nijinsky tells us.[117] For Nijinsky, Tolstoy's "trance" would be evident in his later works (the great novels he mentions only in passing), and of these, the only one Nijinsky names specifically is *Wise Thoughts for Every Day*.[118]

Let me open Tolstoy's book of calendar entries to a date that falls in the time period during which Nijinsky was writing in his diary. I will choose February 3 as a sample. This entry is divided into nine brief sections, with quotations from Saadi Shirazi, Marcus Aurelius, Ralph Waldo Emerson, the Manusmriti, and Tolstoy's own "wise thoughts," including a paraphrase from Arthur Schopenhauer. The first section reads: "We feel that the most important thing by which we live, that which we call our true 'I' is the same thing that exists not only in each person, but in a dog, a horse, a mouse, a chicken, a sparrow, a bee, and even in a tree."[119] Elaborating on this thought in the second section, Tolstoy contends that most people think only of themselves, but that there also exists "reasonable and good people" (*liudi, razumnye i dobrye*), who understand that the lives of other people and even of animals are as important as their own. Such people "live not only in their 'I' but in other people."[120] By the fourth section, Tolstoy gives us this picture of an interconnected world: "All creatures, both people and animals, are connected to each other, so that when one suffers, these sufferings, somehow or another, now or later, spread to everyone. And in the same way the well-being of each and every creature is connected to everyone else, and somehow or another, it spreads to everyone."[121] Notice a parallel in the way well-being "spreads" (*perekhodit*, literally "walks across") in this calendar entry and the way art "infects" (*zarazhaetsia*) others with feeling (*chuvstvo*) in *What Is Art?*[122] It makes me wonder: Can the "kind and intelligent (*umnye*)" dancers who "are capable of all sorts of useful labor" but instead have wasted their lives "learning how to twirl their legs rapidly" (*What Is Art?*) become the same "reasonable (*razumnye*) and good" people who "understand that the lives of other people and animals are as important as their own" (the calendar entry)?[123]

Tolstoy's "Vegetarian Soup for the Soul" may seem an unlikely inspiration for avant-garde trance writing. Yet the message comes very close to what Nijinsky aims to achieve in his diary. The difference is that Nijinsky inserts himself into this interconnectedness not as a wise man but as an "unfinished" person "with mistakes." He experiences this interconnectedness from all sides, with all the drifts, flows, walks, overflights, and psychic mobility that this embodiment entails. In short, Nijinsky's diary is Tolstoy's calendar entry set in motion. If Tolstoy's didactic words give a readable sketch of an interconnected world, Nijinsky's "schizophrenic" ramblings perform a writerly (in the Barthesian sense, *scriptible*) dance into and around a world in flux, where things are perpetually disconnecting and reconnecting. Here I imagine something along the lines of Nijinsky's own choreography in which "movement became an end in itself" and "he broke it down, took it apart and put it back together again."[124] This may seem like an abstract formalist exercise, but movement *in itself* has meaning for a person who *feels that* "God is movement" and "without energy there will be no life."

NOTES

1. Romola Nijinsky, *Nijinsky* (New York: Simon and Schuster, 1934), 424–426.
2. The original manuscript is available for viewing on microfilm at the Jerome Robbins Dance Division (Lincoln Center) of the New York Public Library: Waslaw Nijinsky, *Dnevnik Vatslava Nizhinskogo*, Diary 1918–1919, New York Public Library, Performing Arts Research Collections, call number *ZBD-520. The unexpurgated manuscript has been translated into English by Kyril FitzLyon: *The Diary of Vaslav Nijinsky* (New York: Farrar,

Straus and Giroux, 1999). This translation was followed by a Russian version of the unexpurgated text, prepared by G. Yu. Pogozheva: *Chuvstvo: tetradi* (Moscow: Vagrius, 2000). I used this Russian version, which I checked against the original manuscript. All citations, unless otherwise indicated, refer to this version. All translations are my own, unless otherwise indicated.

3. From Dr. Eugen Bleuler's report of March 6, quoted in Peter Ostwald, *Vaslav Nijinsky: A Leap into Madness* (New York: Carol, 1991), 196.

4. Igor Stravinsky and Robert Craft, *Memories and Commentaries* (Garden City, NY: Doubleday, 1960), 34.

5. There is an inconsistency in the naming of the two parts. On a title page in the original manuscript, Nijinsky wrote "On Death" (*O smerti*), but he wrote in the body text that he wanted to title the book (i.e. part) he was writing "Death" (without the preposition) and the previous one "Life."

6. That is, he never uses the word *dnevnik*. To refer to his work, Nijinsky uses the words *kniga* (book), *rukopis'* (manuscript), *tetradi* (notebooks), *pisanie* (writing), and *zapis'* (note, record). The latter is the singular form of the word *zapiski* (notes) used in the title of Nikolai Gogol's work "Notes of a Madman" or "Diary of a Madman" (*Zapiski sumasshedshego*) and Tolstoy's work of the same name. In Gogol's work, the "madman" uses dated entries in a diary format; Tolstoy's "Notes of a Madman" starts out with a dated entry but leaves the diary format behind in favor of a retrospective memoir. Nijinsky's work is a mixture of these approaches: it is permeated with recollections but has the urgency of the present tense.

7. Maurice Sandoz, "Vaslav Nijinsky," in *The Crystal Salt Cellar* (London: Guilford Press, 1956), 62–77.

8. Hanna Järvinen, "Dancing without Space—On Nijinsky's *L'après-midi d'un faune* (1912)," *Dance Research* 27, no. 1 (2009), 53.

9. Quoted in Millicent Hodson, *Nijinsky's Crime against Grace: Reconstruction Score of the Original Choreography for* Le Sacre du Printemps (Stuyvesant, NY: Pendragon Press, 1996), ix.

10. Tamara Karsavina, *Theatre Street* (New York: Dutton, 1931), 241–242.

11. My focus here is on crossing borders from an artistic and philosophical standpoint. Even a glance at Nijinsky's biography, however, shows that he also crossed state, cultural, linguistic, gender, and sexual borders—border crossings that are reflected in the diary. At the same time, Nijinsky's life reflects the privilege of mobility. His first lover-benefactor, Prince Pavel Dmitrievitch Lvov, may have been "the very first person in St. Petersburg to own a car." See Bronislava Nijinska, *Early Memoirs*, trans. and ed. Irina Nijinska and Jean Rawlinson (Durham, NC: Duke University Press, 1992), 199. This prince-motorist recommended his protégé to the eminently mobile Sergei Diaghilev, the impresario of the Ballets Russes and Nijinsky's mentor-lover for the next five years. During that time, Diaghilev was able to keep his star performer with him in the West because Nijinsky was not allowed to return to Russia unless he did his three-year service in the Russian military. The War Ministry repeatedly denied Nijinsky's petitions for exemption, and from 1910 on, Nijinsky never returned to his homeland even for a visit. Ibid., 483.

12. Introduction to Monika Büscher, John Urry, and Katia Witchger, eds., *Mobile Methods* (New York: Routledge, 2011), 6.

13. Nijinsky, *Chuvstvo*, 77.

14. Ibid., 49, 50.

15. Ibid., 51.

16. For example: "When I say, before the registrar or alter, &c., 'I do,' I am not reporting on a marriage, I am indulging in it." Austin calls this speech act "a performative utterance, or for short 'a performative.'" J. L. Austin, *How to Do Things with Words: The William James Lectures Delivered at Harvard University in 1955*, ed. J. O. Urmson (Oxford: Clarendon Press, 1962), 6.

17. Ibid., 14. When a performative does not follow certain conventional procedures (for example, when one of the parties in a wedding ceremony does not follow the rules), the utterance, according to Austin, is "not false but in general unhappy."

18. Nijinsky, *Chuvstvo*, 224.

19. Ann Hutchinson Guest and Claudia Jeschke, *Nijinsky's Faune Restored: Vaslav Nijinsky's Dance Notation Translated into Labnotes* (Philadelphia: Gordon and Breach, 1991), 5.

20. Ramsay Burt, *The Male Dancer: Bodies, Spectacle, Sexualities*, 2nd ed. (New York: Routledge, 2007), 77.

21. Nijinsky, *Chuvstvo*, 199.

22. Nijinska, *Early Memoirs*, 427.

23. Ibid., 316; See, for example, R. Nijinsky, *Nijinsky*, 165.

24. Nijinsky, *Dnevnik Vatslava Nizhinskogo*. For a more in-depth analysis of vertical/horizontal axes in terms of the structure and language of the diary as connected to Nijinsky's choreography, see Nicole Svobodny, "Tantsovshchik kak pisatel': Vatslav Nizhinskii i telesnost' iazyka" ("The Dancer Writes: Vaslav Nijinsky and the Embodied Word," translated into Russian by Andrei Logutov), *Novoe literaturnoe obozrenie* 135 (2015): 56–67.

25. When one considers Tolstoy's abhorrence of the railroad (remember *Anna Karenina* and *Kreutzer Sonata*), it is rather ironic that Nijinsky was "converted" to Tolstoyanism in a train traveling across the United States.

26. R. Nijinsky, *Nijinsky*, 418.

27. L. N. Tolstoy, *Ispoved'*, in *Polnoe sobranie sochinenii v 90 tomakh* (Moscow: Gosudarstvennoe izdatel'stvo "Khudozhestvennaia literatura," 1957), vol. 23, 58–59.

28. Donald Rayfield, "Last Words," a review of Leo Tolstoy's *The Death of Ivan Ilyich & Confession*, trans. Peter Carson, *Times Literary Supplement*, November 22, 2013, 5.

29. According to Romola, Nijinsky did indeed become interested in yoga while they were in St. Moritz. See R. Nijinsky, *Nijinsky*, 407.

30. Tolstoy, *Ispoved'*, vol. 23, 12.

31. Ibid., 13.

32. Ibid., 14.

33. Ibid.

34. Nijinsky, *Chuvstvo*, 55.

35. Ibid., 57.

36. Ibid., 55.

37. Ibid., 56.

38. Ibid.

39. Ibid.

40. Nijinsky's approach to language definitely has an affinity with the Russian avant-garde movement Zaum, a neologism that could be translated as "beyond the mind," "transrational," or "beyonsense," although there is no direct evidence that Nijinsky knew about this experimental poetry, and he does not directly mention it in the diary.

41. Nijinsky, *Chuvstvo*, 58.
42. Ibid., 131.
43. Ibid., 244.
44. Ibid., 110.
45. Ibid.
46. Ibid., 110–111.
47. Ibid., 71.
48. Nijinsky often uses ellipses in his writing to indicate silence.
49. Ibid., 112.
50. Ibid., 71. In Russian, the word for "language" is also the word for "tongue" (*iazyk*), underlining the connection of speech to the physical body.
51. Ibid., 121.
52. Ibid., 122.
53. Ibid., 77.
54. Ibid., 78. Here there are also references to Tolstoy's 1859 short story "Three Deaths" (*Tri smerti*).
55. Ibid., 82.
56. Eugen Bleuler, *Dementia Praecox or the Group of Schizophrenias*, trans. Joseph Zinkin (New York: International Universities Press, 1950), 356.
57. Ibid., 429.
58. See Edward Denby, "Notes on Nijinsky's Photographs," in Lincoln Kirstein, *Nijinsky Dancing* (New York: Knopf, 1975), 163; and Nijinsky's letter to Stravinsky, cited in Hodson, *Nijinsky's Crime against Grace*, x.
59. Laird Easton, ed. and trans., *Journey to the Abyss: The Diaries of Count Harry Kessler, 1880–1918*, (New York: Vintage Books, 2011), 619.
60. Nijinsky, *Chuvstvo*, 158, 81.
61. Ibid., 79.
62. Ibid., 75, 89.
63. Ibid., 80, 236.
64. See, for example, Jeremy Rifkin, *The Empathic Civilization: The Race to Global Consciousness in a World in Crisis* (New York: Penguin, 2010).
65. Daniel Lerner, *The Passing of Traditional Society: Modernizing the Middle East* (Glencoe, IL: Free Press, 1958), 47.
66. Ibid., 49.
67. Ibid., 50; Stephen Greenblatt, *Renaissance Self-Fashioning: from More to Shakespeare* (Chicago: University of Chicago Press, 2005), 236.
68. Lerner, *The Passing of Traditional Society*, 49.
69. Gilles Deleuze and Felix Guattari, *The Anti-Oedipus: Capitalism and Schizophrenia* (New York: Penguin, 2009), 15.
70. Ibid., 2.
71. Ibid., 84.
72. Romola Nijinsky, ed., *The Diary of Vaslav Nijinsky* (New York: Simon and Schuster, 1936); Deleuze and Guattari, *The Anti-Oedipus*, 84.
73. Ibid., 2.
74. Ibid., 78.
75. Bleuler, *Dementia Praecox*, 53. Deleuze and Guattari mention Bleuler only once. Their main target is Freud's Oedipal mythology.

76. Ibid., 374.
77. Deleuze and Guattari, *The Anti-Oedipus*, 131.
78. Ibid., xiii.
79. I would argue that Nijinsky's writing takes us even further than Deleuze and Guattari. For all their celebration of "something produced . . . not mere metaphors," their theories are ultimately more abstract than Nijinsky's writing, which is grounded in the somatic experience of a *dancer* (not just a "schizo") out for a walk. For a discussion of Deleuze and Guatarri's theories as falling short of the somatic practice of dance, see Kimerer L. LaMothe, "Can They Dance? Towards a Philosophy of Bodily Becoming," *Journal of Dance and Somatic Practices* 4, no. 1 (2012): 93–107. To the question posed in her title, LaMothe answers in the negative: "Without any ability to conceive of the movement specific to a human bodily form, Deleuze and Guattari leave intact a mental sense of self as the sole source of subjectivity" (98). Their concepts "deny what the notion of the rational subject was itself repressing: the creative potency of bodily movement. It remains a clever, abstract thought, guiding us in patterns of self-reflection that promise freedom from the finite materiality of our bodily selves" (99). I am grateful for LaMothe's enthusiastic, careful reading of my manuscript and thank her for pointing me to her article.
80. Nijinsky, *Chuvstvo*, 76.
81. Ibid., 174.
82. Ibid., 210.
83. Ibid., 72.
84. Ibid., 69. Nijinsky repeatedly asserts that he wants to be a person "without habits."
85. Ibid., 174. Nijinsky is speaking in philosophical terms here, but the statement that he had a home everywhere can also be taken literally, in light of his itinerant life. In his early childhood (up to age eight), he traveled all around the Russian Empire with his Polish parents, who were itinerant dancers, rarely living in one place for more than a few weeks. Nijinska, *Early Memoirs*, 22–29. When he began dancing for the Ballets Russes itinerant company at age nineteen, he also did not have a fixed residence but instead lived with his impresario, Sergei Diaghilev, in hotels. To what extent did this migrant life affect his subsequent illness? Bleuler seems to anticipate such a question in his monograph, rejecting the assumption: "One patient became ill because he chose the strenuous and exacting life of an actor; another, because he lived so irregularly; a third, because he traveled too much. Closer scrutiny reveals that there are not even the slightest grounds for such assumptions." Bleuler, *Dementia Praecox*, 344–345. However, a recent epidemiological study suggests that psychosocial stressors, "especially those concerning migrants," may lead to the experience of "social defeat" or "outsider status," which is a risk factor for schizophrenia. Jean-Paul Selten and Elizabeth Cantor-Graae, "Social defeat: Risk Factor for Schizophrenia?," *British Journal of Psychiatry* 187 (2005): 101–102.
86. Ibid., 64
87. Ibid., 73.
88. Ibid., 126.
89. Ibid., 142.
90. Ibid., 73.
91. Ibid., 139.
92. Ibid., 194.
93. Stravinsky, quoted in Richard Taruskin, *Stravinsky and the Russian Traditions* (Berkeley: University of California Press, 1966), 877, 879; Nijinsky, *Chuvstvo*, 195.

94. Nijinsky, *Chuvstvo*, 193.
95. Ibid., 196.
96. Ibid., 127.
97. Ibid., 242.
98. "Ecological visionary"—what George Marshall wrote to me in an e-mail after I sent him the relevant pages of Nijinsky's diary. Marshall also pointed out to me the connection of the "mortality salience" with the psychology of climate change awareness, in light of the fact that most of Nijinsky's writings about the suffocation of the earth occur in Book II ("Death") of his diary. For an exploration of the psychology of climate change denial, see Marshall's *Don't Even Think about It: Why Our Brains Are Wired to Ignore Climate Change* (New York: Bloomsbury, 2014); Nijinsky, *Chuvstvo*, 195.
99. Paul Bloom, "The Baby in the Well: The Case against Empathy," *New Yorker*, May 20, 2013, http://www.newyorker.com/magazine/2013/05/20/the-baby-in-the-well.
100. Ibid.
101. Nijinsky, *Chuvstvo*, 194.
102. Ibid., 242.
103. Burt, *Male Dancer*, 15.
104. Ibid., 58.
105 Nijinsky, *Chuvstvo*, 99, 105. Dr. Frenkel was indeed trying to administer to Nijinsky large doses of chloral hydrate. See Ostwald, *Vaslav Nijinsky*, 175. And, it seems that Romola did plan to institutionalize her husband.
106. Nijinsky, *Chuvstvo*, 164.
107. Ibid., 167–169.
108. Ibid., 169.
109. Ibid., 177.
110. Ibid., 217.
111. Ibid.
112. Ibid., 218.
113. Ibid., 228, 230.
114. Ibid., 245.
115. Ostwald, *Vaslav Nijinsky*, 202.
116. Diagnostic interviews with Nijinsky were conducted in French and German. See ibid., 201.
117. Nijinsky, *Chuvstvo*, 83.
118. Ibid., 92.
119. L. N. Tolstoy, *Na kazhdyi den'*, in *Polnoe sobranie sochinenii v 90 tomakh*, vol. 43, 65.
120. Ibid.
121. Ibid., 66.
122. Tolstoy, *Chto takoe Iskusstvo?*, in *Polnoe sobranie sochinenii v 90 tomakh*, vol. 30, 28.
123. Ibid. Tolstoy believed large theatrical productions (such as ballet) were, like war, a waste of time, money, and energy and sacrificed the lives of young people; Tolstoy, *Na kazhdyi den'*, 65.
124. Lynn Garafola, *Diaghilev's Ballets Russes* (New York: Oxford University Press, 1989), 58.

CHAPTER 4

Russian Resorts and European Leisure
Railroad Vacations, "Native" Sites, and the Making of a Russian (Post)Colonial Identity in Manchuria, 1920s–1930s

Chia Yin Hsu

AN ENGLISH-LANGUAGE HANDBOOK of North Manchuria published in 1924 by the Chinese Eastern Railway (CER), the region's central land transportation network, ran a full-page advertisement for the railway's "health resorts." The CER was constructed in the Chinese territory of Manchuria by the imperial Russian state and completed in 1903. As the final stretch of the Siberian Railroad, it linked European Russia to the Pacific Ocean. The advertised resorts were located at various CER train stations and shared their names: Chalantun, Imienpo, Fularki, Hingan, Laosiaokow and Echo. The page offered scenic images of the resorts and descriptions of their surroundings. Chalantun bordered the Ial River; Imienpo lay "in the mountainous area by the Maiho river," Fularki was "in the plains area by the Nonni river." The advertisement listed the up-to-date amenities of the resorts, which were "equipped with every comfort":

> Electric lighting. Medical supervision and attentive care. Good, varied and nutritious meals are served in the first class restaurants of the health resorts. All forms of sport: rowing, bathing, tennis, football, and others. Walks in the mountains and plains, sunbaths.

The advertisement touted the library at Chalantun, which carried "Russian, English and French books, newspapers and magazines," and promised "complete privacy" to those preferring a quiet vacation. It pointed to the "special lowered rates" for train travel to these resorts, directing interested readers to inquire at the Health Department of the CER.[1]

All the resorts were situated within the former Russian concession, whose concessionary and extraterritorial status was abolished by the Chinese government in 1920. The territory of the concession consisted of a narrow strip of land along the CER tracks, except at the railway stations, where the concession bulged out to allow for a town or a city. Before the Russian Revolution of 1917, the railway concession was a de facto Russian colony, and Harbin, the concession's largest city, resembled a "fine Russian provincial town."[2] As refugees poured into China from Russia during the Russian Civil War, the population that self-identified as Russian in the railway concession grew from around two hundred thousand in 1917 to about four hundred thousand in 1923.[3] This was a small portion of North Manchuria's nearly twelve million inhabitants, but its concentration around the railway—in Harbin as well as in the villages and towns along the line—helped maintain the concession as a Russian place.[4]

Many Russian refugees who fled to Manchuria obtained railroad jobs that maintained them in relative comfort by the standard of the region. But they were perhaps the minority. A good number of the refugees were indigent, presenting to many observers the spectacle of the fall from power of a contingent of the "white" race, and the erosion of colonial privilege conferred by whiteness. A Russian account, for instance, asserted that in China, "the appearance of destitute Russian émigrés ended once and for all the myth of the power and prestige (*izbrannost'*) of white-skinned people."[5] A Japanese diplomat describing Manchuria in the early 1920s portrayed Russians as "a proud race ... now dominated by the very people whom it had lorded over."[6] Such observers, sympathetic or not, invariably saw Russians' plight as degradation.

Heavily subsidized by the Russian treasury before World War I, the railway fell into disrepair after 1914. The CER's resorts were created with the general overhaul of the railway starting in 1920. According to a CER engineer who took part in their creation, the resorts' purpose was to improve the railroad's reputation, publicize its services, and compete with the successful resorts of the Japanese-run South Manchuria Railway (SMR), the southern branch of the original CER line that was ceded to Japan after the Russo-Japanese War.[7] This chapter contends that these railway resorts were meant not only to achieve these goals; they were meant to, and did, do much more. The resorts helped establish a new epistemological order that—mapping the Manchurian terrain for leisure consumption and ethnographic tourism—also reshaped the image and self-understanding of Russian émigrés in China as white and European, against growing perceptions of Russians as destitute refugees whose Europeanness was doubtful. In so doing, the resorts also helped impart to many Russians in post-1917 Manchuria a stance that was necessary for being European in Asia—the sense of existing above and apart from the "natives." This stance constituted a Russian identity that was at once colonial and postcolonial. It was a colonial identity, as it claimed continuity with imperial Russia's domination in North Manchuria, expressed in a belief in Russians' entitlement to the CER; and it was postcolonial—as, confronting Chinese political takeover of the region, Russian views of colonial hierarchies could not be asserted overtly but only by more ambiguous means, such as the cultivation of a particular kind of self and the fashioning of a particular kind of lifestyle.

Spas and health resorts (*kurorty*) in Russia and Europe were well known to educated Russians through literature, their awareness of the elites' habits, and, by the late nineteenth century, increased leisure travel. With the establishment of Soviet power, *kurorty* of the imperial era were turned into scenic and therapeutic sites for "worker leisure" and the "repair of toilers."[8] In the Soviet Far East, bordering Manchuria, efforts to transform the region's forests and mineral springs into *kurorty* began by the early 1920s. As elsewhere in Soviet territory, the far eastern *kurort* advocates envisioned the "broadest masses" as the beneficiaries of the natural "riches" that were to be made available by the new resorts.[9]

The first Soviet *kurorty* predated by over a decade other iterations of mass leisure that resulted from Europe-wide movements to transform holiday travel and leisure "from a regime of privilege to a regime of access"—including *dopolavoro* (after-work) in Fascist Italy, *Kraft durch Freude* (Strength through Joy) in Nazi Germany, and the *congés payés* (paid vacation) for workers in the France of the Popular Front.[10] The resorts in Manchuria, like Soviet resorts, embraced the "regime of access" by making these sites of leisure easily available to Russians in the region. But unlike Soviet resorts, the ones in Manchuria, while purveying mass leisure, also invoked the flavors of privilege and aristocratic life, signaled by the recurring use—by the CER and by the resorts' admirers—of terms laden with a sense of class distinction to describe these resorts and their users, such as "fashionable" and "elegant."[11] These terms conjured up exclusive resorts favored by the cultural and moneyed elite of Europe and Russia both before and after the revolution, such as those in the Côte d'Azur, rather than the Soviet "rest homes" (*doma otdykha*) that turned confiscated villas and estates into proletarian dormitories.[12]

The CER resorts were thus shaped by attempts to ensure both a "regime of privilege" and a "regime of access" in these spaces. The merging of what in Europe and Soviet Russia would have been contradictory aspirations was made possible by the postcolonial condition of Manchuria, reflected in the insistent separation of "natives" from "foreigners" in the perception of many "foreigners" in this region, who gravitated toward the two railway concession zones of the CER and the SMR. That is, in the Manchuria inhabited by Russian émigrés, the class line that guaranteed privilege in European societies and prerevolutionary Russia was redrawn to divide "Europeans" from "natives." The physical environment of the resorts, the leisure habits these resorts cultivated, and the ethnographic knowledge produced by the CER's research societies all worked to redraw this line. In this way, the Russianness that many émigré Russians created in Manchuria was one that did not quite exist in the prerevolutionary society they had known. But, as their writings often attest, the Russianness they invented in Manchuria was presumed to be an unquestionable and unchanging part of being Russian.

THE CER RESORTS

As conveyed by photographic images of the advertised resorts that were sprinkled across the 1924 survey of North Manchuria, the resorts were insistently presented as railway resorts, as if to drive home the modernity of leisure. Fularki, for instance, appeared in that volume with a train crossing an iron-truss bridge in the background. Laosiaokow, south of Harbin, was shown with another iron railway bridge, a strikingly long one. Echo, where not only a resort but also a railway-funded experimental farm was located, was presented with another impressive railway bridge astride the large river bordering the well-kept grounds of the farm.[13]

These resorts were frequently visited by many Russians in Manchuria, especially the émigré population in Harbin, to judge from both contemporary and retrospective mentions of these places. A celebratory history of the CER published in a 1927 special issue of the Harbin paper *Novosti Zhizni* included a photograph of the sanatorium at Fuliaerdi (or Fularki, in the 1924 survey), and another of the resort dining hall at Chzhalan'tun' (also spelled Chalantun, or Chzhalantun').[14] The picture of this dining hall showed a grand interior featuring full-height windows, potted palm trees whose presence invoked perhaps the Côte d'Azur, and linen-covered tables surrounding a broad central aisle left open for a dance floor. One could imagine that such was the décor of elegant restaurant-clubs in any of the metropolises in the West.

According to a former Harbin émigré, K. M. Geishtor, the CER resorts were inspired by the SMR resorts. According to another, B. Kozlovskii, they were intended for answering "the need" of a rapidly increasing Russian population in Manchuria. Led by its new director, B. V. Ostroumov, the railway administration transformed many train stations into what some former émigrés would fondly recall as favorite vacation spots.[15] The CER line consisted of three branches: the eastern segment that connected Harbin to the Soviet border in the direction of Vladivostok; the western segment that led from Harbin to the Soviet Zabaikal region; and a comparatively short southern segment, which remained a part of the CER after the loss of most of this branch of the railway to Japan. *Kurorty* and dacha rentals spread across all three branch lines, usually clustering around train stations. There were about twenty CER resorts: eleven to the east, eight to the west, and one to the south of Harbin.[16]

The resorts along the eastern segment included Ashikhe, Imian'po (or Imienpo, in the 1924 survey), and Ertsen'tsziantszy, nicknamed the "Gateway to the Manchurian Taiga" for the mountain "virgin forest" that distinguished the area. To the west of Harbin the resorts included Fuliarerdi and Chzhalantun'. The first consisted of facilities built "according to the latest fashion" (*po poslednemu kriku mody*), and the second was a "magnificent, fashionable resort (*feshenebel'nyi kurort*)." On the western segment were smaller resorts, such as Lamadtsiantszy, by the Great Xing'an mountain range, and a string of railway station retreats close to the mountain range that were made for "nature lovers." The area around these retreats was "extremely rich in flowers, mushrooms, berries, and nuts," its woods filled with wild game, and its river abundant with fish, Kozlovskii writes. On the southern segment was Laoshagou, like Harbin built on the bank of the Sungari River. This station was set up as a beach resort, surrounded by a restaurant, a dancing hall, and "splendidly appointed dacha buildings."[17]

In the 1920s, the resort at Chzhalantun' was "the favorite place of rest and recreation (*otdykh i razvlechenie*) . . . for many railway employees (*zheleznodorozhniki*)," yet another former Harbin émigré, N. Borislavskii, recalls decades later. He adds that it attracted "the inhabitants of Harbin . . . and [of] other cities" in southern Manchuria and China proper that had a sizable population of Russians and foreigners.[18] As do other émigré memoirists, Borislavskii credits CER director Ostroumov for transforming the railway's stations into resorts. At Chzhalantun', the previously dilapidated railroad station was turned into a "beautiful and spa-like (*kurortnaia*)" destination for vacationers, and the area next to it was landscaped into a park with benches, gazebos, pavilions, and tree-lined alleys leading to a band shell for outdoor concerts. At night, "garlands" of multicolored lamps laced the grounds of the resort and the bank of the Ial River that the resort bordered. Lamps strung across the artificial waterfall at the beach lit up the water from behind. Floodlights illuminated Chzhalantun's beach.[19] Vacationers staying at the dachas nearby (*dachniki*), according to Borislavskii,

> swam and rowed boats, [or] . . . climbed up the mountain trails to the hilltop, to admire the fairytale-like (*feerischeskaia*) nighttime panorama from there. The main walk (*glavnoe gulian'e*) and the [most] boisterous merriment (*besshabashnoe vesel'e*) was around and inside the large, brightly lit veranda spa-hall (*kurzal*), where a string orchestra played, and an elegantly attired (*raznariazhennaia*) public whirled in fashionable dance steps, singing in all keys the favorite foxtrot of that time: "O, Chzhalan'tun', what panorama!! O, Chzhalan'tun', what beauty!!!" And until late at night . . . laughter, ringing young voices were heard.[20]

As presented in photographic images and émigrés' retrospective accounts, the CER resorts commonly featured buildings that resembled European villas and grand hotels; facilities that provided "all kinds of comforts and entertainment" (*vsevozmozhnye udobstva i uveseleniia*); dachas for rent; parks landscaped for tennis, croquet, and other outdoor games; and beaches and riverbanks leveled and sculpted for a variety of aquatic pastimes.[21] Some resorts acquired monikers that suggested their equivalence to scenic locations in Europe and other parts of the West. Chzhalantun' was known as "the Pearl of the East" (*Zhemchuzhnaia Vostoka*), and the Khan'daokhetszy resort on the eastern segment—at a major station that earlier served only the nearby Russian settlement and a Russian timber factory—was called "the Manchurian Switzerland."[22]

The repetition of such terms as "picturesque" and "fairy tale–like," and the comparison of the resorts to places in the West, suggest that these views of the resorts helped assimilate the unfamiliar land of Manchuria with the conceptions of nature and beauty held by the Russian émigrés who were educated, professionals by training, and oriented toward European norms by their outlook. In turn, the repetition and comparison universalized European conceptions of landscape as the norm for transforming local topography.[23] By enabling this reconception and transformation of the Manchurian land, the *kurorty* also enabled the transcendence of geographical difference between Europe and Asia, making it possible to imagine the Manchurian resorts as being anywhere in Europe, and their visitors as no less European than the resorts. Thus, the *kurorty* conferred an identity to a place not by their geographical location but by the style of their architecture and landscape and by the manners and social habits the resorts helped shape. This effort to transcend geographical location was made all the more pronounced by the absence of the Chinese, the vast majority of Manchuria's population, in Russian accounts of these resorts. The resorts remained a Russian space, conceived as part of Europe, and segregated from the "local" population by Russians' leisure practices and consumption habits.

Purveyed by the CER resorts, this sense of leisure, and of living in a manner not too different from Europeans elsewhere, was carried over in the 1930s to the pages of the popular Russian émigré magazine *Rubezh* (Borderlands), which regularly published articles on fashion, sports, and movie stars.²⁴ The weekly magazine extended the mood of holiday leisure to the daily life of Russian émigrés in the city and reinforced their self-identity as urban and European by its emphasis on recreational and consumption trends in the West. An article by Anni Runei, a seemingly made-up French name, for instance, advised readers on the "fashions of the beach," as "beaches everywhere are starting to come alive" with summer approaching. Showing plates of women modeling "contemporary swim suit[s]" and other beach wear, Runei noted that "the distinctive (*svoeobraznaia*) beach life ... [of] our time demands no less elegance and taste than going to the ball." Leaving open whether she meant anywhere in the world or anywhere on the CER line, Runei recommended three essentials to ladies "going to a resort anywhere"—"a travel suit, a ball gown, and an outfit for the beach." Perhaps acknowledging the limited means of her readers, and offering a strategy for economizing, Runei asserted that "it is enough to take along these three pieces of wardrobe," for "in all the chic resorts (*modnye kurorty*) it is acceptable for ladies to appear at the *table d'hôte* (*tabl' d'ot*) in beach clothing."²⁵ Runei's voice was authoritative in matters concerning fashion. In an earlier issue of *Rubezh*, she expounded on the "laws of fashion" for ladies, announcing the arrival of the dress suit. She showcased Parisian fashion houses such as Jean Patou and Elsa Schiaparelli, referring to these designers with a familiarity that suggested the irrelevance of the distance between Harbin and Paris. Describing a jacket from Patou that was worn over a crepe-satin dress "the color of ocean waves," Runei added, "by the way, this is Jean Patou's favorite shade."²⁶

Hunting, a pastime available at a number of the CER retreats, also appeared in the pages of *Rubezh*.²⁷ Reporting on a hunting trip taken by a "popular financier in Harbin," the weekly portrayed hunting as a mode of being that, like fashion, allowed for the geographical difference between Manchuria and elsewhere to be blurred. In this case, the steppe of Qiqihaer, in North Manchuria, was portrayed by the magazine as very much like that of South Russia. Another blurring of geographical difference was suggested by the way the hunters, the financier and his friends, were photographed with their rifles and their chauffeured automobile, the car laden with game, as if to offer a model of European manhood that joined modern mobility to the remembered prerevolutionary Russian elite's presumption of entitlement. The urban, modern, and, implicitly,

European—and perhaps also imperial Russian—character of these men was emphasized in the article, which held hunting to be an inseparable aspect of this character. Hunting, the author judged, "is the best holiday for the man of business (*delovoi chelovek*)," for "at the hunt he almost merges with nature—and she, better than any medicine, calms the nerves that city life enervated."[28] Thus hunting, taken up as a leisure activity, not only recalled aristocratic pleasures of the imperial era but also restored the masculinity of "men of business."

For those unable to go hunting in a chauffeured automobile, athletic clubs that proliferated since the early 1920s provided sports facilities and equipment as another means for engaging in physical exertion as a form of leisure—in contradistinction to physical exertion as a necessity of subsistence, a condition embodied by the coolie and, for many Russians, associated with Chineseness. The existence of these clubs again worked to assimilate Manchuria to the West. Thanks to Harbin's Russian sailing and yachting clubs, for instance, sights ranging from single-scull rowboats to regattas of sailboats, more commonly found on European and American waters, could also be seen on the Sungari.[29]

ZHELEZNODOROZHNIKI AND RAILWAY LIFE

The CER concession was taken over by the Chinese republican government and renamed the Special Administrative Region of the Three Eastern Provinces (SAR) in 1920.[30] But for many Russian émigrés who reminisce about Manchuria in the 1920s and after, this major political change was barely acknowledged. For them, the railway concession remained "Russian" after 1920, a claim that comes implicitly with remembering the life they lived in the former railway concession as, in one way or another, fairy tale–like or dreamlike. This sense of the marvelous is often based on equating pleasure and well-being with the leisure activities dispensed by the CER resorts and other CER-funded facilities.

Geishtor, writing about how Russians lived in the SAR, which for him remained inseparable from the CER and the Russian-dominated railway administration, exclaims: "Nowhere in the world was there a railway like it, and it can boldly be said that life [there] was like a fairy tale." He recalls the "splendidly furnished" resorts, where jazz played and guests brought by special vacation trains "danced until late hours." Many *zheleznodorozhniki*—that is, those with full-time positions at the railway, from administrators and engineers to skilled workers—lived in houses by the Sungari built by the CER, which they rented out to "vacationers" (*dachniki*) in the summer, according to Geishtor.³¹ The *zheleznodorozhniki* enjoyed the low cost of living that Geishtor sees as characteristic of Manchuria in the 1920s. Fancy fare from "crabs, oysters, lobsters," to pheasants and pork was cheap and plentiful; "many restaurants opened," offering "refined menus" and endless "banquets" to a clientele that Geishtor describes as the "public masses" (*massa publiki*).³² Here, refined food, associated with privilege like fashionable holidays, was affordable to a community of the "masses" defined by employment at the CER.

Writing about the early 1930s, A. N. Kniazev remembers: "This time... seems to me like some kind of an unbelievable dream." Kniazev was at that time a student at Harbin's Polytechnic Institute, a technical school founded in 1920 to serve the CER that, by the choice of the school's language of instruction, enrolled mostly Russians.³³ Apart from attending to schoolwork, Kniazev and his cohort took part in student clubs and devoted much time to "sports ... water sports [on the Sungari], excursions (*pokhody*)," and camping. Kniazev marvels at the fullness of this life, which he explains "by our youth, good health, and, evidently (*povidimomu*)," he writes, quoting a saying he seems to believe his readers know well, by an "inextinguishable desire: 'embrace everything and prevail over (*preodolet'*) everything—after all we are Russians, and God is with us!'"³⁴

In contrast to Kniazev's naturalization of privilege as innate to Russianness, Geishtor credits the CER administration for securing a life of relative ease for those connected to the railway by means of generous subsidies. Geishtor notes that railway employees (*sluzhashchie*) enjoyed "free apartments with heating, water, and icebox," and railway workers with full-time positions (*statnye rabochie*)—"even" they—"lived comfortably (*bezbedno*)." The CER administration also set up pension and disability funds for its employees to ensure their continued well-being after retirement and dismissal.³⁵

In fact, writing in 1927, E. Kh. Nilus—who was charged by the CER to compile its history—saw ensuring the "well-being" of the *zheleznodorozhniki* as one of the responsibilities of the railroad, thereby ascribing to the CER the function of a paternalistic company or welfare state. Aiming to define the railway's future agenda, Nilus asked whether the CER had fulfilled its "duty" (*dolia*) to create the "necessary preconditions" for the "material, spiritual, and legal well-being of its numerous agents (*agenty*), and of all the local population that is gravitating toward it." By "local population," Nilus most likely meant Russian émigré-refugees, for whom a central concern was obtaining a legal status that would resolve the legal limbo of statelessness in which they found themselves after 1917. Despite commending the CER for "expend[ing] significant means for the cultural needs (*kul'turnye nuzhdy*) of its numerous employees," Nilus judged that the railway's effort to support its "agents" was inadequate. Pushing the CER to do more, he concluded: "The present directors of the CER still have ahead of them much responsible, cultural work (*kul'turnaia rabota*)."[36]

By calling on the CER to use its resources for the well-being of its "agents"—that is, its employees and workers—Nilus asserted in a veiled way that the railway's beneficiaries should be Russians. Although the CER frequently hired large numbers of Chinese workers, the proportion of Chinese to Russians among its salaried employees and workers remained low. Between 1923 and 1924, CER employees and full-time workers comprised 11,000 Russians and 6,000 Chinese. Following the conclusion of the Sino-Soviet Treaty in late 1924, which transferred the CER's management to the Soviet government, the number of those counted as Russian increased slightly to over 11,000, and that of those counted as Chinese decreased to 5,500.[37] Not only greater in number, Russian *zheleznodorozhniki* were more likely to occupy better-paid technical and professional positions, with greater benefits, while a large part of the Chinese were probably workers.[38] Russian *zheleznodorozhniki*, their dependents, and other Russians who used CER-funded "cultural" facilities thus made up a significant percentage of the Russian population in the region, which was close to 200,000 in 1925.[39]

Inverting the provider-beneficiary relationship, G. V. Melikhov, memoirist and historian of *Russian Emigration in China*, sees the CER as benefiting from the large number of educated Russians who flocked to the railway, thus creating a "high concentration of [émigré] intelligentsia" at the former concession zone and a "corresponding[ly] high level of... cultural life (*kul'turnaia zhizn'*) for all Russian ethnic groups (*rossiiskie natsional'nye gruppy*) and [ethnic] communities (*obshchiny*)" in the "enclaves" of Russian emigration (*rossiiskaia emigratsiia*) in East Asia.⁴⁰ Insisting on the term *rossiiskii* to underscore the unity of émigré ethnic communities, Melikhov nevertheless reveals that perhaps among "Russians" in exile, ethnic Russians and orthodox Christians enjoyed greater influence than other "national groups." He lauds the Russian Orthodox Church for playing an "important unifying role" in educating Russians (*russkie liudi*) in China—a "linguistic, religious, cultural, and moral environment (*sreda*)" that was "completely different in character" from their own.⁴¹ Melikhov's account inadvertently hints at a hierarchy of Russianness, as he indicates that the "cultural life" fostered by the CER was tilted in favor of ethnic Russians, although it included all Russian speakers. Similarly, explaining the high "cultural" level of the former CER concession, Melikhov highlights a status hierarchy at the railway that made the émigré "intelligentsia," meaning the educated and the professionals, a particularly privileged group among émigré-refugees in the region.

Decades later, Russian retrospective accounts referring to the late 1930s and 1940s tended to portray Manchuria and Harbin as a place where Russians lived well, even though a series of major political shifts in the region increasingly curtailed the CER's autonomy and limited the railway's ability to dispense social amenities. These shifts included the Japanese military occupation of Harbin and North Manchuria in late 1931; the creation of the Manchukuo regime by the Japanese government in 1932; the Soviet government's sale of the CER to Japan in 1935; the years from 1937 to 1945—of the Chinese war of resistance against Japan and the Pacific War—during which Manchukuo was plunged into financial crisis; and the resumption of Soviet control over the CER after the defeat of the Japanese army in Manchuria in 1945.⁴²

An example of this persistence of fond memory appears in a 1996 self-published novel about Russians in Harbin by Lidiia Iastrebova, *The Russian Australian*. The novel's two lover-protagonists, having grown up in Harbin, are sent on divergent paths in the mid-1950s, when most of the Russians who remained in China departed either for the Soviet Union or for the American and Australian continents. The story is about young love that blossomed in Harbin and endured, despite the separation of the lovers. It tells of the deep suffering of one protagonist following her "repatriation" to the Soviet Union, and of the mild anomie of the other following his immigration to Australia.[43] To portray Harbin as a place where the young lovers spent their happiest moments, the novel describes their leisure activities in a manner that calls to mind émigré reminiscences and other Russian publications about life in China and Manchuria.

The young lovers, Serezha and Tania, met in a Harbin secondary school whose Russianness—shown in the names of its students, its curriculum, and its after-school events—the novel takes for granted. Like the *Rubezh* articles, the novel, despite setting its story in Harbin and at the Sungari, stresses the features of these places that invite the reader to imagine the story's locale as anywhere in Europe. In the novel, this anywhereness is conveyed in part by referring to music, understood as the standard repertoire of well-known nineteenth-century composers. The author draws on this music to signal Harbin's Europeanness. Tania, a gifted pianist, captivated Serezha's attention playing Chopin. During their walks around Harbin, "whenever the sounds of a piano would come out of a house somewhere, Tania would say: 'Listen, it's the First Concerto of Liszt,' or 'It's Rubenstein's Melody.' Then they would stop and stand under the windows and listen."[44] Emphasizing the presence of European music, the author renders Harbin's streets similar to those of some imagined respectable bourgeois quarter of a nineteen-century European town.

The novel's effort to erase geographical specificity carries over to other parts of the plot. Presenting a picture of how a wealthy Russian family, the Brasletovs, lived in Harbin—even though this section of the novel is set in the straitened times of 1950s China—the author shows Tania and her parents living in a well-appointed residence, their living room "richly and elegantly furnished." Tania's father "worked as chief accountant, but not because he needed the money. He simply liked this work." In his time off "he receiv[ed] guests, visit[ed] theaters and restaurants ... read, listen[ed] to music and play[ed] chess." Conveying the author's idea of a *barin*—one character calls out admiringly after him: "Such a well-dressed gentleman (*kholenyi barin*)"—Tania's father was gentlemanly in taste and bearing, and "could not tolerate physical work." Like the mistress of a bourgeois family—imagined as a variant of the gentry household—Tania's mother "did not work at all, only oversaw the servants." Like the women idealized in the 1930s copies of *Rubezh*, she filled her days with social activities and fashion concerns. She went "to the movies with friends or to cafes. The hairdresser and the manicurist came to her at the house." In the evening, "she met her husband, [when he] returned from work, well-dressed, perfumed and so attractive that he never had any thought of looking at other women."[45] Describing the larger social setting of Harbin, the author acknowledges some external events, such as Stalin's death and the Chinese response to this news at Tania and Serezha's school.[46] But, turning to the domestic space of the family, the author depicts this space as devoid of any sign that could tie the Brasletovs' home to China or Manchuria, except in the muted reference to the servants and in the mention of Brasletov's aversion to physical work. As sketched out by the author, the Brasletovs in Harbin seem indistinguishable from European bourgeois families elsewhere, and—except for some touches that evoke Soviet society in the era of the New Economic Policy—not too different from prerevolutionary bourgeois families in European Russia.[47]

But the novel also lets on that the pockets of carefully curated space of Russianness and Europeanness in Harbin that served as its backdrop—if they existed—were not securely guarded. Tania was forced to give up a new friend. She was, in Tania's words, a "girl who lived [near the dacha], really nice ... And it so happened that she said 'naginat'sia' [instead of *nachinat'sia*, presumably] when papa was there, and he forbade me to be friends with her. You, he says, will pick up wrong words from her."[48] Thus, as presented by the novel, the sphere of bourgeois domesticity in Russian Harbin, which included raising children, resembles what Ann Stoler, studying the Dutch Indies, identifies as the site for the "education of desire"—for shaping the body and habits of the young to ensure their differentiation from the natives and the dubiously European. Through domestic arrangements that mimicked the concerns of the bourgeois family back in the Netherlands, Stoler shows, the Dutch colonial families cautiously tended to their whiteness.[49] In the case of Harbin, what was cultivated, as suggested by the novel, was a Europeanness—synonymous with whiteness in China at that time—that was refracted through asserting Russianness, in order to safeguard the proper Russians from the influence of not only the "natives" but also Russians who had been tainted, to use

Melikhov's phrase, by the alien "linguistic, religious, cultural, and moral environment" of Manchuria.[50] But this Russianness was forged in neither prerevolutionary nor Soviet Russia; it was formed by the colonial and postcolonial predicament of Manchuria. It was a self-understanding that called up fictive aristocratic memories, bourgeois longings, and populist ideals of mass access to privilege. If Tania and her family reflect the first two moods, Serezha represents the third. Despite coming from a family of modest means, he gained entry to the prestigious "Polytechnic Institute" in Harbin, as well as acceptance by the Brasletovs, without class difference ever emerging as an obstacle. In this sense, the Harbin portrayed by Iastrebova was a classless society, albeit one restricted to those speaking unadulterated Russian.

THE "INDIGENOUS" PRIMITIVE AND THE ETHNOGRAPHIC MUSEUM

In Russian accounts of Manchuria that referred to the domestic and intimate realm of family and friends, the Chinese appear in limited guises, usually as servants and laborers. Typical in this regard, Iastrebova's novel *The Russian Australian* barely touches on the Chinese presence in Harbin or in the surrounding area, mentioning it only in passing: for instance, when the Brasletovs took their Chinese cook with them to the dacha in the summers, and when, having decided to "repatriate," Tania's father "hired an entire brigade of Chinese for packing up their polished furniture, crystals, and porcelains."[51]

By contrast, regarding the public, nondomestic realm as perceived by Russians, the Chinese frequently appear in both contemporary and retrospective works, usually as objects of ethnographic study. In late 1922, a new scientific research association based in Harbin, the Society for the Study of Manchuria (*Obshchestvo izucheniia Man'chzhurskago kraia*, or OIMK), was established. As announced by the society's journal, *Izvestiia OIMK*, the society's task was to "help all the cultural forces (*kul'turnye sily*) in the region find a common language, and, by way of amicable efforts, move toward the same goal, toward the all-sided study of the local region."[52] Despite proclaiming its creation as the convergence of "three cultures (*kul'tury*) . . . the Chinese, Russian, and Manchu," the OIMK was primarily a Russian project in both membership and funding. The society brought under its purview natural and social sciences such as geology, ethnography, and trade and industry.[53] The activities of the society—which declared itself as the "breeding ground for education (*prosveshchenie*) and a conduit [for spreading] the scientific knowledge obtained by European culture (*evropeiskaia kul'tura*)"[54]—included publication, expeditions, and museum work. The OIMK was funded substantially by the CER. Between 1922 and 1928, between about 40 percent to 74 percent of the society's revenue came from CER subsidies, which generally increased from year to year.[55] In contrast to the railroad, which was Russian-run, the Chinese-directed government of the SAR did not provide financial support to the society, even though its founders included several prominent Chinese in the SAR.[56]

The new OIMK museum in Harbin—intended for introducing European science to "broad circles of the population" in Manchuria—absorbed over 62 percent of the society's expenses between 1922 and 1925.[57] The ethnographic section occupied a large space in the museum. Explaining the aim of ethnography, a contributor to the first issue of *Izvestiia OIMK* defined the field as a "science" that studied "the culture" (*kul'tura*)—printed in bold in the article—of "primitive (*pervobytnye*) peoples and those strata of civilized peoples which . . . have preserved the traits of a primitive social structure (*pervobytnyi stroi*)." The contributor identified two types of people targeted for ethnographic inquiry: primitive peoples who lived apart from contemporary societies, or who "have already disappeared," and "the least cultured strata (*naimenee kul'turnye sloia*) of the contemporary civilized peoples," which, although living in the present time, still retained "survivals, traces, of [primitive] life." The OIMK museum, according to this author, was to provide the "most unassailable facts" drawn from "the observation of this life," through the exhibition of "ethnographic objects that visually (*nagliadno*) illustrate the life of primitive peoples."[58]

The society's "ethnographic section," later renamed the "historico-ethnographic section," incorporated archaeological discoveries such as those found at the "city of Baichen," an "ancient rampart" near the Ashikhe railway station on the CER's eastern segment. The museum's "historico-ethnographic department" displayed objects divided into collections pertaining to such ethnographic categories as "religion (*kul't*)," "clothing," and "way of life" (*byt*). Religion, according to the museum, meant "lamaist, shamanist, Daoist, etc.," and "way of life" was understood as that of "the Chinese, the Mongolian, the Manchu."[59] Objects such as "Chinese ceramics and ancient bronzes" were shown in glass cases.[60] "Way of life" exhibits were presented in dioramas staging various scenes of social life, using clothing and everyday objects the ethnographers considered specific to the culture of the people in question. The dioramas included "a Mongolian yurt with a group of Mongols inside," "mannequins of Manchus," and, signaling the museum's concern with "disappearing" peoples, a "mannequin of an Orochi in hunting clothes."[61] Representing not the disappearing peoples, but, by OIMK's definition, "the least cultured strata of the contemporary civilized peoples," were dioramas of Chinese social life. One showed "a Chinese peasant family before a Chinese house (*fanza*)." Another depicted "Chinese merchants at a business deal (*za delovym razgovorom*)," with a teacup and an abacus as the representative objects of this scene.[62]

The practice of placing on display the Chinese, the majority of Manchuria's population and themselves recent migrants to a good part of the region, was not unique to the Harbin museum.[63] In Port Arthur, a large city in South Manchuria at the southern tip of the Liaodung Peninsula and the Japanese-run SMR line, a "science museum" similar to that of the OIMK was opened in 1918 by the Japanese military command in the region and financed by the Japanese government. The museum was organized into sections similar to those in the Harbin museum. Like the one in Harbin, this museum was largely concerned with exhibiting artifacts relating to the local population, here defined as that of "Manchuria, Mongolia, China, and, in part, Korea." Visiting the museum in 1933, I. G. Baranov—a "scholar-sinologist," as a Russian émigré memoirist calls him—praised the thoroughness of its Chinese ethnography division.[64] The museum exhibited a great number of items that were "selected very carefully" to "illustrat[e] the way of life (*byt*) of the native population (*tuzemnoe naselenie*) of Kuantung," the Chinese territory in the Liaodung Peninsula that was leased to Japan until its invasion of Manchuria in 1931. The museum's interest in the Chinese was not confined to the ethnographic division. In the zoological division, to portray "Chinese methods for hunting wild birds," what seems to be a diorama, according to Baranov's description, was exhibited: "The hunters with various hunting weapons are represented in small mannequins, as if performing silent scenes."[65]

Tracing his passage through the room of the Port Arthur museum, Baranov revealed how the museum produced knowledge through spatial arrangement, modeling an organizational framework—an epistemological order—that helped the consumers of this knowledge apprehend the unfamiliar and multiethnic world they lived in. Baranov moved from statues taken from currently active Chinese Buddhist temples to "the Indian art of ancient times" displayed next to the statues. After viewing the "Chinese 'mummies'" brought from Eastern Turkestan—by a Japanese expedition, Baranov noted—and prehistoric artifacts, some of which were "obtained by the Japanese at excavations" near Port Arthur, Baranov went on to the division of Chinese ethnography. There he found mannequins in "national dress," women's ornaments made of precious stones and metals, "objects of the Tibetan lamaist religion," and contemporary Chinese objects.[66]

The museum's collections were exhibited in a way that emphasized the irrelevance of differentiation by time period. Conflating the ancient and the contemporary, the mummies and the mannequins, the museum exhibits relegated the imagined "local" to the realm of the timeless and, thus, the primordial. More conspicuously than the Harbin museum perhaps, the Port Arthur museum also blurred the usual boundary between the human and the animal by placing small mannequins of Chinese hunters in the zoological section, suggesting the evolutionary proximity of the Chinese "locals" and the local fauna. Hunting here, depicted as a necessity of survival, was not an activity that differentiated man from nature and animal life—thereby signaling manhood and individual masculinity, as in the pages of *Rubezh*. Both museums clearly distinguished the targets of ethnography from its investigators, however. By establishing a space where Russians and Japanese were absent from the exhibits but present as visitors, these two museums excluded them—along with European and American "foreigners" in the region, the other likely visitors to the museums—from the category of the "local." Thus, either in Port Arthur or in Harbin, the museum provided the space for identifying the primordial with the local, in contradistinction to vacation resorts or the pages of a lifestyle magazine like *Rubezh*, which exhibited the modern and the latest cosmopolitan trends, and offered their consumers access to the "fashionable." Following this ordering of information, hunting, for instance, acquired different meanings depending on the "culture" of the hunters. Whereas the museum turned Chinese hunters—and in Harbin the Orochi hunters—into curiosities, magazines like *Rubezh*, featuring hunters equipped in modern gear, normalized Russian hunters as contemporary models of manhood.

The epistemological order established in the enclosed space of the museum was extended beyond the museum by scholarly or amateur investigators who cast an ethnographic gaze upon the open terrain. Uncovering ethnographic sites embedded in the Manchurian land, the investigator doubled as traveler, conflating the past and present where it concerned the local and turning the open terrain into a vast museum space in which the production of ethnographic knowledge was intertwined with the appreciation of the picturesque. In an article on the "folk beliefs" in the Liaodung region, published a year after his visit to the Port Arthur museum, Baranov praised the ethnographic richness of the land: "The investigator (*issledovatel'*) of southern Liaodung, in the cities as in the villages, stumbles at every step upon a large number and wide variety of religious objects." The article elaborated, "in the cities, as well as [during] outings taken from villages, on the sea shore, at road-crossings, or at picturesque little corners among the mountains, the traveler often finds an ancient Chinese monastery or a lone shrine."[67] Melding the "ancient" with what was practiced "to this day," and counterposing the scientific "investigator" to the "Chinese peasants or merchants" holding "supernatural" beliefs, the article asserted that "all such finds testify visually (*nagliadno*) to the beliefs that to this day reign over the soul of the common Chinese man (*kitaiskii prostoliudin*)," and "give the investigator an idea of the gods to whom the common Chinese man is still praying today."[68]

Some details in Baranov's description worked against the sense of unchanging timelessness he projected onto these "religious objects." For example, the Buddhist shrine near SMR's Anshan station that Baranov documented was renovated several times, the most recent during the republican period, that is, after 1911.[69] But, as the investigator-traveler-tourist,

Baranov delivered what his readers might have expected by setting the Buddhist shrine at Anshan into a legible landscape constructed as serene and undisturbed: "The place chosen for the shrine is very picturesque, with a view on the surrounding mountains, and the bluish ocean below. ... All around it is filled with silence and tranquility, and [even] the sad call of cuckoos is only rarely heard."[70]

Turning to Harbin, Baranov published a pamphlet in 1938 on the two Chinese temples built in the 1920s at the outer edge of the central Russian sector of the city. Perhaps because of his familiarity with the underlying contestations between the Chinese and the Russians over their construction and his faithfulness to detail, Baranov's account of the temples recognized their contemporaneity.[71] Observing the "rather animated" daytime activities outside the Jilesi (Heavenly Shrine), a walled Buddhist monastery compound, Baranov noted that monks, pilgrims, beggars, automobiles, and Russian horse carriages (*izvozchiki*)—which were common in Harbin—crowded about the gates.[72] Describing the main building of the temple-palace complex Wenmiao (Temple of the Letters), also called Kongmiao (Temple of Confucius), Baranov mentioned that its roof rested on "immense red columns made of concrete," a material whose use in nonindustrial buildings was still being pioneered in Europe in the 1920s.[73] Baranov wrote that Wenmiao was, at great cost, "built according to the model of the Temple of Confucius in Peking" and completed by "master craftsmen (*mastera*) commissioned from the former capital."[74] Presenting the temple's construction at this level of detail, the pamphlet also made it possible to read Wenmiao as a Chinese attempt to turn that part of Harbin into a place indistinguishable from "anywhere" else in China, similar to how Russians were envisioning Harbin as a possible "anywhere" in Europe or European Russia.

Baranov's 1938 pamphlet was more a reportage than a translation of an alien culture for Russians touring Chinese sites in Harbin, as it employed more "sociological" than "ethnographic" methods of inquiry. Baranov's nonethnographic approach in this pamphlet was apparently not absorbed by readers such as Elena Taskina, a former inhabitant of Harbin, whose writing reflects a mode of remembering that Russian émigré memoirs are more likely to take up.[75]

Explaining Chinese religious views, Taskina's Harbin memoirs reintroduce a sense of the fantastical and otherworldly that Baranov's 1938 pamphlet had dispelled. "The most interesting layer of the spiritual life of the Chinese is their religious attitude," she claims. "All over the place," she elaborates, "there were innumerable images of spirits and divinities, which, according to Chinese beliefs, accompanied a person everywhere from the moment of his birth right up to his death."[76] Prompted by "curiosity for the people of another culture," Taskina writes, "Russian youth" would visit the Buddhist monastery Jilesi, where the visitors would find themselves "infused by an atmosphere of quiet and contemplation." The monastery's "atmosphere was always friendly," as the young visitors "consistently" showed a respect for "others' religions and others' customs (*chuzhie ustroi*)" that was similar to the "sensitivity and attentiveness toward local religious cults (*religioznye kul'ty*)" shown by Russian railroad builders from the very beginning of the CER's construction, Taskina insists. "Russian engineers, topographers, bridge-builders always upheld the one and same rule—to treat the beliefs of the Chinese thoughtfully and with care, especially their cult of the ancestors ... the places of burial, the sacred groves and woods."[77] By counterposing Russian railroad builders to Chinese sacred sites, and by contrasting the curiosity of young Russians to the quiet of the Chinese monastery, Taskina's memoir asserts yet again the division between the cosmopolitan modern and the timelessness of indigeneity that had been repeatedly traced out in many Russian texts about Manchuria.

CONCLUSION: RACE AND THE RAILWAY EPISTEMOLOGICAL JOURNEY

Russian contemporary and memoir writings about the sites of Manchuria cultivated the active figure of the Russian tourist, who traveled and embarked on excursions. By contrast, these same writings depicted the Chinese, recent migrants to Manchuria themselves, as stationary and bound to the locality, and thus "nativized." Nativizing the Chinese, Russian ethnographic knowledge also preempted the possibility of the nativization of Russians, understood in part as the loss of Russianness. In Iastrebova's novel, this loss was embodied by Tania's misspeaking friend. But linguistic adulteration was perhaps only a way for the author to hint at other forms of nativization that many Russians feared, such as poverty, dire physical need, or falling into a position of servitude in relation to the Chinese or other non-Europeans such as the Japanese.

Russian refugees in Manchuria often found themselves in conditions of material and bodily insecurity. "A good part of the Russian population" in Harbin, Taskina admits, "was without money."[78] Charities and refugee organizations were set up to assist émigré-refugees.[79] This level of want was probably what many Russians in Manchuria experienced. Stories circulated, especially in the 1920s, of formerly well-placed Russians who faced enormous hardship in China. A member of Alexander Kolchak's Siberian Government during the Russian Civil War, P. V. Vologodskii, died impoverished in Harbin.[80] Unknown, but representing the "tragedy" of a generation of educated young Russians, was Nikolai Nikolaevich Zhukov, son of an "agronomist and veterinarian doctor, hereditary nobleman." His death in Shanghai at age thirty was reported in Russian newspapers because he was found destitute, without family or friends, and his burial was to be covered by the municipality.[81]

These stories helped shape Russian understanding of the alienness and inhospitableness of the Chinese social milieu, which various Russian voices characterized in terms of the "almost fabulous cheapness of Chinese labour in Manchuria [which] makes any kind of [labor] competition impossible," or in terms of the condition of "half starvation," which was "the lot of the coolie."[82] This sense of the proximity of the refugee's plight to that of the "coolie" remained imprinted in Russian views. In his late 1990s memoir-history of Harbin, Melikhov, discussing their livelihood, asserts the "impossibility [for the émigrés] to compete in unskilled labor with Chinese day-laborer coolies (*chernorabochie-kuli*)."[83] The fantasies of affluence purveyed by *Rubezh*'s articles and Iastrebova's novel no doubt served to assuage profound anxieties regarding the material insecurity that most Russian refugees faced in the post-1917 decades.

But this fantasy of affluence was given a reality in some of its aspects—leisure activities, recreation, and vacation resorts—which were made available to many Russian émigrés in Manchuria thanks to the CER. This fantasy also involved the distancing of Russians from the "alien" Chinese ways and the destitution Chineseness signaled, which was accomplished by an epistemological order that asserted for Russians a privileged position as the cosmopolitan observers of the locals. Like the fantasy of affluence, this epistemological order was sustained by the CER, because the railway line mapped out and linked such disconnected human settlements as Chinese monasteries, ancient ruins, and Russian resorts. Connected and incorporated into the "railway journey," to use Wolfgang Schivelbusch's term, these disparate expressions of human experience, however alien to Russian views they might have been, could now be grasped by the traveler through the vista put into order by the railroad stations that punctuated this journey.[84]

Kozlovskii offers an example of this ordering of the Manchurian landscape through the "railway journey" in his reminiscence of the CER resorts. Listing those to the east of Harbin, he writes:

> the next popular vacation place was the Ashikhe station.... Not far from the station was the small town of Achen ... distinguished for its beautiful Daoist temples. Near this town were the ruins of the ancient city of Baichen, the former capital of the Chinese dynasty of the Jin, where archaeologists of the Harbin Museum carried out excavations and found many valuable items. Still further to the east was located the larger station of Ertsen'tsziantszy.... At the station, for spa visitors (*kurortniki*) to rest and heal, a large, magnificently designed (*oborudovannoe*) building called "the Ertsen'tsziantszy Resort" was constructed.

Speaking of another major railway station, Maoershan', Kozlovskii continues:

> The surrounding area ... was exceptionally picturesque. The center of delight [there] was the 1000-meter high "Sugar Top" mountain, located at seven kilometers from the station....
>
> Climbing up this mountain was the visitors' favorite excursion.... Set into the very foot of the mountain was a Chinese monastery, where hospitable monks cordially met visitors, showing them the monastery.[85]

As Kozlovskii's enumeration shows, various sites of past and present human habitation, created by alien and distant societies, now fell into place as points of interest in a trajectory traced out as a sightseeing, recreational, resort-hopping tour.

Without this railway epistemological order, what could have emerged as an alternative might resemble the "epistemological crisis" that Anton Chekhov's work on Sakhalin Island presents, as interpreted by Cathy

Popkin. Popkin maintains that facing the "ethnographer's dilemma of turning... 'unruly experience' into 'authoritative written account'"—such as classifying by the rules of "science" an indigenous population that defies ethnographic categories—Chekhov "simply abdicates" from "deliver[ing] a well-crafted description" that would make sense of Sakhalin. Popkin argues that Chekhov's epistemological crisis—"his refusal or inability to deliver" an account that is authoritative and free of contradictions—"makes him a truer witness."[86] By contrast, the railroad, as the author of the text or landscape, inscribed into the Manchurian terrain by its physical presence and the social practices it promoted, persistently produced knowledge that made sense of Manchuria for Russian consumption. If this knowledge brought order to "unruly experience," it did so by suppressing what a "truer witness" would have acknowledged. But, as testified by the nostalgia that émigré reminiscences convey, the epistemological order fostered by the CER's "railway journeys" was one that many Russian émigré-refugees embraced, for it framed the knowability of Manchuria according to the perspective and aspirations of those émigrés whose life revolved around the CER.

NOTES

1. *North Manchuria and the Chinese Eastern Railway* (Harbin: CER Printing Office, 1924), n.p.
2. Rosemary Quested, *"Matey" Imperialists? The Tsarist Russians in Manchuria 1895–1917* (Hong Kong: University of Hong Kong, Centre of Asian Studies, 1982), 255.
3. G. V. Melikhov, *Rossiiskaia emigratsiia v Kitae (1917–1924 gg.)* (Moscow: Institut rossiiskoi istorii RAN, 1997), 8, 58, 213.
4. The date for the population number is 1921, the first time a count of Northern Manchuria's total population was attempted; see *North Manchuria and the Chinese Eastern Railway*, 10–11. For the concession's role in maintaining Russian influence, see Arkhiv vneshnei politiki Rossiiskoi Imperii (AVPRI), f. 301, o. 818/II, d. 79, l. 30b.
5. Petr Balakshin, *Final v Kitae*, v. 1 (San Francisco: Sirius, 1958–1959), 101–102.
6. K. K. Kawakami, *Japan's Foreign Policy: Especially in Relation to China, the Far East, and the Washington Conference* (New York: Dutton, 1922), 268. For Russian and Chinese contestations over extraterritoriality, see Chia Yin Hsu, "Railroad Technocracy, Extraterritoriality, and Imperial *Lieux de Mémoire* in Russian Émigrés' Manchuria, 1920–1930s," *Ab Imperio* no. 4 (2011): 70–76.
7. Melikhov, *Rossiiskaia emigratsiia v Kitae*, 169; K. M. Geishtor, "Kitaiskaia-Vostochnaia zheleznaia doroga s 1921 g. do 1935 g.," 6–7, Columbia University, Rare Book and Manuscript Library (RBML), K. M. Geishtor memoirs, Folder 1-8.

8. Diane P. Koenker, *Club Red: Vacation Travel and the Soviet Dream* (Ithaca, NY: Cornell University Press, 2013), 12, 15; Mary Blume, *Côte d'Azur: Inventing the French Riviera* (New York: Thames and Hudson, 1992), 63–64, 185.

9. I. A. Bagashev, ed., *Kurorty Dal'nego Vostoka* (Moscow: Izd. Dal'ne-Vostochnogo Kurortnogo Upravleniia, 1923), 10, 17; K. Luks, ed., *Kurorty i mineral'nye istochniki Dal'nego Vostoka* (Chita: Dal'ne-Vostochno-Sibirskoe Izdatel'stvo "Knizhnoe delo," 1923).

10. Ellen Furlough, "Making Mass Vacation: Tourism and Consumer Culture in France, 1930s to 1970s," *Comparative Studies in Society and History* 40, no. 2 (April 1998): 252; Gary Cross, "Vacations for All: The Leisure Question in the Era of the Popular Front," *Journal of Contemporary History* 24, no. 4 (October 1989): 599–560. This phrase is used by Furlough to refer to the enactment of the *congés payés*.

11. These terms telegraphed a challenge to proletarianization. By the late 1930s, fashion, luxury, and feminine attractiveness had emerged as a front line for battling communism in Hollywood films. See Helen Laville, "'Our Country Endangered by Underwear': Fashion, Femininity, and the Seduction Narrative in *Ninotchka* and *Silk Stockings*," *Diplomatic History* 30, no. 4 (September 2006): 623–644.

12. Blume, *Côte d'Azur*, chaps. 3–4; Koenker, *Club Red*, 20–22.

13. *North Manchuria and the Chinese Eastern Railway*, 9, 402, 433. For Laosiaokow's location, see B. Kozlovskii, "Kurorty i mesta otdykha vokrug Kharbina i po liniam KVZhD," *Politekhnik* (Sydney, Australia), vol. 10, *Iubileinyi sbornik* (1979), 90.

14. E. Nilus, "Kitaiskaia Vostochnaia zhel. dor. (Istoricheskii ocherk E. Kh. Nilusa)," in *Iubileinyi nomer "Novostei Zhizni" 1907–1927* (Harbin, 1927), 63–64.

15. Geishtor, "Kitaiskaia-Vostochnaia zheleznaia doroga s 1921 g. do 1935 g.," 6; Kozlovskii, "Kurorty i mesta otdykha vokrug Kharbina i po liniam KVZhD," 87.

16. Kozlovskii, "Kurorty i mesta otdykha vokrug Kharbina i po liniam KVZhD," 87–90.

17. Ibid.

18. N. Borislavskii, "Stantsiia Chzhalan'tun' K.V. Zh. D.," newspaper article, n.p., Stanford University, Hoover Institute (HI), Nikolai Petrovich Kalugin Collection, Box 3, Folder 1, microfilm reel 3.

19. *North Manchuria and the Chinese Eastern Railway*, resort advertisement, n.p.; Borislavskii, "Stantsiia Chzhalan'tun'"; Kozlovskii, "Kurorty i mesta otdykha vokrug Kharbina i po liniam KVZhD," 89.

20. Borislavskii, "Stantsiia Chzhalan'tun.'"

21. See, for example, Nilus, "Kitaiskaia Vostochnaia zhel. dor.," 63; Kozlovskii, "Kurorty i mesta otdykha vokrug Kharbina i po liniam KVZhD," 87–90; and "Kurort na st. Ertsendian'tszy," photograph, *Politekhnik*, vol. 10, *Iubileinyi sbornik* (1979), unnumbered page before p. 197.

22. Geishtor, "Kitaiskaia-Vostochnaia zheleznaia doroga s 1921 g. do 1935 g.," 6; Kozlovskii, "Kurorty i mesta otdykha vokrug Kharbina i po liniam KVZhD," 89.

23. I use the term *landscape* or *landscaping* to refer to land that had been altered to suit particular notions of what constituted cultivated and well-kept grounds. To speak of "landscape," as opposed to a piece of land, whether cultivated or not, is to speak of "an aesthetic object," as Christopher Ely notes. Similarly, "scenery," according to Ely, was also an aestheticized object, but it was invented later, in the era of leisure travel. According to Blume, the Côte d'Azur's invention involved the reshaping of preexisting land to suit the taste of the coast's first trend-setting vacationers. The English, for instance, imported their preference for lawns to the Mediterranean coast. Both *landscape* and *scenery* are therefore

expressions of a particular preference—such as, in the case of the Manchurian resorts, that for lawns, beaches, and alpine contours. See Ely, "The Origins of Russian Scenery: Volga River Tourism and Russian Landscape Aesthetics," *Slavic Review* 62, no. 4 (Winter 2003): 667–668; and Blume, *Côte d'Azur*, 31.

24. *Rubezh* began publication in 1927 and at its height in the 1930s had a circulation of close to 2,500 copies, distributed mostly to Harbin and along the CER lines. Iu. Kruzenshtern-Peterets, "O 'Rubezhe,'" *Politekhnik*, vol. 10, *Iubileinyi sbornik* (1979), 185–186.

25. Anni Runei, "Mody pliazha: Rol' kupal'nago kostiuma v nashi dni," *Rubezh* no. 24 (1931): 11, RBML, N. A. Martynov collection, Box 2. Runei's advice was fairly up to date. In 1924, Blume relates, Coco Chanel visited the duke of Westminster in "beach pyjamas" at a resort casino near Cannes. Juan-les-Pins, the town where this casino was located, became "Pyjamaland" by 1930 for "populariz[ing] this convenient and often elegant beach costume," according to a Cannes paper Blume quoted. Blume, *Côte d'Azur*, 90–91.

26. Runei, "Modnyi tualet—kostium: Zakony mody dlia damskogo tualeta.— 'Individual'nyi kostium,'" *Rubezh* no. 20 (1931): 17, RBML, N. A. Martynov collection, Box 2.

27. Kozlovskii, "Kurorty i mesta otdykha vokrug Kharbina i po liniam KVZhD," 88.

28. Argus, "Okhotnichii rai: Za drofami na avtomobile v stepiakh Tsitsikara i Keshania," *Rubezh* no. 24 (1931): 15, RBML, N. A. Martynov collection, Box 2.

29. V. S. Tennisistka, "Sport," *Politekhnik*, vol. 10, *Iubileinyi sbornik* (1979), 277; N. Prokhvatilov, "Vodnyi sport," *Politekhnik*, vol. 10, *Iubileinyi sbornik* (1979), 280–281.

30. See Hsu, "Railroad Technocracy, Extraterritoriality, and Imperial *Lieux de Mémoire*," 69–70.

31. Geishtor, "Kitaiskaia-Vostochnaia zheleznaia doroga s 1921 g. do 1935 g.," 6, 8–9.

32. Ibid., 7–8.

33. See, for example, two curricular bulletins, one for the "Russo-Chinese Technical School" and the other for the "Russo-Chinese Polytechnic Institute," both earlier names of the Harbin Polytechnic Institute. *Kratkii ocherk voznikoveniia i deiatel'nosti Russko-Kitaiskago Tekhnikuma v techenie 1920–1921 uchebnago goda i ego zadachi v budushchem* (Harbin: Tipografiia Kitaiskoi Vostochnoi zheleznoi dorogi, 1921); and *Russko-Kitaiskii Politekhnicheskii Institut v gorode Kharbine* (Harbin: Tipografiia Kitaiskoi Vostochnoi zheleznoi dorogi, 1925), HI: Kalugin Collection, Box 1, Folder 25, microfilm reel 1, sheets 7–38, 39–79.

34. A. N. Kniazev, "Vyderzhki iz dnevnika politekhnika," *Politekhnik*, vol. 10, *Iubileinyi sbornik* (1979): 51, 53.

35. Geishtor, "Kitaiskaia-Vostochnaia zheleznaia doroga s 1921 g. do 1935 g.," 8.

36. Nilus, "Kitaiskaia Vostochnaia zhel. dor.," 64. Nilus might have taken the term *cultural work* from Soviet vocabulary—referring to music, dance, lectures, and other kinds of educational activities—but he used it to mean, more broadly, the welfare of the population for whom the CER was to be responsible. Nilus's obfuscating use of the term *culture* may have been due to the prohibition by the Chinese republican government directed at stripping the CER of its pre-1917 "political"—read governmental—functions. See Hsu, "Railroad Technocracy, Extraterritoriality, and Imperial *Lieux de Mémoire*," 77; and Peter S. H. Tang, *Russian and Soviet Policy in Manchuria and Outer Mongolia 1911–1931* (Durham, NC: Duke University Press, 1959), 130. For Soviet usage of the term *cultural work*, see Koenker, *Club Red*, 47, 155.

37. Nilus, "Kitaiskaia Vostochnaia zhel. dor.," 64; Bruce A. Elleman, "The Soviet Union's Secret Diplomacy Concerning the Chinese Eastern Railway, 1924–1925," *Journal of Asian Studies* 53, no. 2 (May 1994): 476.

38. This imbalance can be surmised from the student composition of the Polytechnic Institute in Harbin, a feeder school to the CER. In 1924, the institute enrolled 437 Russians and 8 Chinese. From October 1924 to January 1925, of the 22 graduating students studying railroad engineering, all were Russian. See "Russko-Kitaiskii Politekhnicheskii Institut k nachalu 1925 goda. Gor. Kharbin," 243, 248; and "Russko-Kitaiskii Politekhnicheskii Institut v gorode Kharbine na 1-go maia 1925 goda i ego pervye vypuski inzhenerov," 20–23, HI: Kalugin Collection, Box 1, Folder 25, microfilm reel 1, 1.25–59 to 1.25–62, 1.25–81 to 1.25–86.

39. V. G. S., "Kharbin: (Istoricheskii ocherk)," *Politekhnik*, vol. 10, *Iubileinyi sbornik* (1979), 102; K. Ocheretin, ed., *Kharbin-Futsziadian': Torgovo-promyshlennyi i zheleznodorozhnyi spravochnik* (Harbin: "Transpechati" NKPS, 1925), 2. Suggesting the variability of population estimates regarding Russians, or the rapid flux of Russians' movement in and out of this region, the 1925 *spravochnik*'s population figure contrasts noticeably with that of Melikhov, who in 1997 gave 400,000 as the number of Russians in the region in 1923 (see note 3).

40. Melikhov, *Rossiiskaia emigratsiia v Kitae*, 202–203.

41. Melikhov, *Rossiiskaia emigratsiia v Kitae*, 202.

42. See George Alexander Lensen, *The Damned Inheritance: The Soviet Union and the Manchurian Crisis 1924–1935* (Tallahassee, FL: Diplomatic Press, 1974); and Louise Young, *Japan's Total Empire: Manchuria and the Culture of Wartime Imperialism* (Berkeley: University of California Press, 1998), 427–430.

43. Lidiia Iastrebova, *Russkii avstraliets: Roman: Kharbin, Avstraliia, Rossiia 1952–1993* (Sydney: Izdatel'svo "Avstraliada," 1996).

44. Ibid., 14, 29.

45. Ibid., 25–26.

46. Ibid., 30.

47. In Vladimir Mayakovsky's play *The Bedbug*, satirizing the materialist climate of the NEP, the author makes the social-climbing fiancée of the proletarian protagonist "a manicurist and cashier of a beauty parlor." Mayakovsky, "The Bedbug," in *The Complete Plays of Vladimir Mayakovsky*, trans. Guy Daniels (New York: Simon and Schuster, 1971), 142.

48. Iastrebova, *Russkii avstraliets*, 24.

49. Ann Laura Stoler, *Race and the Education of Desire: Foucault's History of Sexuality and the Colonial Order of Things* (Durham, NC: Duke University Press, 1995).

50. Melikhov, *Rossiiskaia emigratsiia v Kitae*, 202.

51. Iastrebova, *Russkii avstraliets*, 30–31, 43.

52. A. R., "Obshchestvo izucheniia Man'chzhurskogo Kraia, ego zadachi, struktura i deiatel'nost' (Otchetnyi ocherk)," *Izvestiia Obshchestva izucheniia Man'chzhurskogo Kraia* 6 (March 1926): 6; "Ot redaktsii," *Izvestiia Obshchestva izucheniia Man'chzhurskago kraia* 1 (November 1922): 1.

53. A. R., "Obshchestvo izucheniia," 21; "Ot redaktsii," 1.

54. "Ot redaktsii," 2.

55. "Otchet o deiatel'nosti Obshchestva Izucheniia Man'chzhurskogo Kraia. (5-i god sushchestvovaniia)," *Izvestiia Obshchestva izucheniia Man'chzhurskogo kraia* 7 (December 1928): 77.

56. A. R., "Obshchestvo izucheniia," 43–45; "Otchet o deiatel'nosti Obshchestva," 77. As noted by its journal in 1926, "the OIMK does not receive government subsidy." A. R., "Obshchestvo izucheniia," 31.

57. "Ot redaktsii," 2; A. R., "Obshchestvo izucheniia," 45. The 62 percent includes expenditure for both upkeep and acquisitions, at just above 31 percent each.

58. M. Krol', "Nauka—etongrafiia [sic] i muzei," *Izvestiia Obshchestva izucheniia Man'chzhurskago kraia* 1 (November 1922): 10–12.

59. A. R., "Obshchestvo izucheniia," 26, 35.

60. "Otchet o deiatel'nosti Obshchestva," figure 18 (between pp. 90 and 93).

61. "Otchet o deiatel'nosti Obshchestva," figures 20–21 (between pp. 90 and 93), 26–27 (following p. 97).

62. "Otchet o deiatel'nosti Obshchestva," figure 23 (between pp. 90 and 93), figure 24 (following p. 97).

63. Large-scale Chinese settlement in Manchuria was permitted only after the 1890s. Prior to that, migration from China proper was restricted by the Qing government, and the population in Manchuria was "comparatively static," according to Owen Lattimore. The Chinese in this earlier population largely identified with the Manchus "politically," and could register themselves as Manchu. Lattimore, *Manchuria: Cradle of Conflict* (New York: Macmillan, 1932), 31, 45–47.

64. E. Taskina, *Neizvestnyi Kharbin* (Moscow: Prometei, 1994), 46.

65. I. G. Baranov, "Musei v Port-Arture," *Vestnik Man'chzhurii* no. 6 (April 1933): 70, 72–73.

66. Ibid., 70–73.

67. I. G. Baranov, "O narodnykh verovaniiakh iuzhnogo Liaoduna (Po kumirniam iuzhnogo Liaoduna)," *Vestnik Man'chzhurii* no. 6 (June 1934): 144.

68. Ibid.

69. Ibid., 148, 150.

70. Ibid., 148.

71. This familiarity is shown by the pamphlet's use of internal CER documents to demonstrate Russian support for these projects, as if to rebut contrary views. See I. G. Baranov, *Khramy Tszi-le-sy i Konfitsiia v Kharbine: Istoriia postroiki i kratkoe opisanie* (Harbin, 1938), 4–5, 12–13.

72. Ibid., 6. For the use of *izvozchiki* in Harbin, see, for example, the photographic images showing cars and *izvozchiki* on the street that probably date from the 1930s, in *Polytekhnik* 10 (1979): between pp. 100 and 101.

73. Baranov, *Khramy*, 14. For the early 1920s European architectural view of concrete—that is, reinforced concrete, or, to use a contemporary term, "ferro-concrete"—as the "most modern of building materials," see Henry Russell Hitchcock, *Architecture: Nineteenth and Twentieth Centuries* (Middlesex, UK: Penguin, 1977), 421, 424.

74. Baranov, *Khramy*, 12.

75. Taskina cites Baranov's pamphlet; see Taskina, *Neizvestnyi Kharbin*, 46.

76. Ibid., 44.

77. Ibid., 45–46.

78. Ibid., 43–44.

79. Ibid., 44; Melikhov, *Rossiiskaia emigratsiia v Kitae*, 60.

80. D. G. Wulff, N. S. Lar'kov, and S. M. Lyandres, "P. V. Vologodskii i ego dnevnik," in P. V. Vologodskii, *P. V. Vologodskii: Vo vlasti i v izgnanii: Dnevnik Prem'er-ministra*

antibol'shevistskikh pravitel'stv i emigranta v Kitae (1918–1925 gg.), ed. S. Lyandres, P. Tribunskii, and D. Wulff (Riazan, Russia: Tribunskii, 2006). 44.

81. A. Bel'chenko, "Tragediia russkago cheloveka," *Slovo* (Shanghai), February 19, 1929, HI: Loukashin Collection, Box 15, Folder 3, microfilm reel 15, sheet 57.

82. S. V. Vostrotin, "A Russian View of Manchuria," *Slavonic and East European Review* 11, no. 31 (July 1932): 20, 32; Balakshin, *Final v Kitae*, 101–102.

83. Melikhov, *Rossiiskaia emigratsiia v Kitae*, 59.

84. Wolfgang Schivelbusch, *The Railway Journey: The Industrialization of Time and Space in the 19th Century* (Berkeley: University of California Press, 1986). The journey in this work regards the ways the railroad transformed human perceptions of their social and natural environment.

85. Kozlovskii, "Kurorty i mesta otdykha vokrug Kharbina i po liniam KVZhD," 88.

86. Cathy Popkin, "Chekhov as Ethnographer: Epistemological Crisis on Sakhalin Island," *Slavic Review* 51, no. 1 (Spring 1992): 43–44, 49–51.

PART II

Migrations: People in Motion

CHAPTER 5

Dynamic Bohemians
The Russian Artistic Circle in Paris (Russkii Artisticheskii Kruzhok v Parizhe)

Anna Winestein

THE PERIOD FROM 1870 to 1930 was the heyday of visual artistic exchange between France and Russia, during which countless Russian and later Soviet artists traveled to Paris to visit, study, create, advance their careers, and simply live. They naturally gravitated toward creative compatriots—other artists, poets and writers, musicians, scholars and scientists—but sometimes also turned to political émigrés, revolutionaries, or alternatively diplomats and other representatives of Russian officialdom. The informal networks and structured organizations that emerged not only connected the artists with other Russians in Paris but helped them interact and even integrate into the broader French art milieu. This chapter examines the Russian Artistic Circle in Paris (*Russkii Artisticheskii Kruzhok v Parizhe*, henceforth RAC), also known as the Montparnasse Circle, whose members and leading figures were the most mobile—geographically, socially, and even aesthetically—of all comparable associations.[1] Traveling frequently between Paris and St. Petersburg or Moscow, many of the founders and members served as active conduits connecting the two art worlds, and the RAC was unique in having numerous stakeholders, especially active artists, in both countries. In terms of gender, ethnicity, class, and artistic style or affiliation, the group was more diverse than any other Russian art circle in Paris. Although it existed formally from the spring of 1903 until the end of 1907, the RAC arose from networks formed in the late 1890s and continued to facilitate Russo-French and Russian expatriate to domestic Russian exchange until 1916. I examine the trajectory of the organization; the key personalities and trends that allowed this group to be highly dynamic and flexible, not only geographically but also in terms of its internal organizational and social structures and even aesthetically; and how this adjustability shaped its activities as well as its legacy.

CONTEXT

While in the eighteenth century, it was more common for French artists to travel to Russia to work for the imperial court and also to teach Russian artists, in the nineteenth century the trend reversed. The flow of Russian artists to Paris for study and training increased steadily throughout the 1800s, reaching the critical mass required for the development of a strong artistic community toward the end of the 1860s. The first organization, the Society of Russian Artists in Paris (*Obshchestvo russkikh khudozhnikov v Parizhe*, henceforth SRAP), emerged in the 1870s.[2] Formally established in December 1877, it grew out of a vibrant circle of art, literary, and musical figures that had formed around the painter Aleksei Bogoliubov and the author Ivan Turgenev from 1873 onward. In fact, 1874–1878 was in some ways the liveliest era of the SRAP's history, even if the organization continued to exist into the 1920s.[3] Most of the painters and sculptors involved in founding and running the SRAP were graduates of the Imperial Academy, in some cases sent to Paris to continue their training with the support of imperial fellowships, called pensions. Some of these artists intended to return and develop their careers in Russia, whereas others focused on establishing themselves in France and only occasionally contributed to exhibitions in Petersburg. However, few of these artists, other than Bogoliubov and the sculptor Mark Antokol'skii, deliberately tried to straddle the two art worlds and systematically move back and forth between them.

The flow of imperial pension holders to Paris decreased throughout the 1880s because of the academy's reemphasis on Rome rather than Paris as a suitable destination and increasing interest in German centers. In parallel to this, the artists of the Society of Itinerant Exhibitions (henceforth Itinerants) continued to combat the aesthetic and economic hegemony of imperial art institutions in Russia. As the influence of the Itinerants on the perception and study of art, as well as access to collectors and commissions, improved, artists became less concerned with formally graduating from official art schools as a stepping-stone to their careers. Major structural reforms in state-supported art schools in the early 1890s brought in a new generation of professors, who again encouraged students to travel abroad.

Improved conditions for travel in the late nineteenth century, as well as more artists originating from the middle class, meant study abroad was more accessible. The notion of a trip to Paris and other European centers as part of an artist's training, either to visit exhibitions or to accomplish some brief studying in museums or sketching in an atelier, and at any point during training—not exclusively at the end—became more popular. This generation could afford not only geographic but also institutional mobility, spending time at different art schools within Russia and exploring different academies in Paris. Those who could afford it returned to Paris multiple times after their first visit, taking advantage of previous experiences and increased self-confidence on these latter occasions. Still, new arrivals faced challenges at the time, as highlighted in an early article about the RAC explaining its motivations.

> The number of young Russian artists coming to Paris ... increases each year. Usually having a very incomplete grasp of French and often lacking sufficient resources, they find themselves in a difficult situation in Paris, which they don't know. They also lose a lot of time and energy to get themselves oriented, and end up settling in bad conditions. These preoccupations and these conditions then slow down their work and conversely slow down their return to their homeland. A well-organized effort of solidarity could avoid such inconvenience. It is with this goal that an amicable Circle of Russian artists is organized, whose members commit to helping each other in the greatest possible measure.[4]

Those excluded from or disadvantaged within imperial educational institutions, whether because of their ethnic background or political activism, also flocked to Paris. In the generation of the RAC, they were generally more economically advantaged and less politically involved than the cohort of the next generation, who would form the Académie Russe (Russian Academy) and its offshoots. The circles of the Académie Russe, which existed from 1910 to 1915, included poor Jews from the provinces and members radicalized by the events of 1905–1906 who had experienced jail and labor camps, not just temporary internal exile within Russia, as some RAC members had. Académie Russe members had little interest in leaving Paris once they had arrived there and focused completely on the Parisian artistic space, doing less than the RAC to bring ideas and influence back to Russia until some returned home after the Revolution.

By the time the RAC was founded in 1903, there was also a considerable increase in the number of Russian women traveling to Paris to study, not only art but medicine and other sciences, as well as law. The Imperial Academy and the Moscow School of Painting, Sculpture and Architecture (*Moskovskoe uchilishche zhivopisi, vaianiia i zodchestva*, henceforth MSPSA) had allowed women to audit classes without formally enrolling since the 1870s, whereas in France women's admission to state art schools was constrained till the 1890s and women initially had access only to decorative arts programs. However, with the founding of the Union des Femmes Peintres et Sculpteurs (Union for Women Painters and Sculptors) in 1881, the movement for women's voice in the French art world grew, and private academies quickly discovered a new source of revenue in accepting female students. In the 1890s, Russian women already had more options and better opportunities in Paris than at home, in art training, access to models, and supplies. Furthermore, the freer social environment of France and the respect provided to art as a sphere of activity was especially liberating for women, whose creativity was more validated there than in Russia.

RINGLEADERS

Unlike the vast majority of contemporaneous art societies in Paris and Russia, the four main figures involved in the establishment and running of the RAC were female, and creative women—not society ladies—continued to be represented prominently in its ranks. Women not only had a significant voice and played a major organizational role in the evolution and running of the society, sometimes outnumbering men on the executive board, but they essentially defined its priorities from the start. The group emerged from the social and professional circles of two artists: Elizaveta Kruglikova and Elizaveta Davidenko. They, together with Aleksandra Gol'shtein and Ol'ga Mechnikova, two older, well-established Russian Parisians with extensive networks in French and Russian literary and scientific spheres, were centrally involved in developing the charter of the RAC and gathering its early supporters.

Elizaveta Kruglikova was the unequivocal heart of the RAC and a beacon for innumerable Russian artists and creative figures who came to France between 1900 and 1914. After auditing classes at MSPSA at age twenty-five and studying with several Itinerants, she arrived in Paris in 1895, studying at the Académie Vitti, attending life-drawing sessions at the Académie Colarossi, and traveling for painting *en plein air* in Brittany in 1898. Unlike Muscovite and Russian contemporaries, who mostly studied in the ateliers of stalwarts of the salon such as Fernand Cormon or the more traditional academies, she became passionate about post-Impressionism and especially the School of Pont-Aven through her friendship with the Polish painter Władysław Ślewiński, a friend and pupil of Paul Gauguin. Her new painting style disappointed her parents, who withdrew their financial support in 1898, pulling her back home. Kruglikova returned to Paris in 1900 with help from her brother, settling into her own studio at 17 Rue Boissonade, which she kept until World War I. Gregarious and interested in everything, she acquired friends and acquaintances easily, and the gatherings at her studio were truly international. Within a year, the space became a center of Russian artistic life in Paris, and her weekly parties were the effective birthplace of the RAC in 1903.[5] In contrast to the very discriminating Bogoliubov, head of the SRAP, and the upper-class Russians who kept regular salons in Paris, such as Ivan Shchukin, Kruglikova was receptive to everyone regardless of talent, wealth, fame, or any other outward characteristics. Through her family, her dynamism, and her language skills, she had access to and moved between different social strata and cultural circles. Her father's high military rank and status helped shield her from harassment by Russian officialdom, and she was not afraid to receive individuals who would not have been welcome elsewhere, such as political émigrés.[6]

Although Kruglikova was based in Paris until 1914, she nevertheless traveled regularly to Moscow and the family home in the Tula region, often spending the late summer and early fall in Russia. She remained very involved in the affairs of the RAC during these trips, corresponding actively with other members of the board, advising on key decisions, and raising money and awareness for the RAC. Although her mobility was an asset in terms of building partnerships and recruiting members in Russia, her episodic absence from Paris undermined organizational continuity within the RAC. When Kruglikova was away, there tended to be a loss of focus and follow-through, and several times crises arose that she would have been able to resolve or fight against if she had been present. She also continued to travel in Europe and spend time in Brittany, once traveling there from Paris entirely by bicycle together with a female companion. World War I caught Kruglikova in Russia. Unable to return to France, she lost the entire contents of her studio there, which included most of her works. Nevertheless, in 1916 she published a book of silhouette and monoprint images of Paris, such as the depiction of Max Voloshin on his bicycle (see figure 5.1), in an effort to raise money for Russian artists stranded in Paris by the war.[7] The volume also included poems, stories, and essays by many fellow Russian Parisians, a number of whom had participated actively in the RAC.

By 1903, with encouragement from Victor Joseph Roux-Champion, Kruglikova had set up a printmaking press and was experimenting with *eau-forte*, aquatint, and *vernis-mou*—often in color. Soon she was instructing Russians, French, British, Americans, and Hungarians in the medium. In 1909 and 1910 she even taught *eau-forte* at the Académie La Palette. Kruglikova's teaching primarily stemmed from her desire to share knowledge and aid others, and it is not clear whether she charged anything for it; she also often let friends and students use the press, her supplies, and her studio gratis. Indeed, despite exhibiting in the various Parisian salons and in shows of Russian exhibition societies such as the Western-oriented Mir Iskusstva (World of Art) and similar groups in Moscow, Kruglikova sold little and never depended on her art for income. Her financial freedom allowed her to devote much energy and time to social and philanthropic endeavors, including her salons and the RAC, and to be personally very generous. In fact, she was one of several people

Раздвинувъ локти летѣлъ на велосипедѣ Максъ.

Figure 5.1 *"Max* [Voloshin] flew on his bicycle with his elbows out wide," silhouette by Elizaveta S. Kruglikova, c 1915.
Source: Elizaveta S. Kruglikova, Konstantin D. Bal'mont et al., Parizh Nakanune Voiny v monotipiiakh, Petrograd: Khudozhestvenno-graficheskoe zavedenie "Union", 1916, 45.

who paid the considerable sum of 1,200 francs for a lifetime membership in the RAC at its establishment.

It is a testament to the mobility and adaptability of the RAC that one of its co-instigators, Elizaveta Davidenko, was able to be an active board member despite leaving Paris half a year after the group's establishment. She had been Kruglikova's studio mate from 1900 until the summer of 1903 and was intimately involved in all of Kruglikova's endeavors. Practically inseparable, the two women had a joint nickname: Kruglividenki. They painted together, traveled together around Europe, hosted parties together, and may have been lovers—Kruglikova certainly was bisexual, and occasionally dressed as a man, which likely contributed to her choice to live in Paris. Although Davidenko exhibited a handful of works in Parisian and Russian exhibitions, she was certainly a less notable artist and personality but reliably helped carry out Kruglikova's schemes. Pulled back to Russia for unknown family reasons in 1903, she continued to be heavily involved from St. Petersburg in the planning and implementation of exhibitions of Russian art in Paris and outreach to members based in Russia, and even helped head up a St. Petersburg outpost of the RAC.

Literary scholars and art historians often attribute the second central role in the RAC to the poet and amateur artist Maksimilian Voloshin.[8] Yet an excess of mobility on his part—geographic, institutional, and even aesthetic—ensured that his contributions to the RAC were more limited than most scholarly accounts try to suggest. Although Voloshin helped spark the idea of the RAC, he left Paris less than a month after that and did not participate in any of the key work involved in its establishment and early evolution. The charter was written, the funds to start up and maintain the organization were raised, and events and services were planned and implemented, all without him. Having gone back to Russia in January 1903 intending to continue on to the Far East to study Oriental philosophy and art, Voloshin turned up in Paris again a year later as the art editor and correspondent of the new symbolist literary and artistic publication *Vesy* (The Scales). In 1904 and 1905 he occasionally participated in RAC activities but often failed to come through on his commitments to the organization, being too distracted by his literary and romantic pursuits and the need to earn money as an art critic. His marriage in 1906 took him back to Russia, and unlike Davidenko he did not maintain an active role in the RAC from there. Still, shuttling frequently between Paris, Moscow, and St. Petersburg between 1901 and 1915, and through his editing and writing, he served as an important conduit for the exchange of ideas between Russian literary symbolists and Russian artists in Paris as well as in French literary circles.

Voloshin had first reached Paris in 1901, after a year in exile in Tashkent for political activity at Moscow University. After starting out at the Louvre's school for museum studies, he was jolted from theory and history to practice by meeting Kruglikova in April 1901.[9] Enthusiastic and impulsive, he quickly began visiting her studio and the Académie Colarossi for instruction in drawing, printmaking, and sketching. Voloshin continued to develop his art, his writing, and his criticism in parallel, but the demands of the newspapers and journals for which he came to write and the time he devoted to poetry and literary friendships meant that he turned to his painting and printmaking only during spells of intense activity. At the same time, his wanderlust sent him around Europe by all modes of transportation—by rail, by bicycle, and on foot. He infected his friends, pulling Kruglikova, Davidenko, and others with him on several hiking and bicycle trips.[10] Even in Paris he took them on tours of the Montparnasse countryside, as well as insatiably exploring Paris and introducing his friends to various hidden corners of the city.

Voloshin's future wife, more so than he himself, was deeply engaged in the organization day to day in 1904–1905. A talented young artist with a fragile personality, Margarita Sabashnikova met Voloshin in Moscow in 1903 through literary circles. She was the niece of important Russian publishers as well as of the wife of the poet Konstantin Balmont. Their friendship and courtship occurred between Moscow and Paris, where Voloshin recommended she pursue her studies, and where he assisted her and brought her into the RAC.[11] Between 1903 and 1906, Sabashnikova made several sojourns in France, initially chaperoned by an aunt, later accompanied by a female friend or her brothers, and finally traveling entirely on her own. In 1904 and 1905 she served on the RAC board as a member of the social committee and attended its drawing sessions and events. The pair wed in 1906 and relocated to St. Petersburg, taking both away, but when the marriage fell apart Voloshin returned, alone, to Paris in 1908.

The person who really helped link the RAC to French literary and artistic circles was the writer, editor, and translator Aleksandra Gol'shtein. From the 1880s to the 1920s, salons and literary gatherings at her home were frequented by French and Russian poets and writers, as well as Russian political émigrés. In fact, it was coming from Paris in 1903 armed with letters of introduction from both Gol'shtein and Kruglikova that allowed Voloshin to really expand his literary and art network and professional opportunities in Moscow and St. Petersburg. Born to a Swiss immigrant father and Russian mother in Riazan' province in 1850, Gol'shtein had left for France in the mid-1870s after a brief involvement with peasant populism.[12] She wrote a book on serf life in Russia, translated poetry and literature bidirectionally between Russian and French, and eventually contributed to the journals *Mir Iskusstva* (World of Art), *Zolotoe Runo* (The Golden Fleece), and *Apollon*, and helped facilitate French participation in *Vesy*. She had a strong interest in visual art and was mother-in-law to the talented artist Maria Iakunchikova, who had been living and studying in Paris. After Iakunchikova's tragic death, Gol'shtein helped her son raise awareness for his wife's creative achievements through exhibitions in Europe and Russia. The only board member of the RAC other than Kruglikova to participate from the founding of the RAC to its dissolution, Gol'shtein occupied the role of vice chairman or chairman for most of its existence, giving it much needed stability: however much the other members traveled, she remained resolutely in Paris and served as an organizational and communication hub.

Another established figure who added stability was the artist and scientist Ol'ga Mechnikova, resident in Paris from the 1880s. Less politically engaged and more social, Mechnikova focused on raising funds and also tending to the household side of the society. Her husband, Il'ia, was a prominent scientist of mixed Russian and Jewish ethnicity who was director of the Pasteur Institute in Paris and later a Nobel laureate. Olga helped him with his microbiology research and accompanied him on his travels, but she was also an aspiring artist, studying sculpture with Jean-Antoine Injalbert and painting with Eugène Carrière, as well as exhibiting at the various salons. She had her own purpose-built studio at their home nearby in Sevres, where many of the early meetings about the writing of the RAC's charter took place.[13] She would remain an active board member and contributor for most of its existence and involved her husband, who was the RAC's first honorary chairman, bringing supporters to the RAC and helping arrange for a number of scientific discourses to be delivered in the group's atelier. When the Mechnikovs scaled back their involvement after 1905, the RAC lost key organizational and fund-raising assistance.

OBJECTIVES AND STRUCTURE

Openness, inclusivity, and flexibility were central to the RAC and were at the heart of its charter document. Once the idea of the organization rose in December 1902, it only took until April 1903 for a concise and straightforward charter to be drafted and approved by the twenty founding members of the circle. Beyond setting out the organizational structure, member elections, and fees, the charter specified that "the Circle places at its foundation the widest tolerance for diverse theoretical views on art, without declaring itself to be the representative of any specific school."[14]

The group was to have honorary members, art-lover members, and active members, only the latter of whom would work in the shared studio, take part in shows, and be otherwise beneficiaries. Because the RAC was founded to assist artists from the Russian Empire, the charter stipulated that only Russian speakers could become active members, while other categories of members did not have any exclusions. An earlier formulation of this particular point in the charter, crossed out in the final version, even read "Russians of all nationalities," suggesting that acceptance of people of different ethnic backgrounds was a special concern of the founders. In fact, throughout its existence the group was very tolerant of different ethnic backgrounds; it included numerous Jewish artists and patrons as well as Poles, Georgians, Armenians, and several members from the Baltic regions, although seemingly no Finns. It is unclear why the formulation was altered, but perhaps the focus on Russian language was deemed to allow more inclusiveness. With time RAC's sympathy for people of various political and aesthetic persuasions not approved of by Russian officialdom—political émigrés, active revolutionaries, liberal thinkers and politicians, and "decadents" of all sorts—became clear. It also became a liability that undermined broader economic support from the upper segments of Russian Paris. It is telling, for example, that Aleksandra Gol'shtein's name does not appear in the first announcements, despite her key role in the establishment of the society. It was to prevent Gol'shtein's own past political activism—which had led to her departure from Russia—and her connections with political émigrés from adversely affecting the organization.

The purpose of the RAC was defined similarly to comparable associations in Russia, as "mutual moral and material help among its members."[15] The nature of this help was only partly spelled out in the charter—such as a reading room and shared studio space to organize exhibitions and public readings—since the effort was to create a flexible structure that could evolve with its membership and the members' priorities. In its brief life of four and a half years, the group evolved considerably in terms of its objectives and administrative structure, which testifies to its internal flexibility and reflected the changing corps of its stakeholders. Membership dues and lectures, concerts, exhibitions, and parties were envisioned in the charter as key sources of funding. Indeed, a series of events to raise money and awareness for the organization commenced very quickly, with a May 30, 1903, concert at the Athénée Saint-Germain. The performers included a well-known musical trio from Moscow, as well as Russian opera singers then performing at the Paris Opéra and Opéra Comique. Interestingly, Prince Lev P. Urusov, the Russian ambassador and honorary chairman of the SRAP, and other Russian notables were cited in press reports as having attended the May 30 evening, suggesting that the society was initially well received by official Russian circles in Paris.[16] In June, Il'ia Mechnikov gave a lecture benefiting the RAC at the École Russe des Hautes Études Sociales (Russian School for Social Sciences), the first in a series of scientific discourses he organized for the RAC.[17] However, after one lengthy and very positive article, written by the Russian wife of the prominent French psychiatrist Dr. Pierre Marie, no notices about the RAC appeared in Études Franco-Russes (French-Russian Studies), a publication ostensibly devoted to promoting all aspects of Franco-Russian collaboration and exchange. It seems probable that there was opposition from the government-connected SRAP, whose program of events in this period was much curtailed, and who wanted to stifle the sudden competition. And of course as the political and ethnic openness of the RAC became evident, the organization came to be a threat not just in creative/artistic terms.

LOCATION

Because of the abundance of available studios in Paris, as well as the considerable swings in its fortunes, the RAC itself turned out to be very mobile, occupying four different locations during its almost-five-year existence. Its headquarters always remained on the outskirts of the Left Bank of the Seine, in the 15th arrondissement. Former farmland only recently incorporated into the city, this area was known as Montparnasse. It stood in contrast to the more urban Montmartre, popular with Russians a generation earlier and home of the more conservative SRAP, which was on the Right Bank. Comparable to the Williamsburg area of Brooklyn today, it was abundant in cheap space that was easy to adapt to artist needs and quickly becoming a hotbed of studios, academies, and cafés that attracted artists, intellectuals, poets, and political émigrés from all over Europe and even the New World.

Beginning in September 1903, the RAC rented its first atelier in the same building that housed the Académie Vitti, and a few blocks away from Kruglikova's atelier at 17 Rue Boissonade. It was also near the Rue de la Grande Chaumière, where the Académie Colarossi and other academies actively frequented by Russian artists of this generation could be found. After encouraging growth and success in its first year, the organization relocated to a larger and more expensive space at 3 Rue Joseph Bara in September 1904, only to flee from there without paying rent to 25 Boulevard Montparnasse in January 1905. Two years later, in May 1907, the RAC finally moved to 123 Rue de Sèvres—half a year before being shuttered. In parallel, the venues that the RAC used for fund-raisers and external concerts were mainly in Montparnasse, except when the organization was briefly under the partial control of the SRAP in 1906 and early 1907, during which period events took place on the Right Bank.

PROGRAMS

The RAC quickly commenced the ambitious slate of endeavors outlined in its charter and in early press notices, such as this one in early May 1903.

> Russian artists coming to Paris will find in this circle useful information and a valuable support: the Circle's atelier will be the center of friendly meetings, temporary exhibitions, and gatherings for work. An assistance fund will be organized for the members of the Circle, and it will also have an art library . . . it will endeavor to make Russian art known abroad and to launch artistic personalities whose merit and originality will be to revive the local color of the Russian country. The Circle will organize exhibitions of Russian art, and will also encourage all manifestations of Russian folk art.[18]

To a greater or lesser extent, the RAC accomplished all of these objectives, providing regular low-cost live model sessions and a clublike space that included a library of books and magazines, supporting the exhibition of Russian art in Paris. Geared more toward temporary visitors to Paris than long-term expatriates, unlike the SRAP or Académie Russe, the RAC worked to create a central repository of information and base of support for artists newly arrived in Paris or planning to come, as well as those in Russia who wished to exhibit in France. At one time it even set up a special committee that was dedicated to gathering useful resources and helping find studios or places to live, selecting places to study, and so on, and it had regular office hours where members of the board were on duty to assist members. The RAC also consistently drew on Russian musicians and authors visiting Paris as performers and participants in the social evenings and concerts that brought the artist members together with the broader intellectual community of Paris. The group hosted a concert by Aleksander Scriabin and an impromptu performance by Fyodor Shaliapin, as well as less well-known Russian singers and musicians appearing with local troupes, lectures by Konstantin Balmont, and more. There were, however, also readings by French symbolist poets and authors such as René Ghil, Jean Royère, Sadia Levy, performances by French musicians from the Opéra Comique and other Parisian troupes, and even presentations by scientists, including Marie Curie.[19]

Such was the stream of Russian artists setting their sights on Paris that in 1904 a new competitor, in the form of a Paris outpost of the Russia-based Novoe Khudozhestvennoe Obshchestvo (New Artistic Society, henceforth NAS), appeared on the horizon, creating a novel impetus for the RAC's evolution. The need to maintain and expand membership pushed the RAC to refocus its activities on assisting artists located in Russia who were interested in maintaining a foothold in Paris, as well as the establishment of formal branches in Russia. On the one hand, this was a way to engage with and serve members who had returned home or resided permanently in Russia. On the other, connecting with artist societies based in Russia enabled the RAC to offer its members in Paris some reciprocal advantages. In some sense the Russian outposts of the RAC organically grew out of the return home of devoted members, such as Elizaveta Davidenko and Vladimir Kurbatov. The two became official representatives of the group in St. Petersburg, disseminating information about the RAC, signing up new members and collecting dues, gathering information about artistic opportunities and activities in Russia for their colleagues in Paris, and assisting with exhibition projects. Kurbatov provided an important link between the RAC and the Mir Iskusstva group, with the assistance of his friend and RAC board member Stepan Iaremich as his counterpart in Paris. In Moscow, a larger cluster of artist and collector members and an entire group of volunteers were ready to help. The leadership alone of the

Moscow branch of the RAC consisted of eight people, among them painter and decorative artist Rimma Brailovskaia, wife of fellow RAC artist Leonid Brailovskii, who had studied in Paris in 1895–1898, and the graphic artist and caricaturist Aleksandra Khotiantseva. Others included Savva Mamontov, the artist Nikolai Ulianov, and the architect Ivan Fomin.[20] Most of these actively exhibited with various Russian art societies in parallel to their involvement with the RAC. In fact, many RAC members belonged to various Russian and French exhibition societies at once. The RAC even admitted members of its "rival," the SRAP, a practice that eventually contributed to conflicts that brought about the RAC's dissolution.

Before the establishment of the Moscow and St. Petersburg branches, the RAC had provided informational resources about studios, art schools, and other logistics of Parisian life to Russian artists who had reached Paris on their own, but now the RAC pushed to present the society and especially its leading Russia-based members as resources for those planning to travel to France for study or work. Notices in art journals such as *Mir Iskusstva* and *Iskusstvo* (Art) and presentations to artist groups and art school students were all a part of an effort to generate interest in the society and encourage those envisioning a trip to rely on its aid. And so it was that when Aleksandr Shevchenko and his fiancée arrived in Paris in late January 1905 after Moscow's Stroganov School had been shut down, their first visit off the train was to the RAC's office. Voloshin helped them find and rent and furnish a studio, and advised them about their choices in terms of art academies.[21]

Thanks to improved art transportation options, the RAC also facilitated the movement of artworks as well as creators, allowing artists residing in Russia to be represented in the world's art capital without leaving home. In fact, the RAC was the only Russian-Parisian art society to attempt organizing shows of art by members not resident in Paris. One of the new services the RAC introduced in 1904 aimed at artist members in Russia was assistance for members who wanted to participate in the Parisian art world and art market from abroad. "Wishing to be useful to members residing in Russia," read a notice in the *Mir Iskusstva* journal, "the circle 'Montparnasse' offers its services as intermediary for submission of the works of Russian artists, sculptors, architects and engravers to the Paris Salons."[22] The RAC served as an agent handling shipping, submission of artworks to the Paris salons, and fielding sales. Thus, an artwork sent to the RAC would be submitted by the organization for review, retrieved after the conclusion of the salon or in case of rejection, and then sold locally or shipped back to Russia. The RAC also strove to inform interested parties about upcoming deadlines for application to the Paris salons, a necessary precondition for participating in the French art world but by no means an easy task. The symbolist painter Viktor Borisov-Musatov, who had a deformed back and was homebound in Saratov (although he had spent time in Paris in the 1890s) made extensive use of the service, submitting through the RAC to the salon of the Société Nationale des Beaux Arts (National Society of Fine Art, where he was chosen an associate member) as well as to the Salon des Indépendants, the exhibition *Tendances Nouvelles*, and the Salon d'Automne.[23] His fellow symbolist, Vassilii Denisov, who had studied in private academies in Moscow with Konstantin Korovin and Valentin Serov, did likewise, and there were inquiries from others. For this work, which required sustained presence and attention, Kruglikova relied on the help of the artists Viktor Strubinsky, who resided in Paris year-round, and Konstantin Kuznetsov, who spent summers outside Paris but was otherwise based in the city.

In terms of complete exhibitions, the RAC managed to bring to fruition just one show, of Russian peasant embroideries, held in its own space in May 1904. These were assembled from numerous private collections in Russia and France as well as several Russian *zemstvos* (provincial municipal councils), with some of the items available for sale. Encouraged by the strong attendance and sales for that project, the group worked hard for over a year to organize a follow-up exhibition of a wider range of folk art and crafts in one of the Parisian salons. Although the project had enthusiastic interest from various Parisian salon exhibitions, their efforts were thwarted by external circumstances repeatedly, first of all when the salon of the Société des Artistes Décorateurs (Society of Decorative Artists) in the fall of 1904, for which the show was initially slated, did not take place. By the time the project was reassigned to the Salon of the Société Nationale des Beaux Arts (known as the Salon du Champs de Mars) in the spring of 1905, potential lenders to the show were spooked and preoccupied by the strikes and unrest in Russia.[24] Although the Salon du Champs de Mars allowed a postponement, by 1906 the leadership and priorities of the RAC had changed to such an extent that it was impossible to implement the exhibition. However, with the efforts in preparation of the exhibition, the RAC paved the way for Sergei Diaghilev's 1906 Russian art exhibition at the Salon d'Automne—which came out of an opportunity brought to the RAC in the spring of 1906, communicated by RAC board member Alexandre Benois to Diaghilev.[25] Indeed, numerous RAC members showed works in the Salon d'Automne exhibit, which largely excluded older Russian realists and salon-style artists. The RAC's efforts also anticipated the 1913 exhibition of Russian folk art at the Salon d'Automne that was organized primarily by artists, mostly members of the Académie Russe. At one time, the RAC also envisioned solo and group shows by Russian artists at the RAC's facilities, but none could be successfully organized.

MEMBERSHIP

Looking at the list of members compiled in late April 1905, when the group was at its numeric and probably also programmatic peak, some striking figures emerge.[26] The 213 names constitute a significant number, considering that just 20 supporters had signed the charter two years earlier. Over 180 paid dues, while a handful were honorary members, and a few others did not pay annual dues because of hardship or volunteered their time. Artists represent around half of the official membership, but a fair number more figured regularly in the RAC's activities without having membership. Indeed, since members paid a fee to bring guests to internal social events and, for a period of time, to model sessions, the number of informal stakeholders of the organization was much larger than its official affiliates.

Nearly half the names belong to women, some listed together with their husbands, but many as individual members, and most were engaged in making art or music at a serious level. In 1904–1905, women also represented eleven of the twenty-one board members (and five of eight in the Moscow branch) and filled five of the six executive positions, with Aleksandra Gol'shtein herself occupying the role of chairman in 1905. By contrast the SRAP had no female artists in its first two decades, although the wives of Il'ia Repin and Nikolai Dmitriev-Orenburgskii participated in some of the social and even creative activities. The SRAP did elect as honorary member Maria Bashkirtseva, a wealthy and highly talented painter who received her art training exclusively in Paris, in 1884, after she was catapulted to fame. However, she died six months later without seemingly ever attending the SRAP's events, where her protofeminist ideas would have been quite out of place. In the second half of the 1890s some women artists did appear on the roster of the SRAP, but they were mostly amateurs—daughters and wives of people in the Parisian Russian community—and never played a significant role in running the organization.

Also notable in the RAC membership is the proportion of non-Russian ethnicities, Jews in particular. It is hard to enumerate precisely how many were Jewish since some of them may have had names not clearly identifiable with their ethnicity, but they were represented considerably more strongly than the relative percentage of Jews among Russia's population would suggest. The proportion of Jewish members increased as the overall number of members declined.[27] Implicitly, this shift demonstrates the Jewish members' reduced mobility; they were less likely to return to Russia and had few other options to support themselves.

DOWNTURN

The economic transformations and other disruptions caused by the Revolution of 1905 made themselves felt in Paris quickly. After a small influx of students and others driven to Paris by the closing of institutions and other factors, strikes and social unrest increasingly interrupted mobility and communication, threatening the RAC's activities. Transferring funds between Russia and France became difficult. Moreover, peasant and worker uprisings adversely affected the valuation of Russian stocks and the exchange rate. Members and supporters of the RAC came mostly from the middle rather than upper class, their capital more in domestic stocks and bonds rather than land or other property. Having relocated his family to Paris in January 1905, Alexandre Benois kept a diary that provides a vivid insight into how this jeopardized the RAC and its members. Serious concerns regarding his finances begin to appear in the summer of 1905, with worries about his shares, the freezing or cancellation of projects for which he had counted on being paid, and delayed or withheld payments for work already completed. By October 1905, Benois was afraid that he would deplete his financial reserves within less than a year and reported similar concerns by others, including Aleksandra Gol'shtein.[28] Of course, members in both countries as well as attendees at RAC fund-raisers and events were facing similar difficulties—no income-generating event was held in the fall of 1905. Dues had represented over 60 percent of the RAC's revenue, but now it was a struggle both to find members ready to renew and to collect money from those who were able to pay. Additionally, from August 1905 Kruglikova was stranded in Russia by strikes and upheaval amid the negotiations and battles for civil rights and elected representation in the run-up to the October 1905 Manifesto. It is not clear that she returned to Paris until early 1906.

By December 1905, there were two sources of salvation on the RAC's horizon. One was a proposal to merge the RAC and the SRAP, and the second was a new benefactor, the scion of a merchant family, Viktor Golubev. The person who brought these saviors to the table was the erudite collector and critic Ivan Shchukin, a permanent and visible presence in Parisian Russian circles since the mid-1890s. Shchukin lectured at the École Russe, which was shuttered in 1905 under pressure from Nicholas II, alongside Mechnikov, Kovalevskii, and other intellectuals who were also members of the RAC. He viewed the SRAP with contempt, writing a harsh review of their annual exhibition in 1900, and probably saw in the RAC a new avenue for his energies. The SRAP then had huge endowment funds and an annual government subsidy that gave a combined income of seven thousand francs a year, but only seven or eight artist members.[29] By contrast, the RAC had burned through its cash reserves and tiny endowment, and though reduced, still counted well over a hundred members, many of them artists. At Shchukin's home on December 12, 1905, Alexandre Benois agreed to rejoin the board of the "revamped" RAC, and was introduced to Viktor Golubev, then being groomed for the chairmanship. Recent inheritor of a considerable fortune, Golubev had moved to Paris after completing an art history doctorate at the University of Heidelberg.[30] Aspiring to the role of philanthropist and scholar, and having an energetic wife with ambitions for participating in the world of art, he saw in the RAC an easier vehicle for his social ambitions than the less flexible context of an organization in Russia.

After Shchukin, together with several board members of the RAC, had worked out a detailed proposal for how it and the SRAP could join forces, the plan was brought up at the RAC semiannual meeting on December 16, 1905. However, once Golubev was elected chairman at the meeting, he delayed the merger with fund-raising promises.[31] He tried to gather donations of artworks for a raffle to benefit the RAC but was unwilling to contribute significant funds of his own and was too distracted by collecting art and developing his own project ideas, such as an exhibition of Venetian art, to implement anything concrete. His main accomplishment was to ensure that his selection as chairman of the RAC was announced in Russian art journals such as *Zolotoe Runo*.

By mid-March 1906 a conflict of unclear nature, which Benois described as "the scandal with the blackguard [Serafim] Sudbinin," unfolded within the RAC, driving a considerable portion of the board to quit.[32] The nature of the March conflict remains unclear, but given the vehement reaction from émigré artist members of the Académie Russe to Sudbinin's proposal in 1911 to support the Académie with funds from a mysterious donor, he may have on both occasions been acting as an agent provocateur or informant for the Russian secret police. A former actor, Sudbinin moved to Paris to study sculpture in 1904 with a generous two-year stipend from the merchant Savva Morozov, which ended abruptly after Morozov's death in May 1905. With Russian authorities scared and on their guard throughout 1905 and 1906, monitoring in Paris, an important center for exiles and opposition activists, was at its peak. The Paris police were observing the RAC and kept a file on it, and the Russian secret police almost certainly did likewise.[33] As the number of intellectuals and political activists who fled government persecution for speaking out against the regime or encouraging protests and strikes in Russia increased, many of them made their way to Paris and joined the circle of Gol'shtein and Kruglikova, making the RAC even more suspect. Sudbinin would have been a perfect agent to destabilize the RAC and push it into the arms of the SRAP, since he was not new to the group and, being in financial need, would have been easy to buy off. Sudbinin's actions unraveled Golubev's fund-raising plans and the RAC was forced into a hurried union with the SRAP. By June 1905, more than half of the SRAP artist members had joined the ranks of the RAC, including its chairman, Aleksei Kharlamov. Those who straddled the two organizations included Dmitri Kuznetsov, Countess Maria Eristova, and Leopold Siniaev-Bernstein. With a new board and new imperatives in place, the RAC tried to regain its footing in early 1906. However, the overall economic situation continued to be dire. After the March 1906 resignation of more liberal board members such as Benois and Aleksandr Shervashidze and the weakening of Golubev's position, the balance of power eventually fell to the SRAP. By early May, Boris Matveev, a longtime member and friend of Kruglikova, reported to his mother:

> The board [of the RAC] has now fallen in the hands of the club of right bank artists, that is to say the society that is on a government subsidy and whose first act it was to forbid a lecture by Balmont, who had planned to give a talk on some Saturday about 'the poetry of resistance' and Whitman. Kruglikova is at wits end and all the best people want to eject this unwanted spying [*shpionskii*] element."[34]

In blocking Balmont's lecture, the new leadership repeated the pattern that had developed within the SRAP once it began to receive support from various grand dukes and eventually Alexander III, an arrangement that had been mediated by Bogoliubov, who was close to the Imperial family. Before receiving imperial funds, the SRAP's early events and activities were attended by, and sometimes involved the participation of, liberal and even revolutionary figures from Turgenev's circle. But once the society began to accept governmental support, which later became a permanent annual government grant to the organization, the group was pressured to exclude or considerably lessen the presence of individuals critical of the regime.

Kruglikova and her supporters tried to fight back, and the internecine battles continued to stall the organization for some time. In November 1906 the RAC's social activities revived, and three fund-raising events took place in relatively quick succession, in December 1906, January 1907, and March 1907. All took place deep in the Right Bank of Paris, targeting the wealthy and official community centered on that side of the Seine and following the model of events typically organized by the SRAP.[35] However, despite replenished coffers, the RAC ceased all activity again in May 1907. After moving to a new location in June, it was officially shuttered in late December 1907. During a meeting at Kruglikova's apartment, with

Kruglikova, Gol'shtein, and Mechnikov present, the remaining membership voted to close the organization on December 27, 1907.[36]

After the demise of the RAC, some of its former members and founders continued to serve in the same de facto roles. Kruglikova maintained her regular parties on Saturdays for many years, and she consistently advised visiting Russians and helped them find studios or places to study and understand the system of exhibitions, as well as teaching them (and other foreign students in Paris) printmaking. Likewise, Gol'shtein continued her salon and was an important resource for many. Voloshin, once he resumed his visits to Paris in 1909, was free of his toxic relationship with Sabashnikova and of his editorial duties and spent considerable time inducting young artists and would-be poets into the mysteries of Paris. In addition, he was involved in circles around the Académie Russe, which several junior members of the RAC later joined and actively supported.

CONCLUSION

The RAC benefited greatly from multidimensional mobility. Members and supporters were highly dynamic geographically, able not only to travel from Russia to France, but in some cases to sojourn frequently back and forth, and to travel within France and Europe as a whole. The group displayed social and economic mobility by challenging class conventions and engaging with people of different social groups, ethnicities, countries, and economic means. The membership and stakeholders of the RAC were remarkably diverse, and their various forms of mobility were proxies for adaptability. The members of the RAC had great institutional mobility, frequently changing art schools, affiliations, courses/spheres of study, and exhibiting societies, or combining various memberships in parallel. All the aforementioned fluidity and diversity provided the RAC with vibrancy and allowed it to evolve frequently. But it also undermined continuity, with continuous turnover among the leadership and membership making it difficult to sustain projects and initiatives.

The multifaceted mobility and international reach of the RAC's membership allowed them to create networks of information and professional support that spanned between Paris and Moscow/Petersburg. On the flip side, this made the organization susceptible to disruption by the Revolution of 1905, as it interrupted travel, communication, and the transfer of funds and, in the long term, destabilized the RAC and made it vulnerable to cannibalization by the SRAP. Mobility and dynamism made the RAC and its members suspect to the Russian and French authorities and to members of the Russian community in Paris. Their interactions with the community of émigré revolutionaries or even just liberal thinkers made them subject to monitoring and even potentially intervention. Members and allies traversed and transgressed borders not only of countries but of conventional behavior and even morality, indulging in drugs and nonstandard sexuality. Finally, the bonds between participants, the organization, and mutual commitments to specific missions were often weak, driven more by social needs than aesthetic ones. Having started out from within artistic circles and initially led by and created for people in the arts, the RAC gradually took on a broader membership and support base that brought with it different priorities and a loss of focus and energy. As a result, while the RAC had bright beginnings and some notable achievements, it was the shortest-lasting and, in terms of direct legacy, probably the least successful of the Russian artistic societies of Paris. At the same time, it touched the lives of many artists, musicians, authors, and laypeople and continued to have an afterlife through social networks that persisted for years and decades after its dissolution.

NOTES

1. For instance, the Society of Russian Artists in Paris (1870–1930), various iterations of the Académie Russe and Académie Vassilieff (1908–1914), the Union des Artistes Russes of the 1920s, and so on.

2. Originally titled officially *Obshchestvo vzaimnogo vspomoshchestvovaniia russkikh khudozhnikov v Parizhe*, the group quickly became known to all simply as *Obshchestvo russkikh khudozhnikov v Parizhe*.

3. Anna Winestein, "Building Community: The Origins and Establishment of the Society for the Mutual Aid of Russian Artists in Paris," in *Loyalties, Solidarities and Identities in Russian Society, History and Culture*, ed. Philip Ross Bullock and Andy Byford (London: School of Slavonic and East European Studies, UCL, 2013), 163–181.

4. Daria Marie, "Les artistes russes a Paris," *Journal des Études Franco-Russes* May (1903): 204–205. Author's translation.

5. Maksimilian Voloshin, "Union des Artistes Russes: Russkaia Kustarnaia vystavka v Parizhe," *Rus'*, June 11, 1904, 2. Reprinted in Maksimilian Voloshin, *Sobranie sochinenii*, vol. 5 (Moscow: Ellis Laak 2000, 2007), 436.

6. Aleksandr Bisk, "Russkii Parizh 1906–1908 godov," in *Russkii Parizh*, ed. Tat'iana Buslakova (Moscow: Izdatel'stvo Moskovskogo Universiteta, 1998), 45–52.

7. Elizaveta Kruglikova, Konstantin D. Bal'mont et al. *Parizh nakanune voiny v monotipiiakh* (Petrograd, Khudozhestvenno-graficheskoe zavedenie "Union," 1916).

8. Vladimir Kupchenko, Voloshin's tireless biographer and editor of his collected works, is particularly notable here.

9. An immensely useful guide to Voloshin's life in this period can be found in Vladimir Kupchenko, *Trudy i dni Maksimiliana Voloshina: letopis' zhizni i tvorchestva, 1877–1916* (Sankt-Petersburg: Aleteia, 2002).

10. Elizaveta Kruglikova, "Iz vospominanii o Makse Voloshine," in *Maksimillian Voloshin, Khudozhnik: Sbornik materialov*, ed. R. I. Ponova (Moscow: Sovetskii Khudozhnik, 1976), 98.

11. Margarita Sabashnikova, *Zelenaia Zmeia: Istoriia odnoi zhizni* (Moscow: Enigma, 1993).

12. Lev Weber-Bauler, *From Orient to Occident: Memoirs of a Russian Doctor* (New York: Oxford University Press, 1941).

13. E. Rossinskaia, untitled memoirs of Golubkina in *Pis'ma. Neskol'ko slov o remesle skul'ptora. Vospominaniia sovremennikov*, ed. Anna S. Golubkina (Moscow: Sovetskii Khudozhnik, 1983), 160.

14. "Ustav Russkago Artisticheskogo Kruzhka v Parizhe," copy printed 1905 or earlier, Russian National Library (Rossiiskaia Natsional'naia Biblioteka, hereafter RNB), Rimsky-Korsakov fond (640), item 186, part Ic.

15. Ibid.

16. Daria Marie, untitled article, *Journal des Études Franco-Russes*, July (1903): 292.

17. Untitled notice in *Le Temps*, May 26, 1903.

18. Daria Marie, "Les artistes russes a Paris," 204–205.

19. *Otchet Russkogo Artisticheskogo Kruzhka v Parizhe za vtoroi god ego suschestvovaniia (1904/5)* (Paris: Imprimérie Ch. Noblet, 1905), Gosudarstvennyi Russkii Muzei (hereafter GRM), fond 25, item 249.

20. Ibid.

21. Zh. Z. Kaganskaia, V. N. Zhelabaeva, and T. Z. Lotkina-Ganina, eds., *A. V. Shevchenko: Sbornik Materialov* (Moscow: Sovetskii Khudozhnik, 1980), 99–102.

22. "Russkii Artisticheskii Kruzhok v Parizhe-Mont Parnasse," *Mir Iskusstva* 11–12 (1904), 267 (Khronika supplement).

23. Kruglikova to Borisov-Musatov, March 9, 1905, GRM fond 27, item 55.

24. Matveev to his mother, January 10, 1905, Rossiiskii gosudarstvennyi arkhiv literatury i iskusstva (hereafter RGALI), fond 801, part I, item 9, sheet 32.

25. Aleksandr Benua, *Aleksandr Nikolaevich Benua i Sergei Pavlovich Diagilev: Perepiska 1893–1928*, ed. I. Vydrin (St. Petersburg: Sad Iskusstv, 2003).

26. Register of members sent to Rimskii-Korsakov, April 22, 1905, RNB, fond 640, item 186, part 1b.

27. Account books of the RAC in 1906–1907, RGALI, fond 2479, item 2.

28. Aleksandr Benua, "Dnevnik 1905 Goda," ed. I. Vydrin, I. Lapina and G. Marushina, *Nashe Nasledie* 58 (2001), accessed November 12, 2015, http://www.nasledie-rus.ru/podshivka/5811.php.

29. Ibid., December 1905 entries.
30. Marina Polevaia, *Doma Golubevykh* (St. Petersburg: Almaz, 1997).
31. Benua, "Dnevnik 1905 Goda," various entries.
32. Benua, "Dnevnik 1905 Goda," March 18 entry.
33. Dmitri Gutnov, *Russkaia Vysshaia Shkola Obshchestvennykh Nauk v Parizhe (1901–1906)* (Moscow: ROSSPEN, 2004), 65.
34. Matveev to his sister on May 13, 1906, RGALI, fond 801, part I, item 8, sheet 84–85.
35. Untitled notice in *Le Figaro*, January 18, 1907; untitled notice in *Le Figaro*, March 17, 1907.
36. Protocols of the meeting of December 27, 1907, RGALI, fond 2479, item 4, sheet 1.

CHAPTER 6

Sex at the Border
Trafficking as a Migration Problem in Partitioned Poland

Keely Stauter-Halsted

> "Is it true that they snatch girls off the streets and carry them away to Argentina?"
> "They go there by themselves."
> —Isaac Bashevis Singer, *Scum*, 1991

THE TURN OF the twentieth century was a time of nearly constant human movement out of Eastern Europe. A huge portion of the population of the Polish lands left home during the decades leading up to World War I, with some 8 percent of ethnic Poles crossing international boundaries for seasonal or long-term work.[1] This heightened mobility brought with it chaos, corruption, and anxiety about the fate of loved ones across the sea.[2] Those left behind reserved special concern for the fortunes of single women traveling abroad on their own.[3] Families worried about the vulnerabilities young women suffered during the long journey and the challenges of relocating in a new land. Anxiety over the fate of female migrants fed into contemporary concerns about international traffic in women, a focus of heightened public awareness during this period.

This chapter considers the "white slavery" panic gripping Europe and the Americas at the dawn of the new century by looking at it through the prism of migration. It treats the movement of single women across the Atlantic as part of the much larger wave of labor migrants leaving the

Polish lands. The chapter challenges the historiographical framework that has often been used to assess the problem of sex migration, suggesting that the melodramatic narrative of sexual coercion and captivity was at least partially tied to larger anxieties about the shifting role of women in Victorian-era Eastern Europe. Studying the problem of sex trafficking from a migration perspective sheds light on the treatment of gender in migration history overall and challenges us to rethink our assumptions about human agency among migrants of all types.

Stories of innocent women dragged from their homelands and deposited in foreign brothels captured the imagination of readers worldwide in the years leading up to World War I. Melodramatic exposés featured naïve girls caught in the net of sinister brokers or disappearing off steamers bound for distant ports. Vivid images of sexual danger colored contemporary impressions and helped shape an enduring narrative of sex migration for generations to come.[4] Such assumptions of female vulnerability would later inform scholarly discussions of the cross-border sex trade; the notion that women traveling to work in the prostitution industry lacked autonomy remains commonplace in the historical literature. Researchers continue to refer to sex migrants as a group as "victims of trafficking," "forced migrants," or "prostituted women," labels that simplify their experience and turn all women who sold sex as part of the migration wave into passive participants in their own fate.[5] In many respects, the scholarly framework has tacitly reinforced the contemporary narrative of seduction and abandonment, a scenario that deprives female actors of agency and reduces the chaotic condition of migration and sex trade to familiar comprehensible tropes.

Recent scholarship challenges this narrative, suggesting more complex motivations on the part of female migrants and even proposing that white slavery itself—the pattern of mass-coerced migration to fuel the international sex industry—was to a great extent a construct, "born out of a particular interpretation of sexual danger in a specific social and historical context."[6] Rarely, however, has the phenomenon of cross-border sexual exchange been approached from the point of view of migration studies. Because of the way historians have bracketed the two migration streams, placing single female migrants in a separate category from those traveling as part of families, women who turned to prostitution in their adopted homes are rarely assessed in the context of the larger trends of migration history. We know little about why they chose to leave or how they integrated into their new environments. To address this lacuna, we must look beyond the melodrama of kidnapping and coercion and examine young female migrants in the context of their lives at home before departing, their personal ambitions, and the difficult decisions they were asked to make.[7] Archival evidence suggests that many alleged trafficking victims in this period voluntarily accompanied migration agents, at least on the initial leg of the journey, and that some even understood the activities they would be performing abroad. To be clear, to recognize the element of human agency these migrants exercised is not to gloss over the degree of coercion or trickery they may have experienced along the way. Nonetheless, an examination of the details behind the "captivity narratives" that circulated everywhere at the turn of the twentieth century suggests more individual initiative, more ambition, and more ingenuity on the part of single female travelers than the standard story of passive victimhood implies.

This chapter applies the analytical tools of migration scholarship to the mass movement of single female workers from the Polish lands to the burgeoning cities and port towns of North and South America and the Middle East in the decades before World War I. It treats those labeled as sex migrants as part of a larger wave of human movement and raises important new questions about the genesis of this migration phenomenon and the process by which thousands of women relocated. By placing the moral panic surrounding sex trafficking in the wider context of social anxieties about emigration as a whole, it demonstrates the ways the two migration streams informed one another, shaping public perceptions about the dangers of leaving home. In the end, I suggest, this peculiar form of migration offers rich possibilities for understanding the complexities of female relocation and the role gender plays in the overall movement of peoples.

In migration literature, the global movement of people is profoundly gendered.[8] Women migrate locally in larger numbers than men, but transnational and especially transoceanic migrations are typically weighted in favor of men, who move as a result of the demands of labor markets.[9] Receiving societies impose more stringent controls on female migrants on the assumption that migrant communities will put down more permanent roots in their adopted countries once they establish families. During the great nineteenth-century migrations, according to this picture, women left home to join a spouse or other relative but rarely ventured out as the initial representative of a migration chain.[10] This model of female actors following a male labor migrant has seldom been challenged in migration literature to date. Indeed, as Eleanore Kofman emphasizes, the persistence of this migration paradigm has reinforced "the notion of women as passive followers and dependents, whose employment, where it occurs, is of secondary consideration." Absent from this scenario of "homogeneous phases" of gendered migration are "active female migrants who deploy individual strategies and participate in household decision making."[11]

An understanding of single women making transnational journeys without family ties and with the intention of engaging in labor markets in their new homes suggests that this image needs adjustment. As Adam McKeown has argued, the nineteenth-century liberal state was caught in a quandary as it embraced open borders and free movement of peoples yet discouraged certain categories of people from leaving its borders to protect its citizens from falling into slavery or indentured servitude.[12] Border control agents in Eastern Europe and at ports where suspicious women disembarked carefully policed new arrivals with an eye toward restricting the migration of coerced individuals. At the same time, receiving states, especially after the abolition of institutionalized slavery, worked to prevent captive individuals from settling inside their territory. Yet evidence from sex trafficking files reveals little direct coercion and many examples of adventurous independent female behavior. Voluntary migration and sex migration out of Eastern Europe occurred at roughly the same time; both engendered risks and abuses; and both were subject to imperial measures to control and restrict their impact. Documentary evidence suggests these two migration streams were intertwined in important ways and should be seen as informing one another. At its core, in other words, sex trafficking can be understood at least partially as a migration problem. At the same time, the process of relocating abroad for sex work involved particular forms of exploitation, only some of which overlapped with the challenges migrants of all types faced.

GENESIS OF A PANIC

Nowhere was the panic of white slavery more palpable than in the territories of partitioned Poland and in the Polish émigré communities scattered across North and South America. In the Polish case, contemporary assessments of sex migration were closely tied to an ongoing sense of crisis stemming from repeated waves of labor migration out of the Polish territories. Imperial powers and local communities alike expressed frustration at the loss of labor power, the exodus of military recruits, and the elimination of future citizens who might serve an independent Polish republic. The status of the Polish lands as the site of dramatic rates of outmigration helped drive the panic about white slavery and encouraged the reading public to react with hysteria to stories of virgins shipped off to foreign bordellos. Contemporary activists estimated that tens of thousands of young women "disappeared" from the Polish lands and from the Russian Pale of Settlement each year, most of them of Polish or Jewish background.[13] In the Austrian Polish crownland of Galicia, the terrifying saga of maidens transported abroad and sold into sexual bondage first captured public attention during an 1892 trafficking trial in the provincial capital of Lwów. Spectators in the courtroom and readers of the daily press were treated to vivid accounts of coercion, deceit, and physical abuse the women suffered over a decade-long period.[14] The proceedings captivated the interest of a public preoccupied with the dangers of young women traveling unaccompanied on city streets and helped reinforce anxieties about the explosion of domestic prostitution, the increasingly mobile Jewish population, and rising rates of female emigration.

Accusations of trafficking and stories of abducted women skyrocketed in the decades following the Lwów trial, filling the pages of the mainstream press throughout the Polish lands.[15] Later court cases in Bytom, German Silesia, in 1902 and again in Lwów in 1913 highlighted accusations of abuse perpetrated by ruthless migration agents against traveling women and exposed the entrenched system of corruption and bribery maintained at the borders separating former Polish territories.[16] Proceedings revealed shocking details of the excursions migration agents took into Galicia to "collect" women and transport them abroad. Crossing the border at

Katowice, the women were reportedly sent on to Wrocław, Berlin, London, and then to brothels in Buenos Aires.[17]

Such well-publicized trials fed an anxious public's thirst for colorful and intimate accounts of trafficking operations. White slavery soon became the subject of colorful exposés, editorials, and cautionary tales warning young women to beware of strange young men offering lucrative employment opportunities or marriage proposals.[18] Fears about trafficking reached "epidemic proportions" in the early years of the twentieth century, prompting the birth of rescue societies, international conferences, and multilateral agreements devoted to curtailing the traffic in innocent women and children.[19] By 1914, experts estimated that some one billion pages had been written on white slavery in North America alone.[20] Importantly, this was perceived as a tragedy that befell the Polish territories particularly acutely. Reporters emphasized that public houses in the Near East and Latin America were filled predominantly with girls exported out of the Polish lands, and that some 90 percent of the inhabitants of Latin American brothels were of Polish origin. Even the idiomatic word for prostitute in Portuguese, *polaca*, could be traced to the birthplace of many such pitiful creatures residing in Brazilian bordellos.

MIGRATION FEVER, MIGRATION ABUSES

But white slavery was not the only drama of human movement gripping the Polish territories at the turn of the century. So too were the Polish lands a key source of "voluntary" migration during these decades. A combination of improved railway connections, low transatlantic fares, and effective telegraph communications helped drive the mass exodus from the region. Mediators who helped prospective migrants buy rail and steamer tickets and who became infamous for their fraudulent schemes recruited individuals of all kinds for emigration. Steamship companies hired hundreds of such agents to scour the countryside in search of prospective passengers, while mining and industrial enterprises sent recruiters to locate sturdy laborers.[21] Local entrepreneurs, many of them Jewish, often worked independently, skimming profits by charging inflated ticket prices. The ubiquitous presence of migration agents across the Eastern

European landscape confused the context in which travelers made decisions. Single young women, like their male counterparts, fell victim to fantastical tales and abusive tactics, sometimes agreeing to questionable commitments for positions abroad. The nature of the work and recruitment techniques varied, yet migrants of both genders were vulnerable to trickery, false promises, and even physical danger during their journey. The line between voluntary migration and coercion was very thin indeed.

In the Polish territories, much of the population dreamed day and night of relocating to a wealthier corner of the world. "Argentine fever," in the 1890s, like its earlier cousin, "Brazilian fever," gripped whole communities, leaving villages decimated of population.[22] One consequence of this optimistic attitude toward migration was a tendency for young migrants to act "quite gullible and irresponsible" when presented with advertisements that promised them lucrative positions and tantalizing professional opportunities abroad.[23] Partially because of such enticements, over three-quarters of a million Poles, Ruthenians, and Jews left Austrian Galicia alone during the thirty years preceding World War I.[24] Still others flooded in from the countryside to the sweatshops of Warsaw, Łódź, and Białystok or crossed from Russian Poland and Galicia into Prussia in search of seasonal agricultural jobs and positions in factories.[25] "Throughout the length and breadth of the country," commentators summarized, "in the Polish and Ruthenian villages the population is moving."[26]

The sustained exodus prompted imperial concern about the loss of labor power and military conscripts. Austrian officials complained that the shortage of workers damaged livestock, reduced consumption in the cities, and caused meat to be sold at unprecedentedly high prices since most migrants were peasants who were fleeing land shortages, high taxes, and crippling indemnity payments. Newspapers ran stories describing whole villages turned into ghost towns, emptied of all productive laborers. Government officials circulated elaborate warnings designed to discourage the flow of young workers from European shores. The harsh treatment of migrants en route from Eastern Europe became legion, prompting state bureaucracies to take on increased responsibility for protecting their subjects abroad.[27] Trafficking accusations were but one reflection of imperial anxiety over the loss of personnel and the potential threat to the liberty of their subjects.[28]

Meanwhile, Polish nationalists worried about the impact of mass migration on the demographics of a reborn Polish state. Opponents of emigration warned that the "nation ... should not squander its strength and its blood in the service of foreigners ... or in the improvement of conditions [abroad] that are of no concern to us."[29] Leopold Caro, a Polish lawyer and opponent of emigration, helped popularize the view that migration contributed to a decline in overall morality as families resettled in communities lacking adequate leadership from organized religion.[30] For Caro, migrants were exposed to a host of threats when they left home, including "brutal foreign employers, the neglect of religious practice, the ease of contracting infectious diseases, along with the physical exhaustion." Those who left had no way of foreseeing the impact emigration would have on their health and psychological well-being, Caro argued. More concretely, local economies were adversely affected by the depletion of manpower from native soil. No matter how high the wages émigrés garnered abroad, Caro concluded, they could not possibly make up for "the loss that the national economy must bear through the absence of its most vigorous workers."[31]

Fears about the loss of labor power and rumors of abuse contributed to an increased reliance on the language of captivity to discourage mass migration. Horrifying tales of unscrupulous migration agents appeared in the columns of daily newspapers, many of them characterizing mediators as hyenas who prowled the countryside "seizing poor people and sending them into their misery in exile." Travel agents were described with wolflike characteristics or with stereotypically Jewish features. Newspapers depicted elaborate recruitment ruses for exploiting the defenseless poor designed to "capture the maximum number of emigrants in their nets."[32] As with vulnerable young women swooped up by would-be traffickers, observers stressed that "dark" [ignorant] peasants were willing to accept the "greatest fairy tales about overseas countries" from ingratiating migration agents. Employees of transatlantic shipping companies made themselves indispensible to their clients, arguing that neither the Polish nor Ruthenian languages were adequate for emigrants to negotiate with German officials on the border. The harsh methods many migration agents employed in transporting their clients prompted accusations that they were managing a modern slaving operation. Officials such as Polish Reichsrat deputy Zygmunt Łasocki accused the Galician travel agency Ojczyzna, for example, of "capturing our emigrants, sending them to Canada, and forcing them into slavelike conditions."[33]

A series of high-profile legal cases brought against recruiters helped increase popular unease over the fate of labor migrants. Agents stood accused of charging dramatically inflated prices for steamer tickets, convincing travelers that they needed a special (and expensive) "certificate" to exit, and claiming their services were required for those evading military service to cross the border safely.[34] Since the passport required of émigrés exiting Russian territory was difficult to obtain, mediators promoted their own services as vital to facilitating the border crossing.[35] Among the most widely publicized migration scandals was the Wadowice trial of 1889–1890, which exposed an elaborate system of exploitation established by agents of the Hamburg America steamship line (HAPAG) operating on the frontier between the Austrian, German, and Russian Empires.[36] Details of the trial echoed across Eastern Europe, helping to link labor migration to images of coercion and abuse.[37] Antisemitism also played a role in the proceedings. The accused in the case were sixty-five Jewish travel agents who operated a business in the border town of Oświęcim, at the junction of the Austrian, German, and Russian railway lines.

Prosecutors set out to depict the agents as ruthless human traffickers who had transported thousands of Polish and Ruthenian peasants to hard labor in American factories and mines. They called on images of slavelike conditions similar to those later used in sex trafficking cases. Prosecuting attorneys accused defendants of "introducing a slave trade into the free land of Austria."[38] Newspaper accounts depicted burly "drivers" who surrounded emigrants on the train platform, "beating them with fists and sticks" and forcing them "like cattle" to the agency's offices.[39] Anti-emigration activists soon began using metaphors of slavery to depict the harsh conditions and low wages greeting labor emigrants in the United States and Canada.[40] The Wadowice trial highlighted frightening examples of emigrants who were incarcerated for days, forced to purchase clothing from the company store at exorbitant prices or to pay bribes to physicians conducting medical examinations.[41] Migrants were allegedly imprisoned in locked "pig stalls" and dark basements.

Later trials revealed that subagents routinely detained travelers at the train station in Cracow long enough to cause them to miss their connection to Hamburg and hence their steamer to America (forcing a fine for a new ticket). In the border city of Mysłowice, in German Silesia, travelers were forced to sit for days in the waiting area after being examined by a doctor and were then transferred to a fourth-class train car with no bathrooms or food for the trip to Hamburg or Bremen.⁴² Agents of the Canadian Pacific steamer company were no better. Called "hyenas" and emigration "parasites" by contemporary lawmakers, they operated in cahoots with railway officials and gendarmes, who collectively tricked migrants out of hundreds of crowns, often sending them back home as medically unqualified once their money had been absorbed by border officials.⁴³ At least one Polish Reichsrat deputy was even accused of taking substantial bribes in exchange for channeling migrants to a particular steamer company.⁴⁴ The persistence of such stories helped convince the public that all forms of migration were potentially harmful and risked jeopardizing the liberty of the traveler.

THE TRAUMA OF FEMALE MIGRATION

Part of a much larger movement of people out of Eastern Europe, the pattern of young women traveling abroad on their own was also increasingly prevalent in the early years of the twentieth century.⁴⁵ Economic deprivation in the underdeveloped, underindustrialized Polish territories created a pool of needy young women, many of them recent arrivals from the impoverished countryside to the swelling cities.⁴⁶ Public censure about leaving the homeland fell especially hard on these female migrants. Like their male counterparts, women left home as a result of a wide range of factors and faced a host of potential risks along the way. Despite many shared experiences between emigrants of both genders, however, contemporary observers often singled out independent female travelers for particular criticism.⁴⁷ Country girls were chastised for reaching beyond their station and taking unnecessary risks in their quest for fortunes overseas. Dreams of secure jobs and comfortable lives led them to fall carelessly into the traffickers' traps, nationalist journals warned.[48] Newspaper editors warned that the migration of young women deprived the nation of childbearing women. All of these concerns fed a growing anxiety about single female travelers and encouraged a receptive audience for tales of "white slavery."[49]

Testimonies of women labeled as trafficked out of the Polish lands suggest that for the most part the initial impetus to leave was voluntary, though sometimes based on false or exaggerated information. Migrants chose to venture beyond their native shores for money, for professional advancement, to see the world, to escape the routine of their hometown, or for love. At some stage migration agents may well have employed force or continued deception to maintain control over their charges, yet women who turn up on the rolls of "white slaves" typically took the opening plunge into migration on their own without physical coercion. They may have been coaxed into accompanying a migration agent by promises of employment or the prospect of meeting a wealthy husband, but such commitments are similar to those made to migrants everywhere.

Even in the best of times, migration entailed risks on the part of the traveler, as our examples from the Wadowice case suggest. Migration agents frequently misled their clients into believing secure jobs awaited them. Labor contracts were often cleverly arranged to disguise long-term commitments. Migrants were forced to repay the cost of the journey over many months or years, remaining in semibondage until the debt was paid. Job descriptions were vague and migrants had to be happy with whatever employment they could find upon arriving in a new setting. Such abuses were unfortunate, but they do not in themselves constitute coerced migration. Instead, evidence from diplomatic correspondence, local police files, and the testimonies of returning women suggests at least three ways in which the fate of presumed trafficking victims was misrepresented in the territories of partitioned Poland.

First, women who did not maintain steady correspondence with their families back home were often presumed to have come to a bad end, and their parents complained to their local police officials accordingly. Yet such women were often typical labor migrants wrongly categorized as victims of trafficking or sexual abuse. Especially in Austria, local police were required to file missing-person reports with the Central Police Directorate in Vienna when parents complained about daughters they suspected had been taken abroad by force. Such cases were treated as trafficking episodes, although not all of their subjects ended up in foreign brothels. Sometimes more banal outcomes explained the break in correspondence.

A second explanation for missing teenage girls involves the occupational flexibility to which most migrants are subject. Many female migrants arrived in their new homes intending to find work in shops or factories, but instead turned to prostitution as the best of a range of bad options. Women who traveled abroad and turned to paid sex in their new homes often made the initial decision to leave for reasons similar to those of other travelers. Though coercion may have been involved in their turn to sex work, they were not initially "trafficked" from their hometown or village.

Third and most importantly, professional prostitutes in Eastern Europe migrated to burgeoning cities around the globe in order to pursue work in the sex industry. If their testimonies can be believed, these women traveled abroad in order to improve their fortunes through work in foreign brothels, not because they were forced to do so. As Alain Corbin reminds us, the so-called white slave trade was a "mere corollary of the trafficking officially tolerated by [domestic] regulation" across Europe. The only difference is that there was "no longer unity of place." The international trade in women in many ways represented an extension of local brothel systems in that many of the women and girls involved were well aware of what was expected of them and were mostly willing to be sent abroad.[50] Let us examine each of these scenarios in turn before suggesting some tentative conclusions about the way sex trafficking cases inform the field of migration studies.

Wayward Daughters

The exodus of young people seeking opportunities across the ocean placed significant strains on parent-child relationships. Migrants became preoccupied with their new lives and neglected to write home, leading to suspicions about their fate. Yet not every anxious parent complaining to local police about a "disappeared" daughter located her offspring in an overseas brothel. Consider the case of Maria Klimek, who left her tiny native village of Golanka, in the Galician district of Tarnów, during the summer of 1913 bound for Buenos Aires. Klimek, a twenty-one-year-old serving girl, had taken up with thirty-year-old Stanisław Laszuk. According to her mother, their five-month relationship had "ruined her and caused a scandal" such that the mother happily contributed to the cost of her daughter's transatlantic passage and gave her full blessing to Maria's travel. Laszuk's promise to marry the girl upon their arrival in Argentina no doubt strengthened the mother's support of the trip. Nonetheless, when Maria presented officials in the emigration hall at Hamburg the address of a known brothel as her destination, local police and Austrian consular officials initiated an investigation into possible trafficking charges against Laszuk and warned Maria's mother that her daughter might be in danger. A few months later the mother was relieved to receive a letter from her daughter announcing that she had secured employment as a tutor for the daughters of a wealthy local family. She quickly prevailed upon diplomatic officials to follow up and look into the validity of her daughter's claims.

In reality, as local Argentine police soon discovered, Maria was working as a domestic servant in the family's household. She had exaggerated her professional success in the correspondence with her mother but had nonetheless avoided ending up in a brothel. Klimek had used her relationship with Laszuk to travel abroad but told police that "once she learned of Laszuk's former life, she no longer wanted to have anything to do with him" and so landed a more pedestrian position.[51] Embarking on a transatlantic steamer with a known trafficker did not necessarily suggest that a young woman was being duped or abused; sometimes the trickery could go the other direction and migration agents could be wrong-footed by clever migrants. In Klimek's case, the "suspected victim" left the country voluntarily with the permission of her parent and found "honest" if unglamorous work abroad. She even controlled the narrative of her own story, carefully reporting to her family that she had made improvements to her socioeconomic position. Had Argentine police not investigated her whereabouts, she might have been presumed to be a victim of trafficking. In fact, she was merely guilty of "creating a scandal" at home and fibbing to her mother about the nature of her work in Buenos Aires. As Maria Klimek's case suggests, one side effect of long-distance migration was the loss of contact with loved ones back home. Klimek's story confirms Mark Connelly's argument that sometimes white slavery imagery offered an acceptable explanation for wayward daughters who broke contact with their families after leaving home. "It is possible," Connelly proposes, "that the tragic endings of the white-slave captivities offered an explanation, admittedly macabre, to parents who had lost contact with their daughters."[52]

Volunteerism and False Promises

On other occasions, police and antitrafficking activists tracked girls suspected of having fallen into hostile hands only to find an element of volunteerism that handicapped their ability to prosecute the agents or return the girls to their families. This is the second type of scenario that complicates our understanding of sex trafficking statistics. The struggle for survival prompted some women to turn to unsavory practices such as prostitution after migrating, but this does not mean they were coerced into migrating or forced to take up residence in foreign brothels. The courts recorded countless examples of young women who testified that they had intentionally sought out agents who offered to sponsor their travel abroad and who were well aware of the trafficker's intentions. The story of Fana Aufseher, a young Jewish woman from Eastern Galicia, is a case in point. Fana was tempted after the death of her father to accompany a migration agent to America when he promised her "treasure and wealth." Along the way, however, the man revealed he was really transporting her to Istanbul to work in a brothel. On this occasion, she escaped and returned home. Several years later, however, after Aufseher's mother died, the young woman tracked down the same trafficker at a brothel in Stryj and this time agreed to make the trip, knowing full well what was involved.[53]

Often the potential migrant's only sin was her eagerness to trust a recruiter's rosy promises, a vulnerability of most labor migrants even in the best of times. Typically these false commitments involved the promise of meager but important increments of social mobility, such as the possibility that a peasant girl might find work indoors as a lofty domestic servant, or a maid might be promoted to cashier or shopkeeper. Such elevations of employment status were surprisingly difficult in the Eastern European social economy but could be more easily facilitated in a foreign milieu where one's background and personal circumstances did not serve as markers of success. Migration agents frequently emphasized opportunities for social mobility among women they accompanied abroad. Marya Sabat and M. Kawecka, for example, were approached while working in the fields near the provincial town of Czernowitz and promised positions as household servants if they traveled abroad. Before they knew it, they were on a steamer bound for Constantinople, where they landed in a brothel. Elka Jenner was already employed as a servant in the Wołoczyski region when an acquaintance offered her "good money" if she accompanied him to Istanbul. She agreed to pay an intermediary a five-hundred-złoty fee to make the arrangements and was shipped out of Trieste.[54] Golda Reinerman, in turn, became involved with a group of migration facilitators when one approached her at the Sosnowiec railway station in Upper Silesia, offering her a position as a barkeep in nearby Będzin, along the Russian/German border.[55] In all of these cases, the women were placed in Turkish brothels after arriving in Istanbul. They appear not to have suffered physical coercion at the hands of agents while departing Europe, yet their facilitators clearly were less than forthcoming about the activities the girls would perform after arriving at their destination.

Even relatively pedestrian commitments that agents made to their clients could entail depictions of a luxurious and carefree existence. As Captain Bielski, head of the Będzin district police in Silesia, explained during his 1901 testimony, traffickers played up the suffering and poverty of their young clients, painting idealized pictures of high wages and plentiful jobs in America—not unlike agents seeking workers for colonies abroad. Even the promise of a position as a lowly barkeep or a waitress could be compelling when migrants traveled first class, received housing in luxury accommodations, or were escorted to theater performances on their route out of the country.[56] Emilja Rosentretter, for example, met her contact in Katowice, where he promised her and her friend waitress jobs in Buenos Aires. Along the route out of the country, the agent purchased tickets in the sleeping car of the train and brought them to the theater, activities seen as so luxurious they were highlighted in Emilja's court testimony against her accused trafficker.[57] Personal ambition and a desperate desire to better their material circumstances led each of them to trust unsavory migration agents.

As simple country girls lacking professional skills aspired to jobs in stately homes, fine restaurants, or elegant shops, critics chastised them for taking on the risks incumbent upon single female migrants. Dreams of secure jobs and comfortable lives led them to fall into the traffickers' traps. As one journalist opined, young women were not satisfied with their own social status and so took unnecessary risks to change it. "Their father's background does not suit them, but instead it seems to them that they were born for something better, something higher. They have the desire to cross over into the sphere of the gentry, travel abroad, to pursue their dreams to dress well and to glitter. They want to earn the most possible money. Often they imagine that under foreign skies, in the home of some famous or wealthy family they will have a wonderful party."[58] The crime here appears to have been striving for upward economic mobility, something denied to many young women in Polish territory.

Trafficking and Domestic Prostitution

The third and most difficult scenario for contemporary observers to embrace was that of women working as professional prostitutes in their home countries who emigrated in search of greater economic prospects within the sex trade. Such women did not fit into the neat stereotype of passive and vulnerable female victimhood. For contemporary journalists, images of brash, streetwise sex workers hardly satisfied the public's desire for representations of innocence, naïveté, or passivity that characterized popular accounts of white slavery. Nonetheless, the testimonies of female migrants working as prostitutes suggest they approached emigration as a route to professional advancement. Some believed that relocating to a new environment would offer the chance to start a new life in a more "legitimate" profession. Others wanted to improve their working conditions or increase their profit margin. Contemporary rescue workers had to face the reality that luxurious settings and exotic conditions abroad made the life of a transplanted prostitute attractive, thwarting their efforts to bring migrants back to their native countries. As one British pamphleteer complained, trafficked women often refused the efforts of charity workers simply because the glitter and excitement of their new lives made a return to a "respectable existence" back home unattractive.[59]

Specialists on sex migration have argued that most women who sold sex before leaving home were aware that they would be expected to perform sex work once they relocated.[60] Many of those who left Eastern Europe earlier in the century and made their way to brothels overseas were recruited from houses of prostitution in their native countries. Testimonials from trafficking trials suggest that brothels along the borders of the Polish territories were a key source for those trading in women. The 1901 case against John Meyerowicz for international trafficking held in Bytom, Prussian Silesia, reflects this pattern. Meyerowicz allegedly worked with a phalanx of subagents recruiting prostitutes from across the border in Russian Poland. The bulk of Meyerowicz's "cargo" were recruited from brothels in the border towns of Będzin and Sosnowiec and transported over the border at Katowice, then on to Wrocław, Berlin, and London. As Stanisław Posner emphasized in his study of trafficking along the Prussian/Russian border, the greatest problem was the "link between the domestic brothel trade and the international traffic in women," an issue that was virtually ignored by imperial governments and private charities alike.[61] Polish newspaper accounts of trafficked women often acknowledged that many of them sold sex before they left home, and Edward Bristow points out that among migrants from Eastern Europe in the nineteenth century, "prostitutes were ... increasingly mobile."[62] Their previous activities aside, such women opted to go abroad partially because, like all migrants, "they dreamed and longed for another life."[63]

Prostitutes interviewed at police headquarters often told the same story: they traveled abroad voluntarily in search of opportunities and not as a result of coercion or abuse by international traffickers. Peppi Beiner of Rozdol, Eastern Galicia, for example, insisted she alone was responsible for her decision to relocate internationally. Peppi's mother had died when she was nine, and at age fifteen she left Galicia for Budapest, where she took up work as a professional prostitute. However, "in terms of material conditions," she was not prospering and so after five years she decided "completely on my own" to travel to Constantinople and then on to a brothel in Salonika. According to Peppi's deposition, her migration to the Ottoman Empire had been entirely voluntary, prompted only by the suggestion of an acquaintance at the bordello in Budapest, and she did not use the services of a professional trafficker. Consular authorities in Constantinople doubted Peppi's story, not least because she was carrying false identity papers, which someone no doubt helped her forge. Yet even in the safety of her own consulate (which might well have been convinced to transport her back home if she had so requested), Peppi stuck to her tale of human agency and individual initiative rather than presenting herself as a victim of international trafficking.[64]

Knowledge that the new conditions might entail some sexual activity did not, of course, preclude a whole range of abuses at later stages of migration. Itinerants are always vulnerable to unexpected shifts in their professional situation, and those who labor in the sex industry are not alone in experiencing abuse. Many decided to emigrate only to discover that promises of luxury, wealth, or a stable existence in a "legitimate" profession were unrealistic. As some of these stories suggest, even experienced prostitutes could be duped. Although travelers frequently made the initial decision to migrate abroad willingly, they were nonetheless subject to false promises and entrapment after arriving in their new homes. Agents frequently exaggerated descriptions of wealth to capture the imaginations, if not the bodies, of their prospective clients. Migration literature is careful to stress that serving as a prostitute in one location does not preclude the use of force at some point in the journey to transport women to foreign brothels. Still, we have ample evidence that experienced prostitutes frequently volunteered to relocate. When such cases end up in police files, they reveal a remarkable degree of power on the part of prostitutes.

CONCLUSIONS

Young women who went missing from jobs and homes throughout Polish territory migrated abroad for any number of reasons. Some sought to escape the shame of a personal scandal. Others sought a way out of inherited poverty and limited professional options. Still others were attracted to the opportunity to travel and see the world. Many had worked as prostitutes in their homeland and hoped for better conditions, more money, or a fresh start. Nearly all of them were assisted in some way by a migration agent, who helped supply the necessary papers to cross the border, purchased the rail and steamer tickets, and provided an address for them in their arrival port, without which they would often not be permitted onto a transatlantic ship. Migration recruiters were clever, scrappy, and often corrupt individuals whose first loyalties lay with the companies who hired them and with their own bottom lines. Nevertheless, their behavior and the tactics they used may not have differed significantly among types of migrants. Emigration was a risky business no matter one's destination or background.

Not all of these women ended up in brothels in their new homes, though we know that many foreign bordellos were staffed with women from the Polish lands. These largely unskilled, uneducated young migrants were perhaps guilty of naïveté, ignorance, and a misguided sense of trust. Yet the historical record suggests that they could also be clever, manipulative, resourceful, and pragmatic. During periods of intense overseas migration, such as in the decades before World War I, many such travelers joined the exodus abroad without a clear plan or with an incomplete picture of their future lives. If we use the lens of migration, the experiences of women labeled as "trafficked" appears in a new light, not always so different from that of most labor migrants. Migration studies gives us the vocabulary to look at the peculiar combination of coercion and free will involved in almost every relocation story. The women under examination here need not fall out of that category merely because of the work they may have performed after arriving in their new homes. Once we look beyond the white slavery panic promoted by contemporary actors and reconnect these women with their homes, their families, and their working conditions, we can begin to understand them as an integral part of Polish history. By widening the framework of those histories beyond our usual national borders and by marrying the stream of "legitimate" migration history with the history of so-called sex trafficking, new patterns begin to emerge.

Far from fitting into the neat pattern of step migration, in which women relocated to the New World in order to join a laboring spouse, the lives of the individuals under review suggest more heterogeneous patterns of female mobility. Even as female migrants responded to the call of opportunity along with their male counterparts, nearly every aspect of their migration odyssey was shaped by gendered concerns. From the manner in which they were recruited and the enticements they were offered, including promises of fancy clothing and luxurious accommodations, to the types of work expected of them, from cashier and waitress to kitchen maid and prostitute, the migration journey was coded in gendered terms. Even the flow of information about overseas opportunities was shaped by gender attachments, beginning with the public house gossip through which employment offerings were often transmitted.

Women such as those in our study did not choose to migrate within kinship networks but were recruited independently and relocated among similarly aged women. Setting aside assumptions of family ties allows us to trace a number of unique patterns of female mobility. The women under review, for example, often took up residence with other women or resided with an unrelated family for whom they performed domestic service. Presumptions of marriage and family ties as motivators for mobility in these cases can mask as much as they reveal, and scholars would do well to consider other aspects of a migrant's journey. Finally, our study suggests that women who migrated on their own frequently operated as independent wage earners, rather than as dependent spouses. Female labor migrants could be resourceful and upwardly mobile, even establishing limited financial security and saving for longer-range business adventures. Some were able to set aside funds to establish their own businesses, to marry, or to pursue other opportunities. Moreover, unlike trailing spouses who joined their husbands in staggered-migration scenarios, these women remained physically mobile, relocating repeatedly in a string of related positions or returning to Polish territory with their earnings. Women wage earners sent back remittances to their families in Europe and played crucial roles in the domestic economy back home. As independent wage earners, they had the power to make decisions about the disposition of their earnings, a pattern that should be considered in assessing the broader effects of migration trajectories. In all of these respects, the lessons such cases offer suggest that migration scholars have much to learn from the experiences of this migrant category as they consider wider models of human mobility.

NOTES

1. Annemarie Steidl, Engelbert Stockhammer, and Hermann Zeitlhofer, "Relations among Internal, Continental, and Transatlantic Migration in Late Imperial Austria," *Social Science History* 31, no. 1 (2007): 61–92.

2. John D. Klier, "Emigration Mania in Late-Imperial Russia: Legend and Reality," in *Patterns of Emigration, 1850–1914*, ed. Aubrey Newman and Stephen W. Massil (Lon-

don: Jewish Historical Society of England, 1996), 21–30; Grzegorz Maria Kowalski, *Przestępstwa emigracyjne w Galicji, 1897–1918* (Cracow: Wydawnictwo Uniwersyteta Jagiellońskiego, 2003).

3. Unmarried women represented a substantial minority of those relocating during the great labor migration of the nineteenth century, including some 20 percent of Polish Catholics migrating to the United States. For a breakdown of female migrants to the United States by country of origin, see Donna Gabaccia, "Women of the Mass Migrations: From Minority to Majority, 1820–1930," in *European Migrants: Global and Local Perspective*, ed. Dirk Hoerder and Leslie Page Moch (Boston: Northeastern University Press, 1996), 90–114.

4. On white slavery scares throughout Europe and the Americas at the turn of the twentieth century, see Edward Bristow, *Vice and Vigilance: Purity Movements in Britain since 1700* (Dublin: Gill and Macmillan, 1977); Kathleen Barry, *Female Sexual Slavery* (New York: New York University Press, 1984); Marion Kaplan, "Prostitution, Morality Crusades and Feminism: German-Jewish Feminists and the Campaign against White Slavery," *Women's Studies International Forum* 5, no. 6 (1982): 619–627; Mark Connelly, *The Response to Prostitution in the Progressive Era* (Chapel Hill: University of North Carolina Press, 1980); Egal Feldman, "Prostitution: The Alien Woman and the Progressive Imagination," *American Quarterly* 19 (1967): 192–206; and Donna Guy, "White Slavery, Public Health, and the Socialist Position on Legalized Prostitution in Argentina, 1913–1936," *Latin American Research Review* 23, no. 3 (1988): 60–80.

5. Laura Maria Agustin, *Sex at the Margins: Migration, Labour Markets and the Rescue Industry* (London: Zed Books, 2007), 2–7.

6. Petra de Vries, "'White Slaves' in a Colonial Nation: The Dutch Campaign against the Traffic in Women in the Early Twentieth Century," *Social and Legal Studies* 14, no. 1 (2005): 42.

7. On new approaches to understanding sex trafficking, see Laura Agustin, "The Disappearing of a Migration Category: Migrants Who Sell Sex," *Journal of Ethnic and Migration Studies* 32, no. 1 (2006): 29–47; and Maybritt Jill Alpes, "The Traffic in Voices: Contrasting Experiences of Migrant Women in Prostitution with the Paradigm of 'Human Trafficking,'" *Human Security Journal* 6 (2008): 34–45.

8. On the limitations of research on the gendered components of migration history, see Stephanie Nawyn, A. Reosti, and L. Gjokaj, "Gender in Motion: How Gender Precipitates International Migration," in *Advances in Gender Research*, ed. M. T. Segal and V. Demos (Bingley, UK: Emerald Press, 1997); Eleonore Kofman, "Female 'Birds of Passage' a Decade Later: Gender and Immigration in the European Union," *International Migration Review* 33 (1999): 269–299; Sarah Mahler and Patricia Pessar, "Gender Matters: Ethnographers bring Gender from the Periphery toward the Core of Migration Studies," *International Migration Review* 40, no. 1 (Spring 2006): 27–63; Donna Gabaccia, *From the Other Side: Women, Gender and Immigrant Life in the U.S., 1820–1990* (Bloomington: Indiana University Press, 1994); Donna Gabaccia and Franca Iacovetta, eds., *Women, Gender and Transnational Lives: Italian Workers of the World* (Toronto: University of Toronto Press, 2003); and Pierette Hondagneu-Sotelo, *Gendered Transitions* (Berkeley: University of California Press, 1994).

9. Katharine M. Donato et al., "A Glass Half Full? Gender in Migration Studies," *International Migration Review* 40, no. 1 (2006): 4.

10. Gabaccia and Iacovetta, *Women, Gender and Transnational Lives*.

11. Kofman, "Female 'Birds of Passage' a Decade Later," 271–274.
12. Adam M. McKeown, *Melancholy Order: Asian Migration and the Globalization of Borders* (New York: Columbia University Press, 2011).
13. Ethnicity was a major factor in relations between migrants and those who facilitated their travel abroad. Many migration agents were Jews, a fact that complicated public perceptions of sex migration. For more on the ethnic dimension of trafficking, see Keely Stauter-Halsted, *The Devil's Chain: Prostitution and Social Control in Partitioned Poland* (Ithaca, NY: Cornell University Press, 2015).
14. "Z tajemnic społeczeństwa. Handlarz dziewcząt," *Gazeta Narodowa*, July 9, 1892, 2; "Handlarze dziewcząt," *Gazeta Narodowa*, October 19, 1892, 2. On the details of the trial, see Edward Bristow, *Prostitution and Prejudice: The Jewish Fight against White Slavery, 1870–1939* (Oxford: Clarendon Press, 1982), 80–81; and Keely Stauter-Halsted, "'A Generation of Monsters': Jews, Prostitution, and Racial Purity in the 1892 L'viv White Slavery Trial," *Austrian History Yearbook* 38 (2007): 25–35.
15. See, for example, the cycle of articles under the heading "Naganiacze," published in Warsaw's *Niwa* in 1896; "Handel żywem towarem," *Kurier Poranny*, June 1897; and "Handel dziewczętami," *Słowo*, August 12, 1899, 3.
16. The border crossing at Sosnowiec in Upper Silesia, the so-called three emperors' corner, was an active zone for smuggling of all kinds, from undocumented migrants to contraband publications, armaments, and expensive jewelry.
17. Stanisław Posner, *Nad otchłanią* (Warsaw: Księgarnia Naukowa, 1903), 12–17.
18. The most widely circulated discussions included Posner's *Nad otchłanią*; Augustyn Wróblewski, *O prostytucji i handlu kobietami* (Warsaw: Piotr Laskauer, 1909); and Josef Schrank, *Der Mädchenhandel und seine Bekämpfung* (Vienna: Selbstverlag, 1904).
19. Stephanie A. Limoncelli, *The Politics of Trafficking: The First International Movement to Combat the Sexual Exploitation of Women* (Stanford, CA: Stanford University Press, 2010); Bristow, *Vice and Vigilance*, 190.
20. Bristow, *Vice and Vigilance*, 188–189.
21. Tara Zahra, "Travel Agents on Trial: Policing Mobility in East-Central Europe, 1889–1989," *Past and Present* 222, no. 1 (March 2014): 161–193.
22. On Polish attitudes toward migration to Brazil in the 1890s and Argentina in the early years of the twentieth century, see Benjamin P. Murdzek, *Emigration in Polish Social-Political Thought, 1870–1914* (New York: Columbia University Press, 1977), 61–69, 103–107; and Leopold Caro, *Emigracya i polityka emigracyjna ze szczególnem uwzględnieniem stosunków polskich*, trans. Karol Englisch (Poznań: Drukarnia św.Wojciecha, 1914), 217–218.
23. "Przeciw handlowi dziewczętami," *Nowiny dla Wszystkich*, October 18, 1905, 4. This report on the 1905 Bremen Congress on Combating Trafficking in Women quotes Major Wegener's [sic] reference to Dr. Chatelet's finding that some 59 percent of the girls who resorted to paid sex did so out of hunger.
24. Leopold Caro, *Emigracya i polityka emigracyjna*, 34–35.
25. Between 1885 and 1888, the Prussian government expelled at least thirty thousand Poles and Jews from its territory, arguing that they were unfit for permanent settlement. Tobias Brinkmann, "Why Paul Nathan Attacked Albert Ballin: The Transatlantic Mass Migration and the Privatization of Prussia's Eastern Border Inspection, 1886–1914," *Central European History* 43 (2010): 54; Józef Macko, *Prostytucja* (Warsaw: Nakład Polskiego Komitetu Walki z Handlem Kobietami i Dziećmi, 1927), 347–349.

26. "Ludzie czy szakale: Emigranci a Towarzystwa przewozowe i ich agenci," *Gazeta Ludowa* 6, no. 32 (August 4, 1912): 4.

27. The Habsburg Monarchy passed legislation in 1905 affirming its responsibility to protect migrants even after their arrival overseas. Related to this, a Ministry of the Interior decree dated June 26, 1905, called for the Viennese police directorate to mediate with foreign officials in the battle against trafficking in women. Caro, *Emigracya i polityka emigracyjna*, 324; Nancy M. Wingfield, "Destination: Alexandria, Buenos Aires, Constantinople; 'White Slavers' in Late Imperial Austria," *Journal of the History of Sexuality* 20, no. 2 (May 2011): 303.

28. On Austrian efforts to protect the personal liberty of imperial subjects and others on Habsburg territory, see Alison Frank, "The Children of the Desert and the Laws of the Sea: Austria, Great Britain, the Ottoman Empire, and the Mediterranean Slave Trade in the Nineteenth Century," *American Historical Review* 117, no. 2 (2012): 410–444.

29. Caro, *Emigracya i polityka emigracyjna*, 9. See also Murdzek, *Emigration in Polish Social-Political Thought*.

30. The notion that migration causes disruption of local communities resulting in degeneracy and a collapse of moral standards was later popularized by William Thomas and Florian Znaniecki in their classic work of sociology, *The Polish Peasant in Europe and America*, 2 vols. (Chicago: University of Chicago Press, 1919).

31. Caro, *Emigracya i polityka emigracyna*, 67.

32. *Gazeta Powszechna*, March 24, 1910.

33. Polska Akademia Nauk, Oddział w Krakowie (PAN Kraków), zbiory specjalne, Sygn. 452, "Polskie Towarzystwo Emigracyne, 'Canadian Pacific.'"

34. Kowalski, *Przestępstwa emigracyjne w Galicji*.

35. Brinkmann, "Why Paul Nathan Attacked Albert Ballin," 55–56.

36. On the Wadowice trial as part of a larger campaign to discourage emigration out of East Central Europe, see Zahra, "Travel Agents on Trial."

37. Kowalski, *Przestępstwa emigracyjne w Galicji*, 158.

38. *Der Galizische Menschenhandel vor Gericht* (Vienna, 1890), 205, cited in Zahra, "Travel Agents on Trial," 1.

39. *Galizische Menschenhandel*, 35, cited in Zahra, "Travel Agents on Trial," xx.

40. Friedrich Hey, *Unser Auswanderungswesen und seine Schäden* (Vienna, 1912), 5, cited in Zahra, "Travel Agents on Trial," 175.

41. Caro, *Emigracya i polytika emigracyjna*, 82–86.

42. Ibid., 89–99.

43. PAN Kraków, zbiory specjalne, Sygn. 452, "Polskie Towarzystwo Emigracyne, 'Canadian Pacific.'"

44. Reichsrat deputy Jan Stapiński from the Galician Peasant Party (Stronnictwo Ludowe) was accused in 1912 of having siphoned off huge profits from the sale of steamer tickets on the Canadian Pacific line, an accusation he consistently denied. PAN Kraków, rps 4094, "Materiały Zygmunta Łasockiego dot. Emigracji Polaków do Kanady."

45. On the relative percentage of female migrants out of Europe in the nineteenth century, see Gabaccia, "Women of the Mass Migrations."

46. Ewa Morawska, "Labor Migrations of Poles in the Atlantic World Economy, 1880–1914," in *European Migrants: Global and Local Perspectives*, ed. Dirk Hoerder and Leslie Page Moch (Boston: Northeastern University Press, 1996), 170–208.

47. According to Laura Agustin, "Women who leave their countries and later are found selling sex in someone else's ... disappear from migration studies ... and reappear in criminological [studies] ... where they are called victims." Agustin, "The Disappearing of a Migration Category," 29.
48. "Handlarze dziewcząt," Niwa, October 26, 1896, 729–730.
49. "Przeciw handlowi dziewczętami," 4.
50. Alain Corbin, *Women for Hire: Prostitution and Sexuality in France after 1850*, translated by Alan Sheridan (Cambridge, MA: Harvard University Press, 1890), 285–298.
51. "Maria Klimek, Victim of Trafficking," BPdWA, Prostitution und Mädchenhandel, 1913.
52. Connelly, *The Response to Prostitution*, 124–126.
53. Testimony of Fana Aufseher, "Handlarze dziewcząt," *Gazeta Narodowa*, October 22, 1892, 2.
54. "Handlarze dziewcząt," *Gazeta Narodowa*, October 20, 1892, 2.
55. Posner, *Nad otchłanią*, 19–20.
56. Józef Macko notes that a particular type of trafficker operated between Berlin, Vienna, Moscow, Warsaw, Odessa, and the Baltic ports and always traveled with his clients first class and in a "high style." Many of these were sons of the owners of longstanding trafficking businesses who had learned the trade since childhood. Macko, *Prostytucja*, 351–352.
57. Posner, *Nad otchłanią*, 16–20.
58. "Handlarze dziewcząt," Niwa, October 26, 1896, 729–730.
59. *In the Grip of the White Slave Trader* (London, Offices of the M.A.P., 1911), 100–101.
60. Agustin, "The Disappearing of a Migration Category," 36–39.
61. "Kroniki. St. Posner, 'Nad otchłanią,'" *Nowe Słowo*, March 1, 1903, 114–115; Posner, *Nad otchłanią*, 6–9.
62. "Handlarze dziewcząt," *Gazeta Narodowa*, October 19, 1892, 2; Bristow, *Vice and Vigilance*, 177.
63. "Z tajemnic społeczeństwa. Handlarz dziewcząt," *Gazeta Narodowa*, July 9, 1892, 2.
64. The report from the Austro-Hungarian Consulate in Istanbul notes that Peppi "made this testimony full of lies in order to protect the trafficker from punishment." BPdWA, "Prostitution und Mädchenhandel," 1906/I, Karoline Merczel file, 1.

CHAPTER 7

Evacuation as Migration
The Soviet Experience during the Great Patriotic War

Lewis H. Siegelbaum and Leslie Page Moch

WE LIVE IN an age when large undertakings by states are likely to inspire suspicion if not outright hostility, when the fruits of previous state endeavors wither for lack of commitment to their continuation, and when corporate and other private enterprises reap the whirlwind of profit and power from state retrenchment. The only exceptions to these trends might be war and disaster relief, though states increasingly are privatizing and outsourcing war making, and their relief efforts often take second place to those of nongovernmental organizations (NGOs) or international bodies.

In this respect, perhaps more than any other, the Soviet Union seems to be of another age. The Soviet Union was built for large undertakings. Many of these—such as the collectivization of agriculture, the deportation of whole categories of people, and the destruction of natural resources in the name of industrialization—have attracted scholars' attention and warranted their condemnation. In this chapter, we turn our attention to evacuation during the Great Patriotic War, the term Russians use to refer to the Soviet Union's experience of World War II. We understand migration in general and evacuation in particular as a function of two things: state and administrative policies, practices, and infrastructure designed to both foster and limit human movement on the one hand, and migrants' own practices, relationships, and networks of contact on the other. We refer to the policies, practices, and infrastructure affecting migrants as *regimes* of migration, and migrants' own practices as *repertoires* of migration.

This way of understanding migration is generally applicable in the modern world. What distinguished the Soviet Union was the state's ambitiousness in controlling the movement of people within its borders and thus its outsized role in enacting regimes of migration. Among the forms of migration we address in the larger project, evacuation depended on many of the same institutions and logistical arrangements as the resettlement of rural people and the deportation of entire ethnic groups and other categories of people.[1] We found instances in which officials listed arriving evacuees alongside ethnic German and Polish deportees, and locals referring to evacuees as "refugees" and "exiles." Some evacuees indeed referred to themselves as refugees, thereby emphasizing the gap between the promise of state guardianship and its absence in reality.[2]

To understand these ambiguities and confusions, we must analyze how Soviet evacuation regimes interacted with evacuees' own repertoires. We begin by considering the chronology and scope of the evacuation effort. We then follow the process from the departures of evacuees to their journeys eastward into the interior of the country, their disembarkations and reception, their living and working conditions, and their ultimate destinations. Research on wartime evacuation, long confined to Soviet historians' characteristically heroic narrative of the Great Patriotic War, has recently focused on determining the numbers and ethnic composition of evacuees, the logistics of the operations, and implications for interethnic relations and, particularly, antisemitism during the war and in its immediate aftermath as evacuees sought to return home.[3]

We are the first to place evacuation within the framework of migration. This approach makes it possible to incorporate important contingencies of mobility evident at the time. Such contingencies included the ways that the goal of securing one's own safety coincided or did not coincide with the state's objective of preventing industrial capacity and key personnel from falling into the hands of the enemy; the extent to which institutions fashioned on the spur of the moment could coordinate across thousands of kilometers and internal borders; whether evacuees experienced their displacement as sacrifice or adventure, an interruption or a permanent relocation; and how evacuation related to other forms of displacement during the war.

Our research draws primarily on Soviet archives, including digitized copies available at the US Holocaust Museum. We rely essentially on three kinds of sources—letters to authority, typically requests or appeals (*zaiavleniia*); the myriad forms employed in intrabureaucratic communication detailing the provision of transportation, food, accommodation, and employment; and recollections—in the form of interviews and memoirs—by people who survived not only evacuation but in many cases the Soviet period. None of these sources can bear the weight of reliability; each is partial and otherwise problematic as representative of evacuees' experiences. Nonetheless, taken together and put in conversation with one another, they allow us to analyze crucial dimensions of the repertoires and regimes of evacuation.

"AN OPERATION OF GARGANTUAN PROPORTIONS"[4]

On June 24, 1941, two days after the German invasion, the USSR Council of People's Commissars and the All-Union Communist Party's Central Committee created an Evacuation Council (Sovet po evakuatsii) that immediately set to work moving Soviet citizens, production facilities, and other resources.[5] By December 25, 1941, the director of the Civilian Evacuation Administration reported having successfully removed 10 million citizens to the east, 6.5 million from the Moscow area alone.[6] Movement occurred in two great waves: the first that matched the initial German advance in the second half of 1941, and the second in response to the German occupation of the North Caucasus in the summer of 1942.[7] Soviet historians claimed that as many as 25 million people were evacuated. More recent estimates range between 10 and 17 million. Even these more modest estimates are excessively high, according to Vadim Dubson, who has calculated fewer than 6.5 million evacuees by the end of 1941 to no more than 7.5 million by December 1942. The radical differences among these estimates are a tribute to the difficulty of tracking people who moved with such urgency and often more than once, as well as a function of different interpretations among historians of the motives of evacuation authorities in reporting the number of evacuees.⁸

Whether the state moved 20 million or half that, the feat of relocating so many citizens in such a short period of time had no precedent. Even if we take the lowest estimates, it dwarfed the number of settlers transported to Siberia at the end of the nineteenth and beginning of the twentieth centuries; it also exceeded the combined number of prisoners sent to the Gulag and deportees and exiles confined to special settlements during the 1930s. Moreover, the whole evacuation operation was carried out in a mere eighteen months—from the German invasion to the end of 1942. Nothing occurred on this scale anywhere else in the world.

"Of all the valuable capital the world possesses," Joseph Stalin once said, "the most valuable and most decisive is people."⁹ So profligate with this capital before the war, Stalin was not particularly concerned with coddling Soviet citizens and therefore safeguarding them from Nazi depredations. Rather, because Soviet authorities considered evacuation a key component of wartime strategy, its guiding principles were those that would most effectively underwrite the military effort. The June 27, 1941, decree on evacuation gave first place to the machinery and factory equipment essential for the military struggle. Dismantling, transporting, unloading, and reassembling industrial plants and equipment from areas threatened with occupation was a complicated task involving dozens of state agencies and their shadow party organizations. It also was a calculated risk, for its immediate effect was to cause a substantial decline in output of materials essential for the war effort.¹⁰

Among civilians, priority went to "qualified workers, engineers, and employees with enterprises evacuated from the front" as well as "the population, in the first place youth, fit for military service; Soviet and party leadership cadres."¹¹ A week later, an additional decree authorized the evacuation of the families of high-ranking officials and military officers. In practice, women and children were targeted for evacuation—or to be more specific, women with children, women whose capacities for work were crucial for the war effort, and women whose husbands were elite officials or military officers. Members of the intelligentsia also had priority, along with cultural and educational institutions such as the Bolshoi

Ballet, Moscow State University, and pedagogical institutes. Just as the families of persecuted groups such as kulaks and deported nationalities were punished, so would the families of the Soviet elite be privileged in wartime.[12] The institution of the family would have enormous importance in determining the fortunes of evacuees.

DEPARTURES

Authorities were determined to avoid chaotic flight from war by organizing the orderly removal of the population—or at least certain categories of people. Yet such an organized evacuation regime proved impossible, especially in the first weeks. For one thing, the German invasion caught many people away from home.[13] For another, nobody knew the price of leaving or staying. Abram Tseitlin recalls his father's puzzlement about what to do. When a retreating Red Army unit passed through his native town in Ukraine, he told the commanding officer, "Nobody—neither the *raikom* nor the *raisovet* tells us anything—stay or leave?" and then asked, "If you were in my place, what would you do? I have a wife and three children, the youngest of who is three years old. One more thing. I am a Jew and most of the people you see in the square are Jewish. I have heard that the Germans don't particularly like Jews." The officer replied, "I don't need to be in your place; I know what the Germans do to Communist officers. I don't know what my family has done, whether they have been evacuated, but if I were with them, I would have left. . . . Leave immediately."[14]

Personal experience and recollections from the previous war, rumor and propaganda, one's own nationality—these constituted only part of the "complex web of reasons" that went into each family's decision to stay or leave.[15] Yet another factor was social geography. Residents of major cities had difficulty imagining how evacuation to some unknown, godforsaken collective farm (*kolkhoz*) could be preferable to staying put in the relative comfort, or at least familiarity, of one's own apartment. As Rebecca Manley notes, "in a state in which residence rights were strictly controlled, return to the country's major cities could easily be denied by the state." Moreover, only a few years had passed since "the same state that now proclaimed its desire to protect" members of the intelligentsia had whisked large numbers of urban dwellers away in the dead of night.[16]

But even those most determined to leave needed the means to do so, and in the first months of the war not much functioned as it was supposed to. Thus, many people—how many is impossible to determine—resorted to the repertoire of self-evacuation. Among them was Misha, a Jewish boy of nineteen, who asked if he could hitch a ride with a truck full of Soviet soldiers retreating from Vilna (Vilnius). Although the commanding officer turned him down, the peasant conscripts were more accommodating. With a wink, they helped him clamber aboard. Never again seeing his parents, Misha made it to the Urals, joined the Red Army, and as an officer witnessed the Victory Day parade on Moscow's Red Square. We knew him as Moshe Lewin, one of the greatest historians of Soviet Russia.[17] The "great majority" of civilians who made it to the North Caucasus in the fall of 1941—primarily Jews from Ukraine—were not part of the organized evacuation process but had evacuated themselves—in other words, they were refugees.[18]

In instances where the war found children in summer camps or boarding schools or where no family connections existed, as with orphans, the state assumed responsibility for evacuation without prompting.[19] But the growing numbers of orphans during the war strained the resources and resolve of evacuation and child welfare personnel. Government officials from areas near the front claimed they lacked sufficient food for orphans and pleaded with central authorities to permit their evacuation to the east. Absent the voices of the orphans themselves, we must rely on these officials' letters to convey the dire condition of the "very many children whose parents either were killed by the Fascists or died of hunger under occupation." According to one account from Kalinin oblast, they were found to be "exhausted to the extreme, completely disheveled, louse-ridden [and] living in cellars and holes in the ground of destroyed villages."[20]

Evacuation from the major cities vulnerable to attack began within a week of the invasion. Authorities in Leningrad reported that between June 29 and August 14, 1941, they had evacuated over 469,000 people.[21] Most evacuees left by train for cities to the east. Cherepovets, Vologda, and Iaroslavl' served as both destinations and temporary evacuation points where those in need of medical attention could receive it. After the

Germans cut the last rail connection with the rest of unoccupied Soviet territory in early September, evacuations from Leningrad dwindled but picked up again in November with the opening of the ice road across Lake Ladoga. From January 21 through April 20, 1942, another 550,000 people were thus evacuated from the besieged city. Having endured the first winter of the siege, many were so weak that they did not survive the journey, and even more died in evacuation hospitals.[22]

How did people secure a ticket to leave? Many accompanied their enterprises, helping to dismantle, pack up, and load equipment. Others initially left behind could be included on lists if their bosses were able to persuade evacuation authorities. This was how forty "highly skilled workers" from an armaments plant, evacuated in the summer, followed their colleagues to Ioshkar-Ola in the Mari ASSR in October.[23] We don't know if Ivan Simonov, an engineer employed by the Northern Energy Construction Trust, made it to Sverdlovsk, but at least his boss was willing to seek passage for him and twelve family members (his wife, two teenage sons, his mother, two sisters, three nephews, and three aunts).[24]

Many seeking to leave the city had no sponsors and had to appeal directly to evacuation authorities. Others had received approval for evacuation, but illness—either their own or that of a close family member—had prevented them from departing.[25] As time passed and hunger became more pervasive, illness began to play the opposite role; people increasingly referred to it to underscore the urgency of their evacuation. Marta Raud's story combined both illness and death. The daughter of a military engineer already evacuated from Moscow to Tashkent, she lived with her mother and brother in Leningrad until her brother volunteered for the front two weeks after the Germans invaded and her mother died in January 1942. She and her mother had received the necessary documents for evacuation in August but could not go because her mother's health was failing. Marta had not heard from her brother since his induction. She was fifteen years old.[26]

Other strategies competed for the attention of authorities. One emphasized past contributions and/or the importance of the individual seeking evacuation. Sometimes this strategy was combined with descriptions of the parlous state of one's health or that of family members. For example, O. I. Averichkina, a widowed Leningrader with two children, invoked both her husband's service as head of that city's civil defense organization (*Osoaviakhim*) and the "weakness" of her daughter in appealing for exit by air (see figure 7.1). Likewise, a father serving as battalion commissar asked that his twenty-three-year-old son be evacuated because he had multiple sclerosis and was "one of the most talented young poets of Leningrad."[27] This and many other requests cited family connections in cities to the east because family connections disburdened authorities, relieving them of much of the responsibility of providing evacuees with food and accommodation, and such requests had a decent chance of being approved. We do not know how many tried but failed to obtain passage out of the city, or what proportion of the estimated million who died during the siege had received permission to leave but failed to do so.

As for Moscow, the headquarters of the entire evacuation effort, during a few remarkable days in mid-October 1941 the city itself succumbed to an unseemly scramble among elites who hitherto had stayed put. Once Stalin ordered the evacuation of government offices to the Volga town

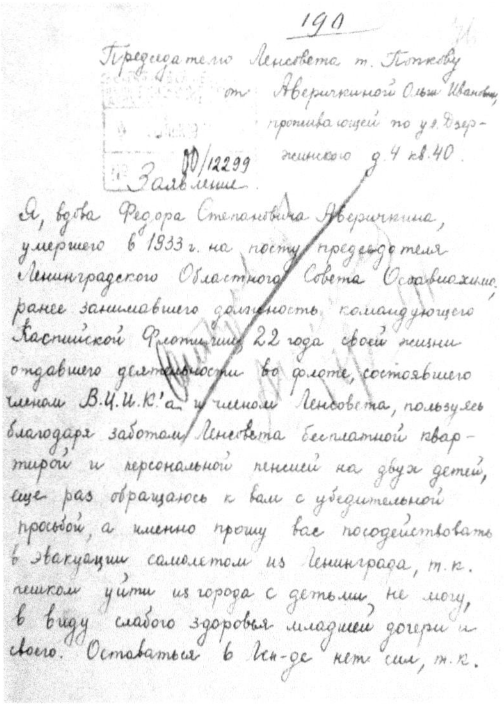

190

Председателю Ленсовета т. Попкову
от Аверичкиной Ольги Ивановны,
проживающей по ул. Дзержинского д. 4 кв. 40.

Ю/12299

Заявление.

Я, вдова Федора Степановича Аверичкина, умершего в 1933 г. на посту председателя Ленинградского Областного Совета Осоавиахима, ранее занимавшего должность командующего Каспийской Флотилией, 22 года своей жизни отдавшего деятельности во флоте, состоявшего членом В.Ц.И.К.'а и членом Ленсовета, пользуясь благодаря заботам Ленсовета бесплатной квартирой и персональной пенсией на двух детей, еще раз обращаюсь к вам с убедительной просьбой, а именно прошу вас посодействовать в эвакуации самолетом из Ленинграда, т.к. пешком уйти из города с детьми не могу, в виду слабого здоровья младшей дочери и своего. Оставаться в Лен-де нет сил, т.к.

Figure 7.1 *Request from O. I. Averichkina to be evacuated from Leningrad with her two children, December 1941.* Source: United States Holocaust Memorial Museum RG-22.033, Tsentral'nyi Gosudarstvennyi Arkhiv St. Peterburga, f. 330 Gorodskaia evakuirovannaia komissiia Leningradskogo gorodskogo soveta trudiashikhsia deputatov, op. 2, d. 81, l. 76.

of Kuibyshev on October 15, the public "fear[ed] that the government had abandoned the population to its fate," and the city "was in the grip of mass panic verging on anarchy." Party and state officials commandeered available transport, and roads out of the city heading east were clogged with vehicles bearing them and their precious household items, barrels of fuel, and cash. Nearly a thousand railway cars left the city's stations during the days of flight.[28] On board were leading personnel of key industries and scientific institutions. October 14–15 saw the exodus of 404 individuals from 24 scientific institutes for Kazan', Sverdlovsk, Alma-Ata, Samarkand, Frunze, and Ashkhabad. The cream of Moscow's theatrical world from ten different companies left on the latter day, some for these cities and others for Magnitogorsk, Karaganda, Tashkent, and Irkutsk.[29]

What if as a result of the haste and inefficiency of evacuation, people got separated from family members? What if some wound up in one city or collective farm and a close relative had been evacuated to another place, perhaps even to another Soviet republic? This was the question that the assistant director of evacuation for Kazakhstan received from a provincial official in November 1941. "Every day evacuees turn to us with requests for train tickets to various places—Fergana, Kokand, Tashkent, Chkalov, etc.—where they have relatives," the official wrote. "Do we have the right to give them?" The answer—"If there is documented proof of relatives living there, then you can distribute tickets"—implicitly endorsed the state's reliance on the family.[30]

JOURNEYS

The extraordinarily privileged, like the aforementioned Averichkina (see figure 7.2) and Leningrad poet Anna Akhmatova, were flown to safety. Others relied on the railroad with occasionally devastating consequences. On June 6, 1942, Aleksei Kosygin, then deputy chairman of the Evacuation Council, received a telegram from Petr Popkov, chairman of Leningrad's executive committee, informing him that a convoy of evacuees had been standing for three days at a station in Kadui, about 310 miles east of Leningrad. For some reason, the evacuees had not received any food or water during this time, and Popkov referred to "much death among them."³¹ Intended to preserve life, the journeys that evacuees took could have the opposite effect. The reason could have been bureaucratic disconnect—evacuation personnel failing to communicate the needs of evacuees to appropriate officials in the commissariats of transport and trade or the regional Soviet government through whose territory the train passed. Sometimes the inadequacy of food or other supplies had to do with the unexpectedly large number of people in need. For example, in August 1942, it was reported from recently liberated Smolensk oblast that two hundred to five hundred people arrived daily, on foot, from occupied territories, overwhelming the little Toropets station on the Kalinin rail line.³²

Sometimes lethal, railroad journeys more often were merely tedious. Most people traveled in a *teplushka* (essentially a boxcar with a stove in the middle). Among the detailed accounts by evacuees that have survived, several reveal instances of cooperation and mutual aid aboard such trains. For example, after Genia Batasheva and her friend Mania had survived the massacre of Jews at Babi Yar in Kiev, they walked all the way to unoccupied territory, where they encountered a Soviet army officer who took them under his wing and provided truck transport. In Voronezh, they joined a convoy bound for Tashkent. Keeping to themselves in the *teplushka*, they went without food for three days until the songs of their fellow passengers moved the two young women to tears. At this point, the evacuees offered them both food and companionship. Abram Tseitlin, whom we left with his father wondering whether to flee or to stay, recounts companionable conversation and traditional road food (bread and butter, onions, hard-boiled eggs, pickles, and boiled chicken) on the train that took his family to Central Asia. On the monthlong journey that ended at Kagan near Bukhara, Tseitlin reports that the *teplushka* became a sort of communal apartment "where each family had its own corner." And, "like every communal apartment, we had our difficulties with each other—over whose turn it was to dispose of garbage and prepare food."³³

Finally, for Anna Dashevskaia, who kept a diary of her journey from Kiev to the Urals via Alma-Ata, the train teemed with human emotion. "On the convoy," she wrote, "a lot of people were arguing, women crying, and men chatting, wiping back tears. As the train slowly pulled away from the station, a great noise went up from our wagon filled with children.

Figure 7.2 *Boarding pass for Averichkina and her two children, January 20, 1942.*
Source: United States Holocaust Memorial Museum RG-22.033, Tsentral'nyi Gosudarstvennyi Arkhiv St. Peterburga, f. 330 Gorodskaia evakuirovannaia komissiia Leningradskogo gorodskogo soveta trudiashikhsia deputatov, op. 2, d. 81, l. 77.

Husbands ran after the train car, waving caps, tears fell uncontrollably on their cheeks—women wailed, pulled at their hair ... then descended into deathly silence, each thinking about herself and quietly wiping away tears...."[34] At stops along the way, Dashevskaia and her sisters kept on bumping into acquaintances—a cousin with his wife and children, a neighbor of their aunt Eva, several classmates—evacuated earlier. At the procurator's office in Alma-Ata, the convoy's last stop, her sister Marusia secured a work assignment to Ural'sk. And so on September 22, 1941, more than a month after they had left Kiev, Anna and her siblings boarded a train for the twelve-hundred-mile journey back across the vast Kazakh steppe. Missing her parents terribly, Anna imagines seeing them at every stop. A week later, she arrived at her "temporarily-permanent place of residence."[35]

DESTINATIONS

Genia Batasheva, Abram Tseitlin, and Anna Dashevskaia all left Ukraine in the late summer and early autumn of 1941 to escape what years later would be called the Holocaust. Many other Jews from Ukraine evacuated themselves to the North Caucasus (the territories of Krasnodar and Stavropol'), where they comprised about 70 percent of the total evacuated population. In these territories, only 9 to 12 percent of evacuees claimed Russian nationality, and 14 percent Ukrainian.[36] The region proved to be a doomed destination, especially for Jews, not so much because the indigenous population sometimes reacted to so many needy evacuees with antisemitic hostility as because it would fall to the Nazis in the summer of 1942.

Elsewhere, Russian-nationality evacuees predominated. They were the clear majority (64 percent) in the Molotov/Perm' territory in the Urals, as of October 1941. Farther east, in Novosibirsk oblast, 41 percent of evacuees were Russian, 11 percent were Jews, and 5 percent Ukrainian—suggesting that many other nationalities were present among evacuees in Siberia. In Kazakhstan, where 45 percent of evacuees were Russian, slightly over a third were Jews, and 11 percent claimed Ukrainian nationality.[37] But as elsewhere, this was a fluid, moving, and growing population. By the time of the next assessment in mid-November, the registered evacuees had shifted in number and nationality.

Many evacuees assigned to a particular destination wound up somewhere else, either through their own doing or because of what frustrated higher authorities referred to as "irregular" (*samovol'nye*) reassignments by regional personnel. Counting on the repertoire of family connections, some evacuees reportedly insisted on being deposited at places where they claimed to have relatives rather than proceeding on to the Altai or Novosibirsk—even when it turned out they did not have any relatives where they claimed they did. The German offensive of the summer of 1942 also precipitated massive reassignments of convoys from the Stalingrad, Saratov, and Kuibyshev oblasts farther east toward the Altai territory and the Novosibirsk and Omsk oblasts.[38] These unanticipated movements left authorities at the receiving end unprepared and evacuees ill served.

If they survived the journey, millions of evacuees found or were assigned places to live. Evacuees accompanying institutions and privileged individuals could count on being accommodated in a city. Manley notes that Muscovites and Leningraders as well as the families of party, state, and military elites enjoyed the additional privilege of settling in any city where relatives or friends were willing to share living space.[39] One such city, Alma-Ata, the Kazakh republic's capital, accommodated cultural luminaries such as Sergei Eisenstein along with the cast and crew shooting *Ivan the Terrible*, leading members of Kiev's Theater of Musical Comedy, the prize-winning Stakhanovite combine driver and Supreme Soviet deputy Maria Demchenko, and the wife of the well-known poet Aleksandr Bezymenskii. When the time came to evacuate from Moscow the family of the Stalin Prize–winning author Sergei Mikhalkov, Lazar Kaganovich, a member of the Politburo and the Evacuation Council, informed the chairman of the Kazakh Council of Ministers. He in turn instructed the city's mayor to provide a suitable apartment.[40] Mikhalkov's wife and son flew to Alma-Ata, where, in addition to the families of cultural figures, "those able-bodied men who did not want to fight sat out the war thanks to 'handy' certificates," as Mikhalkov sardonically recalled in his memoirs.[41]

Among the many children evacuated we single out the odyssey of Lena Jedwab. Sent from Białystok to a Young Pioneer summer camp in southern Lithuania, she and her fellow campmates were evacuated to a children's home in Udmurtia, some 300 kilometers east of Kazan'. A sort of triage followed: the camp counselors went home, the students born in 1924 and 1925 were mobilized, and fifty-five parents came to fetch their children, so that of the 215 children in camp, 160 remained by February 1942. "Did I ever dream that I would be so far from home, in a remote village in Udmurtia? That I would be the ward of a children's home?" she asked.[42] Lena replaced the camp counselors for a while along with two friends, gradually realizing that as much deprivation as she suffered, it was mild compared to what she heard of through letters and visits from people like the children's home director's wife, who arrived from Leningrad in the fall of 1942. Her friends applied to schools in the spring, one entering Moscow State University's Philological Faculty, which had been evacuated to Saratov. Lena stayed on at the children's home through tenth grade in order to qualify for higher educational institutions. She then applied to schools in several cities during the summer of 1943. In the fall, she started at the Bauman Technical Institute in Moscow. It was at this time she learned from other Polish Jews that her entire family—mother, father, brother, and sister—had been killed early in the war.[43]

The least privileged evacuees found themselves in the countryside—on collective farms and state farms—even if they had no experience in farm work. Comprising a majority of evacuees, they were mostly women, children, the elderly, and the handicapped—predominantly people who came without a sponsoring employer. In fact, most evacuees lived in rural areas.[44] For them, everything was more difficult. Letters from rural-based evacuees to local and regional authorities as well as to the Supreme Soviet and its chairman, Mikhail Kalinin, tell a sorry tale of acute material deprivation. "We have received nothing, not even salt," wrote a group of Leningrad evacuees from the Chuvash republic in January 1943. "We are very seriously hungry," complained the Muscovite mother of three children from the republic's Toretskii district in March 1942. "Our situation is not bad, it is desperate," a group of soldiers' wives wrote.[45] Aside from food, petitioners pleaded for dresses, coats, shoes, and cloth. Many simply described themselves or their children as "barefoot and naked."[46] Investigatory reports filed by labor inspectors largely confirmed these complaints.[47] Kolkhoz administrators bore part of the blame: labor-day calculations, the basis for access to resources, slighted evacuees in favor of indigenous members of the kolkhoz. Forced to accommodate the newcomers, host families were at best unwelcoming and at worst aggressively hostile.[48] To be fair, already stretched rural dwellers had to share finite resources with many more people. They needed able-bodied agricultural workers, but that rarely was what they got.

Many evacuees moved more than once and for a variety of reasons—wartime fronts changed with German advances; evacuees sought better conditions elsewhere; family members discovered each other and reunited. Often, travel was interrupted by long waits at evacuation stations, and the final destination was unknown. Civilians sent to the Donets Basin, for example, had to pack up their belongings again and continue their journey eastward as the Germans approached. Some fourteen thousand evacuees arrived in Novosibirsk in November and December 1941. Among the Leningraders who arrived in the same city in the latter half of 1942, some continued their journeys to the Altai krai, Kazakhstan, the Krasnoiarsk krai, Irkutsk oblast, and Kyrgyzstan.[49]

Itineraries easily get lost in the aggregated data. We learn about the possibilities from the family of Abram Zakharovich Shteingol'ts. In charge of the bakeries of Minsk, Shteingol'ts was evacuated to Tambov. His wife, son, and two daughters who followed by truck and train found him working and living in a bakery. In November 1941, after an arduous trip during which food "ran out," the family relocated to a small village in the northeast corner of Kazakhstan. From there Abram was called to the front only to return in 1942 because of a stomach ulcer. He then worked in the rationing administration for the district and eventually directed a factory in Alma-Ata. The family joined him in 1944 along with relatives from Leningrad who had survived the blockade.[50] Despite their many moves, this family found a way to reunite and stay together.

High mobility and family regathering also occurs as a *leitmotif* in the story of Genia Batasheva. When we last left her, Genia was en route to Tashkent with her girlfriend Mania. There, the evacuation station assigned them as minors (Genia was eighteen years old at the time) to an *artel'* (cooperative) some 25 kilometers southwest of the city. But, having been told of rampant typhus in the area, the girls boarded the first convoy that came along. They traveled over 2,500 kilometers to the northwest to Chkalov oblast, where they took up residence on the steppe in a former Cossack settlement. Genia did indeed take ill but was nursed back to health on a kolkhoz where she helped the director with correspondence and learned how to harvest grain. Eventually, she established written contact with an aunt who had been evacuated to Omsk in southern Siberia and who invited her to come. Another journey of 1,700 kilometers brought her and Mania to Omsk, where they got jobs at a shipbuilding factory that had been evacuated from Leningrad earlier in the war. There they learned from the radio that their native Kiev had been liberated. Unusually, both girls' fathers survived the war, but not their mothers. Mania joined her father in Kiev; Genia reunited with hers in Rubtsovsk, a town in the southern Altai where the Khar'kov Tractor Factory that employed her father had been evacuated in 1941.[51]

RETURNS

Soviet evacuees—like most people displaced during the war elsewhere in Europe—wanted to go home. However, going home was not a simple matter. All across Europe, the war had destroyed villages and large swaths of urban residential areas.[52] In the Soviet Union, where an urban place of residence was privileged and permission to live in a major city difficult to come by, city dwellers were especially eager to return home. None outdid evacuees from Moscow who, as soon as the danger of bombardment and occupation abated in early 1942, were seized by "suitcase moods." Alarmed reports reached the Evacuation Council from Penza, Riazan', and other provincial towns of central Russia about Muscovites crowding railroad stations and, despite prohibitions against doing so, demanding tickets for Moscow.[53]

The reevacuation regime imposed by Soviet authorities could be quite stringent. Whereas rural dwellers could reclaim their homes without obtaining a residence permit, restrictions applied to urban residents.[54] In the case of Voronezh, cited by Manley, the city soviet "simply abolished all rights to previously occupied living space." Authorities elsewhere, faced with the prospect of a flood of returnees and reduced housing stock, tried to impose expiration dates on tenants' rights or distribute living space to them from the pool of less-than-full accommodation.[55] As for Moscow, the city council decreed on June 2, 1944, that only those who had paid rent all along—in absentia, in wartime—and who could find their way back to the city within sixty days of receiving notice could reoccupy their former apartment.[56]

Some could not wait to receive notice. Take the indignant Dr. Roman Shakhnovich, a Kremlin physician, who until his evacuation to the Chuvash republic had lived in an apartment on the highly desirable Gorkii Street. Shakhnovich wrote in November 1942 that his wife and sons had vacated the apartment to join him in evacuation. Even though he continued to pay rent, he reports, his neighbor decided to occupy the apartment without authorization (*samovol'no*). Understandably distressed, Shakhnovich sought to have his neighbor ousted, but city authorities rejected his request, insisting that he was still on assignment in Chuvashia.[57]

Struggles over the return of evacuees were not simply between state authorities and the evacuees themselves, but often triangular. In some areas, such as Saratov oblast, regional officials were keen to hold on to evacuees at least through harvest time but were enjoined to release them by central authorities as well as those in other parts of the country starved for labor.[58]

According to an official from the Resettlement Administration responsible for reevacuation in the Russian Soviet Federative Socialist Republic (RSFSR), the total number of evacuees in the republic, which had stood at a little more than 4 million on January 1, 1944, dropped to 2.14 million by the beginning of 1945, and 1.68 million by April 1. In other words, within fifteen months, 2.3 million evacuees had been returned to their homes.[59]

For some, returning home could be a long, drawn-out process. According to a resettlement official from the Bashkir ASSR, of the more than 80,000 evacuees in the republic at the beginning of 1945, over 50,000 had been reevacuated, but that still left some 28,000 at year's end. As late as 1947, nearly 2,500 families of evacuees in Ulianovsk continued to depend on the material assistance of resettlement authorities.[60] Many evacuees had no home to go to and no surviving relatives. But some—it is impossible to determine how many—decided to make a go of it where they were. The Steingol'ts family, whom we left in Alma-Ata during the war, had the opportunity to return to Minsk but stayed put. The father, Abram, directed the bakeries of the Kazakh capital; his wife, having learned Kazakh, directed a school. They remained in Alma-Ata for the rest of their lives.[61]

CONCLUSION

Thanks to the war and their evacuation, many Soviet citizens experienced their country in a new way. Although nerve-racking at the time, their odysseys could take on a romantic hue in retrospect. Lydia Chukovskaia recalled Anna Akhmatova exclaiming as she gazed out the window of the train taking them from Kazan' to Tashkent, "I'm glad to be seeing so much of Russia." For those who were children, the wondrousness of the Soviet Orient created lasting images. Tseitlin's description of the little Uzbek town of Kagan includes aural as well as visual recollections—the rumbling of passing trains and the whistles of their locomotives, the measured roar of the cotton mill, the "mournful singing" of the muezzin calling the faithful to prayer, "the penetrating cries" of the donkeys, the nocturnal howling of jackals. Together the sounds "produced a peculiar symphony that no composer could have recreated," and no impressionable youngster could forget.[62]

Whether evacuees perished, found new homes, or returned at war's end, they demonstrate that World War II is the central event of twentieth-century Russia's migration history. When we add to them their military compatriots, the deportees, and those repatriated at war's end, we see an entire nation on the move, and a state struggling to apply myriad regimes of migration. Evacuees themselves depended on the state's regime of evacuation but also sought to mitigate its inadequacies and perceived injustices. They did so by beseeching authorities, moving on their own initiative, bonding with fellow travelers, and relying on connections with relatives both close and distant—repertoires familiar to students of migration throughout the world.

NOTES

1. Rebecca Manley, "The Perils of Displacement: The Soviet Evacuee between Refugee and Deportee," *Contemporary European History* 16, no. 2 (2007): 495–507.

2. US Holocaust Memorial Museum (hereafter USHMM) Record Group (hereafter RG) 74.002, Reel 1 (Tsentral'nyi Gosudarstvennyi Arkhiv goroda Almaty [hereafter TsGA A] op. 6, d. 1279, ll. 180, 191; op. 6, d. 1278a, ll. 20–21).

3. See, for example, Marina N. Potemkina, "Evakonaselenie v Ural'skom tylu: opyt vyzhivaniia," *Otechestvennaia istoriia* 2 (2005): 86–98; Vadim Dubson, "Toward a Central Database of Evacuated Soviet Jews' Names, for the Study of the Holocaust in the Occupied Soviet Territories," Research Note, *Holocaust and Genocide Studies* 26, no. 1 (2012): 95–119; Rebecca Manley, *To the Tashkent Station: Evacuation and Survival in the Soviet Union at War* (Ithaca, NY: Cornell University Press, 2009); Kiril Feferman, "A Soviet Humanitarian Action? Centre, Periphery and the Evacuation of Refugees to the North Caucasus, 1941–1942," *Europe-Asia Studies* 61, no. 5 (2009): 813–831; and Anna Shternshis, "The Role of Ethnic Identity in the Survival of Soviet Jewish Civilians in 1941," paper presented at "Russian Jewish Migration across Borders, across Time," Harriman Institute Conference, Columbia University, October 2012.

4. Manley, *To the Tashkent Station*, 28.

5. For the decree, see "Iz istorii Velikoi Otechestvennoi voiny: nachalo voiny," *Izvestiia TsK KPSS*, no. 6 (1990): 201. On the absence of prior planning for evacuation, see Manley, *To the Tashkent Station*, 28; I. Grinberg, G. Karataev, and N. Kropivnitskii, eds., *Evakuatsiia v Kazakhstan: iz istorii evakuatsii naseleniia zapadnykh raionov SSSR v Kazakhstan, 1941–1942* (Almaty: Fortress, 2008), 11, 24–25.

6. Feferman, "A Soviet Humanitarian Action?," 816.

7. For an alternative periodization with specific reference to Jews and their differential rate of survival, see Mordechai Altschuler, "Escape and Evacuation of Soviet Jews at the Time of the Nazi Invasion: Policies and Realities," in *The Holocaust in the Soviet Union and*

the Sources on the Destruction of the Jews in the Nazi-Occupied Territories of the USSR, 1941–1945, ed. Lucjan Dobroszycki and Jeffrey S. Gurock (New York: Sharpe, 1993), 77–104.

8. For useful summaries of the estimates, see Manley, *To the Tashkent Station*, 1, 50, which gives a figure of 12 million by the end of 1941 and 16.5 million by the fall of 1942; and Potemkina, "Evakonaselenie v Ural'skom tylu," 86–87. See also Dubson, "Toward a Central Database of Evacuated Soviet Jews' Names," 96, 99–101. Dubson argues that administrators systematically inflated the numbers; on the other hand, Kristen Edwards explains why the Resettlement Administration figures are low in "Fleeing to Siberia: The Wartime Relocation of Evacuees to Novosibirsk, 1941–1943," Ph.D. diss., Stanford University, 1996, 50.

9. Iosif V. Stalin, *Sochineniia*, vol. 14 (Moscow: Pisatel', 1997), 62.

10. On this point, see Wendy Goldman, "10,000 Boxcars a Day! Evacuating People, Food, and Factories," unpublished paper presented at the annual conference of the Association for Slavic, East European, and Eurasian Studies, Boston, November 22, 2013.

11. *Izvestiia TsK KPSS*, no. 6 (1990), 208.

12. Manley, *To the Tashkent Station*, 35–38.

13. USHMM RG-31.053, Memoirs of Abram Tseitlin, "Evacuation," 15; USHMM RG-31.113, Anna Dashevskaia Diary, 6; Lazar' Rafael'evich Tsents, "I Remember/ia pomniu: Vospominaniia veteranov VOV," accessed February 12, 2013, http://iremember.ru/artilleristi/tsents-lazar-rafaelevich.html, 1. For families separated because one or more members had been traveling to distant locations when the war broke out, see USHMM RG-22.027M, Reel 48 Gosudarstvennyi Arkhiv Rossiiskoi Federatsii [hereafter GARF] f. A-327, op. 2, d. 70, l. 70; d. 73, l. 29).

14. Memoirs of Abram Tseitlin, "Evacuation," 14, 17.

15. Anna Shternshis, "The Role of Ethnic Identity," 10.

16. Manley, "The Perils of Displacement," 498.

17. Ronald Grigor Suny, "Living in the Soviet Century: Moshe Lewin, 1921–2010," *History Workshop Journal* no. 74 (Autumn 2012): 194.

18. Feferman, "A Soviet Humanitarian Action?," 823.

19. *Moskva prifrontovaia 1941–1942: Arkhivnye dokumenty i materialy*, ed. M. M. Gorinov (Moscow: Mosgorarkhiv, 2001), 251. See also Lena Jedwab Rozenberg, *The Girl with Two Landscapes: The Wartime Diary of Lena Jedwab, 1941–1945* (New York: Holmes and Meier, 2002).

20. USHMM RG-22.027, Reel 45 (GARF f. A-327, op. 2, d. 43, ll. 112, 114, 122). These letters and memoranda date from July–October 1942.

21. Aleksandr Mikhailovich Tiranin, "Nedavno rassekrechennye dokumenty blokadnogo Leningrada," accessed March 3, 2013, http://artofwar.ru/t/tiranin_a_m/text_0190.shtml (Tsentral'nyi Gosudarstvennyi Arkhiv Sankt-Peterburg [TsGA SPb] f. 7179, op. 53, d. 58, l. 30).

22. Mikhail Frolov, "Evacuation from Leningrad to Kostroma in 1941–42," in *Life and Death in Besieged Leningrad, 1941–44*, ed. John Barber and Andrei Dzeniskevich (Houndmills, UK: Palgrave Macmillan, 2005), 73, 79.

23. USHMM RG-22.033 (TsGA SPb f. 330, op. 1, d. 4, ll. 4–6, 24, 31–33).

24. USHMM RG-22.033 (TsGA SPb f. 330, op. 2, d. 81, l. 47, 89).

25. See, for example, USHMM RG-22.033 (TsGA SPb f. 330, op. 2, d. 81, ll. 78, 108; d. 82, l. 39; d. 83, l. 170); USHMM RG-22.030 (TsGA SPb, f. 7179, op. 11, d. 814, l. 217).

26. USHMM RG-22.033 (TsGA SPb f. 330, op. 2, d. 83, l. 182).

27. USHMM RG-22.033 (TsGA SPb f. 330, op. 2, d. 82, l. 95).

28. Quotation from John Barber and Mark Harrison, *The Soviet Home Front, 1941–1945: A Social and Economic History of the USSR in World War II* (London: Longman, 1991), 64. See also Manley, *To the Tashkent Station*, 59–63; Gennady Andreev-Khomiakov, *Bitter Waters: Life and Work in Stalin's Russia* (Boulder, CO: Westview Press, 1997), 163–182.

29. *Moskva prifrontovaia*, 254–257, 260.

30. USHMM RG-74.002 (TsGA A, f. R- 1137, op. 6, d. 1284, ll. 134–35).

31. USHMM RG-22.027, Reel 46 (GARF f. A-327, op. 2, d. 50, l. 14). Kosygin was Popkov's immediate predecessor as Leningrad executive committee chairman.

32. USHMM RG-22.027, Reel 40 (GARF f. A-327, op. 2, d. 2, l. 78).

33. USHMM RG-50.226.0008, Oral History Interview with Genia Batasheva, Part 6, 3:30–27:00; Memoirs of Abram Tseitlin, "Evacuation," 21, "Kermine," 26. Batasheva and her friend survived by telling a German soldier that they were not Jewish and had wandered to Babi Yar out of curiosity. They were driven back to Kiev and released. For testimony Batasheva gave in 1980, see Tat'iana Evstaf'eva and Vitalii Nakhmanovich, eds., *Babii Yar: Chelovek, vlast', istoriia: dokumenty i materialy v 5 knigakh* (Kiev: Vneshtorgizdat Ukrainy, 2004), 106–108, 321–322.

34. Dashevskaia Diary, 7–8.

35. Ibid., 18–22.

36. Feferman, "A Soviet Humanitarian Action?," 820. Feferman uses resettlement department data.

37. Ibid., 820; Grinberg et al., *Evakuatsiia v Kazakhstan*, 100.

38. USHMM RG-22.027, Reels 48, 46 (GARF f. A-327, op. 2, d. 68, l. 15; op. 2, d. 50, ll. 33, 103–06). Reassignments occurred from the beginning; in early October 1941, Kazakhstan had steeled itself for over sixty thousand evacuees from Moscow, but less than nine thousand arrived because "evacuation stations in Novosibirsk, Chkalov, Kuibyshev, Saratov and elsewhere irregularly reassigned evacuees." USHMM RG-74.002 (TsGA A f. 1137, op. 9, d. 141, ll. 75–76).

39. Manley, *To the Tashkent Station*, 151.

40. USHMM RG-74.002 (TsGA A f. 1137, op. 6, d. 1279, l. 18; d. 1280, ll. 13, 42–43).

41. S. V. Mikhalkov, *Ot i do…* (Moscow: Olimp, 1997), 134. USHMM RG-74.002 (TsGA A f. 1137, op. 9, d. 142, l. 66). The son, Andrei, born in 1937, would become a film director and screenwriter under the name Konchalovskii, his mother's maiden name.

42. Rozenberg, *Girl with Two Landscapes*, 15, 70, 75. Quotation is from page 15.

43. Rozenberg, *Girl with Two Landscapes*, 85, 87, 92, 103, 145, 169.

44. Of 6.9 million evacuees registered as of January 1942, 3.4 million (48 percent) were sent to rural areas, compared to 2.7 million (39 percent) sent to cities. The remaining 13 percent are not accounted for. See Natalie Belsky, "'Hiding behind the Name of Evacuee One Cannot Sit and Remain Idle in the Soviet Union': The Struggle for Employment of 'Unorganized' Evacuees," paper presented at Midwest Russian Historians Workshop, Northwestern University, March 16, 2013. By April 1943, roughly two-thirds of 663,290 evacuees in the oblasts of Saratov, Gor'kii, and Kirov lived in villages. In the predominantly black-earth Penza oblast, 84 percent of the evacuees resided outside cities, but in the more urbanized Novosibirsk oblast, only 38 percent did so as of January 1943. USHMM RG-22.027, Reel 42 (GARF f. 327, op. 2, d. 26, ll. 25, 35, 49, 73); Edwards, "Fleeing to Siberia," 5, 231.

45. USHMM RG-22.020 (Gosudarstvennyi istoricheskii arkhiv Chuvashskoi Respubliki, hereafter GIAChR), f. 827, op. 1, d. 599, l. 19; f. 1041, d. 599, l. 46; f. 1263, op. 1, d. 51, l. 180).

46. USHMM RG-22.020 (GIAChR f. 835, op. 1, d. 354, ll. 3, 9, 11, 13, 14, 17–170bv, 20, 22, 37, 45, 113, 125, 134, 205, 217, 261, 302).

47. For such reports from the Chuvash republic, see USHMM RG-22.020 (GIAChR f. 835, op. 1, d. 354, l. 37; f. 1263, op. 1, d. 51, ll. 73–75, 153, 179–80; d. 78, ll. 2–3).

48. USHMM RG-22.020 (GIAChR f. 1263, op. 1, d. 51, ll. 18, 53, 101, 128, 212, 2370bv, 243).

49. Edwards, "Fleeing to Siberia," 108–111.

50. Grinberg et al., *Evakuatsiia v Kazakhstan*, 43–47.

51. USHMM RG-50.226.0008, Batasheva, Part 6, 28:00–49:00.

52. See, for example, Leora Auslander, "Coming Home? Jews of Postwar Paris," *Journal of Contemporary History* 40, no. 2 (2005): 37–59; and Annette Wieviorka and Floriane Azoulay, *Le Pillage des appartements et son indemnisation* (Paris: La Documentation Française, 2000).

53. Manley, *To the Tashkent Station*, 240; USHMM RG-22.027 (GARF f. A-327, op. 2, d. 68, ll. 10, 13). According to G. A. Kumanev, forty-six of the sixty-five resolutions about reevacuation that the State Defense Committee and the USSR Council of People's Commissars adopted between January 3 and March 9, 1942, concerned Moscow. See his "Evakuatsiia naseleniia iz ugrozhaemykh raionov SSSR v 1941–1942 gg.," in *Naselenie Rossii v XX veke, istoricheskie ocherki*, vol. 2 (Moscow: ROSSPEN, 2001), 77.

54. As cited in USHMM RG-22.020 (GIAChR f. 1263, op. 1, d. 81, l. 39).

55. Manley, *To the Tashkent Station*, 256–260.

56. USHMM RG-22.020 (GIAChR f. 1263, op. 1, d. 81, ll. 47, 52, 55).

57. USHMM RG-22.020 (GIAChR f. 1041, op. 1, d. 599, l. 206).

58. Cf. GARF A-327, op. 2, d. 710, ll. 35–37, and d. 713, op. 2, l. 85.

59. GARF A-327, op. 2, d. 710, ll. 38–42; d. 423, ll. 4–32.

60. GARF A-327, op. 2, d. 428, l. 70; USHMM RG-22.027 (GARF f. A-327, op. 2, d. 440, l. 229).

61. Grinberg et al., *Evakuatsiia v Kazakhstan*, 46–47.

62. Memoirs of Abram Tseitlin, "Kermine," 8.

CHAPTER 8

Far from Home
Soviet and Non-Soviet Railway Workers' Experiences during the Construction of the Baikal-Amur Mainline Railway (BAM), 1974–1984

Christopher J. Ward

While traveling through the People's Republic of Cuba, young BAM laborers endeavored to strengthen the fraternal solidarity of the Cuban and Soviet peoples in the struggle against imperialism and reaction while promoting the dual concerns of democracy and social progress.[1]
—*BAM Builder* (newspaper), 1976

Unfortunately, Komsomol [Young Communist League] BAM Headquarters has just now learned, based on an unexplained and belated receipt of information from the Bureau of International Youth Tourism Sputnik, that certain youth selected to participate in the first Druzhba [Friendship] voyage to Cuba were not the best representatives of BAMer youth. We have received no explanation from Sputnik regarding these deficient young people.[2]
—Report of the Komsomol Central Committee, 1981

To tell the truth, we got along fairly well with the [East] Germans despite their poor command of Russian and their obvious displeasure at having to spend their summers in our mosquito-infested and sweltering camp. Their refusal to share their cigarettes with us really irked us, though.[3]
—Nikolai V. Nikitin, former BAM laborer

THIS CHAPTER EXPLORES the efforts of the Soviet administration, particularly members of the Komsomol (the USSR Young Communist

League) and the USSR Ministry of Transport Construction, to complete the Baikal-Amur Mainline Railway (BAM) by propagandizing the mainline among the peoples of the Soviet Union's allies and through the use of foreign labor in the area in which the railway was being constructed, which is known as the BAM Zone.[4] In the eyes of the project's managers, this accomplishment would serve as a catalyst in increasing trade between the European USSR and the Pacific Rim, particularly with Japan, and thus help reduce the Soviet economy's dependence on trade with Western Europe and the United States.[5] In order to complete the ambitious goal of driving the nearly 2,500-mile mainline across Eurasia, BAM officials made two fundamental decisions. First, they chose to use the incentive of foreign travel, higher pay, and automobile vouchers in an attempt to encourage generally ineffectual domestic cadres to build the railway more quickly and efficiently. Second, BAM administrators used ideological and practical inducements to attract international laborers, most of whom were already studying in the Soviet Union, to assist in the project's construction.[6]

These decisions resulted in the dispatching of thousands of railway construction workers (known as BAMers) who traveled outside the USSR as ostensible ambassadors of Soviet achievements. In addition, BAM officialdom's choices led to the creation of a propaganda campaign that heralded BAM as a showcase of international solidarity and cooperation. Based on my findings in the archives, most importantly the former Komsomol archive at the Russian State Archive of Social-Political History (RGASPI), I hold that the approximately ten thousand BAMers who journeyed abroad damaged the reputation of the project and the Soviet Union in the eyes of some of their hosts. I have also discovered that those from the so-called fraternal nations who encountered the BAMers during their travels outside the USSR learned that their Soviet counterparts were not doctrinaire do-gooders but instead kindred spirits who shared their interest in informal socializing, which often included the use of alcohol and sexual experimentation. Rather than promoting BAM and Soviet state socialism, many BAMers abroad deflected attention from the project through their interactions with other young people. In addition, they gained personal knowledge of the world outside the Soviet Union that possessed different customs and attitudes. Upon their return home, the BAMers related their experiences to their comrades.

In exploring the creation and dissemination of the BAM "myth" as a showcase of international solidarity and cooperation, this chapter also demonstrates that non-Soviet BAMers labored on the project in a distinctly unequal capacity in comparison to their Soviet counterparts. In reaction to the unreliable nature of domestic BAMers, mainline administrators turned to these foreigners, most of whom were recruited from a number of socialist countries or "fraternal nations," to help meet the unrealistic demand that BAM be completed within a decade of its start in 1974. Although the project's leadership used gentle but persistent pressure to convince the heads of a large number of socialist nations to send their youth to BAM in return for Soviet economic and political assistance, non-Soviet youth who worked on the mainline were frequently surprised and even disgruntled at being segregated from their Soviet counterparts while toiling on low-prestige but nevertheless important infrastructure construction assignments, many of which were located in the project's hinterlands.

To the state's considerable embarrassment, these international BAMers witnessed the mainline's corruption, gross inefficiency, and colossal waste of resources firsthand. Later, these individuals undoubtedly related their experiences to those back home, as had the Soviet youth who ventured abroad. Evidence suggests that the foreign BAMers' generally negative impressions of their time on BAM further damaged both their and their countrymen's opinions of the Soviet Union as a political and economic model worthy of emulation. This contributed to a loss of faith in Soviet-style state socialism. It may also have led to a widespread discrediting and, in some cases, an outright rejection of Soviet military and humanitarian assistance in a number of developing nations, particularly among a number of Soviet "client states" in southern and eastern Africa.[7]

FRATERNIZERS AND ENTREPRENEURS: BAMERS ABROAD

I now turn to consider the BAMers who traveled to several nations outside the USSR between 1974 and 1984 onboard special *Druzhba* (Friendship) and *Zvezdnyi* (Starlit) trains and also on cruises.[8] Under Komsomol control, the Druzhba and Zvezdnyi trains were managed not by high-level bureaucrats but by middle-ranking and relatively young Komsomolers, most of whom were under age thirty. While the avowed purpose of the Druzhba and Zvezdnyi journeys was to use foreign travel as a reward for laborers who exceeded their production quotas, Komsomol BAM Headquarters also expected that the recipients would propagandize the mainline's accomplishments. While ostensibly engaging in "socialist fraternization" with the youth of the host nations, Soviet BAMers abroad participated in decidedly nondoctrinaire conversations and occasional drunken soirées that, in the eyes of the mainline's bosses, served the unintended function of casting the BAMers and the Soviet Union in a negative light. For example, railroaders from the western BAM segment who exceeded their production norms by the greatest percentage traveled to East Germany in October 1975 onboard the Zvezdnyi, a special agitational-propaganda train operated from the BAM Zone administrative center of Tynda and various regional headquarters.[9] These 340 individuals were selected according to recommendations submitted to the project's leadership by their peers and supervisors. In addition, all potential travelers required the final approval of Moscow-based Sputnik, the Soviet Bureau of International Youth Tourism, and the Komsomol BAM Construction Headquarters in Tynda.[10] Nearly all of the participants had surpassed production norms that GlavBAMstroi had established with little or no understanding of the varying work conditions at the project's construction sites.[11] Komsomol BAM chief Valentin Sushchevich remarked that the most outstanding of the chosen workers had surpassed their rail-laying and dormitory construction quotas by some 200 percent, lauded the equal division of travel permits between BAMer men and women, and emphasized the fact that many of the most successful builders came from Moscow and Leningrad.[12] Yet he also admitted to his superiors in Moscow that the influence of personal connections (*blat*) and a desire to impress officials in the center also played a role in deciding who got to journey abroad. Problems during the voyages of the supposedly "pacesetting" BAMers arose almost immediately after their travels began. In fact, Sushchevich's deputy Iurii Galmakov felt compelled to apologize to Egon Krenz of the East German Union of Free Youth (FDJ) for some BAMers' behavior during their tours of the Lenin Museum in Leipzig and Frederick the Great's Sans Souci palace in Potsdam. Somewhat embarrassedly, Galmakov admitted to Krenz that Soviet youth had "defiled" the palace's gardens by frequent spitting and urinating in public. Galmakov also noted that certain unnamed travelers "violated social order" and "failed to adequately serve as agitators for the project" by neglecting to engage in a discussion of BAM with their socialist comrades. Instead of inspiring the East Germans to follow the Soviet example and undertake such a "grand exploit" as BAM, Galmakov confessed that the young travelers drank to excess and participated in "immoral behavior" (one guesses that this included sexual activity) with East German youth while visiting Berlin, Leipzig, Weimar, and Dresden.[13]

Writing in 1976, Sushchevich displayed a decidedly more negative attitude toward the BAMers abroad than he had in the previous year. The Komsomol BAM chief noted that the young people who had traveled aboard a Druzhba train to East Germany and Hungary "violated social order" by "fraternizing with members of the opposite sex" in both nations.[14] In the same report, Sushchevich stated that several participants confessed to frequent intoxication during debriefings with their Komsomol chaperones, most of whom were ten to fifteen years their senior, after returning to the Soviet Union.[15] The generational dynamic is important to note, as archival documents reveal that the chaperones and the younger workers often did not interact socially. Instead, at the conclusion of a day's structured activities in a particular town or city, they divided themselves into separate groups, both of which apparently consumed large amounts of local alcoholic beverages. Undoubtedly, the older BAM representatives "allowed" the younger cohort to socialize more or less freely with local youth because the workers outnumbered their chaperones by an average of twenty to one.[16]

In the eyes of the project's administrators, the behavior of BAMers chosen to travel outside the Soviet Union did not improve in the 1980s. In 1981, Sushchevich's successor, Iurii Verbitskii, criticized the actions of some two hundred BAMers who boarded the first Druzhba train to steam through Cuba after arriving in Cuba from the Soviet Union. Verbitskii reported that bribe-accepting Sputnik functionaries permitted BAMers "who [are] not the best examples of 'pace-setting' young workers" to slip through the project's personnel selection system and to travel to the island. Verbitskii went on to the describe the BAMers' conduct in Cuba as "frequently impolite" and "unduly familiar" vis-à-vis the local population, noting the damage done to Soviet-Cuban relations by the BAMers' boorish behavior, specifically their complete lack of Spanish-language skills and general ignorance of Cuban culture. Verbitskii lamented the BAMers' ignorance of Cuban history after the 1959 popular revolution led by Fidel Castro and Ernesto "Che" Guevara in the USSR's closest ally in the Caribbean and Latin America.[17]

Another objective of the BAMer abroad campaign was not only to improve relations with the youth of the "fraternal nations" but also to boost those nations' impression of the visiting Soviet youth. In no country was this more obvious than in Hungary, whose population still possessed a fresh memory of the 1956 Soviet intervention. In 1975, the Komsomol BAM apparatus arranged for fifty-six winners of a "First Year of the Tenth Five-Year Plan: A Pacesetting Finish" competition to meet Hungarian youth studying in the USSR, listen to a series of lectures on the history of the Magyar people, and view a number of films on Hungary's geography and culture in an effort to foster "international friendship" in preparation for their voyage to Hungary onboard a Druzhba train the following year.[18] This group of BAMers, however, was not to travel to Hungary with a small number of overextended chaperones. In an attempt to put the best possible face on both BAM and the Soviet people for the Hungarians, the Komsomol chose some thirty-three party members, each of whom was involved in the staging of a decidedly unpopular exhibit of paintings by a number of Hungarian artists the previous year in the BAM Zone towns of Severobaikal'sk and Shushensk, to accompany the competition winners to Hungary and serve as a "stabilizing force" to prevent further embarrassment.[19]

Despite the presence of the dutiful party members, the winners of the campaign fared no better than their fellow BAMers in creating a favorable impression of their project and nation among the Hungarians. Writing in 1976, Sushchevich noted that many of those who traveled to Hungary were guilty of repeated "violations of production discipline and social order."[20] Sushchevich also remarked with considerable alarm that a significant portion of those selected for travel had, in their haste to exceed production quotas and receive permission to travel outside the Soviet Union, contributed to "deficiencies in dormitory construction."[21] Another ill-fated trip abroad consisted of a 1981 voyage by a mixed group of young

Komsomolers and professional railroaders to Cuba, Vietnam, North Korea, and the Philippines on board a Druzhba steamer, with which the Komsomol intended to cement ties between the Soviet Union and these socialist nations (with the exception of the Philippines), each of which sold goods to the USSR at fixed prices.[22] In exchange for being hosted by the Cubans, BAMers would assist in the construction of the Havana to Santiago de Cuba–Central Railway while on the island and also work with Vietnamese railway authorities in Hanoi and Ho Chi Minh City (commonly known as Saigon).[23] The promised assistance of the BAMers while traveling through these countries never materialized, however, as the Komsomol BAM Headquarters blamed the Union of BAM Transport Workers for creating a poorly organized itinerary and allowing "less than desirable elements" to participate in the trip.[24] Because of the organization's lax standards, the Komsomol apparatus was as much to blame for the poor ideological quality of those selected for the cruise to Asia and the Caribbean, since it had the final say on who was to leave the country.

In another effort to combat the BAMers' glacial construction pace and lax labor discipline, the project's Komsomol managers arranged for prize-winning laborers of such socialist competitions as the "I Am the Master of the Project" campaign to travel to a number of Soviet bloc countries, including East Germany, Hungary, Poland, and Cuba.[25] This movement and similar competitions were plagued by the same problems of "undisciplined" BAM cadres who cast themselves, the project, and the USSR as a whole as much less doctrinaire and industrious than intended by Soviet officialdom. The "I Am the Master of the Project" campaign received the brunt of official criticism. In 1983, Vladimir Shcherbinin, head of the Komsomol BAM Headquarters, singled out young BAMers who had traveled to Cuba and Hungary for the purpose of publicizing the mainline and "providing an example of Soviet achievement in railway construction worthy of emulation."[26] Shcherbinin also castigated these individuals for failing to sufficiently foster a "sense of socialist competition" among their Cuban and Hungarian comrades by expressing more interest in imbibing local spirits than trumpeting their construction achievements. Furthermore, Shcherbinin noted with great concern, as Sushchevich had earlier, that many participants in BAM promotion campaigns in both Cuba and Hungary displayed "irresponsibility" toward their socialist obligations as representatives of the project by failing even to mention BAM to their Cuban and Hungarian comrades.²⁷ Interestingly, Shcherbinin placed the blame for the failure of the campaign not with the Komsomol but with his organization's convenient target, the USSR Ministry of Transportation's Union of BAM Transport Workers, which he hinted permitted known "violators of social order" to go abroad by accepting "favors" (i.e., bribes) from competition participants. Shcherbinin boldly accused the union of exaggerating descriptions of its members' accomplishments and withholding information of criminal wrongdoing by supposedly "outstanding" transport workers whom it had selected to travel to Cuba and Hungary.

Older BAM representatives (those older than the Komsomol cutoff age of thirty-five) also ignored official expectations regarding their behavior while overseas. The Komsomol archive contains dozens of reports of high-level *apparatchiki* (a commonly used pejorative term for bureaucrats) who rewarded themselves with travel to nations located outside the "fraternal circle," shopped for goods that were in short supply at home, and obtained scarce building materials for their work brigades. For example, in 1981 and again in 1984, a "special group" of high-level mainline administrators spent over two weeks in Japan.²⁸ These individuals' purported purpose in visiting the island nation was to meet with "young Japanese socialists" to discuss Tokyo's stance on the disputed "Northern Territories" after the 1973 visit of Japanese prime minister Kakuei Tanaka to Moscow failed to resolve the longstanding territorial issue.²⁹ Reports made after both groups' return from Japan, however, indicated that members of the BAM delegation ignored their official purpose and instead purchased electronic equipment and discussed trading Soviet timber for Japanese tractors and cranes with representatives of well-known *keiretsu* while supposedly "bolstering fraternal relations with our Japanese communist comrades."³⁰ In fact, these reports made no mention of any contact whatsoever between BAM officials and pro-Moscow Japanese communists.³¹

While the intended purpose of the Druzhba train trips and cruises and the higher-level "special groups" was to propagandize BAM and to encourage platonic "socialist fraternization" with the youth of the host nations, the fact that the BAMers who participated in such journeys often engaged in unapproved activities revealed the average BAMer's lack of ideological dedication that cast the BAMers and the USSR in a different light than that desired by the state. For the young people who witnessed and participated in the BAMers' debaucheries, the "Path to the Future" led not to communism but to something far more desirable. Indeed, the opportunity to leave the Soviet Union, if only for a short time, was a prize for exceptionally productive BAMers and undoubtedly served as a motivational tool for those eager to see the outside world for themselves. The fact that most BAMers acted as typical young people and not as buttoned-down ambassadors of Marxism-Leninism came as a surprise or a disappointment to the dedicated Komsomol BAM officials who strove to enlist foreign support for BAM.[32]

"ALL WE DO IS INSTALL TOILETS!": FOREIGNERS ON THE MAINLINE

I now turn to the experiences of approximately ten thousand non-Soviet youth who labored on BAM between 1974 and 1984.[33] First, the BAM administration worked hard to include foreign workers on the railway for both political and economic reasons.[34] Second, the older generation of BAM officials remembered the efficient and cost-effective forced labor undertaken by German and Japanese prisoners of war who had toiled on an earlier BAM attempt from 1943 to 1953.[35] During the mainline's heyday, the project's leadership assumed that foreign youth might be induced to help build BAM not through coercion but with the promise that they would receive valuable hands-on training and education in their respective professions or academic disciplines while toiling on the mainline. In its desperation to complete BAM within a decade, the project's Komsomol apparatus actively recruited foreigners who were already studying in the USSR as well as young people not in the Soviet Union. In turn, it consciously risked discrediting the USSR in the foreigners' eyes by exposing them firsthand to the railway's (and the entire nation's) serious deficiencies. By and large, foreigners' brigades toiled on projects of little or no prestige and were generally segregated from the Soviet detachments with which they were supposed to be cooperating. While BAM propaganda ignored the fact that Soviet and foreign construction columns often worked apart from one another, the image of a "multinational" (*mezhdunarodnyi*) endeavor was in reality an environment where Russian was the lingua franca and the interaction between workers from supposedly "fraternal" socialist nations and the USSR was heavily curtailed by the state.

LATIN AMERICAN BAMERS

Archival sources also point to the preponderance of official attention within the BAM bureaucracy given to actively recruiting young people from the so-called fraternal circle of nations. In particular, the project's leadership viewed Latin American and Caribbean youth as fertile sources of potential labor because of the close relationship between the Soviet Union and the emerging socialist governments of the region, particularly Cuba. BAM officials were encouraged by the seemingly inexorable spread of socialism among the peoples of Latin America and the Caribbean as evidence of the increasing popularity of Soviet- and Cuban-aided "peoples' fronts" in Nicaragua, Chile, and Argentina during the early 1970s.[36]

In order to encourage Cubans already in the Soviet Union and those still in Cuba to take an interest in coming to the BAM Zone, project chief Valentin Sushchevich initiated a "mutual exchange program" between BAMers and laborers on Cuba's Havana to Santiago de Cuba–Central Railway, which ostensibly would strengthen social and professional ties between railroaders of both nations.[37] In reality, however, the "mutual exchange program" evolved into an elaborate façade that concealed a decidedly one-way transfer of Cuban young people to the USSR in return for Soviet humanitarian and military assistance. The job of enticing the Cuban Comité Nacional de la Unión de Jóvenes Comunistas (National Committee of the Union of Young Communists), also known as the UJC, to send its members to the BAM Zone fell to deputy director Vladimir Mukonin of the Komsomol BAM Headquarters. As part of the effort to convince Havana to part with a substantial portion of its best young workers, Mukonin wrote in 1977 that the "pride of the Soviet people in BAM mirrors that of the Cuban nation in the Havana to Santiago de Cuba–Central Railway," and that despite obstacles in the process of completing both lines, both BAM and the Cuban Central Railway would serve as the Komsomol and UJC's "gifts to their [respective] peoples."[40] Mukonin proposed an "exchange of party materials and personnel," requesting that the UJC send Cuban volunteers to help build BAM as a part of a "socialist competition campaign" between the young people of each nation.[38]

In 1977–1978, José Esquina of the UJC agreed to arrange the details of a "socialist competition" between the builders of the Havana to Santiago de Cuba–Central Railway and BAM *after* members of his organization currently in Cuba and those already studying in the Soviet Union had been dispatched to the BAM Zone. Esquina's only stated condition for sending members of his organization to BAM was that representatives of the UJC's daily Juventud Rebelde (Rebellious Youth) be allowed to accompany their comrades in order to cover "the BAMers' successful rail-laying methods."[39] Esquina also invited Soviet BAMers to the Eleventh World Festival of Youth and Students in Havana, which the UJC sponsored. The festival, which the Castro government named the Festival of Anti-Imperialist Solidarity, Peace and Friendship, was held in honor of the sixtieth anniversary of the October Revolution and in commemoration of the twenty-fifth anniversary of the July 1953 assault by young Cuban revolutionaries, including Castro himself, on the Moncada barracks in Santiago de Cuba.[40] By attending the World Festival of Youth and Students, Esquina maintained that youth from "the birthplaces of José Martí and Vladimir Lenin" would strengthen the already close ties between the Soviet and Cuban peoples.[41] What Esquina did not mention, however, was that his organization wanted the fifty-odd Soviet BAMers attending the festival to remain in Cuba after the end of the event and help with the construction of the Havana to Santiago de Cuba–Central Railway. Vladimir Mukonin acquiesced to Esquina's recruitment tactic with the implicit understanding that the exchange of the labor of fifty of his workers for the skills of the several thousand Cubans who came to work on BAM served the purposes of both men. Another result of the Mukonin-Esquina correspondence was a "Joint Soviet-Cuban Agreement on Socialist Competition between the Young Builders of the Baikal-Amur Mainline Railway and the Central Cuban Railway," in which Leonid Brezhnev and Fidel Castro affirmed both nations' commitment to completing their respective railways.[42] UJC officials eventually sent more than ten thousand Cubans to BAM over a ten-year period, a time in which Soviet technical aid to Cuban railroaders laboring on the Havana to Santiago de Cuba–Central Railway line increased markedly. This spike in Soviet aid to the embryonic Cuban railway system can certainly be viewed as "compensation" for the use of so many young Cubans, some of whom did not return to their homeland for several years after their stints in the USSR on BAM.

WARSAW PACT BAMERS

Students from the Warsaw Pact nations, and East Germany in particular, played an important and, in relation to the Latin American BAMers described earlier, a more publicized role in BAM construction. Accounts in the BAM Zone media tended to profile youth who echoed the official positivism regarding the project and, most importantly for the propagandists' purposes, allowed themselves to be photographed on the job.[43] For example, in the summer of 1975, correspondent V. Popov of *Vostochno-Sibirskaia pravda* (East Siberian Truth) described the dormitory-painting exploits of East Germans Heiner Seifert and Dieter Lindig, students at the Leningrad Polytechnic Institute who had volunteered to become BAMers.[44] Curiously, Popov's story does not contain interviews with Seifert and Lindig themselves but rather is written from a distant perspective in which the reader learns nothing about the two East Germans except that they painted one side of a five-story building in just one week. In this fashion, Popov's contribution differs markedly from similar profiles of Soviet BAMers, which invariably contained detailed descriptions of the workers themselves, including their hometowns, opinions of life in Siberia, and impressions of the project.[45] The journalist now faced the prospect of not writing the article at all and risking condemnation from his superiors, who wished the foreign component of the mainline emphasized. Instead, he chose to pen a personality-free account that focused on the Germans' tasks instead of their opinions of BAM.

As with Popov, the BAM "hagiographer" Tatiana Tomina chose her subjects based on their nationality rather than their importance or uniqueness as individuals. In the 1983 edition of *BAM—A Panorama of a Multinational Project*, Tomina related the story of one Vladek Zaichek, a Czechoslovak Communist Party official and BAM veteran who met with the head of GlavBAMstroi. In her essay "Vladek Is Going to BAM

Again," Tomina ignored the achievements of Zaichek and his brigade of Czechoslovak railroaders. Instead, Tomina emphasized the sense of privilege and "deep honor" Zaichek felt after his "brotherly conversation" with the leader of the BAM hierarchy.[46] The mainline's administration also encouraged foreign BAMers who could write well in Russian to contribute articles to newspapers across the BAM Zone and Soviet Union. Aspiring East German engineer Kristian Brückner wrote in *Vechernii Kishinev* (Evening Kishinev), the newspaper of his "adopted hometown," that his experience in building the BAM settlement of Zvezdnyi alongside other foreigners endowed him with "socialist fire" and strengthened his character despite the primitive living and working conditions at his team's worksite.[47] As with Popov's story, Brückner's submission defied the convention of most BAM newspaper articles, but for different reasons. First, the fact that Brückner mentioned the harsh circumstances of daily life confronted by all BAMers is unusual. Normally, the genre of BAM worker profiling tended to marginalize the climatic and topographical impediments to BAM construction, while Brückner devoted an entire paragraph to describing the swarms of insects that bedeviled him and his comrades, which other writers dismiss as temporary annoyances that will soon be eliminated as part of the inevitable Promethean triumph of Soviet technology over nature. Second, Brückner's article appeared not in a BAM Zone publication likely to be read by the workers themselves but in a newspaper for the residents of Kishinev in the far-off Moldavian Soviet Socialist Republic. This piece never appeared in the BAM Zone or national press, probably because Brückner's frank description of his brigade's frustrations with Siberian mosquitoes and mud led the Komsomol leadership in Moscow to believe that such an article might weaken the already fragile morale of the BAMer cadres, Brückner's expression of his "socialist fire" notwithstanding. The impressions of East German Roland Grosse in the newspaper *Severnaia pravda* (Northern Truth) confirmed that "no language barrier" existed between German, Mongolian, and Soviet youth within a *Start* (Start) brigade based at the BAM town of Udokan. Grosse, along with the other members of *Start*, learned to sing songs "about BAM, friendship, and peace" in Mongolian and German in addition to Russian.[48] According to Smirnova's report, Grosse beamed with pride when describing the "East Germany Day" held by the German contingent, and noted that the Udokan authorities promised Grosse's co-nationals and the Mongolians a tour of the cities of the Soviet Union after completion of their work.⁴⁹

Despite such representations as Popov's, Brückner's, and Grosse's, some who visited and worked on BAM did remark on the discontent and occasional disillusionment of non-Soviet BAMers. East Germans Heino Westfal and Dieter Ostertag viewed BAM as a project that would help the Soviet Union reach its "glorious communist future" by expediting the flow of goods and raw materials between the eastern and western USSR.⁵⁰ Westfal and Ostertag, however, were confused and disappointed that their assignments did not include any railway construction assignments. As with the Chileans, the East Germans did not lay track alongside their Soviet comrades as they had been promised, but installed plumbing as a part of a brigade of Czechoslovaks, Poles, and Hungarians in which Russian was the only lingua franca, albeit a decidedly weak one for many.

Another factor that compounded the foreigners' dissatisfaction was the communication problem within such ethnically diverse brigades composed of youth who spoke little or no Russian and whose native tongues were often unrelated to one another. This lack of mutual intelligibility resulted in the formation of national cliques that worked and socialized apart from those of other nationalities, Soviet or non-Soviet.⁵¹ The differentiation by language among the youth of the supposedly "multinational" BAM revealed the fiction of a unified, linguistically homogenous labor force that used Russian in its construction of the "Path to the Future" instead of the realities of cultural and linguistic separation.⁵² The Komsomol archives show that BAM administrators were cognizant of and concerned with the foreign workers' less-than-rosy opinions of BAM. In a representative report to the Komsomol BAM Construction headquarters, A. D. Kniazev of the agitational-propaganda train *Komsomol'skaia pravda* (Komsomol Truth) reported that "several dozen" students from a number of Warsaw Pact and developing nations working within a particular Vitiaz' (Champion) detachment frequently complained to him about their current assignment, which consisted mainly of installing toilets and painting buildings in the newly founded settlements of Lena and Taiura in the summer of 1975.⁵³ When the foreigners expressed a strong desire to be transferred to a different worksite where they could actually lay rails,

Kniazev was unable to accommodate them after explaining that "all construction billets [were] currently full."[54]

What Kniazev could not admit to his charges was that the foreign BAMers under his supervision were prohibited by the Komsomol from laboring on the railway itself because of official concerns that they would learn of its casual construction pace firsthand.[55] Kniazev also reported that other Soviet advisors working with the Vitiaz' detachment reported their embarrassment at having to explain the lack of functional construction equipment and knowledgeable supervisors to their foreign guests, who in many instances knew more about their jobs than their bosses.[56] The exclusion of foreigners from meaningful assignments at a time when the mainline needed as much skilled labor as possible not only impeded construction progress but also further discredited BAM in the minds of many youth from abroad, all of whose primary knowledge and opinions of the Soviet Union derived from their experiences on the project. Consequently, the disillusionment of all BAMers, Soviet and non-Soviet, began well before the Gorbachev era as other observers have argued, although this disenfranchisement was not publicized until the mid-1980s, by which time the mainline had lost the nation's (and much of the world's) interest.[57]

In addition to those who worked on BAM under the direct supervision of the Komsomol, international students enrolled at the Patrice Lumumba Peoples' Friendship University (Universitet Druzhby Narodov imeni Patrisa Lumumby) in Moscow also contributed to the endeavor.[58] During their summers away from school, these students served as members of the International Student Construction Brigade, known colloquially as the "Friendship Brigade."[59] As with the Vitiaz' detachment mentioned earlier, the Lumumba University students worked in an unequal capacity vis-à-vis their Soviet counterparts. Beginning with the Friendship 1975 program, some three hundred students from Lumumba University undertook such disparate tasks as fire station construction, school renovation, warehouse construction, sewage system installation, and dormitory erection. The Friendship Brigade served as a cheaper labor force than Soviet workers.[60]

BAM administrators split the hundreds of Lumumba University students who arrived in the BAM Zone each summer into two groups. The first cohort included BAMers who possessed at least a modicum of Russian-language training (generally Poles, East Germans, Hungarians,

Mongolians, Bulgarians, and Czechoslovaks), while those lacking any Russian language skill whatsoever (including Latin Americans, Africans, and South and Southeast Asians) were sent to a separate location and given the dirtiest and most arduous assignments in Siberia's sweltering summer temperatures, amid clouds of insects. The archives do not reveal why those who could not speak Russian were segregated and given the most difficult tasks, but it is plausible that BAM Headquarters, not knowing exactly what to do with the developing world BAMers, sent these individuals to jobs that required the least instruction and supervision.[61]

Both BAM Zone and national media outlets strove to publicize members of the Friendship Brigade whose ideological profiles matched the state's image of the ideal BAMer as a committed socialist who was zealous in his or her desire to complete the mainline. One such individual was Bolivian Gonsalo Alvarado, who was among the first wave of Lumumba University students to reach the BAM Zone in the summer of 1974. Alvarado's father, a prominent Bolivian communist, was killed by "fascist bandits."[62] Subsequently, Gonsalo fled Bolivia to pursue an engineering education in the USSR.[63] Along with other Friendship Brigaders from Nigeria, Bangladesh, and India, Alvarado's detachment labored to build structures along the Abakan-Taishet BAM segment at the project's western terminus. Journalist Iurii Petruk proclaimed that the Friendship Brigaders' activities "increase[d] the technical knowledge of all people, not just Soviet citizens."[64] In reality, however, the topographical and geologic conditions of BAM Zone construction differed markedly from the environs of Alvarado's comrades. As a result, the Brigaders' skills learned in Siberia would prove to be of little value back home.[65]

In addition to luring foreign youth to join BAM with promises of a technical education, BAM administrators also courted foreign industrial magnates and political dignitaries from abroad in an effort to secure more laborers. For example, the bosses of Nizhneangarsktransstroi regularly invited Hungarian officials to visit the BAM Zone between 1974 and 1984 in a bid to form "sponsorship agreements" between the mainline and Hungarian industries.[66] In reality, these relationships were used by the BAMers to acquire high-quality finished goods from Soviet client states for little or no cost and without Moscow's knowledge. This process was reflected in a 1977 visit to Severobaikal'sk by a group of administrators from the Videoton electronics factory in Budapest. During this trip, BAM officials received a number of "gifts" in the form of record players, televisions, and other items from Videoton representatives. Not completely placated, the Nizhneangarsktransstroi bosses requested that young workers from Videoton come to the BAM Zone the following summer for a "tour of the area" in order to "further strengthen fraternal relations and improve social contacts."[67] This was never intended to be a vacation, of course, as the young Hungarians were assigned to BAM construction soon after their arrival. Records of similar visits by delegates, including the Soviet-controlled Committee of European Youth Organizations, reveal why the Hungarians from the Videoton factory and other visiting foreign groups agreed to what appears at first glance to be such an unequal relationship with their Soviet hosts. First, the BAM apparatus always provided the delegations' transportation to and from the BAM Zone free of charge, and not by rail as one might expect, but by much more expensive airplane. Once in the area, BAM administrators treated their foreign guests to "complimentary production examples" (i.e., free samples) of foreign-made cigarettes, mineral water, and alcohol purchased by BAMers while overseas. These bribes also included luxury food items that neither the foreigners nor their Soviet hosts could easily locate at home.[68] In addition, BAM officials made certain that visiting dignitaries collected "stipends" (often various amounts of foreign currency) ostensibly for "the purchase of BAM souvenirs and books," which in reality were nothing more than kickbacks.[69] Both the "production examples" and "stipends," along with the "comradely company" of the project's young female secretaries, helped ensure that the foreign dignitaries took home positive impressions of BAM that helped reduce their hesitation about sending their youth to help build another country's railway.

Although bribed foreign officials directed some "volunteers" to the mainline, the project suffered from a constant shortage of qualified and motivated builders. Despite this deficiency, not all foreign students who wished to participate in the construction of BAM were allowed to do so. In 1974, East German high school student Kirsten Radtke wrote the Komsomol Central Committee in Moscow to express her desire to travel and possibly work in the BAM Zone. In an undated reply, administrator V. Aldokhin applauded Radtke's enthusiasm but informed the youngster that she had to wait two years and receive training in an occupation required by the project. Only then, Aldokhin stipulated, could Radtke apply to come to BAM as a member of an East German student construction brigade. Another letter, this one a November 1974 communication from a group of Dresden students, eagerly requested a copy of the Komsomol-published book *BAM—nachalo* (BAM—The Beginning) and asked about the feasibility of working on the mainline. The Komsomol chose to ignore the Dresdeners' request because of a fictional "shortage of BAM publications," which it produced in the hundreds of thousands.[70] Apparently, Makarov could not confirm the "political reliability" of the East Germans (i.e., their membership status within the Komsomol-like Union of Free German Youth), and thus their attempt to join the mainline was ended abruptly.

Two Czechoslovak students petitioned the Komsomol in 1978 to allow them and a small group of others to work on the railway and then tour the BAM Zone and other regions of the USSR. The Czechoslovaks stated that their classmates were interested in the "construction of BAM itself, but also in what kind of people are working there and what working conditions are like in the BAM Zone generally."[71] The youth organization's curt response was that "construction in areas approved for visitation ha[d] not yet begun," and in a blatant misrepresentation of fact remarked that "the Komsomol [could] not invite any foreign students to the region."[72] The BAM administration rejected dozens of similar requests to visit the BAM Zone. Bulgarian students wrote the offices of the newspaper *BAM* in 1979 after hearing about BAM. The Bulgarians had studied the project and composed a lecture titled "BAM—The Project of the Century," which they delivered to a combined audience of over five thousand people. After learning of the students' desire to see the BAM Zone for themselves, BAM chief Valentin Sushchevich chose not to respond directly and instead forwarded the letter to the Komsomol's sister organization in Bulgaria.[73] When asked to comment on his treatment of this and other requests by foreigners to visit and work on BAM, Sushchevich replied that "they [the young foreigners] were not serious in their desire to come to the BAM Zone ... [and] that their requests to come to the Soviet Union were possibly motivated by 'external influences.'" Sushchevich's use of this term indicated his suspicion that the West or other enemies of the

USSR sought to place spies within the USSR with the ultimate objective of learning more about "the Mainline of the Century."[74]

INTERNATIONALISM ACHIEVED?

In conclusion, the state's dual-pronged strategy to both publicize BAM and recruit labor for the endeavor failed to achieve its intended goals. The mainline's administration rewarded even haphazardly chosen, less qualified domestic workers with travel outside the Soviet Union. In addition, many young BAMers shirked their officially mandated "social responsibilities" and instead used the opportunity of relaxed adult supervision to "eat, drink, and be merry," as many given such new freedoms often do. Instead of providing the world's socialist nations with shining examples of industrious and socially conscious young people, the "BAMer abroad" program had the reverse effect of either sullying or altering non-Soviet citizens' opinions of BAM, and by extension the USSR in general. In sum, the Soviet state, through the Komsomol and other official organizations, failed to employ BAMers who traveled abroad as ambassadors of Soviet achievements. This was due in no small part to the railroaders' less than admirable but nevertheless completely understandable behavior. Furthermore, the lack of competent and dedicated Soviet BAMers compelled the project's supervisors to recall the efficient and cost-free labor of German and Japanese POWs on the earlier BAM with nostalgia. Viewing the young people within the Soviet Union's "fraternal circle of nations" and the Warsaw Pact as an economical and highly motivated pool of labor, the Komsomol strove to lure foreign students of the 1970s and 1980s to the BAM Zone. Its promise to the foreigners that their education would be enhanced by laying track alongside the USSR's BAMers, however, proved ultimately hollow.

While most foreign BAMers never enjoyed the opportunity to toil alongside their Soviet comrades, the project's administration was unable to shield them from the blatant inefficiency and waste on what the Komsomol and CPSU heralded as the most important public works project of the Brezhnev years. Perhaps even more importantly, the government's utter inability to convince either foreign or Soviet BAMers of the mainline's progressive nature and international flavor starkly pointed to the lack of dynamism and flexibility within the official propaganda machine that churned out the BAM "myth" during the era of "developed socialism." By the mid-1980s, the state's grasp on this component of the BAM "myth" slipped as frustrated and apathetic BAMers from both the Soviet Union and abroad returned home to tell family and friends about the dead ends that defined the "Path to the Future."

NOTES

1. V. Vezbakh, "Miting druzhby i solidarnosti," *Stroitel' BAM*, August 5, 1976, 4.
2. Russian State Archive of Social-Political History, Moscow (hereafter RGASPI), f. 27-M, op. 1, d. 299, l. 9.
3. Nikolai V. Nikitin, former BAMer and student at the Tomsk Polytechnic Institute, interview by the author, April 19, 2000, Moscow.
4. For a broader perspective on the history of BAM construction during the Brezhnev years, see Christopher Ward, *Brezhnev's Folly: The Building of BAM and Late Soviet Socialism* (Pittsburgh, PA: University of Pittsburgh Press, 2009). Portions of this chapter appeared earlier in that work.
5. RGASPI, f. 27-M, op. 1, d. 279, l. 6.
6. For a standard explanation of the ideological precepts behind Soviet relations with developing countries both inside and outside the so-called circle of fraternal nations (a commonly used term describing an array of mostly socialist countries in Eastern Europe, Africa, Asia, and Central and South America), see B. Ponomarev, "Aktual'nye problemy teorii mirovogo revoliutsionnogo protsessa," *Kommunist* 15 (October 1971): 37–71; and R. Ul'ianovskii, "Nekotorye voprosy nekapitalisticheskogo razvitiia osvobodivshikhsia stran," *Kommunist* 1 (January 1966): 109–119. Both Ponomarev and Ul'ianovskii state that the developing nations of Latin America, Africa, Asia, and the Caribbean count on the Soviet Union's assistance in throwing off the dual yokes of capitalism and colonialism. Furthermore, both theorists declare that the USSR will assist all developing nations in rejecting foreign intervention through the granting of economic and military assistance.
7. I submit the nations of Angola and Mozambique (both Portuguese colonies from the 1890s until 1974) in southern Africa, and Ethiopia (under titular Italian control between 1895 and 1939) in eastern Africa, as representative examples of former Soviet "client states" that in the middle of several divisive conflicts during the 1970s and 1980s began to question the viability and practicality of Marxism-Leninism as a reputable developmental paradigm for postcolonial Africa. See Richard B. Remnek, "Soviet Policy in the Horn of Africa: The Decision to Intervene," in *The Soviet Union in the Third World: Successes and Failures*, ed. Robert H. Donaldson (Boulder, CO: Westview Press, 1981), 125–149.
8. RGASPI, f. 27-M, op. 1, d. 299, l. 9.
9. RGASPI, f. 1-M, op. 65, d. 28, ll. 34–35.

10. RGASPI, f. 27-M, op. 1, d. 39, ll. 2, 16.

11. GlavBAMstroi, a division of the USSR Ministry of Transport Construction, was responsible for overseeing and completing all BAM-related rail and building construction.

12. RGASPI, f. 27-M, op. 1, d. 39, l. 16.

13. RGASPI, f. 27-M, op. 1, d. 77, l. 82–85; RGASPI, f. 27-M, op. 1, d. 74, ll. 33–34.

14. RGASPI, f. 27-M, op. 1, d. 77, ll. 82–83.

15. Ibid.

16. Ibid.

17. RGASPI, f. 1-M, op. 65, d. 438a, l. 29.

18. RGASPI, f. 27-M, op. 1, d. 105, l. 165; RGASPI, f. 1-M, op. 65, d. 28, l. 123; RGASPI, f. 27-M, op. 1, d. 100, ll. 17, 79, 81.

19. RGASPI, f. 27-M, op. 1, d. 74, ll. 62–63; RGASPI, f. 27-M, op. 1, d. 77, ll. 3–4. BAM deputy chief Iurii Gal'makov criticized Ivan Rekhlov, director of the Shushensk Portrait Gallery, for failing to publicize the Hungarian art exhibition, thus leading to the show's paltry attendance.

20. RGASPI, f. 27-M, op. 1, d. 105, l. 165.

21. RGASPI, f. 27-M, op. 1, d. 32, l. 1–2.

22. Soviet ties with Vietnam were especially close after the Southeast Asian nation's invasion of Kampuchea/Cambodia in 1978 and China's retaliatory attack on Vietnam the following year, which the Vietnamese viewed as an assault on their national sovereignty and an aggressive strike of Sinoization. See Douglas Pike, "The USSR and Vietnam," in Donaldson, *The Soviet Union in the Third World*, 251–266. Furthermore, both Cuba and Vietnam served as members of the Soviet-controlled Council for Mutual Economic Assistance (CMEA) and were recipients of generous economic assistance from the USSR. See Ramesh Thakur and Carlyle A. Thayer, *Soviet Relations with India and Vietnam* (New York: St. Martin's Press, 1992), 3, 5, 13.

23. RGASPI, f. 27-M, op. 1, d. 252, ll. 21–22.

24. RGASPI, f. 27-M, op. 1. d. 253, l. 122, 124.

25. Hilary Pilkington remarks that BAM's "socialist competition drives" served as the model for such campaigns nationwide. See Pilkington, *Russia's Youth and Its Culture: A Nation's Constructors and Constructed* (London: Routledge, 1994), 95; and Thomas O. Cushman, "Ritual and the Sacralization of the Secular: Social Sources of Conformity and Order in Soviet Society," Ph.D. diss., University of Virginia, 1987, 122–124.

26. RGASPI, f. 27-M, op. 1, d. 300, l. 22.

27. Ibid.; RGASPI, f. 27-M, op. 1, d. 299, l. 10.

28. The need to strengthen trade with Japan occupied an important position in the regime's effort to legitimize the mainline. At a 1974 meeting of the Trade Unions Central Committee, USSR minister of transport construction E. F. Kozhevnikov stated that "credits from Japan" were necessary to ensure the project's on-time completion. In a secret document dated September 19, 1974, the Khabarovsk krai CPSU organization stated that "the second transcontinental way [i.e., BAM] with its connection to the ocean will assist in the improvement of economic ties between the Soviet Union and the countries of the Pacific basin." See State Archive of the Russian Federation (GARF), f. R-5474, op. 20, d. 8199, l. 124; and RGASPI, f. 27-M, op. 1, d. 2, l. 15.

29. After World War II, the Soviet Union and Japan began an as of yet fruitless process of negotiating ownership of the three southernmost islands in the Kuriles chain (Etorofu, Kunashiri, and Shikotan), and a group of islets (the Habomais), which were seized by

the Red Army in 1945. For a detailed discussion of the Northern Territories controversy, see Kimie Hara, *Japanese-Soviet/Russian Relations since 1945: A Difficult Peace* (London: Routledge, 1998), 13–33 and 113–150.

30. This Japanese term describes large, family-owned monopolies such as Mitsubishi, Sony, and Sumitomo that played a strong economic and political role in the Japanese oligarchical system.

31. RGASPI, f. 27-M, op. 1, d. 253, l. 123; RGASPI, f. 27-M, op. 1, d. 332, l. 10.

32. Nikolai N. Shtikov, Irkutsk Pedagogical Institute and former BAM Zone resident, interview by the author, May 7, 2000, Irkutsk.

33. Ponomarev, "Aktual'nye problemy teorii mirovogo revoliutsionnogo protsessa," 37–71; R. Ul'ianovskii, "Nekotorye voprosy nekapitalisticheskogo razvitiia osvobodivshikhsia stran," *Kommunist* 1 (January 1966): 109–119.

34. Nikitin and Shtikov interviews.

35. Olga P. Elant'seva, "Iz istorii stroitel'stva zheleznoi dorogi Komsomol'sk-Sovetskaia Gavan' (1943–1945 gg.)," *Otechestvennye arkhivy* 3 (1995): 90–100. The BAM railway examined in this chapter was the third Baikal-Amur Mainline railway. The original BAM was built between 1932 and 1941 by Gulag prisoners, while the second project, constructed by labor camp inmates and prisoners-of-war, began in 1943 and ended with Stalin's death in March 1953.

36. Regarding the official optimism of the early to mid-1970s in Moscow and Havana on the growing appeal of socialist ideas among the peoples living within an area that the USSR once considered firmly within the United States' sphere of influence, see V. Alekseev, "Problemy BAMa v burzhuaznoi istoriografii," *BAM* (July 13, 1984), 2; Harry Gelman, *The Soviet Union in the Third World: A Retrospective Overview and Prognosis* (Santa Monica, CA: Rand/UCLA Center for the Study of Soviet International Behavior, 1986); Leon Gouré and Morris Rothenberg, *Soviet Penetration of Latin America* (Washington, DC: Monographs in International Affairs, 1975); Richard Lowenthal, "Soviet 'Counterimperialism,'" *Problems of Communism* 25, no. 6 (November–December 1976): 52–63; and Rajan Menon, *Soviet Power and the Third World* (New Haven, CT: Yale University Press, 1986).

37. This railway, somewhat condescendingly labeled the "Cuban BAM" by BAM administrators, was designed with the help of Soviet railway professionals and would link the island's two major cities by rail for the first time.

38. RGASPI, f. 27-M, op. 1, d. 123, l. 71; RGASPI, f. 27-M, op. 1, d. 138, ll. 158–160.

39. RGASPI, f. 27-M, op. 1, d. 160, ll. 1–14.

40. The United States–supported and authoritarian leader Fulgencio Batista (1902–1975) dominated Cuban politics from 1933 until Castro's populist 26th of July Movement overthrew Batista's regime in January 1959. See Nicola Miller, *Soviet Relations with Latin America, 1959–1987* (Cambridge: Cambridge University Press, 1989), 43–44.

41. RGASPI, f. 27-M, op. 1, d. 160, ll. 1–14.

42. RGASPI, f. 27-M, op. 1, d. 116, ll. 21–22.

43. Olga P. Elant'seva, "Mesto foto-kinodokumentov v osveshchenii istorii stroitel'stva BAMa," in *Arkhivy Dal'nego Vostoka Rossii na puti v novoe tysiacheletie: Materialy regional'noi nauchno-praticheskoi konferentsii, posviashchennoi 80-letiiu so dnia prinitiia dekreta Soveta narodnykh komissarov RSFSR "O reorganizatsii i tsentralizatsii arkhivnogo dela v RSFSR,"* ed. V. P. Bondarenko (Vladivostok: Rossiiskii gosudarstvennyi istoricheskii arkhiv Dal'nego Vostoka, 1998), 232–238.

44. V. Popov, "Iz 42 stran," *Vostochno-Sibirskaia pravda*, August 15, 1975, 2.
45. See, for example, N. Andreev and V. Sungorkin, "Novosel na BAMe," *Komsomol'skaia pravda*, June 4, 1980, 2; S. Arokhorov, "Na dalekom 167-m," *Gudok*, June 18, 1974, 3; A. Bobrovskii, "Ul'kan prinimaet gostei," *Komsomol'skoe znamia*, October 7, 1975, 4; Aleksandr Iakovlev, "Trassa: Pis'ma, dnevniki, zapiski nashego sovremennika," *Komsomol'skaia pravda*, December 2, 1975, 2; Valentina Serezdinova, "Khorosheet rodnaia Sibir,'" *Izvestiia*, November 6, 1975, 2; and E. Volina, "Obyknovennaia romantika," *Gudok*, August 17, 1974, 3.
46. Tat'iana Tomina, "Vladek snova edet na BAM," in *BAM—zemlia komsomol'skaia: Panorama vsenarodnoi stroiki. Vypusk odinnadtsatyi—1983 god* (Blagoveshchensk: Khabarovskoe knizhnoe izdatel'stvo, Amurskoe otdelenie, 1984), 263–265. See also "Pesnia—Tozhe oruzhie," in ibid., 265–267.
47. Kristian Brückner, "Trudovoi semestr na BAMe," *Vechernii Kishinev*, October 6, 1975, 1.
48. N. Smirnova, "Internatsional'nyi studencheskii otriad na BAMe," *Severnaia pravda*, August 25, 1984, 4. The impressions of Soviet BAMers who worked with international brigades corroborates the fact that the use of any language besides Russian was frowned upon.
49. Ibid.
50. S. Kolesova, "Magistral' druzhby," in *BAM—zemlia komsomol'skaia: Panorama vsenarodnoi stroiki: Vypusk chetvertyi—1977 god* (Khabarovsk: Khabarovskoe knizhnoe izdatel'stvo, 1978), 61–64.
51. Nikitin interview.
52. A 1975 article by K. Privalov describes the "bonds of socialist competition forged between Soviet and foreign BAMers" but also clearly states that these groups worked and socialized in separate tent communities. See K. Privalov, "Byla by v Indii Sibir,'" *Moskovskii komsomolets*, August 21, 1975, 1.
53. RGASPI, f. 27-M, op. 1, d. 82, ll. 15–16.
54. Ibid., l. 15.
55. Ibid., l. 16.
56. Ibid.
57. Hilary Pilkington, for instance, notes that both CPSU and Komsomol observers reported that Soviet BAMers also remarked on the primitive level of their housing conditions, but that this phenomenon began only after Gorbachev's rise to power in 1985. See Pilkington, *Russia's Youth and Its Culture*, 99.
58. Established in 1960, the Patrice Lumumba Peoples' Friendship University was named for Patrice Emergy Lumumba (1925–1961), a prominent African socialist and first prime minister of the Republic of the Congo, who was assassinated with the collusion of the Congo's former Belgian colonial masters and, some scholars maintain, the United States.
59. "Interotriad—BAMu," *Amurskii komsomolets*, July 9, 1975, 1; RGASPI, f. 1-M, op. 39, d. 555, ll. 5–17. The International Student Construction Brigade was a part of the eight-thousand-member and ethnically diverse All-Union 30th Anniversary of Victory Student Construction Brigade, whose members labored on summer projects across the Soviet Union from the early 1960s to late 1980s.
60. Iurii Petruk, "Tri kontinenta na BAMe," *Moskovskii komsomolets*, January 24, 1975, 2.
61. Nikitin and Shtikov interviews; and Dr. Michael Waganda, former Patrice Lumumba Peoples' Friendship University student, interviews by the author, October 15, 1999, and March 9, 2000, Moscow.
62. Petruk, "Tri kontinenta na BAMe," 2.

63. India enjoyed increased Soviet support after fighting an inconclusive border war with the Soviet Union's ideological rival China in 1962.

64. Petruk, "Tri kontinenta na BAMe," 2.

65. Waganda interview.

66. Based in the BAM Zone town of Nizhneangarsk, Nizhneangarsktransstroi was a construction subdivision that was organizationally similar to Angarstroi.

67. RGASPI, f. 27-M, op. 1, d. 128, l. 36.

68. RGASPI, f. 27-M, op. 1, d. 279, ll. 140–41.

69. Ibid., l. 141.

70. RGASPI, f. 1-M, op. 45, d. 297, ll. 41, 43, 135, 137; Galina Mironova, editor at the *Molodaia gvardiia* publishing house, interview by the author, December 2, 1999, Mytishchi.

71. RGASPI, f. 27-M, op. 1, d. 207, l. 7.

72. Ibid., l. 8.

73. RGASPI, f. 27-M, op. 1, d. 207, ll. 13–14.

74. Valentin A. Sushchevich, BAM Society founder, interview by the author, October 4, 1999, and April 19, 2000, Russian Youth Organizations Headquarters, Moscow. Sushchevich told me that the United States, other unnamed "Western powers," and Israel secretly placed spies within the BAMer population to observe and even delay the project's progress.

PART III

Narrations: Literatures of Migration and Mobility

CHAPTER 9

TRAUMATIC MOBILITY
Motivating Collective Authorship in Siberian Narratives of Polish Exiles from the Inter-revolutionary Epoch (1832–1862)

Elizabeth Blake

THE VARIOUS LABELS *deportees*, *exiles*, and *Sybiracy* (Siberians) do not adequately express the violent and traumatic dislocation experienced by generations of nineteenth-century Polish revolutionaries, when they were arrested, imprisoned in citadels, and forced to march, often in shackles, across vast expanses of the Russian Empire as part of the process of being relocated to prisons and fortresses in a land governed by officials speaking another tongue.[1] Polish exiles from the *epoka międzypowstaniowa* (inter-revolutionary epoch), sentenced between the 1830–1831 November Uprising and the 1863 January Uprising in the Congress Kingdom of Poland, comprised a particularly mobile group of *Sybiracy*, since they benefited from Alexander II's 1856 general amnesty allowing these exiles to return to their homeland.[2] Their journeys of exile often commenced beyond Russia's western border, with arrests of Polish and Lithuanian revolutionaries commonly occurring in Austrian and Prussian territories, and ended in Irkutsk or in the mines of Nerchinsk in the Zabaikal'sk region of Russia. These political exiles were linked to prominent conspiracies and uprisings in Warsaw, Galicia, Cracow, Vilnius, and Hungary.

They participated in Szymon Konarski's Stowarzyszenie Ludu Polskiego (Association of the Polish People); the Towarzystwo Demokratyczne Polskie (TDP, the well-connected Polish Democratic Society), supported by representatives of the Great Emigration; Father Piotr Ściegienny's populist agitation with ties to Henryk Kamieński's Związek Narodu Polskiego (Union of the Polish Nation); and the Związek Bratni Młodzieży Litewskiej (Union of Lithuanian Youth) led by the brothers Dalewski.[3] As a result of Nicholas I's suppression of Polish dissent following the execution of Konarski in 1838, the arrest and deportation of Father Ściegienny in 1844, and the sentencing of Polish conspirators in the wake of the 1846 Cracow uprising and the 1848 Hungarian Revolution, Polish *Sybiracy* encountered the opportunity to record extensively their experiences of solitary confinement in dark citadels, severe floggings, hard labor, and indeterminate Siberian exile.

Yet because this generation's Siberian experience was abbreviated by the amnesty of the Tsar-Liberator Alexander II, the exiles enjoyed multifarious opportunities for collaboration with fellow Poles not only in prison fortresses, during forced marches through the Siberian wilderness, and in remote settlements in Russia but also after their return to the Polish homeland. Envisioning, writing, editing, and circulating their manuscripts in Siberia and Poland, and within émigré circles in the West, *Sybiracy* also saw their texts subjugated to the forces of mobility with the resultant loss (sometimes by confiscation) and fragmentation of the documents themselves. Nevertheless, *Sybiracy* in East and West preserved the substance of their experience in the form of prison graffiti, notes in personal albums, (clandestine) correspondence, notebooks, personal papers, or even manuscripts that, when published, enjoyed a diverse readership. Even when a deportee recording his experiences failed to survive Siberian exile, his accounts could be retained in partial manuscripts (*rękopisy*), letters (*listy*), and papers (*karty*). In this manner, the established insular Polish communities in Siberia as well as the camaraderie among those returning after the amnesty helped safeguard testimonies to this Siberian chapter of Polish intellectual history.[4] Émigrés in London, Paris, and the Swiss cantons as well as Poles living in Cracow and Poznań disseminated this exile history by publishing remembrances of Siberian captivity in daily and weekly newspapers (particularly those with liberal or democratic leanings) as well as in bound volumes.

The movement of the authors along with their writings from East to West exposes their manuscripts to a hybrid textual culture, namely the manuscript norms of the *Sybiracy* (which flourished in Russia) and the standards of a well-established print culture in Western Europe whose multilingual readership had already devoured the memoirs *Le mie prigioni* (*Memoirs of My Imprisonments*, 1832) of accused Carbonaro and dramatist Silvio Pellico, incarcerated by the Austrian Empire.[5] As a result, the reader of these accounts, in addition to the usual challenge of navigating the experiencing and remembering selves that accompanies memoirs, must also consider the circumstances in which the reminiscences were composed, circulated, and published. The editing of manuscripts published posthumously and the appearance of original manuscripts in compilations or even in their comrades' remembrances (at times without attribution) raise complex issues of authorship and composition in narratives recognized as historical eyewitness accounts in their own time.[6] The inclusion of oral narratives from additional unnamed sources in these Siberian accounts further complicates issues of authorial responsibility and ownership of experience. However, an analysis of the manuscript culture of the highly mobile inter-revolutionary *Sybiracy* will demonstrate that its norms of coauthorship allow for multiauthored eyewitness narratives without delegitimizing their established value as authentic historical records of the Siberian experience.

NINETEENTH-CENTURY MANUSCRIPT CULTURE

Although nineteenth-century Russia witnessed the "eclipse of the traditional scribal culture," manuscripts still circulated widely in the empire owing to the restrictions imposed by tsarist censors, and allusions to such manuscripts appear in prominent literary works of the period.[7] For example, the functionary Maksim Maksimych in Mikhail Lermontov's *Geroi nashego vremeni* (*A Hero of Our Time*, 1839), plans to use the manuscript of the Byronic Grigory Pechorin, situated in the Caucasus (Lermontov's place of political exile), for military cartridges until the unnamed editor of Pechorin's journal decides to disseminate it even though it requires him "to place his own name on another's work."[8] Nikolai Gogol and Fyodor Dostoevsky use the word "notes" (*zapiski*) in the titles of their respective works that discuss incarceration, "Zapiski sumasshedshego" ("Notes of a Madman," 1835) and *Zapiski iz mertvogo doma* (*Notes from the House of the Dead*, 1860–1862).[9] Gogol embeds in the final entries of the diary of his madman surreptitious references to the practices of the Third Section, such as the shaving of heads or its interrogation techniques for which it was characterized as the Spanish Inquisition, as he underscores with Aksenty Poprishchin's observation: "Haven't I fallen into the hands of the Inquisition, and the one, whom I took for the chancellor, isn't he the Grand Inquisitor himself."[10] Dostoevsky, author of a famous legend about a Grand Inquisitor who incarcerates heretics, draws on his Siberian notebooks to create in his autobiographical novel *House of the Dead* a narrative composed primarily of the remembrances, "Stseny iz Mertvogo doma" ("Scenes from the Dead House"), written by former convict and exile Alexander Gorianchikov. After Gorianchikov left this manuscript amid his posthumous "papers" (*bumagi*), the narrator, who had been fascinated by the misanthropic exile, discovers them and presents them to the reader with the warning that "three-fourths of these papers were empty, meaningless scraps" with the exception of "one little notebook" with an "incoherent" description of prison life that is sometimes interrupted "with some sort of strange, horrible remembrances" and contains passages "written in madness."[11] These literary examples suggest a link between prison or exile and a manuscript tradition with a heightened awareness of the way in which the fragmentation of narrative arises from the brokenness of the author, the intrusion of an editor, or the physical (de)composition of the discovered text.

On the other hand, the Polish *Sybiracy*, having endured imprisonment and exile alongside Russian political prisoners, tend to focus on articulating a national trauma rather than underscoring the formal composition of a manuscript. The ambiguous concept of authorship in *Sybiracy*'s manuscript culture allows for a collective authorship sharing diverse methods to create an authentic narrative that preserves the memory of exile while exposing the punitive Russian penal system. Unlike for the aforementioned Russian authors, the focus for the Polish writers is not the composition of an original text that must withstand the rigors of the tsarist censor. Since several manuscripts were published posthumously and outside Russia, frequently in serial form in Polish-, French-, and Russian-language newspapers, their authors betray little regard for the censor. However, by partnering with other dissident groups in Warsaw, Paris, London, Geneva, and other European cities, the authors of the composite remembrances respond to the challenge of appealing to the appetites of a European readership with diverse manuscript fragments, references to famous tyrants and conspirators, and fascinating tales of adventure or escape. This readership was primed to accept Polish impressions of the barbaric Russian Empire, since it had already encountered Pellico's images of a belligerent Austrian Empire with several references to the kindness of his Polish jailers, such as Kunda, who attempted to supply the Italian prisoner with supplementary rations, and the compassionate guard Kubitzky, who marked the grave of Pellico's deceased compatriot so that his family could recover the body.[12] In some respects, the Polish literary images of Siberian exile in the works of the Romantics, such as Adam Mickiewicz's *Dziady* (*Forefathers' Eve*) or the poetry of Zygmunt Krasiński, thwarted attempts by *Sybiracy* to establish a historical record of exile, because these works defined archetypal images of persecution that inspired a "Siberian mythopoesis," which resonated particularly well with the Polish political exile community.[13] The conflation of former exile Rufin Piotrowski's memoirs with Mickiewicz's drama as well as the identification of Agaton Giller with Christological martyrology instead of Siberian history in Stanislaw Eile's *Literature and Nationalism in Partitioned Poland* attest to this confusion of the creative nonfiction characteristic of Siberian memoirs with Polish nineteenth-century fiction engaging cultural identity.[14]

These memoirs as nonfiction reflect the authors' desire to preserve the memory (out of a sense of duty to survivors and victims) of injustices not redressed and so reflect what Paul Ricœur describes as an "attestation-protestation" whereby "the historian-citizen" is placed "in a situation of responsibility as regards the [traumatic] past."[15] Because the remembrances of Piotrowski, Giller, Józef Bogusławski, and Szymon Tokarzewski—usually discussed by scholars as a single survivor's personal account of Siberian hardship—represent hybrid narratives for their inclusion of the oral and manuscript histories of other *Sybiracy*, a reader seeking to discern an individual's eyewitness testimony in their recollections not only must address the remembering self of the author but also must explore the presence and motivations of the contributing authors. The well-known texts of these four famous *Sybiracy*, written primarily during the interrevolutionary period, display historical and thematic similarities that motivate the presence of secondary authors even though their primary authors are in Siberian regions and communities distant and distinct from those of the secondary authors. In other words, in an effort to demonstrate a shared trauma, authors incorporate others' personal histories into a single narrative, thereby emphasizing the interconnectedness of localized Polish exile communities in Siberia, whose links extend not only to their common homeland but even to émigré circles in the West. Hence, the impact of the authors' movement through space on the texts does not end with the writing during the Siberian journeys but continues through the gathering, editing, and publication processes for those representing a community that adopted laborious measures to copy, conceal, and preserve its notes, papers, letters, and notebooks relating to exile, as evidenced by the Czartoryski archives and manuscript collection in Cracow, which houses the archives from the Hôtel Lambert linked to the Great Emigration in Paris.[16] This shaping of texts, vividly displayed when multiple accounts are dedicated to a similar historical time and geographical space, underscores the need to approach even a seemingly *"unprocessed historical record"* with a hermeneutics of suspicion as a result of the fragmentation that accompanies not only the process of remembering but also the preservation of the written word by a mobile group of exiles, many of whose members are prevented from publishing their uncensored remembrances.[17] For this reason, comrades, loved ones, and historians discovering these fragments sought to give voice to their testimony, even if the attestation required overlooking the processed nature of the text or its editing with the addition of footnotes, narrative emplotment, or fusion of the fragments with other written accounts.

RUFIN PIOTROWSKI'S MODEL NARRATIVE

With his remembrances of an escape from Siberia, *Pamiętniki z pobytu na Syberyi* (*Memoirs from a Sojourn in Siberia*, 1860–1861), written in 1849–1850, Rufin Piotrowski captivated the European imagination in the 1860s with "one of the most romantic nineteenth-century biographies," as indicated by the rapidity with which they were translated into French and German (1862) and then English (1863).[18] From the beginning of the memoir, he writes as a representative of an exile community with links to the TDP and to a leader of the Great Emigration, Prince Adam Czartoryski of the Hôtel Lambert—connections that ensured the rapid translation and dissemination of his memoirs, especially through journalist Julian Klaczko's French translation.[19] For this reason, Piotrowski's own narrative of flight appears against the backdrop of similar infamous attempts to quit Siberia by members of the Polish community, most notably the aborted rebellion in Omsk plotted by the priest Jan Sierociński and the failed escape organized by a leader of the 1830 Uprising, Colonel Piotr Wysocki, which are described both in Piotrowski's publications from the 1840s and in his memoirs.[20] The importance of Sierociński for Piotrowski's story and the political position of the émigrés may be gleaned from an article-length handwritten manuscript dated 1851, "Martyre du Prieur Sierocinski" (The martyrdom of Priest Sierociński).[21] The legendary figures of Wysocki and Sierociński are subsequently discussed in the Siberian remembrances of Giller and Bogusławski as well as in the research of Maksimov in a way that suggests that Piotrowski's memoirs serve as a thematic model for subsequent interrevolutionary Siberian reminiscences, even though the portrayal of the exiles connected to famous conspiracies, but unknown to the author personally, seems tangential to Piotrowski's individual Siberian sojourn.

Piotrowski establishes his connectedness to Omsk, and therefore to the infamous *Omskoe delo* (Omsk Affair), by maintaining that while the incident preceded his arrival in the region, he "knew those who sat together in the prison with Father Sierociński."[22] Because Sierociński and his fellow conspirators were flogged to death in Omsk, the administrative headquarters for Western Siberia visited by Piotrowski and located not far from the Siberian factory to which Piotrowski was sentenced, the testimony about Sierociński appears accurate. This story, which serves a narrative purpose in Rufin's memoirs by providing historical background to geographic areas of Western Siberia, nevertheless appears amid a discussion of Piotrowski's own desire for escape—a desire characterized as universally Polish with a reference to an escapee, Maurycy Beniowski, who was sentenced for his links to the Konfederacja Barska (Confederacy of Bar, 1768–1772) to Kamchatka in the Russian Far East, from where he fled in 1771. The presence of Beniowski and Father Sierociński in Piotrowski's narrative thereby establishes a dramatic thematic parallel for Piotrowski's personal experience instead of constituting part of the latter's eyewitness testimony depicting Polish Siberia. Likewise, the flogging and harsh imprisonment of Colonel Wysocki in the fortress of Akatui offers a parallel to the brutal execution of Father Sierociński and enhances the readers' sense of danger directly before Piotrowski relates the perils of his own successful flight.

As he begins these accounts in the third volume, Piotrowski is conscious that his readership, "the civilized world," will conclude that these stories, written in 1849 in Vienna, will seem to be exaggerated, but he underscores their truthfulness directly before his account about Colonel Wysocki.[23] Here, Piotrowski clarifies that exploration of truth, with God as a witness, motivates his writing: "I write only to give homage and truthful testimony, to submit to righteous posterity a sorrowful keepsake of misfortune and martyrdom."[24] All the same, since he was not in Eastern Siberia near Nerchinsk where Colonel Wysocki served his sentence, Piotrowski's account does not display the same detail or source history evident in his description of Father Sierociński's conspiracy but instead contains references to his limited information about the flight and clarifies that only after the author's return from Siberia to France in 1846 does he prove "with certainty" the whereabouts of Colonel Wysocki near Irkutsk.[25] Thus, the history of Colonel Wysocki seems removed from Piotrowski's individual Siberian experience (even though while in Siberia he saw "one soap dish of his work with the signature: P. W. Akatui") and even contains information gathered after his Siberian period. Such moments in his memoirs indicate that he includes tales of physical torment related by other Polish exiles to emphasize a shared national trauma, perhaps because his individual witness to the hardships of servitude did not include the corporal punishments characteristic of oral Siberian narratives recorded by Piotrowski.

AGATON GILLER'S HISTORY OF THE COLLECTIVE SIBERIAN GEHENNA

The collective nature of the Siberian sojourn particularly informs the narrative of Giller, a prominent member of the Komitet Centralny Narodowy (National Central Committee), which played a leading role in the 1863 January uprising in which many former *Sybiracy* participated. Giller's dedication to Polish independence may be gleaned from Alexander Herzen's observation that Siberian escapee Mikhail Bakunin introduced Giller as a "battle-hardened fighter" who "from Poland took a walk in shackles to the mine and, as soon as he returned, set about the business anew."[26] Giller's promotion of national liberation motivates the tragic "emplotment" of his Siberian narratives, in which he remains ever conscious of his *nation*'s conflict with imperial Russia.[27] Giller's Siberian remembrances, his *Lista Wygnańców Polskich do roku 1860* (List of Polish exiles before 1860), and his extant correspondence with former exiles demonstrate how he actively continued to gather materials after the failed uprising while residing in the West.[28] Indeed, the time between his 1860 return to Warsaw and the appearance of his publications about Poles in Siberia allowed him many opportunities to share manuscripts and oral histories with his fellow *Sybiracy*, who joined him in the uprising and continued to correspond with him after his flight westward. Consequently, his movements from Siberia to Warsaw and from Warsaw to Switzerland inform his exilic narratives as he offers a vision of Siberia formed not only by himself but also in dialogue with his compatriots.

The mobility Giller invokes as a cause for the fragmented nature of his *Podróż więźnia etapami do Syberyi w roku 1854* (Journey of a prisoner by stages to Siberia in the year 1854, 1866) also reminds the reader of his own story of dislocation as he moves from Kazan' to Irkutsk, from Irkutsk to Warsaw, and from Warsaw to Swiss exile, where he wrote the prologue in 1865. He presents a partial record of his sixteen-month journey to Siberia and relates how his initial copy was taken from him during an inspection at a guardhouse in Kazan', so the present memoir, unchanged since he wrote it during his exile in Nerchinsk, was derived from his memory of the first. His early inclusion of references (in a recollection of Warsaw in 1846) to other *Sybiracy*—Karol Ruprecht, Michał Mirecki, and Stefan Dobrycz—who were all sent to the Nerchinsk region suggests the importance of the locale for the writing of the manuscript.[29] Giller thereby displays a conscious understanding of the distance between lived experience and his own remembrances, which is further evident in his disclosure that one of his notebooks (which survived Siberia intact) was lost during the 1863 uprising, so there is a narrative gap in the Lithuanian leg of his journey.[30] Throughout *Journey of a Prisoner*, Giller's own voice dominates the narrative with few additions from other contributors with the rare exception of quoted conversation with those he encounters, but he does supplement his travelogue with highlights from chaotic periods in Russian history such as the Napoleonic invasion, the internecine strife caused by seventeenth-century pretenders, and the rebellion led by Emelyan Pugachev, who often makes his way into Siberians' writings because of his connection to Orenburg.[31] His discussion of the tortuous martyrdom and "miraculous halo of legend" of Konarski, many of whose co-conspirators shared Giller's years in Eastern Siberia, personalizes the narrative's links to the inter-revolutionary generation.[32] Furthermore, like Piotrowski, Giller mentions locales significant for the typical exiles' journey such as the Warsaw citadel or Viatka, where Giller recalls that Henryk Kamieński spent his exile as the latter described in *Le Temps* (The Times).[33]

A year after F. A. Brockhaus, a printing house in Leipzig with a history of Polish-language publications, had released the memoir of Giller's 1854 journey, Brockhaus published Giller's *Opisanie zabajkalskiej krainy w Syberyi* (A description of the Zabaikal'sk region in Siberia, 1867) drawing on his experience serving in the 14th Battalion and living in the settlements in the Nerchinsk region.[34] Although two substantial tours of the Zabaikal'sk region (in 1856–1857) provided him with a detailed picture of the local communities, his focus remains on the history of Polish exiles in Eastern Siberia. He supplies the reader with general observations about the exiles, statistical analyses about their presence (out of the 14,000 living in Cossack settlements of soldiers, 2,500 are Poles), personal accounts of Polish exiles, and records of their burial places.[35] The dedication page, on which Giller honors all of the Polish exiles who died in Nerchinsk, reveals an early connection between his narrative and the escapes recounted by Piotrowski, owing to the references to a fellow conspirator of Father Sierociński, Dr. Ksawery Szokalski (d. 1844), and one of a deportee, Major Franciszek Malczewski (d. 1852), who tried to escape with Colonel Wysocki. The presence of their detailed backgrounds in his description of the Zabaikal'sk region demonstrates that Giller depended on secondary sources, likely oral histories, to provide information about famous exiles even though Giller frequently neglects to credit the sources and continues to structure his narrative around the places that he visits.³⁶

After completing the second volume, in which Giller records a visit to Akatui where he meets Wysocki, the reader is introduced to a potential source for the descriptions he includes of Malczewski's Siberian imprisonment and Dr. Szokalski's suicide in Akatui. In the account of the visit, Giller provides a brief history of Colonel Wysocki's imprisonment, exile, and attempted escape in addition to paraphrasing and directly quoting the famous exile, who read parts of his work to Giller—including "a description of the 29th of November"—the day Wysocki attacked the Warsaw citadel (1830) and Malczewski led a battalion of sappers to the arsenal.³⁷ However, already in the first volume when Giller comes upon the grave of Malczewski in Nerchinsk-Zavod, he supplies the reader with a detailed history of Wysocki and Malczewski's shared imprisonment for three years, their subsequent sentence served in Aleksandrovsk (in the Irkutsk region), their punishment for an attempted escape in the silver mines of Akatui, and their mutual home in the settlement nearby—the location of the visit between Giller and Wysocki.³⁸ In Akatui, Wysocki was also with Dr. Szokalski, whose suicide Giller introduces in order to provide a history for a house in Kara: "In the house in which Ksawery Szokalski (martyr of the nation's affair, a respectable and devoted soul) shot himself, an altar was quickly arranged, before which Father Jurewicz for three days led mass and heard confessions of the faithful."³⁹ This physical space then motivates Giller's discussion of Dr. Szokalski's past involvement with Father Sierociński in a narrative that misspells the name of a co-conspirator (Melodini for Włodzimierz Milidin) and admits memory lapses, for example, "if my memory does not deceive me."⁴⁰

Such details present in the "recollections" about the deaths of Dr. Szokalski and his co-conspirators indicate that Giller remains at least one step removed from these events, thereby demonstrating that the eyewitness to Siberian trauma may exploit a sense of place to invoke memories of those victimized in order to articulate authentically the exilic experience. Giller's description of the Zabaikal'sk region has been recognized as an authoritative historical source by several nineteenth- and twentieth-century historians of Siberia, who have not noted its multiple levels of authorship.

For example, the third volume of Maksimov's groundbreaking study of the imperial Siberian prison system, *Sibir' i katorga* (Siberia and penal servitude, 1871), draws substantially on Giller's portrait of the Poles in exile to relate "The Unhappy Fate of Colonel Wysocki, Father Sierociński, and Doctor Szokalski" and other stories in which the studies of both Giller and Piotrowski are cited.[41] Giller's research is listed regularly in the source history for individual entries in the bibliographic guides on nineteenth-century Polish revolutionaries and exiles by Vladimir D'iakov and Wiktoria Śliwowska.

Because Giller served as a soldier and Piotrowski served his partial sentence in a distillery, they escaped the harshest punishments associated with Siberian penal labor (*katorga*) that ruined the health of many compatriots; instead they returned to the West robust enough to produce and publish writings about their experiences. Since Giller and Piotrowski survived in freedom into the 1860s, when Europe turned anew to the Polish Question, they enjoyed a widespread readership for their chef-d'oeuvres on the Siberian exile experience, even when they included the remembrances of the deceased.[42] Other *Sybiracy* who did not live to see either the completion or publication of their manuscripts relied on their compatriots, or even fellow exiles, to edit, conclude, circulate, or publish the accounts so that the writings remained subject to the forces of mobility. This remains true of two writers depicting Western Siberia— Bogusławski and Tokarzewski—who shared the Omsk prison fortress with the Russian novelist Fyodor Dostoevsky and returned following the 1856 amnesty but did not live to see the publication of their memoirs. The manuscript "Sybirski pamiętnik Józefa Bogusławskiego" (A Siberian memoir of Józef Bogusławski) recopied by historian Eustachy Heleniusz Iwanowski's copyist was donated by Iwanowski to Jagiellonian University's library collection in 1898, following its publication in two redacted versions (1894 and 1896) and long after Bogusławski's death in Częstochowa in 1857, in spite of treatments for his health in Carlsbad, Bohemia.[43] Tokarzewski's published memoirs *Siedem lat Katorgi: Pamiętniki Szymona Tokarzewskiego 1846–1857 r.* (Seven years of penal servitude: Remembrances of Szymon Tokarzewski 1846–1857, 1907) appeared more than fifteen years after his death and fifty years after his imprisonment in Omsk.[44]

THE WELL-TRAVELED MANUSCRIPT
OF JÓZEF BOGUSŁAWSKI

The complex publication history of Józef Bogusławski's recollections attests to the challenge of establishing an authoritative version of certain manuscripts from the inter-revolutionary period. Even before the publication of his memoirs, Bogusławski's conspiratorial legacy was well established within the Polish exile community, since he was connected not only to the infamous Konarski (for which he was arrested in 1839 and sent to Tambov) but also to the 1846 Lithuanian group linked to Jan Röhr, which included Apolin Hofmeister and Anicety Renier, with whom Bogusławski was hauled around Vilnius in "the wagon of delinquents" before being stripped of noble rights on a scaffold, as Giller describes.[45] There likely arose renewed interest in this Lithuanian group in the 1890s, because Nikolai Berg's 1873 study *Zapiski N. V. Berga o pol'skikh zagovorakh i vosstaniiakh, 1831–1862* (Notes about Polish conspiracies and uprisings, 1831–1862), which provides a history of the interconnected networks of various 1846 Polish conspiracies (including Röhr's), appears in a second Polish edition in Cracow in 1894.[46] The political activities of the Polish Siberians sent to Nerchinsk—Ruprecht, Mirecki, and Dobrycz— and mentioned in Giller's *Journey of a Prisoner* are discussed by Berg here as well.[47] Furthermore, considering the former exiles' connections to the Polska Akademia Umiejętności (Polish Academy of Learning), formed in 1872, and the relocation of the Czartoryski manuscript collection to Cracow in 1874, the publication of Bogusławski's memoirs in 1894 and 1896 appear to reflect a general late-nineteenth-century trend in Austria-Hungary of promoting research about Polish Siberians.

The earliest-known published citations from Bogusławski's text are extant in historian Eustachy Heleniusz Iwanowski's *Wspomnienia polskich czasów dawnych i późniejszych* (Remembrances of Polish times, long ago and more recent, 1894).[48] Iwanowski had already displayed an interest in other Konarski conspirators by publishing parts of Franciszek Sawicz's memoirs in an 1874 collection *Wspomnienia lat minionych* (Remembrances of bygone years), so Iwanowski's partial inclusion of Bogusławski's words in a chapter that largely paraphrases and selectively cites from the Siberian's narrative has a precedent in the historian's scholarship.⁴⁹ In fact, Iwanowski valued Sawicz's manuscript because of an ability to authenticate it, since it had been given to the editor of the memoirs, the poet Aleksander Groza, by Sawicz himself.⁵⁰ The fragments of Józef Bogusławski's manuscript cited in Iwanowski's chapter "Więźniowie i wygnańce roku 1848" (Imprisonment and exile of the year 1848) are not supplemented by attempts to account for the provenance of Bogusławski's remembrances but instead refer to infamous historical events, such as the floggings of Father Sierocinski and Dr. Szokalski, in order to connect with the reader. In some respects, the chapter appears as a compilation, with Iwanowski including large sections of Bogusławski's passages on Tara and Tomsk without crediting him and then placing quotation marks acknowledging citations from Bogusławski beginning with the account of Ust'-Kamenogorsk.⁵¹ Such editorial practices have exposed Iwanowski to scholarly criticism for his "trimming" and "distorting" of Bogusławski's text.⁵²

Iwanowski recognizes the limitations of Bogusławski's unfinished memoirs and underscores his removal from the lived experience of the Omsk prisoners by admitting: "The memoirs of Bogusławski, condemned to the hard labor of an exile, are not finished. How long he stayed in Omsk, when he returned to his nation, and what was the fate of his comrades, Professor Żochowski and Aleksander Mirecki; what happened to them, did they return, we do not know."⁵³ His ignorance as to Mirecki's fate further indicates that he had not read Dostoevsky's *House of the Dead*, even though it was by this time known to *Sybiracy*, because Dostoevsky alludes to Mirecki's release from prison into the settlement.⁵⁴ Since Iwanowski had no direct connection to Bogusławski and displays little knowledge of Western Siberia, the recollections selected for inclusion in *Remembrances* appear out of context and with little historical background on Bogusławski's compatriots in Siberia. Iwanowski's lack of shared experience with Bogusławski becomes problematic in his discussion of Tomsk when he concentrates on famous conspirators located in the region—for example, a Konarski collaborator (Tomasz Bułhak) and a Ściegienny conspirator (Kwasery Stobnicki)—but connects the latter to Bogusławski instead of Tokarzewski, in contrast to the original manuscript.⁵⁵ Thus, in the reconfiguration of the memoirs with the purpose of narrating the Siberian trauma rather than preserving the memory of an individual's experience, Iwanowski reauthors the documentary moment.

An edited version of Bogusławski's manuscript published as a series of brief articles appeared under the title "Wspomnienia Sybiraka: Pamiętniki Józefa Bogusławskiego" (Recollections of a *Sybirak*: Memoirs of Józef Bogusławski, 1896) in the Cracow liberal-democratic daily *Nowa reforma* (New reform).[56] When Bogusławski's unfinished manuscript was published, the editor (identified as Józef Tokarzewski in the introduction but widely accepted to be Szymon) did not attempt to create a holistic biography of his Siberian experience.[57] Rather, the publication's unfinished nature and its reflection of Bogusławski's preoccupation with establishing a record of places and names linked to the Polish Siberian experience suggest that the editor, even though he "copied and supplemented" the manuscript, preserved the sense of fragmentation evident in the account that Bogusławski left behind. The manuscript material was rearranged according to theme and location for publication, emphasizing traumatic mobility through the frequent chapter divisions with descriptive titles highlighted in italics and additional footnotes (written by multiple authors) providing background for some of the people, places, and customs mentioned in the narrative. Bogusławski's participation in multiple conspiracies and his knowledge of Russian allowed him to establish contacts in various locations through which he passed in Western Siberia, including several (Tobol'sk, Tomsk, Ust'-Kamenogorsk, and Omsk) with significant Polish exile populations. As in the reminiscences of Piotrowski and Giller, Bogusławski's recollections mention several famous conspirators, including Petrashevtsy (Sergei Durov and Fyodor Dostoevsky), the Konarski collaborator Bułhak, agitators for Father Ściegienny (Stobnicki and Hipolit Raciborski), comrades of Father Sierociński, and future 1863 insurgents (Tokarzewski and Cyriak Accord, brother-in-law of memoirist and January conspirator Jakób Gieysztor). Hence, scholars of nineteenth-century Siberia cite from the 1896 remembrances to verify the historical accuracy of other primary texts, despite Tokarzewski's editing of the original manuscript, thereby suggesting that the manuscript can remain authoritative even when altered by a fellow *Sybirak*.[58]

TOKARZEWSKI'S POSTHUMOUS MEMOIRS: A PROCESSING OF BOGUSŁAWSKI'S HISTORICAL RECORD

However, scholars have been more critical of the recycling of Bogusławski's reminiscences without attribution in both the 1907 and 1918 editions of Tokarzewski's *Seven years*, which also include multiple passages from fellow inmate Dostoevsky's *House of the Dead* in a lengthy footnote, intimating some textual dependency on Dostoevsky's famous depictions of Omsk.[59] Tokarzewski's 1867 letter to Giller detailing individuals being deported to Siberia and his role as preserver and editor of Bogusławski's "Recollections of a *Sybirak*" are difficult to reconcile with the image of an author compiling a Siberian narrative dependent on contributions from the writings of those who shared his experience.[60] The fact that Bogusławski's individual confrontations with Dostoevsky and the Polish exile's personal assessments about Siberia are reassigned to Tokarzewski in *Seven years*, in which they are embellished with inserted dialogues, has encouraged recently a closer examination of the role played by his wife, Halina, in the preparation of his manuscript. Yet her tendency to elaborate on fragments gathered from other remembrances shows that she immerses herself in a generic tradition of exile literature, well established by the early twentieth century, in an effort to highlight her husband's place within the Siberian martyr narrative. Her husband's life of frequent migration within the Russian Empire and the resultant loss of personal papers allow Halina the authorial space to create a seemingly credible account of individual witness to Siberian trauma, with the consequence of complicating the historian's task of discovering the "documentary moment and its generating matrix of presumed truth—that is, the testimony of those who declare their having been there where things happened."[61]

In the accounts attributed to her husband, Halina exploits the fragmentation or disappearance of papers and manuscripts accompanying the life of exile in order to account for gaps in the narrative or interjections of the editor's voice into the account. For instance, Jan Trynkowski, noting the references in *Ciernistym szlakiem* (*By a Thorny Path*, 1909) to lost papers and the need to reconstruct remembrances from a distance (after the 1860s), alludes to Halina's "confabulations, artful tales, or also reconstructions based on flimsy foundations" when discovering her fabrication of a ten-page account of her husband in Omsk.[62] Knowing this, can one really accept Halina's explanation that *Seven years* (like *House of the Dead* and Bogusławski's manuscript) breaks off after a detailed account of Omsk because of missing pages that had been left with a curator of Wawel Cathedral in Cracow?[63] Indeed, only the 1918 edition acknowledges that Halina organized and copied her husband's notes (*notatki*), possibly motivated by Tadeusz Korzon's recollection in *Mój pamiętnik przedhistoryczny* (My prehistoric memoirs, 1912) that Tokarzewski, on his return from the first exile through Moscow, had met with a group of Polish students with whom he had left "his memoirs of prison and flogging in Zamość as well as his sojourn in Omsk in that same *Dead House* which was famous throughout all Europe thanks to the talented Russian Dostoevsky."[64] Although Korzon remarks that the manuscript was lost "amidst the turmoil of 1863" but found after Tokarzewski's death—a likely scenario given the time gap between the 1890 death and the 1907 publication of *Seven years*—Halina contends that there were two copies of the manuscript written during the first exile.[65] She indicates that the second copy, which was returned to Tokarzewski after his arrival in Warsaw in 1883, had been preserved by a fellow author and Siberian Teresa Bułhakowa (misspelled Buthakowa), about whom Tokarzewski writes in *W ucieczce: Opowiadania wygnanka* (*Into flight: Stories of an exile*, 1911).

However, this claim also reflects the habit in *Seven years* of connecting Tokarzewski with famous exiles, starting with a hagiographic moment in the first chapter of *Seven years* that outlines how his deacon uncle, having read out in a Zamość cathedral the names of those belonging to the Świętokrzyżcy (Holy Cross) exiled to Nerchinsk, elicits an oath from Tokarzewski to go with these deportees as a convict.[66] The second chapter then places Szymon within the Tokarzewski lineage of conspirators with the disclosure that his ancestor was one of those linked to the Confederacy of Bar, a movement opposed to Catherine II's occupation of Poland. When she invokes the name of the well-regarded Teresa Bułhakowa as guardian of her husband's manuscript, Halina *consciously* applies this tendency to invoke the famous, which has a precedent in the Tokarzewski-Bułhakowa connection appearing in *Into flight*, where it relies on previously published biographical information drawn from Maryan Dubiecki's 1895 biography of Bułhakowa.[67] Therefore, it is important to note that

Wiktoria Śliwowska, the distinguished historian on Siberian exile, clarifies in "Prawda i fikcja w opowieściach Szymona Tokarzewskiego" (Truth and fiction in the stories of Szymon Tokarzewski) that the popularity of *Seven years* encouraged Halina to intertwine "invented names" and stories with survivor testimony to authenticate her creations.[68] Thus, because of the time lapse between her husband's first exile and the publication of *Seven years*, histories and accounts written by inter-revolutionary exiles provided Halina with enough information to create a narrative out of the notes on Siberia left behind by her husband and his fellow inmate.

However, her description of the manuscript preservation, coupled with Tokarzewski's movement, obscures the provenance of *Seven years*, whose writing is linked to the circles of exiles who returned in the late 1850s. In both the preface to *Seven years* and the notes to "Recollections of a *Sybirak*," the name of Emilia Gosselin (spelled Goslin in the latter) appears, thereby suggesting a link between the reminiscences and the circle of women in Warsaw, which included Narcyza Żmichowska and Gosselin (who died in 1864), with whom Tokarzewski had contact after his first return from exile.[69] The note in "Recollections of a *Sybirak*" identifies Szymon Tokarzewski as being an owner of a Warsaw women's shoe store—his profession and location after returning from his first exile—to which *Seven years* alludes with a reference to him as a master cobbler.[70] The group's connection to Bogusławski's manuscript may be surmised not only from Gosselin's note but also from Żmichowska's presence in Carlsbad in 1858 and her 1860 letter in which she lets Gosselin know that she is seeking out a Miss Bogusławski to hand over a box but then writes that she is not passing on to "Szymon [Tokarzewski] a good word" since she will soon return.[71] With his connections during this period to former Siberians now conspiring in Warsaw, such as Giller, Ruprecht (linked to Tokarzewski's prison comrade Aleksander Mirecki), Gerwazy Gzowski, and Zygmunt Sierakowski (connected to a fellow deportee to Orenburg and co-conspirator of Bogusławski, Bronisław Zaleski), Tokarzewski could have gathered additional background information about his fellow Omsk inmates.[72] Because of passages found in both Bogusławski's manuscript and *Seven years* (but not in "Recollections of a *Sybirak*"), such as a literary debate with Dostoevsky over Eugène Sue's novel *Le Juif errant* (*The Wandering Jew*, 1844–1845), it seems most likely that the author or compiler of *Seven years* had access to the manuscript of *A Siberian memoir*, which Bogusławski maintains was written in Carlsbad in 1857.[73] Therefore, the Siberians' post-exilic experience before Tokarzewski's second deportation impacts the text of *Seven years*, so it is unlikely that a manuscript copy, written in Siberia and returned after 1883, became the main source for the reminiscences. Instead, *Seven years*, in attributing the trauma experienced by Bogusławski to Tokarzewski with text taken from *A Siberian memoir*, not only violates the flexible norms of the *Sybiracy*'s understanding of authorship but also affirms Halina's influence on the composition of the recollections.

REMEMBERING SIBERIA: SHAPING THE DOCUMENTARY RECORD

The *Sybiracy*'s formation of mobile communities and the shared desire of Polish exiles and 1863 insurgents to encapsulate the experience of Siberian imprisonment and settlement allowed for the exchange and editing of manuscripts, for collaboration on written accounts, and for the inclusion of unattributed oral tales in survivor narratives. Therefore, despite the resultant shaping of eyewitness testimony, the fusing of individual oral narratives recalled by *Sybiracy* into a compiled account for the authentic preservation of a collective traumatic experience is embraced by members of the inter-revolutionary generation. All the same, the concept of authorship in these narratives is developed to the point that when one acts as an unacknowledged compiler, there are frequently clues in the text pointing the reader to their original sources, such as Iwanowski's eventual citation of Bogusławski or Giller's account of a visit to Colonel Wysocki that establishes a source for his information about Malczewski. Stories about Father Sierociński by Piotrowski and Bogusławski, who both write from witness testimony, are shrouded in anonymity, but this appears motivated by a desire to protect a fellow Siberian from potential harm rather than from the exploitation of another's experience. Nevertheless, the fact that several of these narratives from the inter-revolutionary period by Piotrowski, Giller, and Bogusławski contain references to the Omsk affair, which their authors did not witness, challenges their claims to present a verifiably accurate historical record, since they are removed from these events spatially and temporally.[74] The omission of this affair from *Seven years* further attests to Halina's influence on the reminiscences with her failure to appreciate the infamous nature of the event arising from her indirect knowledge of the inter-revolutionary generation's deportation and exile experience, which produces only secondary trauma for her.

Beginning during their confinement in citadels and their interrogations by tsarist commissions, text for the *Sybiracy* remained an important component of their traumatic dislocation, with the elaborately detailed sentences by the commissions (sometimes signed by the accused), the confiscation of personal papers, and individuals' attempts to record the fate of fallen comrades, which often were clandestinely passed to friends and traveling merchants so that they reached contacts in Poland or the West. Siberian exile for the inter-revolutionary generation translated into movement across vast expanses on foot and in kibitkas as well as multiple migrations eastward and westward so that written observations preserved in letters, notebooks, and loose papers traveled with the author and his compatriots. Yet the physical tribulations endured by some writers during penal servitude sometimes resulted in premature death, thereby preventing the completion of manuscripts, which were entrusted into the care of others, circulated among co-conspirators, and then edited by family, friends, or Siberian comrades for publication in newspapers and bound volumes. By the 1890s, however, the ethical imperative to preserve the documentary record of the midcentury's Siberian trauma allowed editors—whether historians or loved ones—to disregard the integrity of extant textual fragments. By this time the significant temporal distance between the historical referent and its narrative representation notably impacts *Seven years*, because the documentary moment that generates a "matrix of presumed truth" has competing truth claims in the established record by Bogusławski and in the historical imagination of those reading *House of the Dead* as Dostoevsky's thinly veiled autobiography.[75] Nevertheless, the need for "attestation-protestation" that addresses an "event itself so monstrous as to put to flight all the modes available to representation" is a way in which the relatives of exiles express their secondary trauma, which offers some justification for Halina's imaginative re-creation of her husband's penal servitude that masks his manuscript's connections to inter-revolutionary Warsaw.[76]

NOTES

1. In *Zesłańcy polscy w Imperium Rosyjskim w pierwszej połowie XIX wieku* (Warsaw: Wydawnictwo DiG, 1998), Wiktoria Śliwowska records approximately 2,800 biographies of Polish Siberians in the first half of the nineteenth century; in *Ucieczki z Sybiru* (Warsaw: Wydawnictwo Iskry, 2005) Śliwowska estimates that 40,000 Poles were sent to Siberia after 1863 (18), whereas Sergei Maksimov, *Sibir' i katorga* (St. Petersburg: Tipografiia A. Transhelia, 1871), places this number at approximately 19,000 (3:80).

2. Śliwowska notes that during the inter-revolutionary period, 310 Poles were sent to penal servitude, 573 were sentenced to service in special army corps, 453 were relocated into settlements, and 62 were restricted to monasteries, often in remote regions of Russia (*Ucieczki z Sybiru*, 12).

3. For a brief summary of Polish conspiracies from the 1830s and 1840s, see Maksimov, *Sibir' i katorga*, 3:36–37. For further information on Father Ściegienny and Kamieński as well as on Franciszek and Aleksander Dalewski, see Agaton Giller, "Lista wygnańców Polskich do roku 1860: Spisana przez Agatona Gillera na Syberyi," in *Album Muzeum Narodowego w Rapperswyll*, ed. Władysław Plater (Poznań: Nakładem J. K. Żupańskiego, 1872), 393, 404, 428; Włodzimierz Djakow, Adam Gałkowski, Wiktoria Śliwowska, Włodzimierz M. Zajcew, *Uczestnicy ruchów wolnościowych w latach 1832–1855 (Królestwo Polskie)* (Wrocław: Wydawnictwo Polskiej Akademii Nauk, 1990), 207–208, 442–443; and Śliwowska, *Zesłańcy polscy*, 120–121, 256–527, 613–615.

4. Maksimov, in the third part of *Sibir' i katorga*, subtitled *Politicheskie i gosudarstvennye prestupniki* (Political and state prisoners), finds that Giller credits such Polish communities in Eastern Siberia with the safe return of Polish exiles (3:52).

5. Alina Witkowska notes the significance of Pellico's memoirs for nineteenth-century Polish memoirists in Alina Witkowska and Ryszard Przybylski, *Romantyzm* (Warsaw: Wydawnictwo Naukowe PWN, 2000), 603.

6. For instance, in "Kilka o wygnaniu syberyjskiém szczegółów," in *Wspomnienia lat minionych* (Cracow: Skład główny w Księgarni Katolickiéj W. Miłkowskiego, 1876), Eustachy Heleniusz Iwanowski relies on Giller to verify biographical information of *Sybiracy* and characterizes Maksimov's treatment of Polish Siberians as fair and without "national hatred" (2:247).

7. Hugh Olmsted, "Modeling the Genealogy of Maksim Grek's Collection Types: The 'Plectogram' as Visual Aid in Reconstruction," in *Medieval Russian Culture*, ed. Michael S. Flier and Daniel Rowland, California Slavic Studies XIX (Berkeley: University of California Press, 1994), 2:109.

8. M. Iu. Lermontov, *Sochineniia* (Moscow: Izdatel'stvo "Pravda," 1990), 2:498.

9. Since in the Omsk prison fortress, Dostoevsky read *The Posthumous Papers of the Pickwick Club* (*Zamogil'nye zapiski Pikkvikskogo kluba*) by Charles Dickens, in which Mr. Pickwick must endure his own incarceration, the Russian novelist may have drawn on this title for the naming of his autobiographical novel.

10. N. V. Gogol', "Zapiski sumas shedshego," in *Polnoe sobranie sochinenii N. V. Gogolia* (Berlin: Slovo, 1921), 7:380. Aleksander Herzen, for example, invokes similar images of the inquisition, as is discussed in the fifth chapter of Elizabeth Blake's monograph, *Dostoevsky and the Catholic Underground* (Evanston, IL: Northwestern University Press, 2014).

11. F. M. Dostoevskii, *Zapiski iz mertvogo doma*, in *Polnoe sobranie sochinenii v tridtsati tomakh* (Leningrad: Nauka, 1972), 4:8.

12. Silvio Pellico, *Memoirs of My Imprisonments* (London: Henry Washbourne, 1850), 190, 217. Pellico's remembrances also penetrated the Russian capital, since a copy in French translation was found in Aleksander Pushkin's library.

13. Stanislaw Eile, *Literature and Nationalism in Partitioned Poland, 1795–1918* (New York: St. Martin's Press, 2000), 77.

14. Ibid., 79.

15. Paul Ricœur, *Memory, History, Forgetting*, trans. Kathleen Blamey and David Pellauer (Chicago: University of Chicago Press, 2004), 259.

16. Correspondence and manuscripts from Polish exiles connected to the Orenburg fortress (Bronisław Zaleski and Edward Żeligowski) as well as a manuscript from Rufin Piotrowski are located in this collection.

17. Hayden White, *Metahistory: The Historical Imagination in Nineteenth-Century Europe* (Baltimore: Johns Hopkins University Press, 1973), 5.

18. Śliwowska, *Ucieczki z Sybiru*, 148.

19. Julian Klaczko's translation for *Revue des deux mondes* under the title "Souvenirs d'un Sibérien" first popularized Piotrowski's remembrances in Western Europe; the preface to an 1863 English edition, *The Story of a Siberian Exile* (London: Longman and Green, 1863) clarifies that the translator is using Klaczko's version (viii).

20. Śliwowska, *Zesłańcy polscy*, 463.

21. "Martyre du Prieur Sierocinski," 1851, Archiwum Hotelu Lambert, MS 5660, Biblioteka Czartoryskich w Krakowie (B. Czart.).

22. Rufin Piotrowski, *Pamiętniki z pobytu na Syberyi*, 3 vols. (Poznań: Nakładem Księgarni Jana Konstantego Żupańskiego, 1860), 3:23. In a list of his Siberian compatriots at the beginning of the third volume, Piotrowski suggests a potential local source for his account of the affair when highlighting Adolf Januszkiewicz's presence in Omsk in the 1840s and 1850s (3:5). His posthumously published memoirs, *Żywot Adolfa Januszkiewicza i jego listy ze stepów kirgizkich* (The life of Adolf Januszkiewicz and his letters from the Kirgiz steppes), appeared in 1861.

23. Piotrowski, *Pamiętniki*, 3:18.

24. Ibid., 3:20.

25. Ibid., 3:22. It is possible that Giller is the source of this confirmation, since Giller and Piotrowski share a mutual acquaintance in Gerwazy Gzowski, whom Piotrowski met in 1845 while Gzowski was passing through on his way to Eastern Siberia. For their connection, see Jakób Gieysztor, *Pamiętniki z lat 1857–1865*, ed. Tadeusz Korzon (Vilnius: Księgarnia Stowar. Nauczycielstwa Polskiego, 1921), 1:197.

26. A. I. Gertsen, *Sobranie sochinenii v vos'mi tomakh* (Moscow: Izdatel'stvo "Pravda," 1975), 7:350.

27. White, *Metahistory*, 7. White here refers to the structure, that is, tragedy, romance, comedy, or satire, engaged by the historian to narrate his story.

28. For example, Tokarzewski's 1866 letter to Agaton Giller includes a list of Siberian exiles (Fragment korespondencji Agatona Gillera z lat 1867–1887, MS 7138, Biblioteka Jagiellońska [BJ]), and Giller's letters to Bronisław Zaleski (Archiwum Hotelu Lambert: Bronisław Zaleski. Korespondencja. Listy od Agatona Gillera, MS 6370, B. Czart.) contain various references to his Siberian period.

29. Agaton Giller, *Podróż więźnia etapami do Syberyi w roku 1854* (Leipzig: F. A. Brockhaus, 1866), 1:5–6; Śliwowska, *Zesłańcy polscy*, 135, 392, 522–523. They are all mentioned in Agaton Giller's *Opisanie zabajkalskiej krainy w Syberyi* (Leipzig: F. A. Brockhaus,

1867), 1:255; 2:109. Giller wrote a biography of Ruprecht as well: *Karol Ruprecht: Szkic biograficzny* (Lwów: Nakładem autora, z drukarni J. Dobrzanskiego i K. Gromana, 1875).

30. Giller, *Podróż*, 1:vii.

31. Bronisław Zaleski makes this connection in "Wygnańcy polscy w Orenburgu," *Rocznik Towarzystwa Historyczno-Literackiego* (Paris: Księgarnia Luxemburgska, 1867), 77; also, Bakunin's 1862 article presents Pugachev's importance for anti-tsarist movements, including those of Polish origin, in "Narodnoe delo: Romanov, Pugachev, ili Pestel'?," in *Polnoe sobranie sochinenii* (St. Petersburg: Izdanie I. Balashova, 1907), 1: 230, 234.

32. Giller, *Podróż*, 2:221.

33. Ibid., 1:59, 63; 2:139; Śliwowska, *Zesłańcy polscy*, 257. Appearing as Kamiński in Giller, Kamieński's biographical information (son of a general, connection to Lubelsk, 1846 exile to Viatka, and writing career) demonstrates that Giller is referring to Kamieński, who appears under entry #385 in "Lista Wygnańców Polskich" and whose remembrances were published as "Mémoires d'un prisonnier" (1865).

34. In *Sybir Romantyków* (Poznań: W drodze, 1993), Zofia Trojanowiczowa lists his cities of residence from 1864 to 1870 as Dresden, Leipzig, Bendlikon, and Paris (468).

35. Giller, *Opisanie*, 1:18.

36. In his article published in the same year, Giller's fellow Siberian exile and correspondent Zaleski refers to "the conspiracy of Father Sierociński and doctor Szokalski" as being known all over Siberia ("Wygnańcy Polscy," 85).

37. Giller, *Opisanie*, 2:107; Śliwowska, *Zesłańcy polscy*, 361. Curiously, this remembrance coincides with the publication of Colonel Piotr Wysocki's publication of *Memoir of the Uprising of November 29th, 1830* (*Pamiętnik o powstaniu 29 listopada 1830 roku*, 1867).

38. Giller, *Opisanie*, 1:258–261. According to V. A. D'iakov, D. B. Katsnel'son, and B. S. Shostakovich, in "Petr Vysotskii na Sibirskoi katorge (1835–56)," *Ssyl'nye revoliutsionery v Sibiri* 4 (1979), Malczewski was in Nerchinsk-Zavod with a former Konarski conspirator Doctor Beaupré who treated Dr. Szokalski (26).

39. Giller, *Opisanie*, 195. For a recollection of Dr. Szokalski by his fellow surviving conspirator Franciszek Knoll, see Anna Brus, Elżbieta Kaczyńska, and Wiktoria Śliwowska, *Zesłanie i katorga na Syberii w dziejach Polaków 1815–1914* (Warsaw: Wydawnictwo Naukowe PWN, 1992), 245–248.

40. Giller, *Opisanie*, 196–197; Śliwowska, *Zesłańcy polscy*, 388.

41. Maksimov, *Sibir' i katorga*, 29, 45, 46. Later in 1870, Giller published *Z wygnania* (From exile), which reflects a more thorough examination of the Polish exile community in Eastern Siberia and includes a series of biographical accounts of its prominent members. This indicates that Giller had access to secondary sources on Eastern Siberia before he published his own memoirs.

42. For example, see Giller's *Polska w walce: Zbiór wspomnień i pamiętników z dziejów naszego wyjarzmienia* (Poland in combat: A collection of remembrances and memoirs from the history of our unyoking, 1868).

43. See Sybirski pamiętnik Józefa Bogusławskiego, 1898, MS 5913 III, BJ. Whereas Giller lists Bogusławski as dying en route from Carlsbad to Częstochowa in 1859 ("Lista Wygnańców Polskich," 388), the publisher's introduction to "Wspomnienia Sybiraka: Pamiętniki Józefa Bogusławskiego," *Nowa Reforma* (1896) 249:1, situates his 1857 death in Częstochowa.

44. Although the preface to the first edition dates Tokarzewski's death to 1900 instead of 1890, an announcement of his death in the July 5, 1890, issue of *Gazeta Warszawska*

(Warsaw Gazette) and an obituary in *Kurjer Warszawski* (Warsaw Courier) on the same day confirm that he died on July 3, 1890—the same date that appears in the preface to the second edition of *Seven years* (1918). I am grateful to research librarians Jan Adamczyk and Barbara Bułat for helping me locate these sources.

45. Giller, *Opisanie*, 2:77.

46. For more on Röhr, see N. W. Berg, *Pamiętniki o polskich spiskach i powstaniach 1831–1862*, trans. W. Ralex (Cracow: Nakład G. Gebethnera i Spółki, 1894), 69, 74–75, 77, 81, 85. Karol Ruprecht is also mentioned in connection with the conspiracy (83).

47. Berg, *Pamiętniki*, 83–98.

48. Heleniusz was a pseudonym used by the author.

49. For letters (1877–1882) written to Iwanowski by another former Konarski conspirator, Gaspar Maszkowski, relating to the historian details about Siberian exile life, see Korespondencja, materiały do pracy i papiery Eustachego Iwanowskiego. Korespondencja, L-F, vol. 2, MS 5931, BJ.

50. Iwanowski mentions this in the description (Spis rękopisów, darowanych bibliotece [Jagiellońskiej] dnia 17 VI 1887 przez Eust [achego] Iwanowskiego, MS 4545, BJ) of his 1887 donation to Jagiellonian University, which included a copy of Sawicz's memoirs (Pamiętnik Sawicza, syna ks. unickiego, MS 4509, BJ).

51. [Eustachy Iwanowski], *Wspomnienia polskich czasów dawnych i późniejszych* 2 vols. (Lwów: w komisie księgarni Gubrynowicza i Schmidta, 1894), 2: 109–110; Szymon Tokarzewski, *Siedem lat katorgi: Pamiętniki Szymona Tokarzewskiego 1846–1857 r.*, 2nd ed. (Warsaw: Gebethner i Wolff, 1918), 47–48.

52. Śliwowska, *Zesłańcy polscy*, 539.

53. Iwanowski, *Wspomnienia polskich czasów*, 2: 129.

54. Dostoevskii, *Zapiski iz mertvogo doma*, 4:217. For instance, the *Sybirak* Stanisław Krupski claims that an eighth chapter of Dostoevsky's novel was banned by the censor for its account of the Omsk affair—"that bloody episode which Piotrowski recalls"; for further details, see Śliwowska, *Ucieczki z Sybiru*, 275; Krupski, *Luźne karty pamiętnika zbiega z Sybiru*, vols. 1–2 (Leipzig: F. A. Brockhaus, 1877), 1: 264.

55. Iwanowski, *Wspomnienia polskich czasów*, 2: 111; Sybirski pamiętnik, MS 5913 III, fol. 22.

56. Jerzy Myśliński, "Prasa Polska w Galicji w dobie autonomicznej," in *Prasa Polska w latach 1864–1918* (Warsaw: Państwowe Wydawnictwo Naukowe, 1976), 124.

57. Bogusławski, "Wspomnienia Sybiraka," 249:1; Śliwowska, *Ucieczki z Sybiru*, 350–351. In her discussion of the mystery surrounding the authorship of this text, Śliwowska confirms that Szymon Tokarzewski is the only possible *Sybirak* to have edited the manuscript, even though the manuscript currently held in the library at Jagiellonian University is not written in Tokarzewski's handwriting.

58. For example, Bogusławski's published recollections from *Nowa reforma* are frequently cited in the research of D'iakov and Śliwowska. Also, with the acknowledgment of the previous partial publication of Bogusławski's memoirs, the 1896 editor recognizes an earlier variant of the manuscript, whose prior existence must necessarily limit his ability to revise and supplement "Recollections of a *Sybirak*."

59. Szymon Tokarzewski, *Siedem lat katorgi: Pamiętniki Szymona Tokarzewskiego 1846–1857 g.*, (Warsaw: Gebethner i Wolff, 1907), 160–162; Tokarzewski, *Siedem lat*, 1918, 125, 172–173. In *Dzieje polaków na Syberji* (Cracow: Krakowska Spółka Wydawnicza, 1928), Michał Janik points out that Tokarzewski either "took" some of his fellow inmate's

remembrances or at least "reconciled" his own with those of Bogusławski (221). Zofia Bobowicz-Potocka discusses similarities in "Kto był właściwym autorem rozdziału poświęconego Dostojewskiemu w książce Szymona Tokarzewskiego *Siedem lat katorgi?,*" *Przegląd Humanistyczny* 8 (1975): 91–94. For a summary of the critical reception of *Seven years* in the Russian press for its similarities with *House of the Dead*, see Elizabeth Blake, "Portraits of the Siberian Dostoevsky by Poles in the *House of the Dead*," *Dostoevsky Studies, New Series* X (2006): 60–62.

60. Jan Trynkowski, "Z Zabajkala, przez Chiny, do Szwajcarii: List Szymona Tokarzewskiego do Agatona Gillera z 13 czerwca 1866 roku," in *Zesłancy postyczniowi w Imperium Rosyjskim*, ed. Eugeniusz Niebelski (Lublin: Wydawnictwo KUL, 2008), 160–162.

61. Ricœur, *Memory, History, Forgetting*, 254.

62. Trynkowski, "Z Zabajkala," 158.

63. Tokarzewski, *Siedem lat*, 1907, 212; Tokarzewski, *Siedem lat*, 1918, 218.

64. Tokarzewski, *Siedem lat*, 1918, 231; Tadeusz Korzon, *Mój pamiętnik przedhistoryczny* (Cracow: Skład główny w księgarni G. Gebethnera i Sp., 1912), 58.

65. Korzon, *Mój pamiętnik*, 58; Tokarzewski, *Siedem lat*, 1918, 231.

66. Tokarzewski, *Siedem lat*, 1918, 10. The Swiętokrzyżcy (e.g., Gerwazy Gzowski, Gustaw Ehrenberg, and Michał Olszewski) had links to Konarski's Association of the Polish People, but Gzowski also had connections to Kamieński's Union of the Polish Nation according to Śliwowska in *Zesłańcy polscy* (202).

67. Shimon Tokarzhevskii, *Sibirskoe likholet'e* (Kemerovo: Kuzbassvuzizdat, 2007), 452–467; Maryan Dubiecki, *Teresa z Wierzbickich Bułhakowa: Wizerunek pośmiertny z jej pamiętników, listów, notat* (Krakow: W Drukarni "Czasu" Fr. Kluczyckiego I Spółki, 1895), 36–44.

68. Śliwowska, *Ucieczki z Sybiru*, 353.

69. This is evident from Narcyza Żmichowska's extant correspondence, the article attributed to *Gazeta Polska* in the 1907 preface to *Seven years*, and Tokarzewski's account found in *Bez paszportu: Z pamiętników wygnańca* (Warsaw: Getherner i Wolff, 1910), 24–26.

70. Tokarzewski, *Siedem lat*, 1918, 6; Bogusławski, "Wspomnienia Sybiraka," 249:1. For a similar description of Tokarzewski in an 1858 letter, see Narcyza Żmichowska, *Listy* vols. 1–5 (Wrocław: Zakład imienia Ossolińskich, 1957–1967), 2:126.

71. Żmichowska, *Listy*, 2:372.

72. Gieysztor recalls seeing all of these Siberians in Warsaw in the early 1860s (*Pamiętniki*, 1:197). Aleksander Mirecki was imprisoned along with Dobrycz and Michał Mirecki, according to Walerian Staniszewski, *Pamiętniki więźnia stanu i zesłańca*, ed. Adam Gałkowski and Wiktoria Śliwowska (Warsaw: Instytut Stosowanych Nauk Społecznych UW, 1994), 17. In [B. Zaleski], *Notatka o powstaniu 1863 r[oku]*, in *Bronisława Zaleskiego i Kajetana Cieszkowskiego nieznane relacje o powstaniu styczniowym*, ed. W. Caban and R. Matura (Kielce: Wyższa Szkoła Pedagogiczna im. Jana Kochanowskiego, 1997), 27, Zaleski himself remembers the public punishment of Bogusławski in an account with some general similarities to that in Bogusławski's "Wspomnienia Sybiraka" (249:1) and Giller's *Opisanie* (2:77).

73. *Sybirski pamiętnik*, MS 5913 III, fol. 2, 24, 26.

74. This is also arguably true of *House of the Dead*, as Blake discovers in *Dostoevsky and the Catholic Underground* (47–48).

75. Ricœur, *Memory, History, Forgetting*, 256.

76. Ibid.

CHAPTER 10

Technology, the City, and the Body
Bergelson and Shklovsky in Berlin

Harriet Murav

FOR VIKTOR SHKLOVSKY, the Russian-language Formalist writer and critic, and for David Bergelson, the Yiddish prose author, the city of Berlin, the place of their temporary exile in the 1920s, presented a fascinating spectacle of city life and technological sophistication, as well as the horrific traces of World War I. Both refer to the so-called broken men, veterans who had suffered severe and dramatically visible bodily disfigurement. In the "postscript" to *Zoo, or Letters Not about Love* (written and published in Berlin), Shklovsky notes that the "streets are filled with terribly subdued cripples."[1] The protagonist of Bergelson's "Among Refugees," a veteran of World War I, has a mutilated face, recalling Otto Dix's painting of a young soldier after a skin graft operation.[2] Berlin, like other urban centers of this time, displayed unmistakable evidence of the impact of technology on the human body. The city also provided a fresh impetus for Shklovsky and Bergelson's literary experimentation. Shklovsky had already written his critical manifesto *Art as Device* before arriving in Berlin; however, he developed and elaborated this concept in his Berlin-era work by linking literary and technological devices. Bergelson, like Shklovsky, was fascinated by technology and gadgetry of all kinds, including earlier innovations, for example, the bolting mill, which assumes the role of a character in *Der toyber* (*The Deaf Man*), written in

1906. In addition, the train, telegraph, and camera appear prominently in his pre–World War I work; his 1913 novel *Nokh alemen* (*The End of Everything*) includes a detailed description of a medical inhalation device.[3] His 1929 novel *Mides-hadin* (*Judgment*) takes this interest in technology in a new direction by inserting images of a new type of collective or mass subject that is vulnerable to the workings of power.[4]

The question of the body and the machine was the central question of much twentieth-century thought; Henri Bergson's study of laughter, the futurists' love affair with machines, Vsevolod Meyerhold's biomechanics, and Taylorization are examples.[5] Technology offered the possibility of a positive transformation of the human being, new conditions for work and recreation, and new freedom from the tyranny of material necessity and human incapacity. In 1925 Sigmund Freud wrote that when man put on all his prosthetic devices, he was "truly magnificent."[6] World War I also revealed the opposite—what technologically enhanced battle could do to the "tiny, fragile, human body," as Walter Benjamin put it in "The Storyteller" in 1932.[7] The machine occupied a prominent place in the new utopias and new artistic and literary practices, aimed at the transition from art to life. The Yiddish-language critic Daniel Tsharni, as I show, refers to the cinema of the 1920s as a model for the building of socialism. Raymond Williams's observations about the circumstances giving rise to the emergence of modernism illuminate my point. In his essay published posthumously in 1989, *The Politics of the Avant-Garde*, Williams writes, "There is a virtually unprecedented emphasis on the most evident features of a modern urbanized industrialized world: the city, the machine, speed, space—the creative engineering, *construction of a future*."[8] This chapter explores the intersection of technology, migration, and literary innovation in Shklovsky and Bergelson.

I am not arguing that Shklovsky and Bergelson were personally acquainted or knew each other's work directly. My claim is that they were thinking along parallel lines, derived from similar sources, and that the broad issues they engage—dislocation, the body and its relation to the machine—are better understood in a fluid framework of comparison and contiguity, rather than in the more limiting one-to-one model of influence.[9] Both writers experienced the dislocation, violence, and upheaval brought by the great historical events of the Russian Revolution and Russian Civil War. Both were fascinated and delighted by the new technologies and new forms of art of their time—including cinema. While historical transformation does not in itself engender new aesthetics, parallels can be noted between the disruptions of everyday life and the embrace of disruption as a form of art in the work of both Bergelson and Shklovsky. I begin with some general remarks about the life paths of the two authors before turning to a discussion of their use of what I call literary technology. One of the most important points of intersection is their shared ambivalence about the capacity of the machine and the new socialist order to improve human life. Both Bergelson and Shklovsky questioned notions of historical progression and the teleology that it implies. This is yet another sense in which they are preoccupied with movement and its success or failure.

TWO JOURNEYS

Viktor Shklovsky was born in St. Petersburg in 1893.[10] In *Sentimental Journey*, he describes himself as "the son of a Jew and of half-Jewish blood."[11] He was a student at the University of St. Petersburg when he became interested in Futurism. One of the founders of OPOIAZ (*Obshchestvo izucheniia poeticheskogo iazyka*, The Society for the Study of Poetic Language), Shklovsky fought in the tsarist army during World War I, training recruits in the use of armored cars—a biographical fact that is important for his literary work. The movement of the plot in works of fiction and the movement of objects in space in the realm of daily life are directly linked in Shklovsky's thought. After the October revolution and civil war, the Bolsheviks began arresting Socialist Revolutionaries, the party to which Shklovsky belonged, and in 1922 put them on trial. It was at this time that Shklovsky fled, first to Finland and then Berlin.[12]

Unlike Shklovsky, the Yiddish prose writer David Bergelson, born in Ukraine in 1884, received no formal secular education, except for his sporadic attempts at the Kiev dental school. He read widely, however, in Hebrew, Yiddish, and Russian and was well acquainted with the new ideas of his time. By the time he arrived in Berlin in 1921, Bergelson was highly reputed as a Yiddish modernist innovator.[13] In the years 1914–1919,

Bergelson moved from city to city in Ukraine, settling in Kiev. In 1918 Bergelson was one of the founders of the Kiev Kultur-Lige, an association that promoted Yiddish modernist culture in multiple media, including theater, visual art, and literature. Bergelson was first exposed to Cubo-Futurist art in Kiev, because of his contact with the painters Alexandra Exter and Issacher Ber Ryback.[14] The new style of painting sought to introduce movement and rhythm in the traditionally immobile pictorial space. In Kiev, Bergelson also undertook the editorship of several short-lived Yiddish literary journals, including *Eygns* (Our own), in which he published *Opgang* (Descent) and *Yoysef Shur*.

In Berlin, Bergelson was the co-editor of the Yiddish-language modern art journal *Milgroym* (The Pomegranate). Ryback's cubist portrait of an old Jewish man and a clock appeared in its first issue, the same issue in which Bergelson published his own short story "Onheyb Kislev 1919" ("The Beginning of Kislev 1919"). Bergelson wrote for the New York Yiddish newspaper *The Forward*, later changing to the more leftist *Morgen frayhayt* (Morning Freedom). He authored dozens of short works, some set in Berlin—for example, *Tsvishn emigrantn* (Among Refugees) and *Blindkeyt* (Blindness), others set in the *shtetlekh* (market towns) of Ukraine. Bergelson remained in Berlin until 1933, when Hitler came to power; he traveled in Europe and returned to the Soviet Union in 1934.

Neither Shklovsky nor Bergelson sought refuge from anti-Jewish violence in Berlin. Both, however, describe the anti-Jewish violence perpetrated during the Russian Civil War. For Bergelson, the crisis came at the end of 1919, when the author could no longer find work in Kiev, and the threat of violent death from ongoing pogroms became very real. Bergelson participated in an appeal to "friends of Yiddish" in America, seeking help in relocation to the United States, but nothing came of his request.[15] He spent 1920–1921 in Moscow, traveling to Berlin in 1921 at the invitation of a publisher. The plot of "Among Refugees" and other Berlin-era work also directly concerns anti-Jewish violence. Bergelson's story "The Beginning of Kislev 1919," published in *Milgroym* in 1922, paints a bleak picture of a dead Jew, thrown from a train and lying frozen and lifeless on the ground. In *Sentimental Journey*, for example, Shklovsky also describes the killing of Jews by soldiers (61), the murder of trainloads full of Jewish refugees (163), and the murder of his brother, a doctor working on a hospital train, who was beaten to death (156). Both writers transform the train—the symbol of historical and technological progress par excellence—into a killing machine.

Regardless of the difficulties that had to be overcome, especially for Shklovsky, in order to arrive in Berlin, neither he nor Bergelson felt particularly at home there. Shklovsky's *Sentimental Journey*, published in Russian in Berlin in 1923, ends as follows: "Now I live among emigrants and am myself becoming a shadow among shadows" (Ia seichas zhivu sredi emigrantov i sam obrashchaius' v ten' sredi tenei).[16] The last line of Bergelson's "Among Refugees," written while the author was living in Berlin and first published in Kiev in 1927, reads: "I'm an emigrant . . . among emigrants. . . . I don't want to be one anymore" (Ikh bin an emigrant . . . tsvishn emigrantn. . . . ikh vil es mer nisht) [ellipsis in the original].[17] The speaker in Bergelson's text is the would be "Jewish terrorist," the unnamed protagonist with a crooked face who plans but fails to carry out the killing of a pogromist with whom he shares temporary living quarters in Berlin. The fact that both Shklovsky and Bergelson experienced dislocation in the same urban setting at the same moment, a moment full of echoes and aftermaths—of World War I, the Russian Revolution, and the Russian Civil War—enters into their common articulation of the experience of diaspora.[18] To be an immigrant in both Shklovsky's and Bergelson's texts is to live a secondary existence as the mere shadowy reflection of an imagined fuller, richer life lived at a home that no longer existed.

TECHNOLOGY, LITERARY AND OTHERWISE

Shklovsky is best known for *Iskusstvo kak priem* (*Art as Device*), first published in 1917, in which he argued that the task of literary art is not to reflect history, psychology, sociology, or the biography of its creator. The purpose of literary art is to awaken perception, dulled by habitual responses to the world; art "make[s] a stone feel stony" again.[19] Literature accomplishes this goal by impeding the recognition of objects and experiences—the famous "defamiliarization" or "estrangement" (*ostranenie*). Shklovsky was also fascinated by the new technologies of his time, including film and the automobile. Like his more well-known German contemporaries Benjamin and Siegfried Kracauer, he was interested in the way that technology changes consciousness. The tools we use use us:

> A tool not only extends the arm of a man, but also makes it an extension of himself.
> They say that a blind man localizes his sense of touch in the end of his cane.
> I feel no attachment to my shoes, but they are, all the same, an extension of me; they are a part of me....
> What changes a man most of all is the machine.
> ...
> The machine gunner and the contrabassist are extensions of their instruments.
> Subways, cranes, and automobiles are the artificial limbs of mankind.
> (ellipses added) (*A Sentimental Journey*, 114–115)

Shklovsky's notion of the prosthesis is not limited to the artificial limb that substitutes for an injured or missing part of the body. Not merely a replacement, the prosthesis is rather an extension of the body. This is also true the other way around: the human being in contact with the instrument is the extension of the instrument, as if the instrument had its own autonomous life. The way I move in space and, indeed, my entire interaction with the surrounding world changes because of the prosthetic. The machine that produces speed changes the human being who uses it, because, as Shklovsky puts it, "speed requires a goal" (119). If we have the capacity to drive at great speeds, we invent reasons for doing so; behavior and consciousness change because the technology makes new forms of behavior and consciousness possible.

There is a connection between Shklovsky's notion of art as device and his model of the human being as prosthetic extension. In his *Theory of Prose*, the device is the supplement that replaces character, emotion, biography, history, psychology, and every other dimension of artistic prose that up until the Formalists was taken as the central core of the artistic work. When Shklovsky says, "speed requires a goal," the attribution of agency to velocity itself decenters the human subject. Shklovsky writes in a similar way about the artistic device that creates content. A subplot, for example, serves the purpose of slowing down the action. The preoccupation with the enhanced speed of physical objects in space goes hand in hand with slowed motion and impeded perception in the aesthetic realm. In both literary and real-life instances, the mechanism, whether linguistic or physical, takes over and extends the function previously attributed to the human author, understood in both the literary and existential sense of authoring oneself and one's own actions. Shklovsky's penchant for one-sentence paragraphs, as in the examples quoted earlier, contributes to the overall effect of the decentering of the author. Short bursts of utterance replace the flow of expression, suggesting the image of Shklovsky as a speaker disconnected from himself.

Shklovsky's growing doubt about his ability to author his own life emerges in *Sentimental Journey* when he says that the forces moving him were external to him: "I am only a falling stone" (133). In *Art as Device*, the function of art is to make us perceive and not merely recognize the particular qualities of the stone as a stone, as an object whose own existence is separate and strange to the human being; in this text, in contrast, the stone's capacity to fall is a metaphor for the author's own powerlessness.

In *Judgment*, written in Berlin, Bergelson describes the new Bolshevik order as a regime of strict justice: "There the first fires blazed up high against the horizon . . . they are the cold fires of judgment . . . fires of a strange new harsher world."[20] The novel traces the establishment of Bolshevik power in a border town, where recalcitrant Jews and non-Jews smuggle people, goods, and anti-Bolshevik literature across the border. A former monastery serves as the jail, interrogation center, and place of execution, presided over by Filipov, the so-called ambassador of history. Among the inmates is Yuzi Spivak, arrested for his anti-Bolshevik activities on behalf of the local Socialist Revolutionaries. This is the party that Shklovsky belonged to. By the end of the work, Spivak has gone over to the Bolshevik side, and Filipov has heroically sacrificed himself for the Bolshevik cause.

The chief interest of the work does not lie in its improbable and conventional plot. What is remarkable is Bergelson's innovative style, especially with regard to the image of the decentered human individuals and their reformulation as a mass subject. This change is parallel to the dispersion of human subjectivity into various prosthetic devices, as I argued earlier with regard to Shklovsky. Massification, however, is not the same as prosthetic transformation. Before examining the mass subject and its implications in

Bergelson's text, a few words of introduction will be helpful. My discussion relies on one of the foremost theorists of mass phenomena, Siegfried Kracauer.

In his essay *The Mass Ornament*, Kracauer interpreted popular entertainment of the 1920s in light of the twin forces of capitalism and technology. He considered the synchronized movements of the dance group the Tiller Girls as "the aesthetic reflex of the rationality to which the prevailing economic system aspires." The calculations of the movements of the factory worker and the Tiller Girls take as their smallest unit arms and legs and not the individual body of the worker or dancer. The result is a rational and aesthetically pleasing but nonetheless violent dismemberment of the human body. Each part of the body goes into the composition of the work as a whole; each body part corresponds to "fractions of a figure." Kracauer goes on to critique the mass ornament as the figure of fascism.

What Kracauer criticized as the negative effect of capitalism on human consciousness and the human body, Russian Constructivism and the theory of biomechanics lauded as a means of producing a new human collectivity and a renewed relation to the surrounding world.[21] Consciousness could be changed by working from the outside inward, from the movement of the body to thought and emotion. In *Judgment*, Bergelson uses the same set of aesthetic elements deployed by Russian constructivist literature, art, and theater. These devices include the formation of a visible figure by the coordinated action of more than one individual, the synchronized movement of a mass of people, and the disaggregation of the human body.

In the opening of the novel, for example, the commandant Filipov orders three men to go on their regular ten p.m. patrol. As the scene opens, two of the men are sitting in a room; one plays the accordion, another taps his feet in time to the music. Then:

> Suddenly the accordion stopped playing.... The wall started to shake from dull, blunt, heavy blows. The blows seemed at first to come from far away, from deep under the earth. But the more they repeated the closer and more stubborn they seemed....
> Then they rode away from the courtyard, in a triangle-shaped formation that looked like the Hebrew vowel *segol*.
>
> Di harmoshke hot ofgehert tsu shpiln.... Di vant hot aroysgegebn toybe, tempe un shvere klep. Di klep hobn fun anheyb zikh gedakht vayter vi zey

voltn kumen tif fun under der erd. Nor vos mer zey hobn zikh ibergehazert
alts nenter hot zikh gefilt di ekshones, mit velkher zey faln in der vant....
Itst rayt men aroys fun hoyf, vi in a segol.²²

I'll call this "action by remote control." The actions of individuals get displaced onto their instruments; for example, the accordion stops playing of its own will. Shklovsky's characterization of "the machine gunner" and the musician as "extensions of their instruments" applies well to this scene. The exchange between human beings and technology goes beyond objects that we would conventionally consider tools, instruments, or devices, however. It is not Filipov who hammers the wall with his fist; it is rather the wall itself that gives out blows. Finally, the end result of this remote trigger is the triangle-shaped formation of the three riders. Each individual rider is merely a point in the figure.

The site of the prison itself provides opportunities for the description of mass phenomena. It is significant that the Moscow State Yiddish Theater's staging of the work in dramatic form included "mass scenes."²³ Bergelson animates the inanimate prison building and renders inanimate the crowd of people gathered at its entrance:

> Out of boredom the peephole in the heavy door yawned with its mouth half open. The doors lazily opened and shut. Sleepily they grabbed a woman and took her in to her husband, and ten minutes later they spit her back out and snatched another woman.
>
> Fun langvaylikayt genetst mit a halb moyl der 'kuker,' vos in di shvere toyern. Foyl efenen zikh di toyern un farmakhn ikh bald vider. Farshlofenerhayt khapn zey arayn a yidene tsu ir arestirtn man un in tsen minut arum shpayen zey zi fun zikh aroys tsurik afn plats un khapn arayn a tsveyte.²⁴

The inanimate objects in the passage move, act, and take on human qualities, including sleepiness and laziness, whereas the human beings resemble passive objects that are moved from place to place not by their own agency. The women are grabbed up and spit out. The whole building seems similar to a giant artificial human being, a *golem* (to which Bergelson refers elsewhere in the work) with eyes (the peephole), a mouth (also the peephole), and limbs (the doors). The functions of the eyes and mouth are deliberately confused: the peephole, the eyes, open into a yawn, like a mouth.

Bergelson continues his exploration of the human body as an amalgamation of individual parts in another scene, in which prisoners, arrested for speculation, wait to be executed. They discuss a man who, "before his death, removed his own rubber dental plate with five gold teeth" to send to his wife ("hot farn toyt aroysgenumen fun moyl a kautshukukove gumen mit goldene tseyn").[25] Although this image for a post-1945 reader seems to be prescient, Bergelson could not have anticipated that the Nazis would harvest gold teeth and hair from the Jews they killed. Turning one's own body into a source of valuable products, a form of self-commodification, suggests the transformation of the person into sheer materiality, a way of using oneself up in the most literal sense. Bergelson read and reworked Franz Kafka's *The Hunger Artist* into his own Berlin story, "Far tsvelf toyznt dolar fast er fertsik teg" ("For 12,000 Bucks He Fasts Forty Days: Scenes of Berlin").[26] Bergelson writes, "In the very heart of Berlin, which is always teeming with heretics from all over the globe, a boy had been fasting."[27] Berlin serves as a global destination for intellectuals of every nationality. Both the Kafka and the Bergelson stories feature what we now call "performance artists," who starve themselves in exchange for payment, thus taking the principle of the alienation of one's labor to its grotesque extreme and laying bare the device of capitalism.

In his study of train travel, Wolfgang Schivelbusch uses the term *machine ensemble* to encompass the aggregated, interlocking system of transportation and communication—including the train and the telegraph—that completely changed the nineteenth-century European landscape.[28] This term captures well the intermeshing of human and mechanical action in *Judgment*. My final example of the machine ensemble is the scene of Filipov's medical examination. It begins with the sound of a clock (a prominent element in the Ryback portrait I discussed earlier):

> Tick-tock, tick-tock.
> Its beat is like cold drops dripping in the stillness. And the stillness is hard, like stone.
> ...
> It seems that:
> The cheap alarm clock is counting out his last minutes.
>
> Tik-tak, tik-tak.
> Vi kalte tropns tripn zayne klep in der shtilkayt. Un di shtilkayt iz hart, vi shteyn.

...
Es dakht zikh:
Der biliker vek-zeyger tseylt im oys zayne letse minutn (ellipsis added).²⁹

The rhythm created by the sound of the ticking of the clock—"tik-tak" ("tick-tock") is transformed into "tropns tripn" (drops dripping); as the scene continues, the ticking of the clock is repeated twice more. The cold drops dripping become the "cold fingertips" of the doctor as he feels his patient's pulse, an internal bodily rhythm.

Bergelson adds yet another rhythm to the scene, as the doctor feels the goiter on the sick man's neck and throat. It seems to the doctor that the patient says "Tapst mikh . . . tapst mikh . . . mikh hot men shoyn genug arumgetapt" (Tap, tap me, you've tapped me out). In both the Yiddish original and my translation, "tap" repeats three times in one line. The tapping rhythm works both extradiagetically, on the reader, and diagetically, within the world of the novel. The tapping rhythm is so overpowering that even when Filipov interrupts the exam by sitting up in bed, the doctor's fingers continue to palpate his neck:

> And the doctor's tapping fingers foolishly remained hanging in the air, stubbornly dancing their pointless dance.
>
> Un dem doktors arumtapndike finger hobn baleydikt un lepish a tants gegebn in der luft un zenen narish geblibn hengen.³⁰

The sound of the clock, "tik-tak," in the previous passages and the sound of the doctor's "tapping" fingers interact with one another to create another new rhythm. Dialogue is superfluous here, because what interests Bergelson is the acoustical choreography that the ticking clock sets in motion, the "dance" performed by the doctor's fingers. The effect that this scene creates on the reader provides an instance of what Shklovsky would call "tactile perception," or "texture," that is, the accentuation of sound qualities that disrupt the flow of easily recognizable meaning. Shklovsky characterizes both verbal art and painting as the creation of a "continuous palpable thing, a textured thing."³¹ The repeating "tik-tak" and "tap" produce a mechanized verbal texture in a scene devoid of human voices.

Before the Berlin period, Bergelson served for a short time as editor of the Yiddish journal *Di yidishe velt* (The Jewish World). In 1913 this journal included an article that closely paraphrased the French philosopher Bergson's essay on laughter.[32] Bergson defined the comedic as something mechanical superimposed on life: "We laugh every time a person gives the impression of being a thing" (58). A vivid example is the eating machine in Charlie Chaplin's 1921 *Modern Times*. Chaplin, trussed up in a device that mechanically sends food to his mouth, looks both comical and frightened. The famous dance of the dinner rolls in *The Gold Rush*, in which Chaplin's head and hands fuse seamlessly with the forks that hold the rolls—offers a more positive view of the interaction between the body and technological devices, in this instance, forks. As Tom Gunning points out, a charming new human being is created, consisting of Chaplin's head; the forks, which replace his legs; and the rolls, his feet.[33] In Bergelson's text, in contrast, the dancing fingers are out of sync with the rest of the scene.

Chaplin was extraordinarily well known and widely commented on in the Americas, Europe, Russia, and the Yiddish-speaking world. While in Berlin, Shklovsky wrote an article on Chaplin and planned a longer study of Chaplin and Bergson, which he never completed. Marc Chagall's 1929 pen-and-ink drawing of Chaplin includes the comic actor's bowler hat and cane but also represents Chaplin's feet as chicken legs, suggesting the famous scene from *Gold Rush* in which a starving fellow miner imagines Charlie as a chicken ready to be slaughtered and cooked.[34] Daniel Tsharni, Bergelson's close associate and friend, who also spent time in Berlin in the 1920s, wrote a critical article about the Moscow State Yiddish Theater that specifically and strikingly references Chaplin as *the* image par excellence of "modern times." In the film, Chaplin, a factory worker, steps away from the conveyor belt for a break, but his body continues to perform the same jerky movements as if he were still at the line. For Bergson, as I have shown, the dehumanized body as automaton is a source of humor. For Tsharni, it is the fulfillment of the new social and political order. The new way of life in Russia, according to Tsharni, which is creating the "mass-person," is "jerky" (*tsapldik*) like Chaplin and cinematographic."[35] The new art and the new society break down the natural flow of human movement into its component parts, as if re-creating them in the manner of the frames of film; reorganize them; and produce a new form of human collective life.[36] Life itself is like the work of art in the age of mechanical reproduction. The assimilation of the body into the image of the machine is part of the socialist bright future, which was already being enacted in theater, film, and real life.

In Bergelson's 1929 novel, in contrast, the question of the body and the machine takes on darker overtones. The tyranny of the clock drives the rhythm of the doctor's dancing fingers; his gestures are merely automatic, not transformed into some new harmony. In *Judgment*, clock time, revolutionary time, and the span of a human life conflict with one another. The doctor's fingers are left hanging in the air, a fragment, perhaps, of the *luftmentsh*, literally the "person of the air," the person without an income, made famous by Sholem Aleichem's writing. In the 1925 film *Evreiskoe schastie* (*Jewish Luck*), Solomon Mikhoels plays Sholem Aleichem's hero Menakhem Mendl in the style of Charlie Chaplin, with a bowler hat, walking stick, and bobble walk. The new Bolshevik order, however, declared the *luftmentsh* obsolete. The new harsh justice unfolds in its own time, subordinating human beings, including "history's ambassador," to its demands.

Shklovsky went on to proclaim himself to be out of sync with the times and with the new technology of life generally. Instead of providing a source for the creative extension of human capacity, in *Third Factory* (1926), the "factory," the image of the dominant force of the historical moment—is oppressive; it "processes" Shklovsky. He cannot keep his place on the factory line, so to speak. Unlike Tsharni's enthusiasm for the human cog whose movement has become jerky, like Chaplin's in *Modern Times*, Shklovsky's emotions toward the new requirements of the time are far more ambivalent:

> The time cannot be mistaken; the time cannot have wronged me.
> It's wrong to say: "The whole squad is out of step except for one ensign."
> I want to speak with my time, to understand its voice.[37]

For both Bergelson and Shklovsky, this desire was never realized.

I have traced the physical movement of two individuals, Bergelson and Shklovsky, each of whom traveled across physical and geographical boundaries to arrive in the same place, the city of Berlin, at the same time. Each writer contemplated the metamorphosis of the body in light of both new technologies and the new ideological emphasis on the mass subject. The reformulation of the body as yet another mechanical device, another cog in the machine, had both positive and negative valence in the broad philosophical context of the time. The very nature of the body's movement was reconceptualized in terms of mechanical action, and this altered vision of human life was realized in new forms of life in society and new art forms, including new literary technologies. And yet the engineering of a new future ultimately left both Bergelson and Shklovsky behind.

NOTES

1. Viktor Shklovsky, *Zoo, or Letters Not about Love*, trans. Richard Sheldon (Normal, IL: Dalkey Archive Press, 2001), 136.

2. See Harriet Murav, "Bergelson, Benjamin, and Berlin: Justice Deferred," in *The Russian Jewish Diaspora and European Culture (1917–1937)*, ed. Jörg Schulte, Olga Tabachnikova, and Peter Wagstaff (Leiden, Netherlands: Brill, 2012), 201–220.

3. For the English, see David Bergelson and Joseph Sherman, *The End of Everything*, New Yiddish Library (New Haven, CT: Yale University Press, 2010), 93. For the Yiddish, see *Mides-hadin* (Vilnius: B. Kletskin, 1929), 120.

4. For a discussion of Bergelson and Berlin in a similar light, see Shachar Pinsker, *Literary Passports: The Making of Modernist Hebrew Fiction in Europe* (Stanford, CA: Stanford University Press, 2011), 135–137.

5. For a study of the "human motor" and modernity, see Anson Rabinbach, *The Human Motor: Energy, Fatigue, and the Origins of Modernity* (New York: Basic Books, 1990).

6. For a discussion of the prosthetic god in Marinetti and Windham Lewis, see Hal Foster, "Prosthetic Gods," *Modernism/Modernity* 4, no. 2 (1997): 5–38.

7. See Walter Benjamin, *Illuminations: Essays and Reflections*, trans. Harry Zohn (New York: Schocken, 1969).

8. Raymond Williams, *Politics of Modernism* (New York: Verso, 2007), 53.

9. Sasha Senderovich also compares Shklovsky and Bergelson's Berlin periods in "In Search of a Readership: Bergelson among the Refugees," in *David Bergelson: From Modernism to Socialist Realism*, ed. Joseph Sherman and Gennady Estraikh (London: Legenda, 2007), 150–165. For a compelling articulation of the notion of "contiguity" as opposed to "influence," see Dan Miron, *From Continuity to Contiguity: Toward a New Jewish Literary Thinking* (Stanford, CA: Stanford University Press, 2010).

10. For a discussion of Shklovsky's work in relation to his life experience, see Radoslav Borislavov, "Viktor Shklovskii—Between Art and Life" (Chicago: University of Chicago Press, 2011); see also Svetlana Boym, *Another Freedom: The Alternative History of an Idea* (Chicago: University of Chicago Press, 2010).

11. Viktor Shklovsky, *A Sentimental Journey: Memoirs, 1917–1922* (Normal, IL: Dalkey Archive Press, 2004), 65. Henceforward, citations will be given in the body of the text.

12. I base my account on Sidney Monas, "Historical Introduction," in Shklovsky, *A Sentimental Journey*.

13. His decision to move to Berlin from Moscow in 1921 was probably driven at least in part by the desire to take advantage of the opportunities for writing and publishing in Yiddish. Moscow in 1920 was a challenging physical environment.

14. See Gennady Estraikh, "The Yiddish Kultur-Lige," in *Modernism in Kyiv: Jubilant Experimentation*, ed. Irena R. Makaryk and Virlana Tkacz (Toronto: University of Toronto Press, 2010), 201.

15. See Joseph Sherman, "David Bergelson (1884–1952): A Biography," in Sherman and Estraikh, *Bergelson: From Modernism to Socialist Realism*, 24.

16. For the English, see Shklovsky, *A Sentimental Journey*, 276.

17. The Yiddish is cited from David Bergelson, *Geklibene verk*, 8 vols, vol. 5 (Vilnius: B. Kletskin, 1930), 199; and the English from David Bergelson and Joachim Neugroschel, *The Shadows of Berlin* (San Francisco: City Lights, 2005), 43. I have modified the English translation.

18. Galin Tikhanov emphasizes the importance of the war on the formulation of Shklovsky's notion of defamiliarization; see Tikhanov, "The Politics of Estrangement: The Case of the Early Shklovsky," *Poetics Today* 26, no. 4 (2005): 666–696.

19. Viktor Shklovsky, *Theory of Prose* (Normal, IL: Dalkey Archive Press, 1990), 6. I have modified the translation.

20. For another discussion of this work, which also discusses "estrangement," see Mikhail Krutikov, "Narrating the Revolution," in Sherman and Estraikh, *David Bergelson: From Modernism to Socialist Realism*, 167–182.

21. For a broad-ranging article that discusses Russian constructivist theater in this light, see Nick Worrall, "Meyerhold's Production of 'The Magnificent Cuckhold,'" *Drama Review* 17, no. 1 (1973): 14–34.

22. Bergelson, *Mides-hadin*, 6–8. All translations are taken from this edition and, unless otherwise noted, are my own. I give the Yiddish original because it is less likely to be familiar to the reader.

23. See Jeffrey Veidlinger, *The Moscow State Yiddish Theater: Jewish Culture on the Soviet Stage* (Bloomington: Indiana University Press, 2001), 134.

24. Bergelson, *Mides-hadin*, 170.

25. Ibid., 130.

26. See Bergelson and Neugroschel, *Shadows of Berlin*, 57–64.

27. Ibid., 59.

28. See Wolfgang Schivelbusch, *The Railway Journey: Trains and Travel in the 19th Century*, trans. Anselm Hollo (New York: Urizen Books, 1979), 24.

29. Bergelson, *Mides-hadin*, 86.

30. Ibid., 89.

31. Shklovsky, *Knight's Move*, trans. Richard Sheldon (Normal, IL: Dalkey Archive Press, 2005).

32. For the article, see Sh. Rudnyanski, "Henri Bergson vegn estetik," *Di yidishe velt* 8 (1913): 82–86.

33. See Tom Gunning, "Chaplin and the Body of Modernity," *Early Popular Visual Culture* 8, no. 3 (2010): 237–245.

34. The Yiddish press carried articles written by Chaplin and translated into Yiddish; see Charlie Chaplin, "In vos bashteyt der sod fun mayn derfolg," *Literarishe bleter* 3 (1925). For a discussion of the Chagall and the significance of Chaplin generally in Russian experimental art, see Yuri Tsivian, "O Chapline v russkom avangarde i o zakonakh sluchainogo v iskusstve," *Novoe literaturnoe obozrenie* 5 (2006): 99–142.

35. Daniel Tsharni, "A briv fun Moskve," *Tealit* 5 (1924): 22–23.

36. For a discussion of Russian Cubo-Futurism, biomechanics, and film that makes a similar point, see Worrall, "Meyerhold's Production of 'The Magnificent Cuckhold,'" 14–15.

37. Viktor Shklovsky, *Eshche nichego ne konchilos'* (Moscow: Federal'naia programma knigoizdaniia Rossii, 2002), 8; Viktor Shklovsky, *Third Factory* (Normal, IL: Dalkey Archive Press, 2002), 8.

CHAPTER 11

ANDRZEJ STASIUK AND THE MYTH OF THE LITERARY *GASTARBAJTER*

George Gasyna

A BARD OF POSTCOMMUNIST POLAND

Andrzej Stasiuk, born in 1960 in Warsaw, ranks among postcommunist Poland's most successful cultural exports. His novels and his persona have achieved cult status both in Poland and elsewhere, especially in Ukraine and the Balkans. Despite only one reading tour of North America, in 2010, Stasiuk is a relatively familiar name in the United States, specifically in academia. Indeed, no syllabus for a college course on postcommunist European fiction would be complete without at least one work by Stasiuk on it—most often, the novel *Tales of Galicia* or collections of essays/stories such as *Fado* or *My Europe* are included. While perhaps not a household name like Milan Kundera or Czesław Miłosz, or other luminaries hailing from what was till recently referred to as the *Other Europe*, Stasiuk can be considered a known quantity in North America and Western Europe. However, Stasiuk has had a rather difficult relationship with one region—twenty-first-century's Poland's immediate neighbor to the west, Germany, the subject of his quasi-autobiographical quasi-travelogue *Dojczland*, published in 2007. Here I read the work in a dual context to take into account, first of all, the mythologies and discourses of modern Polish (e)migration to the west and, perhaps less centrally, the difficulties and discontents of the historical relationship between Poland and Germany (and I shall return to the pidgin spelling of the novel's title shortly). I argue that Stasiuk's program of self-marginalization, undertaken through an ostensibly autobiographical *récit* whose posited objective is to track, catalog, and evaluate his numerous public appearances in Germany as a respected and widely published author, both works to undermine the processes of cultural rapprochement between Germany and Poland today and propagates a template or paradigm of mutual incompatibility and incomprehensibility between these neighboring European states. In order to "counter" or oppose Germany—more specifically, the mythos of Germany as the realm of a former occupier, as a kind of (anti-Polonian) primal force, and as a difficult neighbor—Stasiuk reverts to a palette of stereotypes and deeply subjective half-truths that purportedly speak to the all-but-inevitable isolation that the (e)migrant Pole is bound to suffer in Germany. However, any residual value such narratives may once have held as instances of communal memory, or even as cautionary tales for fellow compatriots contemplating such a move, is undercut if not refuted outright (or is in any event quickly exposed as constituting a mere historical residue) in light of the actual experience of Polish migrants in Germany in the twenty-first century. This chapter, then, tries to think through Stasiuk's strategies of marginalization and offer a kind of coda to what we can today historicize as a twentieth-century syndrome of migrant self-abnegation.

Even after Poland's accession to the European Union in 2004 and the subsequent opening up of the UK, Ireland, and selected Scandinavian countries to Polish labor, Germany remained an attractive—perhaps inevitable—destination of migrant outflow, typically placing first or second in rankings.[1] According to Polish migration researchers, as many as three hundred thousand Polish workers made Germany their temporary home each year from 2000 to 2007, "migrant" in such instances defined as remaining in the target "receiving country" for at least two months, though not necessarily intending to remain indefinitely—or at the very least, making no explicit declaration of such an intention to pollsters.[2] Put another way, nearly a third of the entire Polish labor exodus (or brain drain or muscle loss) of the new millennium has chosen Germany as a provisional or permanent place of residence. This was the case even after the opening of the UK labor market to Poles in 2004, coincident with accession to the EU—although the constituent regions of the UK eclipsed

Germany as the EU's top receiving country for Polish labor, temporary or otherwise, by the end of 2006.[3] The image of Germany as the preferred European destination, EU membership or no, for outmigrating Poles was far more pronounced during the previous two decades. Indeed, from 1980 to 1999, anywhere from 55 percent to 69 percent of all ethnically Polish emigrants chose West Germany (before reunification) or Germany (after reunification) as an adoptive, and sometimes permanent, home for themselves and their children.[4] For some of these travelers, whether seasonal or irregular laborers, advanced students or professionals seeking career placement, hopeful nomads, or economic or political refugees, Germany, as always (that is, both before and after Poland's accession to the EU) symbolized a special, though in some cases only a proximate, land of opportunity and personal freedom. For others, the choice in a matter like this would above all have been a pragmatic one, based on geographic proximity to the homeland and friends and family members remaining there, language proficiency or skill set, the degree of fit with the real needs of the labor market in the hosting country, and ease of access to Poland, including availability of reliable air connections and convenience of ground transportation options, and even such factors as the relative ease of receiving German citizenship for those who could claim a genealogical filiation to the German lands.

IMAGINING THE MIGRANT SELF

In the interest of semantic precision but at the expense of mythopoeia perhaps, Andrzej Stasiuk "in Germany" is not, properly speaking, an immigrant or even a migrant worker. Rather, his peregrinations and also his privations are those of participants of reading tours or travelers of the academic conference circuit.[5] For all that, from a Polonist's perspective, what's immediately striking about this text, Stasiuk's first travel work not devoted to journeys through the eastern or southern regions of Europe such as *Fado* or *On the Road to Babadag*, is that in *Dojczland* he preemptively delineates for himself, as well for other migrants from Poland who might work in the "cultural arena" and thus find themselves in Germany, the subject-position of the Other. On the surface, the work's conceptual platform could be illustrated thus: a Polish visitor to Germany, even someone such as himself—that is, a noted author and publisher whose extensive travels are funded by a major publishing house, the prestigious Berlin-based Suhrkamp Verlag—is akin to a barbarian from the wilds making awkward though determined steps in the garden of the civilized world.[6] Of course, this is not the first time a gambit of this kind has been deployed as a tactical or ironic defense of Polish marginality in the West, or perhaps something less anodyne. The German Slavist Dirk Uffelmann contends that Stasiuk's narrative strategy consists in part of "a sarcastic, subversive stylization" and as such can be seen as a kind of general "meta-language for inscribing alterity," Polish and otherwise, and I entirely agree.[7] Uffelmann also refers to this narrative mode as a form of self-Orientalization, meaning that the specific form of alterity one confronts when one thinks of Poles or Slavs in Germany is *subalternity*. While I would concur that the cultural binary of—or projected wall between— West and East and also that of metropole versus periphery is certainly in place in Stasiuk's "subject-construction" practices, their actual dynamics as articulated in *Dojczland* are somewhat differently accented and more complicated, proceeding as they do from a distinct set of assumptions.[8]

WITOLD GOMBROWICZ'S CHILDREN, OR, HOW TO NAVIGATE THE PERIPETEIAE OF (E)MIGRATION

In the modern Polish case in particular—or the context of thinking Poles who sought to make sense of the Western metropolitan centers in which they found themselves by intention or by chance—Witold Gombrowicz's three-volume *Diary* (*Dziennik*), written throughout the 1950s and 1960s, constitutes the key cultural touchstone. It is the urtext, both index and archive of the conceits and practices of Polish exilic/emigrant self-inscription (and self-perception) and a sort of handbook on Polish— and generally "Eastern" European—émigré comportment in the West in the Cold War era. Gombrowicz's position is that the typical forms of conduct are ineffectual and even counterproductive as far as advancing one's position is concerned, in large part due to their (oft-desperate) overreliance on Romantic or romanticized notions of Poland's importance, real or symbolic, in the community of Western nations. The text's central goal was to imagine a pragmatics of articulation of Eastern European cultural immaturity and formal insufficiency as a means of destabilizing or even inverting the binaries. *The Diary*, then, tenders a clear-headed counterindication to the hapless maneuvers on behalf of various parts of the emigrant community (specifically, the Polonia of the post–World War II period) to leave some kind of mark on the Western cultures that were hosting them.[9] Gombrowicz's own three-decade exile from Poland took him first to Buenos Aires in 1939, then to West Berlin on a Ford Foundation Fellowship in the early 1960s, then to Paris and finally Provence (in Vence, just northeast of Nice), where he died in the summer of 1969. In the matter of the order and trajectory of his peregrinations, Gombrowicz had little choice; these paths were largely determined by the eruption of World War II and the partition of Poland by Nazis and Soviets in 1939, the subsequent vagaries of Cold War politics post-Yalta (in the wake of which Poles returning from abroad almost invariably faced mistreatment, and sometimes far worse fates, at the hands of the new Soviet-installed regime), and the largesse of Western cultural agencies, ranging from publishing houses to organizations assisting refugees.[10]

Rejecting both the cosmopolitan identity of a figure like Vladimir Nabokov—or in the more local Polish context, Czesław Miłosz—a free agent flamboyantly "forgetting" or, at the very least, selectively foregrounding and reinscribing his own traumatic past, and the homesickness and paralysis of a figure like Jan Lechoń or Marek Hłasko, two would-be Polish cultural ambassadors whose personal and *national* traumatic pasts effectively crushed them while they were abroad, Gombrowicz chose a third way of exile as an exercise in autonomy of form. A self-appointed representative of Europe's "younger" cultures, he embarked on a project of diagnosing the pathologies of East European migrations to the moribund West. The three volumes of the *Diary* proposed that the volatility of identity of the itinerant/migrant Pole could function as a cultural weapon if properly deployed; this was, after all, *the last thing* that the West was expecting. What the West was expecting, rather, was a kind of determinate object: a docile emigrant already convinced of his own subalternity, a "poor relation" (as Gombrowicz memorably put it in his *Diary*) who was thrilled by the mere fact of being invited to the same table as the cultural potentates. Alternately, what the West could expect was an exasperating interloper—someone, on the contrary, insisting that the European East and its collective achievements (or "gifts" to the world) were just as good as the heritage of the West.[11] Both are predictable positions, and the *Diary* mercilessly rebukes fellow Polish émigrés who would compile laundry lists of Poland's cultural achievements and "unleash" them on their unsuspecting hosts. Not only was a comparison with the storied cultural heritage of the West absurd, in light of the fact that the Eastern European artistic forms or literary practices were commonly belated or epigonal imitations of the mainline movements and ideas from the West; the very ambition to engage in it was symptomatic of a provincial's acute lack of couth:

> To compare Mickiewicz to Dante or to Shakespeare is to compare fruit to preserves... a meadow or village to a cathedral or city; an idyllic soul to an urban one which is loaded with knowledge about the world of the human race.... [A]s things stand, Chopin and Mickiewicz serve only to emphasize your own narrow-mindedness, because, with the naïveté of children, you prance out your polonaises under the noses of a bored foreign audience just so you can strengthen the impaired sense of your own worth and endow yourselves with meaning. You are like the poor wretch who claims that his grandmother had a large estate and traveled to Paris. You are the poor relations of the world, who try to impress themselves and others.[12]
>
> Porównywać Mickiewicza z Dantem lub z Szekspirem, to porównywać owoc z komfiturą... łąkę i wioskę z katedrą lub miastem, duszę sielską z duszą miejską, naładowaną wiedzą o świecie rodzaju ludzkiego.... Szopen z Mickiewiczem służą wam [Polakom] tylko do uwypuklenia waszej małostkowości—gdyż wy z naiwnością dzieci potrząsacie przed nosem znudzonej zagranicy tymi polonezami po to jedynie, aby wzmocnić poczucie własnej wartości i dodać sobie znaczenia. Jesteście jak biedak, który chwali się, że jego babcia miała folwark i bywała w Paryżu. Jesteście ubogimi krewnymi świata, którzy usiłują imponować sobie i innym.[13]

Gombrowicz's dialectics of cultural essences dictated that, to the contrary, the (European) marginal East possessed in abundance what the West lacked: the vitality precisely of its own incompleteness. It had not been formally refined, reworked, drained of its pure juices: in the comparison between "fruit and preserves," the East could brandish unadulterated forms, their "value" conjoined precisely to their attendant potentiality. Thus youth and immaturity, the promise of unfinished Eastern European forms, the incomplete and perhaps only temporary victories over nature, in short, the fractional triumph over the environment and over the self—these were to be procured for battle with the bourgeois and (Gombrowicz contended) wilting cultures of the post–World War II West. The foundation of an alternative subjectivity to be deployed to combat the West was of the utmost import to Gombrowicz, for a host of reasons. The chief motive, perhaps, was innately linked to his identity politics and his concern for his place in the wider modernist canon as a writer of youth, immaturity, ex-centricity, and queerness, one who felt himself compelled to represent or even *reform*—in an iconoclastic way, but not discounting the very real potential for personal gain—his increasingly isolated and sociopolitically reactionary former homeland of the post–World War II era.[14]

A LITERARY "GASTARBAJTER"

Although Stasiuk and, in fact, his entire generation of Polish writers establish Gombrowicz as an almost Olympian avatar and prescient precursor for surviving and maybe even thriving in the West, his own strategies for negotiating marginalization (real and imagined) engage none of the preceding protocols precisely. He is neither a docile body, a boastful gatecrasher, nor for that matter a quicksilver, possibly vampiric Other—trafficker of the youth potion. Moreover, the willful barbarian persona constitutes little other than an expedient pose/mask at most, insofar as the text gives no evidence of it having been employed in order to destabilize his hosts—there are, in other words, no signs of potential violence coming from *this* particular Other, now. Rather, the dominant mode of his engagement is ironic disengagement, a policy of preemptive *self-exclusion*. This Groucho Marx approach can, in principle, tender deliciously seditious payout but only if the principle of dialogism still holds. Still, a binary opposition between the European West and the East is delineated just as starkly in Stasiuk as it had been in Gombrowicz, though now its polarities have been inverted. In *Dojczland*, as in nearly all of Stasiuk's writings and the many interviews on the subject, the European East is clearly best.

However, for Stasiuk Poland does not strictly speaking belong in *Eastern Europe*. Apart from the rural east and the highlands of the south—that is, the old Polish-Lithuanian commonwealth's former provinces of Galicia and Transcarpathia—Poland embodies an intermediary, liminal space; it is the zone on the borderland, a neither-nor. Confronted with concretized forms of either Eastern or Western "essence"—he mentions Paris and Moscow—the Poles' own core identity for Stasiuk tends to *wash out*; they become unsure of their footing, "torn" (*rozdarci*) within themselves.[15]

But while Poles—if they really stop to think about it—may sense themselves to be liminal misfits vis-à-vis the conventional cultural polarities of East and West, a Pole who has found himself in *Germany*, for Stasiuk in any case, constitutes an always already overdetermined entity: a subject disciplined into a normative space by matters of *form* and, precisely, ideals of proper comportment. On the face of it, *Dojczland* seems to offer a platform for playing an intersubjective formal game of assimilation and otherization. Stasiuk, though, seems to declare that that particular game is rigged when it comes to Germans and Poles, and a priori refuses to be welcomed. The idea of Germans serving as hosts for visiting Poles is rejected on its face. The gift of welcoming is not returned; more precisely, the act of giving, apart from its economic context or rendering, is not reciprocated but is instead reduced to an exchange of values. Specifically, the relationship between the Polish cultural "guest worker" and his German hosts and moderators is immediately reconceptualized into a "horizon of reciprocity"—one grounded purely in monetary exchange.[16] The starkness of this relationship is made clear in the blurb on the back panel of the Polish edition—which like many of Stasiuk's books is self-published, or more precisely, issued by a publishing house that he runs, Wydawnictwo Czarne (which implies that he has full control over the content of the cover). It is actually on the back cover of the original edition that the label "literary gastarbajter" initially appears, in a passage that is the author's endorsement of his own work (in the third person). With this self-affixed label, a reduplication of his otherness via a discourse of essential Slavic-Germanic incommensurability, Stasiuk situates himself as, at best, a visitor who is tolerated because he is potentially useful. He contends, for instance, that his German audiences come to see him principally because, as he puts it, through him they are better able to "acquire knowledge, shape a view" (*przychodzili, by wyrobić sobie pogląd*).¹⁷ Alternatively, he is useful because his presence allows the audience to determine for itself "whether I was lying or to ascertain whether my humanity was similar to theirs ... or perhaps to satisfy their need to be in the presence of otherness" (*przychodzili sprawdzić, czy nie kłamię ... Albo po to, by zbadać, czy moje człowieczeństwo jest podobne do ich człowieczeństwa. Albo też po to, żeby zaspokoić potrzebę obcowania z odmiennością*).¹⁸ In exchange for his primary service of "amusing" the public, as he would have it, Stasiuk receives cash (*zabawiałem publiczność, brałem kasę*), which he counts and recounts in his hotel room as a form of meditation.¹⁹ Rather implausibly, Stasiuk's narrator goes so far as to suggest that especially in the smaller towns, he might very well have been the first Pole, "a real Pole," that his readers had seen in person.

And just what *is* a real Pole? Stasiuk's answer forthwith: a real Pole, such as he himself, is a figure divorced from German stereotype or legend: neither the easily categorized and forgotten seasonal worker, construction worker, or plumber, nor the more mythical thief of BMWs and Mercedes-Benzes.²⁰ Sponsored by his publisher and a host of cultural institutions, Stasiuk in Germany is also the nonresident alien, perhaps even one of "exceptional ability," but not a cultural ambassador (a position he flatly refutes); as a guest worker, moreover, he is contractually obligated to perform a concrete and tangible but temporary service.²¹ A cog in the "entertainment" industry broadly defined, the most a Polish literary "gastarbajter" can expect in Germany is guarded curiosity of the locals, not dialogue; loneliness and isolation are his true companions, and a robust internal monologue emerges, of necessity, as his principal solace.²² Stasiuk writes, for example, that while he was sitting in his hotel room one afternoon, drinking from a flask of Jim Beam and preparing for yet another public reading in a German town the name of which he cannot immediately recall, his predicament was "akin to that of lone African travelers waiting with their bundles for the next train at little provincial stations." With the flamboyant claim of possessing "a black soul" underneath his "white skin," Stasiuk sets about to performatively embody the Other:

> My situation was not entirely different from that of the Black Africans waiting for their trains at forgotten little stations. My skin was white, but I had a black soul. If you want to experience true loneliness, you should

visit Germany. You should travel fifteen times between Frankfurt and
Cologne, and wake up in the middle of the night in the town of Hamm,
on the seventh floor of a hotel where the railings are gilded. And stare
out into the night. And you need to go to Krefeld and Hagen, and to
Duisburg, all this so that once in Stuttgart, at the train station you could
finally relax, because there you would finally be reminded of the Gara de
Nord.

    Moja sytuacja nie różniła się aż tak bardzo od sytuacji tych samotnych
Murzynów na zapomnianych stacyjkach. Miałem białą skórę, ale czarną
duszę. Jeśli chcesz przeżyć prawdziwą samotność, powinieneś pojechać
do Niemiec. Powinieneś piętnaście razy pokonać koleją drogę między
Frankfurtem a Kolonią i zbudzić się w środku nocy w Hamm na siódmym
piętrze hotelu z poręczami obitymi złotą blachą. I w środku nocy patrzeć
w ciemność... I trzeba być w Krefeld i w Hagen, i w Duisburgu, by dopiero dworzec w Stuttgardzie przyniósł ukojenie, przywołując wspomnienie
z Gara de Nord.[23]

Loneliness, anonymous hotel rooms, a resolute awareness of the palimpsest of local history and this particular (Polish) subject's unenviable place in it, which becomes increasingly difficult to cut through with sarcasm or irony: these are, it seems, the true signposts for reading this work. Viewed through such a lens, *Dojczland* becomes a repository of gestures of self-abnegation and marginalization, calling out for readerly empathy (to the acts of witnessing recorded therein) without offering a full solution to the problem of navigating one's own otherness in realms of postmemory and the era of (at the time of this writing) open borders, or of reconciling the many discontents of a national traumatic past, all of which come into painfully sharp relief in the course of travel to the heart of the mainland of the former occupier/brutalizer. But Stasiuk resolves to push twentieth-century history to the background rather than to set it up as a frame or prism for his experiences (not always successfully). More precisely, he resolves to live in the present, almost weightlessly floating over the land—partly out of concern that constantly reminding his hosts or fellow German travelers of Poland's tragic fates at the hands of the German Nazis might be awkward and perhaps seen as rude, even if the reflex or "impulse" (*odruch*) to do so remains and needs to be actively checked.[24] However, despite or perhaps because of these efforts, *Dojczland* offers another, deeper layer of encounter, almost despite itself, a kind of countertext to the dramas of self-preservation (amid generally welcoming, curious audiences and—from his own descriptions—remarkably neutral public spaces).[25] To place this narrative properly, one must consider the broader cultural frame of modern Polish-German relations, from the perspective of the Polish *homme sensuel moyen*: on the one hand, Germany can remain unknown or unknowable only because, and to the extent that, it is actually almost too well *known* by Poles, not only as a problematic neighbor and former occupier and now, for the foreseeable future, a political and economic partner in the building and maintenance of the supranational European state, but also as a nodal point for Polish migrations ever since the Romantic bard Adam Mickiewicz composed the best part of his drama *Forefathers' Eve* in Dresden (the Saxon capital) back in the early 1830s. Indeed, the term "going to the Saxons" (*jechać na Saksy*) for example, has been slang for economic migration from the late nineteenth century until recently. German lands—and more specifically the Reich and the areas annexed to it—are also the site of forced labor by millions of Poles who had been imprisoned by the Nazis in 1939–1945—not an immediate or even an inevitable chain of association for most Poles, but one that is inextricable from the communal memory of Poles. On the other hand, it could be argued that Poles know the Germans all too well while not really knowing them at all, because their knowledge is the knowledge of the silent refugee: an itinerant knowledge, concerned mainly with surfaces and impressions, undergirded by an anxiety about survival. Such, Stasiuk claims, is his own acquaintance with Germany: toward the end of *Dojczland* he declares that despite his numerous voyages throughout the country, the only local Germans he actually "knows" are his German readers.[26] Apart from them, there are only a "few others," but those are *not* actually Germans (*Niemcy*) but rather "friends and acquaintances"; all the other Germans that constitute his knowledge base are individuals encountered in public spaces such as train compartments or cafés, Germans observed and described—but not *known*.[27] Thus, punning on the demonym (in Polish *Niemiec*, masc. pl. *Niemcy*, fem. pl. *Niemki*, means literally "a mute" and suggests a "stranger," an unknown person in the sense of an unknown quantity) constitutes Stasiuk's strategic way out of the entanglements of the discourse of alterity, a crucial component of which is the assumption that contemporary Germans taken as a whole do not actually know that much about their neighbor to the east, apart from received ideas and persistent stereotypes of their own. The text then pushes readers toward a structuralist type of quandary, a binary opposition between self and other, and the way to resolve the differentials is to attend closely to the text's own contextual performativity and its inner contradictions.

The cultural position of relative intimacy due to contiguity and the interpenetrations of "History" but yet an ultimate unknowing is actually something that Stasiuk's narrative has difficulty parsing out. First of all, for him (that is, for Stasiuk's narrator, though the text insists on a close proximity between author and the I-voice that speaks in *Dojczland*), Poland's "nearest" neighbors are not Germans but Slovaks and Ukrainians, while his most intimate European locus is a toss-up between marshy Romania of the Danube delta, where he felt most "European," and the highlands on the Slovak-Ukrainian border.[28] In *Dojczland*, as an apotheosis of Eastern European housedness, Stasiuk points to the Gara de Nord train station in Bucharest (as opposed to a site like the Hauptbahnhof in Frankfurt or particularly Berlin—the latter station not only less remote from Poland geographically but also a site used by thousands of them, including his Polish readers, on a regular basis, and thus palpably "known" by them).[29] In a text in which train stations and related transportation and communication nodes figure conspicuously, and can be viewed almost idealistically as sites of humanizing contact, the Bucharest structure is the archetype of "softening" and humanization forces at work that mark the entire region, Stasiuk's "home district": it is a specimen of monumental architecture to be sure, but one whose forms have been distinctly tempered, whose spaces have been reterritorialized by local use. Stasiuk's zero point, his longed-for Gara, is a locus in which the Roma child violinist is a figure not *out of place*. The dozens or scores (both are Stasiuk's quantifiers) of train stations he encounters subsequently during his German peregrinations, no matter how structurally pleasing, architecturally impeccable, or convenient to use they may be for a weary traveler, are lacking in this human regard.[30] This ostensible lacuna bespeaks a certain nostalgia for a mythical and vanished past, for an erstwhile community whose members used to congregate within and around such ad hoc nodes, a community that has since become atomized or, more to the point, modernized, as the pace of life increased. The realities of travel in the twenty-first century in the

West, however, have required the interfaces, and thus our spaces and our expectations for their use, to change, and change dramatically. The train stations encountered by Stasiuk in Germany, for example, represent multimodal public spaces that seem to hold more in common with modern airports (which also figure in Stasiuk's account, as he does fly into and out of Germany, but apart from the Frankfurt airport they seem "grey" and abstract to the tale he is interested in relating) than with ersatz market squares of old, where one could pause and from which one could ponder the world, undisturbed, as the hours passed.[31] But truth be told, there is nothing homey or comforting about the sight of a Roma child violinist at a Bucharest station, or anywhere else for that matter: this is a prime signifier of exclusion from the European commons and its modern family of nations; it is a figure of abjection.

The second and more significant reason why the gift of welcoming has to be refused according to the text's logic is that Stasiuk (or his narrator) is keen on offering readers to share in the experience of a Dojczland. Indeed, to a significant extent the land described here *is* Dojczland, not Germany (note the Polish spelling). What is a Dojczland? The short answer would be: an imaginary projection of the migrant Pole, a defense mechanism, a mythopoeic spatiality. To cultural anthropologist Przemyslaw Czapliński, who reviewed this work when it first appeared in Poland and found its narrator's subject-position remarkably puzzling, a Dojczland constitutes "an intermediary entity"—a kind of emotive prosthesis for the Pole. Above all it is an iconography composed half of desire and half of prejudice, and mediated—to the extent that it may be mediated at all—through a foreign semiotic system.[32] On the synchronic level of myths and their creation, Polonizing the name of the host nation can help a migrant strategically obtain a comfort of reterritorialization via language; by the same token, though, in so doing he or she is foreclosing the true lived reality of the Other. Such a feat would require a willful surrender to the alien semiotic system, the foreign language of signs and iconographies, something to which Stasiuk himself refuses to consent. For instance, he keeps resisting the idea that in advanced parliamentary democracies such as Germany's, protest movements, even abhorrent ones like the neo-fascists whose rally he witnesses in Berlin, should be allowed to use the public agora. He would rather they be removed from sight, cleared from the common spaces of the *polis* rather than being treated with dignity and even respect by the "besieged" authorities.[33] Or, with dogged insistence he focalizes the former Nazi significance of the towns through which he is passing or cities where he might have a train transfer, while the present-day contexts of those places in the lived culture (or politics, or economics) elude him (or he ignores them).[34] And he wonders why Germans generally will *not* smoke under placards that state "no smoking"—to an extent that the sight of groups of Germans actually smoking under such a sign proves a delight worth pausing on—and what else this portends in the context of their famed ability to follow orders.[35]

CAN CONTESTED MEMORY LEAD TO A EUROPEAN COMMONS?

Still, despite this ideational double retrenchment behind veils of mutual incommensurability and (semiotic) impenetrability, Stasiuk's insistence on the mythos of difference signals a paradoxical space of hope, pointing toward a shared understanding or a common "European" fate, of a Continent united, at root, by the memory of World War II and the Holocaust.[36] The text subtly gestures at such "openings"—in the body politic and even in Stasiuk's own imaginary of the Teutonic other, saturated as it is with overdetermined symbols ranging from the medieval Battle of Grunwald-Tannenberg to the *Panzer* tank of more recent memory—but generally stops short of investigating them, and this despite the proviso that "Germany" of all places cannot be visited lightly or *innocently*.[37] Letting his guard down too frequently might confirm Stasiuk as the emotional, sentimental Slav (or Eastern European, or some other subaltern or "Other"), someone refusing to leave the past behind. Yet wherever he impulsively reverts to ossified stereotypes vis-à-vis the other—for example, in the protracted discussion of Teutonic pursuit of formal "institutionalized perfection," as well as the related image of the Pole-in-Germany as an escapee from form who frantically tries to avoid being corralled by it—Stasiuk is denying *himself* the opportunity of a new, deeper, self-knowledge.[38] He is back at the Gara de Nord, inserted into a semiotic system he can master (or in which he can feel as a master), but the train, so to speak, has long left the platform.

This is due not only to the specific past with which this part of the world is freighted, but also to the fact that Germany holds its secrets; unlike Stasiuk's congenial "brotherlands" in Eastern and southeast Europe, a visit to Germany is not only never innocent, it demands real exertion to comprehend.[39] Specifically, it calls for a type of memory work that can prove decentering for the subject, possibly exposing the migrant worker, whether an expert in "asparagus cultivation" or a visiting novelist, to instances of cathartic *postmemory*—to the images that the next generation living in a specific time and place has *constructed* and via which it too remembers the sins and atrocities committed by their immediate forebears.[40] As mentioned, Stasiuk cites several examples of localized reuse of German and particularly the Nazi past, but in all cases he seems to hit an impasse of preprogrammed reactions (his own) to what he has been witnessing. His personal memory, his Polish communal past, and even his family's memories of "Germans" all become entangled with the local German experience and (post-)memory, without a viable way forward.[41] He would prefer it if the Germans could find a way to meditate on the Nazi past of their country in a more explicit and durable fashion, in the public space—something apart from, as a *supplement* to, the "masochistic subconscious manifestations" of their own "catastrophe" at the end of World War II.[42] Reporting on an allegorical reenactment of the German defeat at the hands of the Allies and the Soviets in 1945, which was being staged by actors/activists in front of Brandenburg Gate, he wonders why no figure of a Nazi has been included in the passion play—and indeed, why there are no signs at all of exemplary Nazi regalia such as the swastika or a black SS cap, only the Soviet soldier and the American GI. The critique offered is rather oblique, however: "if you are going to say A, you also need to say B, and if there is going to be 'maso,' there should at least be *a dash of 'sado.'*"[43] Nonetheless, absent such iconic signifiers, testimony to an erstwhile German ambition of dominion over its neighbors, any "vision" of the German past on offer at the *Platz* for local and touristic consumption (tourists can take pictures of themselves with one of the figures, he informs the reader) remains incomplete, quite apart from the fact that the wearing of Nazi uniforms or similar public displays of Nazi symbols by private individuals is subject to criminal persecution in Germany today.[44] And while he is generally skeptical and indeed rather alarmed at the fact that neo-Nazi groups are able to organize rallies unmolested, in this particular instance the question of authenticity (and also completeness) of historical (post-) memory, even or perhaps *especially* if staged spontaneously by activists for a pedagogic purpose, seems to trump the cultural terror or at the very least the deep distaste associated with the symbols and icons themselves.

To avoid a general entanglement between competing narrativizations of communal memory, and the point of *Dojczland* seems to be that for his or her own good, the Pole in Germany would do best to avoid this, the migrant must seek forms of temporary diversion:

> It's impossible to travel from Poland to Germany while completely sober. Let's not kid ourselves. This is a kind of trauma, after all. And it affects asparagus farmers and writers in equal measure. It is impossible to go to Germany and relax. *A journey to Germany is like psychoanalysis.*... Yes, reined-in *melancholy mixed with alcohol in reasonable doses*—that's the only way to neutralize this land psychologically. It's the only way to survive a literary journey from Munich to Hamburg.
>
> Nie da się na trzeźwo pojechać z Polski do Niemiec. Nie oszukujmy się. To jednak jest trauma. W równym stopniu dotyka specjalistów od uprawy szparagów i pisarzy. Nie da się do Niemiec pojechać na luzie. *Jazda do Niemiec to jest psychoanaliza.*... Tak, trzymana na uwięzi *melancholia i alkohol w rozsądnych dawkach*—tak tylko można przetrwać literacką trasę z Monachium do Hamburga.... Tylko tak można zneutralizować psychicznie ten kraj.[45]

As a mainline technique of the self, in addition to confronting the "trauma" in an alcohol-fueled haze, fleeting amnesia is expedient as well, as is self-censorship and paradoxical muteness. Stasiuk-narrator keeps reminding himself that *next time* around, he will attempt to concentrate on the Germany of Thomas Mann and on Lübeck as opposed to the Germany of Himmler and Nuremberg, and that he will refrain from asking his hosts whether their grandparents had ever served in the Wehrmacht.[46] Yet certain sites, and therefore certain memories, cultural or communal— such as war monuments reconstructed historical districts, or the aforementioned kitschy tourist attractions on Potsdamer Platz (which had once been bisected by the Berlin Wall), and around the new "glassy"

Reichstag—are impossible to avoid.[47] In the end, Stasiuk's own vision re-presents a cognitive mapping of juxtaposition and of incomplete integration: striking images are deployed to hover for a time, imprinting themselves on the readerly consciousness—such as the "sado-maso" imagery of Nazi female officers, breeders of the new master race, clad in black leather (to offer just one)—but then Stasiuk reports that he will be departing to a new town, to service a new audience.[48] After all, he is doing this "labor" principally for cash, and the tickets have already been paid for.[49] And the reader is encouraged to forget the image as the narrator does (or pretends to).

BETWEEN INSIGHT AND AMNESIA

On the lookout for a sympathetic reader—despite the fact that *Dojczland* and selected other works have been translated into German and Stasiuk enjoys attention there, this imagined reader strikes me as a *Polish* reader—Stasiuk selectively reengages his masculinist persona and seems to settle on the tried-and-true solution of anesthesia via alcohol.[50] However, he is not imbibing local drink such as beer or schnapps or even classic masculine "Polish" spirits like vodka or cognac straight up, but rather American hard liquor (an inevitable libation for the American troops stationed in Germany, and perhaps a liquid signifier of the political and current hegemon). The more central question has to do with the justification of anesthesia through alcohol offered in the text. Why should a Polish traveler/migrant in Germany wish to forget, and what? Here, Stasiuk responds with a stratagem and a tautology: Germany, he notes, "is *impossible to gauge correctly while sober.*"[51] Thus, a flask of Johnnie Walker, or if all else fails, a box of train station wine purchased at 3 a.m., forms the cornerstone of his survival strategy. Its other component: do not leave your hotel room or your publisher's guest apartment, unless absolutely necessary.[52] Proceed directly to the location of the reading and then return directly from the location of the reading. Do not look people in the face, not even the clerk at the train station store, unless he or she happens to be of immigrant origin, preferably Balkan or Central Asian or perhaps Russian. *Then* and only then is empathy possible again, humanity (even though this is the "lesser, weaker" type of humanity) returns, and a smile can be tendered as part of the transaction.

In philosopher Giorgio Agamben's typology of contemporary "political life," *the ban*, typically established by a sovereign power center—that is, from above, as a constitutive part of the Law—forms a critical tool for regulating cultural and political forms of participation by the Other. The ban thus emerges as an instrument of general policing of biopower—typically through exclusion or capture, often by prescribed killing—that reifies the modalities of otherization and, to the extent that it is voluntarily observed, self-otherization:

> Ancient Germanic law was founded on the concept of *peace (Fried)*, and the corresponding exclusion from the community of the wrongdoer, who therefore became *friedlos*, without peace, and whom anyone was permitted to kill without committing homicide. The medieval ban ... presents analogous traits: the bandit could be killed ("to ban someone is to say that anyone may harm him") or was even considered to be already dead: "Whoever is banned from his [the Sovereign's] city on pain of death must be considered as dead." Germanic and Anglo-Saxon sources underline the bandit's liminal status by defining him as a wolf-man (*wargus, werwolf*). *What has been banned is delivered over to its own separatedness and, at the same time, consigned to the mercy of the one who abandons it*—at once ... removed and captured.[53]

Agamben's definition masterfully combines onomastics and power reification, that is, the act of naming and regulating crime—both of which require a kind of proximity if not intimacy. What is troubling about Stasiuk's text is that the logic of *the ban* is in full operation, even if its motive force seems to stem not from the power center but rather from the inside, from authorial self-indictment: declaring oneself as a Pole in Germany is to define oneself a subject "without peace." A notable derivation of the notion of the ban is, of course, the bandit, and it is *not* tautology to note that the bandit as outlaw, that is, a figure innately outside the common Law, or as a liminal being, demands preemptive regulation by the Sovereign, by Law.[54]

However, in 2007 (and equally in 2016, if not more so), there are few obvious signs of exclusion of *Poles* from Germany or bans established against them, not even for the car thieves of legend—the true bandits operating in Germany who might with good reason find themselves barred. And indeed, traveling freely in an era of relatively open European borders (fully unrestricted between Germany and Poland), holding the correct— EU-issued, supranational—kind of passport, Stasiuk does not mention having encountered any. Yet as part of his archaeology of peripherality, wherein Polish culture as a semimarginal entity is set off in a dialectic with cultural hegemons in the West and the destabilizing but aleatory discourses of "true" liberating Eastern essences (to the Russians, were he to travel there, he would present himself and be perceived as a Western Slav, that is, *almost* a German), Stasiuk enacts a cultural ban against himself by rejecting the promises of hybridity, plainly on offer in daily life in the host nation in the first decade of the new millennium.[55] That rejection is not equivalent to wallowing in the tragic though insular Polish past or fearing a soulless and technocratic Teutonic future. Stasiuk, seemingly always on the lookout for comforting essences—and this is one exilic lesson from Witold Gombrowicz *not* fully assimilated in *Dojczland*—finds to his frustration that Germany's has continually eluded him. He admits as much in one of *Dojczland*'s most striking sections, which juxtaposes the idea of the (in)ability to capture the true character of a people with a meditation on hordes of tourists taking snapshots of celebrated sights and sites, such as former homes of philosophers and poets.[56] In response to the existential confrontation with Germanness ("the mystery of the German soul was giving me no respite"; *zagadka niemieckiej duszy nie dawała mi spokoju*), and a realization that the eastern part of Germany was somehow less foreign, home to a greater number of recognizable humanizing elements, particularly as one travels east of Berlin but also east *within* Berlin, where the hybridization with or inflection by Slavicdom has been especially palpable, Stasiuk ultimately settles on a metonymic reading.[57] Germans, he concludes, historically the most dogged contributors to the grand civilization of Europe, are in truth somewhat like Americans—but "with the volume turned down somewhat" (*na nieco wolniejszych obrotach*).[58] They are "like Americans who had Luther, so they know they were not born yesterday. Like Americans who had Hitler, so they know that they cannot rush full steam ahead into the future."[59] Just as with the United States, where he may have spent a few weeks at most, Germany for Stasiuk represents "a pent-up force, an accumulated energy" of the inevitable hegemon; it is a site of pure potentiality.[60] Superficial associations with the discourse of political and cultural superiority aside, this would suggest that Germany today, like the United States during its own (midtwentieth) "century," is inherently unfixed and mutable. "Germany had been changing its skin like a snake," he notes in one particularly evocative passage—and he shudders at the thought of it.[61]

In the guise of a *gastarbeiter* laboring toward a semblance of a literary truth (not to say essence), beyond snapshots and superficial impressions of the average traveler, Stasiuk thus places himself in an unenviable position: preoccupied with finding endorsements or confirmations for the myth of an immutable German inhumanity and otherness, he misses the fact that the object of his search, Germany, has meanwhile discreetly (or maybe not so discreetly) detached itself from all but the most persistent stereotypes and has transformed itself into something new and unexpected—emblematized by the glassy new core of Berlin, which to Stasiuk, who in this section imagines himself as an Eastern European "Gypsy" wanderer, is "blank" and "weightless," ready to be "inscribed with new content."[62] Proceeding from the premise that most Poles "are *still* afraid of Germans," and expecting to be regarded as an "immigrant"—it is difficult to determine just what that means for Stasiuk, but it certainly implies some form of a self-imposed ban that precludes the feeling of "being at peace"—Stasiuk is uncertain how to classify the true newcomers in Germany, the Turks, Balkan Slavs, and Central Asians, as well as the "Black Brothers," whom he encounters in train stations, on subways, in hotels, on the street.[63] Immigrants and migrants all, or nearly, they seem neither abject nor excessively resigned—they attend to their own business, mostly. Their numerosity in public spaces, metro and train stations for one, suggests that thanks to the forces of globalization Germany is becoming, if not a melting pot precisely, then at least a hybridizing space.[64] In any event, he instinctively affiliates with those he considers to be most disenfranchised—in this case because of the color of their skin (recall that Stasiuk avers possessing a "black soul"). Yet, reverting to the comforts of his own prejudices, Stasiuk fails or perhaps refuses to see how these disruptive new Germans, hiding in plain sight, could signify anything other than mute and fearful strangers as he himself pretends to be. And it appears that he never asks.

The final irony of the text, then, is compound. Not subject to the ban, able to enter and peacefully move across the land with no restriction as a political body, and clutching a return plane ticket to his (home)land of unfinished forms, the privileged guest qua autonomous subject enjoys not only full protection by (international and local) law but also the largesse of cultural institutions and can even, to return to Agamben, ask the Sovereign for at least one favor. Yet he takes nothing from the encounter ... apart from money.

Dojczland thus represents a remarkable departure in Stasiuk's oeuvre—an oeuvre whose devotion to inscriptions of heterogeneity and contact is legendary, an oeuvre jubilantly and self-consciously grounded in fundamental ideas and ideals of dialogue and exchange. Confronted with a mythos of Germany as an inhospitable and form-driven and yet somehow quicksilver place, a mythos he chooses to challenge only partially and at his own convenience, this seasoned traveler ceases to speak, refuses the invitation for a deeper experience of cultural immersion—or even to try to authoritatively declare his views on what "makes them tick." What's being promoted here, then, is a new ecology of travel: abandoned to his own devices but abandoned by choice, as a kind of self-quarantine (or self-ban, in anticipation of being denied peace by the authorities?), Stasiuk's narrator treads so lightly that not only does he *not* take pictures—apart from mental snapshots—he does not even help himself to that extra bar of soap from the hotel bathroom or that second cup of coffee, even though they are being offered to him as *gifts*, free for the taking. At a period in cultural history when eighty thousand fiercely passionate German football fans on any given Sunday may holler the surname "Lewandowski" every time Bayern Munich's talisman Polish striker scores a spectacular goal (and he had more than one of those in the last few Bundesliga seasons), this seems like a particularly unfortunate moment to insist on locking oneself in.

NOTES

1. Up to two million Polish emigrants and migrant workers (variously defined) were living in those countries in the mid-2000s, with the UK attracting the lion's share; see

Bela Galgoczi, Janine Leschke, and Andrew Watt, "Intra-EU Labour Migrations—Flows and Policy Responses," in *EU Labour Migration since Enlargement: Trends, Impacts and Policies*, ed. Bela Galgoczi, Janine Leschke, and Andrew Watt (Farnham, UK: Ashgate, 2009), 1.

2. Agnieszka Fihel, "Post-Accession Migration from Poland: A Quantitative View," in *Contemporary Polish Migrant Culture and Literature in Germany, Ireland, and the UK*, ed. Joanna Rostek and Dirk Uffelmann (Frankfurt: Peter Lang, 2011), 30–31; Marek Okólski and Dariusz Stola, "Migrations between Poland and the European Union: The Perspective of Poland's Future Membership of EU," University of Warsaw, Institute of Social Studies, Working Paper no. 25, 1999, 5.

3. See Fihel, "Post-Accession Migration," and Okólski and Stola, "Migrations between Poland and the European Union," 190–191. Germany was historically the dominant European "destination country" pre-EU accession, attracting 32.1 percent of Polish migrant outflow, including seasonal workers variously defined, while the UK, at 31.4 percent of Polish migrant outflow, ranked (by 2006) as the top European (and eventually, global) destination postaccession, and with the subsequent derestricting of the local labor markets to Poles.

4. And the United States was the second most popular choice; see Okólski and Stola, "Migrations between Poland and the European Union," 8–9. The preceding statistics are compiled exclusively from Polish government tallies of migrant outflow. As Okólski and Stola point out, the data in "countries that receive migrants from Poland" vary considerably; indeed, they contend that "the number of Polish migrants is several to several dozen times higher than that shown in Polish statistics." They note, moreover, that "the migrants' countries of destination have various definitions and principles of recording immigration, and the completeness of their records is far . . . from perfect"—further complicating the final tally; ibid., 5.

5. Daniel Schümann, "Lost in Migration: Literary Images of Poles in Germany by Stefan Żeromski and Andrzej Stasiuk," in Rostek and Uffelmann, *Contemporary Polish Migrant Culture*, 53–54.

6. See Andrzej Stasiuk, *Dojczland* (Wołowiec, Poland: Wydawnictwo Czarne, 2007), 70; his own word is *wieśniak* (villager or peasant). Stasiuk claims to have visited as many as 216 German "cities and villages" during his lecture tours, though it appears that these numbers include his visits as a "freelance" tourist as well, in addition to scores of towns in Austria and in the German-speaking part of Switzerland. This figure is revised several times over the course of the narrative, see Stasiuk, *Dojczland*, 61.

7. Dirk Uffelmann, "Self-Orientalisation in Narratives by Polish Migrants to Germany (by Contrast to Ireland and the UK)," in Rostek and Uffelmann, *Contemporary Polish Migrant Culture*, 106–107.

8. Ibid., 106.

9. See, for example, George Gasyna, *Polish, Hybrid, and Otherwise: Exilic Discourse in Joseph Conrad and Witold Gombrowicz* (New York: Continuum, 2011), especially chap. 3, "Life Writing."

10. After his West German fellowship sojourn (he was based in West Berlin), Gombrowicz stayed in a writer's residence in France on several occasions, courtesy of various agencies of *la République*. See, for example, the third volume of *The Diary* (Dziennik), on his stay at Royaumont in the spring and summer of 1964: Witold Gombrowicz, *Dziennik III: 1961–1969* (Cracow: Wydawnictwo Literackie, 2001), 186–189.

11. See Witold Gombrowicz, *Diary, Volume I*, trans. Lillian Vallee (Evanston, IL: Northwestern University Press, 1988), 6–7, on the dynamics of (especially exilic) collective appropriation of individual cultural achievement. The plural pronoun *you* in quotation marks should give one pause: how much, exactly, did the individual Poles carrying forth on the cultural achievements of their nation actually have to do *with* these achievements? How much does "Mr. Kowalski have in common with Chopin?" Gombrowicz asks, before pointing out that they, the Mr. Kowalskis of the nation, as individuals charting their way toward an individual future—and its potentialities—are "more important" than Chopin, or Mickiewicz, or any other luminary in the national pantheon that they might care to name; see ibid., 5–6.

12. Gombrowicz, *Diary, Volume I*, 4–6.

13. Witold Gombrowicz, *Dziennik I: 1953–1956* (Cracow: Wydawnictwo Literackie, 2000), 11–13.

14. See, for example, Gombrowicz, *Dziennik III*, 123–126, 172–174, 208–212; and *Diary*, volumes I and II, especially Gombrowicz, *Dziennik I: 1953–1956*, 26–38.

15. Stasiuk, *Dojczland*, 57.

16. See Jean-Luc Marion, "The Reason of the Gift," in *Philosophy of Communication*, ed. Briankle G. Chang and Garnet Butchart (Cambridge, MA: MIT Press, 2012), 516–518, on the difference between the gift, gratuity, and givenness (as prerogatives or phenomena of exchange), and the construct of the "horizon" of reimbursement. Stasiuk's value exchange rationales, especially the a priori rejection of gestures of welcoming, remind one of the type of exchange described by Marion wherein "I give to an enemy"—a gift without the expectation of receiving something of value in return, a gift that when offered can lead to further humiliation or insults (a gift that is seen as "an affront"), because hatred forms an inextricable part in the logic of the exchange; see ibid., 519.

17. Stasiuk, *Dojczland*, 87.

18. Ibid., 87.

19. Ibid., 92, 62–63.

20. Ibid., 88.

21. And thus, somewhat analogous to a holder of the American EB-2 visa, made available ("given") to foreign nationals who are artists, performers, poets, and the like; see US Department of Homeland Security, "Employment-Based Immigration: Second Preference EB-2," accessed January 6, 2014, http://www.uscis.gov/working-united-states/permanent-workers/employment-based-immigration-second-preference-eb-2.

22. Stasiuk, *Dojczland*, 27–28, 92.

23. Ibid., 20.

24. Ibid., 29–30.

25. See, for example, ibid., 12–15, 28, 32–33.

26. See ibid., 88.

27. Ibid., 88.

28. Stasiuk's award-winning 2004 philosophical travelogue, *Jadąc do Babadag* (*On the Road to Babadag*, 2011) is the most eloquent expression of this worldview.

29. See in particular Stasiuk, *Dojczland*, 97–98.

30. See ibid., 7–11, and *passim*.

31. Ibid., 42–45.

32. See Czapliński's "Barbarzyńca na zagrodzie." *Tygodnik Powszechny*, October 26, 2007, accessed June 20, 2015, http://ksiazki.onet.pl/barbarzynca-na-zagrodzie/bkqe5.

33. Stasiuk, *Dojczland*, 101–102.

34. One such site is Nuremberg, which he describes as "a key word association imprinted on the Slavic mind by the very word *Germany*"; see ibid., 81. See also his descriptions of his meanderings in central Berlin (97–101), a concatenation of sites (also of memory) which he variously describes as a glassy underwater city and a postexpressionist collage straight out of a Chagall landscape; ibid., 98.

35. See ibid., 94–95.

36. See ibid., 17, and the section on the "German Pope" (Benedict XVI) praying at Auschwitz, figuratively assuming all the sins of his countrymen, seeking general absolution, toward the end of the narrative (109–110).

37. See the discussion in Schümann, "Lost in Migration," especially 56; Stasiuk, *Dojczland*, 17; my emphasis.

38. Schümann, "Lost in Migration," 56; Stasiuk, *Dojczland*, 83.

39. See for example his *Fado*, a volume of philosophical musings and travel reflections, in which Stasiuk develops the idea of an alternate, fraternal east-central European "union" based on the proximity to the Carpathian Mountains, their "spine"—which starts in Poland and Slovakia and, moving southeast and then southwest again, forms a semicircle that culminates in Romania and the Balkans—constituting the nucleus of this imagined transnational space, a "separate continent"; see especially *Fado,* trans. Bill Johnston (Champaign, IL: Dalkey Archive Press, 2009), 57–60.

40. See Marianne Hirsch, "The Generation of Postmemory," *Poetics Today* 29, no. 1 (Spring 2008): 103–108.

41. See Stasiuk, *Dojczland*, 28–30, as well as 89–90, where Stasiuk recalls the story of his grandmother who was just about to be executed ["*już stała pod ścianą*"] but was then spared thanks to an SS officer's caprice.

42. Ibid., 100.

43. Ibid., 101, my emphasis.

44. See ibid., 101–103.

45. Ibid., 27, 38; my emphasis.

46. Ibid., 19.

47. According to Marianne Hirsch, the term *postmemory* indicates the relationship that the "generation after" bears to the personal, collective, and cultural trauma of those who came before—to experiences they "remember" only by means of the "stories, images, and behaviors" among which they themselves grew up; see Hirsch, "The Generation of Postmemory," 103.

48. See Stasiuk, *Dojczland*, 100.

49. Ibid., 99.

50. See, for example, "Wir brauchen alle eine Therapie" [We all need therapy], an interview with Andrzej Stasiuk in *Die Welt*, March 14, 2007, http://www.welt.de/politik/article760654/Wir-brauchen-alle-eine-Therapie.html; Schümann, "Lost in Migration," 54.

51. Stasiuk, *Dojczland*, 27; my emphasis.

52. As part of the archaeology of gift giving, it is worth noting that the apartment, which Stasiuk uses free of charge, is always well supplied with food and drink for the duration of the author's stay; see ibid., 33–34.

53. Giorgio Agamben, *Homo Sacer: Sovereign Power and Bare Life*, trans. Daniel Heller-Roazen (Redwood City, CA: Stanford University Press, 1998), 104–105; 110; my redaction and emphasis.

54. Ibid., 104.
55. See Stasiuk, *Dojczland*, 73–75.
56. See ibid., 49–60.
57. Ibid., 56, 60, 75. These humanizing elements include such items as "gold teeth, old women with bleached hair, knock-off jewelry, leisure suits, pimples on broad necks... and provincial and post-Soviet design [*dizajn* in the original, another lazily Polonized foreign term] straight out of Chisinau" (59).
58. Ibid., 53.
59. Ibid., 50.
60. Ibid., 70.
61. Ibid., 98.
62. Ibid., 97–98.
63. Ibid., 53–54; my emphasis.
64. See Schümann, "Lost in Migration," 53.

CHAPTER 12

Journeys of Identity
From Soviet Jew to German Writer

Adrian Wanner

SINCE THE TURN of the millennium, a striking new phenomenon has appeared on the German literary scene: Soviet-born native speakers of Russian who immigrated to Germany and write fiction in German for a German audience. As a country that used to define itself in ethnically homogeneous terms, Germany has only belatedly and reluctantly come to acknowledge its status as a destination for immigrants. While narratives of immigration have long been at the core of America's cultural mythology, no comparable tradition exists in Germany aside from the relatively recent phenomena of *Gastarbeiterliteratur* (*guest worker literature*) and Turkish-German literature. Russian speakers have now replaced the Turks as Germany's largest immigrant group. Since the collapse of the Soviet Union and German reunification, about 2.5 million "repatriated" Russian Germans and about 200,000 Russian-Jewish refugees have relocated to Germany.[1] It was only a matter of time before some of these newcomers began to write in the language of their host country. Even though the number of Russian Germans far exceeds that of Russian Jews, it is the latter group—on average more educated, urban, and more attuned to literary culture—that is largely responsible for launching the genre of Russian-German immigrant literature.[2] This is similar to the situation in North America, where Gary Shteyngart's bestselling 2002 novel *The Russian Debutante's Handbook* signaled the advent of a fashionable new trend of Russian-Jewish-American immigrant fiction. Both the Russian-German and Russian-American authors belong to a global cohort of "translingual" Russophone émigrés that has sprung up as a result of the Jewish exodus from the Soviet Union and its successor states.[3]

Unlike the dual identity of the typical diaspora Jew, Russian-Jewish émigré authors in Germany have at least a tripartite identity, combining a Russian linguistic and cultural origin, a Jewish "ethnicity" (in most cases without a religious allegiance), and German citizenship and use of the German language as a medium of literary expression. The "Russian" label seems to have trumped thus far the other identities as a promotional strategy adopted by their publishers, be it because of the relative novelty of Russian immigration, the prestige of Russian high culture, or the totalitarian mystique associated with the former communist superpower. An additional complicating factor for these authors is the fraught legacy of German-Jewish relations in the twentieth century, raising the question whether it is even appropriate for a Jew to move to Germany and become a writer in the "language of the perpetrators." In this chapter, I investigate the oeuvre of several Russian-speaking Jewish immigrant writers in Germany and Austria, including Lena Gorelik, Vladimir Vertlib, Olga Grjasnowa, Katja Petrowskaja, and, somewhat more briefly, Wladimir Kaminer and Jan Himmelfarb.[4] The multiple identities of these authors assume an increasing level of complexity, ranging from an impersonation of Russianness over an oscillating and blurred ethnic identification to an openly contrarian stance that questions received ideas of integration and acculturation. Strikingly, images of railroad travel surface in many of their narratives as a symbol of transnational mobility, uprootedness, and shifting identities. This is perhaps not surprising, given that the railway system, in Todd Samuel Presner's words, "represents the organizing principle, the material reality, and the cultural metaphor for ... modernity as a story of mobility," making it "arguably the most iconic association of both the splendor and horror of German/Jewish relations."[5]

The originator and self-proclaimed mascot of the "Russian" brand in German fiction is Wladimir Kaminer. Born in Moscow in 1967 and living in Berlin since 1990, Kaminer emerged as a "shooting star" of German literature with his *Russendisko*, a collection of vignettes about Russian émigré life in Berlin published in 2000. The book became an instant bestseller and has been translated into many languages, including English.[6] Kaminer has since published twenty more books in rapid succession, and his Russian Disco at Kaffee Burger in the former East Berlin has become a legendary fixture of Berlin's nightlife. Kaminer's staged Russianness (or Sovietness) is a (self-)ironic performance that both mobilizes and mocks ethnic stereotypes. In his frequent public appearances, he refers to himself as "*der Russe vom Dienst*" (loosely translatable as "the Russian from central casting"). Kaminer's Russian Disco with its Red Star logo, schmaltzy Slavic tunes, and uninhibited frenzy can be enjoyed both as a celebration of Russianness and as a postmodern parody of earlier German stagings of Russianness such as those practiced by the pseudo-Russian singer Ivan Rebroff.[7] Kaminer's Jewish background plays a much more muted role in his public persona. While he is not hiding his Jewishness, Kaminer prefers not to dwell on it either. "Russian," rather than "Jewish," is the common denominator that he uses for immigrants from the former Soviet Union. Nevertheless, an important, largely unmentioned factor contributes to his popularity with the German public: as a Jew who has happily embraced the German language and culture, he is helping to burnish the image of the new Germany as a philosemitic rather than an antisemitic nation.

LENA GORELIK

More recently, Kaminer has received competition from several younger female immigrant authors, who project an equally "cool" Russian persona. Like Kaminer, they have used their Russianness as a tool of self-identification and self-promotion, but, unlike Kaminer, they are more attuned to the implications of their Jewish identity. The most prolific among them is Lena Gorelik, who was born in Leningrad in 1981 and emigrated to Germany in 1992. Since 2004, she has published five novels—*Meine weißen Nächte* (*My White Nights*, 2004), *Hochzeit in Jerusalem* (*Wedding in Jerusalem*, 2007), *Verliebt in Sankt Petersburg: Meine russische Reise* (*In Love with St. Petersburg: My Russian Journey*, 2008), *Die Listensammlerin* (*The Collector of Lists*, 2013), and *Null bis unendlich* (*Zero to Infinity*, 2015), as well as two books of nonfiction: *Lieber Mischa* (*Dear Misha*, 2011) and

"Sie können aber gut Deutsch!" ("But Your German Is Really Good!," 2012). Gorelik's self-representation in her fiction and essayistic writings has vacillated over the years between a Russian, Jewish, and, most recently, a sort of generic immigrant identity.

Anya, the heroine of Gorelik's early fiction, is a young woman who came to Germany as a child and clearly functions as the author's alter ego. In the first chapter of *My White Nights* we see her taking leave from her relatives and friends at the St. Petersburg railway station in May 1992. When the train begins to move, the thought flashes through Anya's head that she probably won't see her city of birth, her friends, or her beloved dog ever again. Luckily, she is distracted from this gloomy thought by a new, "authentic" Barbie doll, a last-minute gift from an American visitor. This toy embodies for her the promise of life in the West. Unlike their stiff Russian knockoffs, American Barbies are supposed to be able to bend their legs. After some initial frustration, Anya is indeed able to bend the doll's legs with her brother's help. She asks her aunt, who has accompanied the family as far as the border and is taking the next train back to St. Petersburg, to call all her friends and tell them the sensational news.

This episode, couched in gentle irony, symbolically anticipates the gist of Gorelik's narrative: after some initial disappointment and hardship, and with the required effort, life in the West will indeed deliver on its promises. The narrative perspective and chronology of the novel alternate between the eleven-year-old Anya, who looks at Germany with the eyes of a newcomer and a naïve child, and the grown-up Anya, who speaks German without an accent and seems fully integrated into German society. Nevertheless, a residual "foreignness" remains, which can surface in special situations, for example when Anya tries to attract the interest of a good-looking stranger at a party by drawing attention to her Russian origin. The ethnic identity highlighted in *My White Nights* is Russian rather than Jewish. Gorelik delves only briefly into the touchy issue of immigrating to Germany as a Jew. As in Kaminer's books, antisemitism, if mentioned at all, is presented as a Russian rather than a German problem. Even though Anya's father initially declares that he would never agree to live in Germany, he changes his mind when he becomes the victim of an antisemitic attack in a St. Petersburg suburban train.

Overall, the immigration to Germany appears retrospectively justified as the right decision. The choice between a Russian and a German identity and lifestyle becomes symbolically embodied in Anya's amorous dilemma, which takes up the bulk of the novel. She is torn between her German boyfriend, a rather prosaic but reliable and caring character, and her flamboyant former lover, a fellow Russian-Jewish immigrant. At the end Anya opts for the German, who is willing to make certain gestures of accommodation to her Russianness—for example, he acquires a book about mushrooms. In fact, almost all German characters in the book seem rather benevolent toward the Russian-Jewish immigrants, which may have been part of the novel's appeal to German readers.[8]

In Gorelik's second novel, *Wedding in Jerusalem,* Anya engages in a more thorough exploration of her Jewish identity but with no conclusive result. We learn that her interest in Judaism was only a passing adolescent whim. Even though she feels at ease in Israel, she does not consider it her true home, and she is annoyed when other members of her extended family, especially those who have settled in the United States, reproach her for living in Germany. If there is a problem at all in the German attitude toward Jews, according to Gorelik, it manifests itself in an exaggerated *Gutmenschentum,* that is, an ostentatious philosemitism as a compensation for past guilt. Gorelik's third book, *In Love with St. Petersburg,* where the narrator, seemingly identical with Gorelik herself, travels to St. Petersburg to show her city of birth to a German friend, does not address the heroine's Jewish identity at all. Gorelik's hospitable and warmhearted St. Petersburg relatives appear as paradigmatic "Russians" without any reference to their ethnic background. Interestingly, while *In Love with St. Petersburg* foregrounded Gorelik's Russian origin at the expense of her Jewishness, in her next book she performed the exact opposite operation by focusing squarely on her Jewish identity and barely mentioning her Russian roots. *Dear Misha* is written in the form of a letter to her newborn son. The baroque subtitle gives a good impression of the book's satirical tone: "Dear Misha, . . . whose name almost would have been Schlomo Adolf Grinblum Glück, I am so sorry I couldn't spare you this: You are a Jew." Adorned with Talmud-like side glosses and oscillating between Jewish pride and Jewish self-mockery, the book lampoons a gamut of clichés ranging from the Jewish nose to the Jewish mother to the Jewish world conspiracy.

What unites Gorelik's first three novels is the good-natured persona of her first-person narrator, a traveler and mediator between the geographic and cultural spaces of Russia, Germany, and Israel who addresses differences in mentality and behavior with gentle humor. Her book "*But Your German Is Really Good!*" presents a clear break with this pattern. It bears the polemic subtitle "Why I don't want to be grateful anymore for being allowed to live here, and why tolerance doesn't help us further." Partially as a response to Thilo Sarrazin's best-selling pamphlet *Deutschland schafft sich ab* (*Germany Abolishes Itself*, 2010), which lamented the destruction of German culture and the degradation of the German gene pool by uneducated Muslim immigrants, Gorelik offers a spirited appeal for a more inclusive society in which foreign-born citizens are accepted as fellow Germans rather than merely "tolerated." In particular, Gorelik expresses resentment at her own status as a *Vorzeigeausländer* (literally, a "foreigner for show," a term with similar implications to the American "model minority"). She resents being complimented for her good German and makes clear that she has become fed up with being touted as a role model for other immigrant groups, mainly Muslims, who are judged to be insufficiently willing to integrate.

VLADIMIR VERTLIB

Gorelik's sense of unease demonstrates an awareness that her integration into German society may not have been as smooth and unproblematic as initially assumed. In this sense, her position has become more distant from Kaminer, and perhaps closer to that of another Russian-speaking Jew who has become a successful writer in German, Vladimir Vertlib. Born in Leningrad in 1966, Vertlib settled in Austria at age fifteen after a ten-year odyssey that involved numerous border crossings and residence in multiple countries, including Israel, Holland, Italy, and the United States, where he and his family lived in New York's Brighton Beach neighborhood and later in Boston before they were deported as illegal aliens.[9] Vertlib's literary persona is that of the alienated outsider rather than the happily integrated immigrant. Unlike Lena Gorelik's protagonist Anya, who displays her patriotism by rooting for the German soccer team at the world championship, the German-Jewish hero of Vertlib's novel *Letzter Wunsch* (*Last Wish*, 2003) has a more complex attitude. When simple souls subject him to an inane loyalty test by asking which side he would support in a hypothetical soccer match between Germany and Israel, he varies his answer according to the questioner. To a German he invariably says "Israel," but if the questioner is a foreigner, especially a Jew, he says "Germany."[10]

Becoming a writer in German, a language to which he only gradually developed a more positive attitude, finally freed Vertlib from the compulsive need for further emigration, as he explained in a 2004 interview.[11] Nevertheless, Austria has not become an unproblematic "home" for him. Unlike Kaminer, who tends to avoid the topic of German antisemitism, Vertlib is well aware of the baggage that he carries as a Jewish author writing in German, especially in a country that has been reluctant to confront its own Nazi past. Just as Gorelik does in her most recent books, Vertlib's account suggests that the conspicuous philosemitism of the Germans masks an underlying unease. The feisty protagonist of the novel *Das besondere Gedächtnis der Rosa Masur* (*The Special Memory of Rosa Masur*, 2001), who is modeled on Vertlib's own grandmother, observes that "as we know, the Germans nowadays love the Jews, at least as long as the Jews don't behave as Jewishly as they believe Jews are capable of but should rather not."[12]

Vertlib's unsettled identity is expressed in the central metaphor of train travel, signaling an existence that remains forever in transit and on the move. The title of his autobiographical novel, *Zwischenstationen* (*Intermediate Stations*), evokes the predicament of a journey with an endlessly deferred arrival. Railway stations not only serve as a symbolic marker for the different chronological and geographical phases of the hero's biography; they also provide the literal backdrop for some of the story's crucial scenes. The book's opening chapter shows the narrator's arrival at St. Petersburg's Finland Station for his first return to his city of birth in 1993. This is followed by a flashback to his departure from Leningrad as a five-year-old child twenty-two years earlier. In between the two scenes, Vertlib inserts an atmospheric lyrical evocation of train rides and nightly railway stations, which is introduced with the comment: "As long as I have been able to think, riding trains has always held a special attraction for me."[13]

The railroad was indeed the preferred means of transportation for the Russian Jews who emigrated to Germany in the 1990s. The opening chapter of Kaminer's *Russendisko* shows the hero's arrival at East Berlin's Lichtenberg station in 1990, while his autobiographical novel *Militärmusik* (*Military Music*), a sort of prequel to *Russendisko*, ends with his train trip from Moscow to Berlin. As already mentioned, Lena Gorelik begins her debut novel with an account of her train journey from St. Petersburg to Germany in 1992, with a later chapter relating her arrival at Berlin's Ostbahnhof (East Railroad Station). In addition to these accounts of the railroad as a facilitator of fateful transnational migration, Vertlib and Gorelik both describe suburban train rides in the St. Petersburg region where they become witnesses of antisemitic aggression. In Vertlib's *Intermediate Stations*, trains turn into an all-pervasive leitmotif. In a later chapter we see the adolescent hero aimlessly riding streetcars all over Vienna, taking his infatuation with railroad travel to an obsessive level. The book ends with another train scene, featuring the narrator's arrival in Salzburg, his new permanent home in provincial Austria. The first thing he does after leaving the train station is to purchase a Tyrolean hat and to break into a cheerful yodel. His multinational odyssey thus ends on a faux note of Austrian folklore.

OLGA GRJASNOWA

Olga Grjasnowa, eighteen years younger than Vertlib, is another widely traveled Russian-Jewish author with a complex and conflicted literary persona. Her debut novel *Der Russe ist einer, der Birken liebt* (*A Russian Is Someone Who Loves Birch Trees*) was published in 2012 by the prestigious publisher Hanser Verlag.[14] Grjasnowa, a graduate of the Institute of German Literature in Leipzig, was born in Baku in 1984 and immigrated to Germany with her parents in 1996. Maria (Masha) Kogan, the novel's protagonist and first-person narrator, also hails from Azerbaijan and arrived in Germany in 1996 as a Jewish refugee. Thoroughly traumatized from witnessing the anti-Armenian pogroms and other atrocities in Baku, she remains alienated from German society in spite of her perfect command of German (and fluency in a bewildering array of further languages, including Arabic). Like Lena Gorelik, Masha refers to herself cynically as a "perfectly integrated *Vorzeigeausländer*."[15] Her attitude toward mainstream German culture is characterized by resentment and rage. After her German boyfriend dies from the consequences of a soccer accident, the closest people in her life are her former lover, a German Arab, and her homosexual best friend, a German Turk (with whom she is able to converse in Azeri). In the second half of the novel, Masha relocates to Israel (not permanently—as she explains, she would never want to give up her German citizenship) to work as an interpreter for a German government-funded organization. In Israel, too, she remains an outsider. Her relatives find that she doesn't look Jewish. A security employee at Ben Gurion Airport destroys her laptop computer with gunshots because the glued-on Arabic letters on the keyboard raise suspicion. The guard takes her for a *Schickse* (non-Jew) before he is informed by Masha's Israeli companion that her grandmother was a Holocaust survivor (241). Her fluent knowledge of Arabic, paired with her ignorance of Hebrew, causes universal bafflement. After an unsuccessful relationship with a lesbian Israeli peace activist, Masha suffers a mental breakdown. We last see her in a Palestinian refugee camp in the occupied West Bank, where she is overcome by her traumatic childhood memories of ethnic strife in Baku.

The ironic title of Grjasnowa's novel, echoed by an epigraph from Chekhov's *The Three Sisters*, seems to parody the current craze for Russianness among German readers and publishers. In reality, the book frustrates such expectations. The only mention of birch trees and Russians occurs in the sarcastic comment of a Palestinian in Ramallah (265). Even though Masha speaks Russian natively, when one of her German professors asks her whether she is Russian, her answer is "Ein wenig" ("a little," 37). The multicultural identity that Grjasnowa constructs for her heroine is traumatic rather than harmonious. Masha's compulsive learning of different languages looks like a desperate attempt to find the "home" that she perhaps never had in the first place. Almost instinctively, she always gravitates toward the stigmatized "other," be it Armenians in Azerbaijan, Turks in Germany, Palestinian Arabs in Israel, or homosexuals everywhere.[16] The identification with the Turkish immigrant population in Germany makes the novel stand out from other works by Russian-German writers. In Wladimir Kaminer's writings the German Turks play at best a folkloric role, and sometimes they even serve as the target of condescending ethnic derision.[17] Grjasnowa's heroine, by contrast, clearly identifies with the Turks as fellow victims of German xenophobia.

The German Slavist Dirk Uffelmann has noted that successful immigrant writers in Germany seem to follow a two-pronged strategy—on the one hand, they emphasize their integration into the host society; on the other they construct themselves as exotic foreigners. In this manner, they manage to work simultaneously with the two paradigms that define the discussion on immigration and multiculturalism—assimilation versus difference. Uffelmann argues that by accommodating both sides in a divided public, they have succeeded in covering "the entire segment for migrant literature on the German market."[18] A danger they incur with this strategy, of course, is to turn into harmless providers of orientalizing entertainment and *Kuschel-Ausländer* (*cuddly foreigners*, to use a term coined by the group Kanak Attak to denounce immigrants who let themselves be co-opted by a phony German multiculturalism).[19] Olga Grjasnowa takes her unease with this situation to new extremes with her depiction of an "immigrant overachiever" who is chafing under the German demand for integration with its implied patronizing condescension toward anyone with a *Migrationshintergrund* (*migration background*, a word that her character can't stand, as we learn early on in the novel [12]).

The irony, of course, lies in the fact that although Grjasnowa rallies against the clichés of migrant literature, her own background as a Russian-speaking Jew from Azerbaijan, which she shares with her fictional heroine and which is prominently advertised on the book's dust jacket, may be precisely the feature that makes her novel attractive to German readers. Grjasnowa's rather disappointing second novel, *Die juristische Unschärfe einer Ehe* (*The Legal Indeterminacy of a Marriage*, 2014), looks like an attempt to further cash in on her "exotic" background. It relates a love triangle involving Leyla, a lesbian former Bolshoi ballerina from Azerbaijan who is now living in Berlin; her husband Altay, a gay psychiatrist wedded to Leyla in a marriage of convenience; and a female American-Israeli art history student named Jonoun. Part of the plot takes place in Baku. Altay and Jonoun travel there to free Leyla from an Azerbaijani jail, in which she has landed because of her participation in an illegal car race, whereupon the two women engage on a road trip through Azerbaijan, Georgia, and

Armenia, the main purpose of which seems to be to regale the German readers of Grjasnowa's novel with a picturesque panoply of post-Soviet Caucasian landscapes and characters.

KATJA PETROWSKAJA

The rather facile clichés of Grjasnowa's second novel are all the more disconcerting when we contrast them with another book published in the same year, Katja Petrowskaja's *Vielleicht Esther* (*Perhaps Esther*, 2014). Petrowskaja, the latest Russian-German-Jewish literary star, was born in Kiev in 1970. She studied Russian philology in Tartu and Moscow, where she lived until moving with her German husband to Berlin in 1999. In 2013 Petrowskaja received the Ingeborg Bachmann Prize, the most prestigious literary award in the German-speaking world, for her story *Perhaps Esther*, an account of the murder of her Jewish great-grandmother by the German Wehrmacht in Kiev. The book with the same title, in which the story becomes part of a larger textual framework, came out a year later with Suhrkamp Verlag, the leading German publisher, and earned the author universal critical acclaim. *Vielleicht Esther* is not a novel but an investigation of the history of Petrowskaja's far-flung family, taking the narrator on a trip through time and space involving multiple locations ranging from Berlin, Vienna, Warsaw, and Kiev to the Mauthausen concentration camp, where her Ukrainian grandfather was imprisoned at the end of World War II.

As with some of the other authors discussed here, the railroad plays an important symbolic function in the book. The opening prologue shows Petrowskaja in Berlin's glitzy new Main Station waiting for the train that will take her to Warsaw (which is the birthplace of her maternal grandmother, as we find out later). The bombed-out wasteland in the middle of the German capital immediately evokes associations with the war, which are ironically reinforced by the gigantic letters *Bombardier Willkommen in Berlin* on display below the station's vaulted roof. When a confused American traveler of Iranian-Jewish provenance asks Petrowskaja about the meaning of the sign, she makes up a story on the spot, claiming that it is an advertisement for a successful French musical. Only when she looks up the word on Google afterward does she discover that "Bombardier" is the name of a multinational aerospace and transportation company. As it turns out, the American and his wife, whose grandmother emigrated a century ago from a Belorussian village to the United States, are also taking the Warsaw Express in search of the lost world of their ancestors.

The episode puts into relief several important strands of Petrowskaja's narrative. The locus of the train station points to travel, migration, and displacement as crucial themes. Later in the book, a chapter titled *Der Zug (The Train)* describes the harrowing journey in a cattle car across the Soviet Union of Petrowskaja's then six-year-old mother, who, together with her mother and sister, is being evacuated from Kiev, where the German occupiers soon will murder her grandmother and the other remaining Jewish relatives. The scene, told to Petrowskaja by her mother, becomes indelibly etched in her memory. The trope of Jews being transported in cattle cars evokes very specific associations, but, as Petrowskaja notes, "the word 'cattle car' did not particularly preoccupy me, because I knew that they were going in the other direction, not in the direction of death, but into the unknown."[20]

The structure of Petrowskaja's book follows spatial and associative principles rather than a chronological order. In that sense, it resembles a railway network as described in Todd Samuel Presner's *Mobile Modernity*: "Stations are infinitely connectable; the tracks are, by definition, bidirectional; the system is nonlinear, acentric, and open-ended; connections are based on the contingency of contiguity; and movement is synchronous."[21] The account of Petrowskaja's trips across Poland and Austria in search of lost traces of her family gives her book the character of a travelogue and detective story. The initial episode with the "Bombardier" sign at the Berlin train station indicates the importance of language for Petrowskaja's project: words and names are never "innocent" but come with their own mental and associative baggage. We learn that Petrowskaja's own Russian-sounding last name was an alias adopted by her paternal grandfather in the Bolshevik underground and passed on to his descendants. His actual name was Shimon Shtern (meaning "star"), which in Petrovskaja's interpretation becomes a symbolic evocation of the Star of David.[22]

The lost past can only be approached through the telling of stories. *Geschichten (Stories)* is in fact the subtitle of Petrowskaja's book. *Geschichte* is also the German word for "history," and the different stories unfolding in the book trace a panorama of twentieth-century European history in all its tragic complexity. Storytelling involves a creative act, as demonstrated by the invented explanation of the "Bombardier" sign at the Berlin train station, which, as Petrowskaja explains, should by no means be considered a "lie." As she puts it, "he who doesn't lie cannot fly" (9). Even though Petrowskaja insists that nothing in her book is invented, *Perhaps Esther* is a carefully crafted, self-consciously literary text, suffused with allusions and quotes from the Russian and German poetic canon and written with a passionate lyric intensity that sometimes turns into a dreamlike stream of consciousness.

Some of the quotes included in the text stage a sort of German-Russian literary dialogue. The beginning of Heinrich Heine's *Fichtenbaum* poem ("Ein Fichtenbaum steht einsam"—"A fir tree stands lonely") serves as the epigraph to the chapter on Petrowskaja's family tree. This poem has acquired particular prominence in Russia thanks to Mikhail Lermontov's creative transposition. Later in the book, when Petrowskaja retraces the fifty-five-kilometer death march of her Ukrainian grandfather from the Mauthausen concentration to the town of Gunskirchen, she quotes the opening of Mikhail Lermontov's poem *Vykhozhu odin ia na dorogu* (*Lonely I go out on the road*) both in Russian and in the German translation by Rainer Maria Rilke (*Einsam geh' ich auf dem Weg*), without ever identifying Lermontov or Rilke by name (243). The citation of Alexander Blok's poem *Night, Street, Lantern, Pharmacy* in German translation at the end of the book also remains unattributed (281–282). These poets, as it were, have become an integral part of the fabric of Petrowskaja's own Russian-German lyric consciousness and therefore need no separate identification.

Petrowskaja's mastery of German is all the more impressive as she only began to learn this language at age twenty-six. The "foreignness" of the linguistic medium in which her story is told becomes itself a topic of reflection in her book. As she writes:

> My German remained in the tension of unreachability and saved me from routine. As if it were the smallest coin I paid back my past in this language that I acquired late, with the passion of a young lover. I desired German so much because I could not melt together with it, driven by an unfulfilled longing, a love that knew no object or gender, no addressee, because

there were only sounds that could not be captured, they were wild and unreachable. (79)

As Petrowskaja points out, the Russian word for German, *nemetskii*, is etymologically related to *nemoi* (*dumb, mute*). For the Russians, a German is someone "who cannot speak." Interestingly, her maternal grandmother, her great-grandfather, and many more members of that side of her family tree were directing schools for the deaf, first in Austria and Poland, and after World War I in the Soviet Union. Petrowskaja likens her acquisition of the German language with her ancestors' ability to make deaf people express themselves in an idiom that they were not deemed capable of mastering. German becomes for her a "wishing rod in the search for my people, who for centuries taught deaf-mute children to speak, as if I had to learn the mute German in order to be able to talk" (79). The outcome is a personally liberating experience that is helping her cope with historical and personal trauma: "My German, truth and deception, the language of the enemy, was a way out, a second life, a love that does not pass, because one never reaches it, gift and poison, as if I had freed a bird" (80).

The expression *Gabe und Gift* (*gift and poison*) contains a possible bilingual pun involving the conflicting English and German meanings of the word *gift*. It demonstrates both Petrowskaja's sensibility to semantic polyvalence and a lingering unease about her status as a German writer. Elsewhere in the book she likens her writing in German to a cross-gender performance with a glued-on male organ (118). Her own sense of identity remains fluid and problematic, and it also fluctuates according to her location. As a "Russian from Germany," she feels like a "representative of the occupying powers" when she visits Poland (101). As she explains: "Nowhere have I felt as perfectly lost as here in Warsaw. I thought in Russian, looked for my Jewish relatives, and wrote in German. I had the good fortune to move in the fissure of languages, in the exchange, the confusion of roles and perspectives. Who conquered whom, who belongs to my people, who to the others, which shore is mine?" (115).

This experience of nonbelonging did not arise only with Petrowskaja's emigration to Germany, it also had been a feature of her former life as a Russian-speaking Jew from Kiev studying in Estonia and later living in Moscow. As she told a journalist from the Berlin newspaper *Der*

Tagespiegel: "In Estonia I am a Russian occupant, in Moscow a Ukrainian provincial. To be a semi-stranger everywhere is difficult. Better to be a total stranger in Germany."[23] Calling herself a "total stranger" is an overstatement, of course, but Petrowskaja does look at German society from an outsider's perspective, and, even though she is nonobservant and, as she puts it, "rather accidentally Jewish" (10), she cannot help pondering the implications of her Jewishness in the context of German history. In one of her book's more poignant moments, we see her and her eleven-year-old daughter at the German Historical Museum in Berlin accidentally stumbling on a tour guide who is explaining the complex racial categorizations of the Nuremberg Laws displayed on a chart from the 1930s. Petrowskaja is thrown off guard by her daughter's whispered question, "Where are we on this chart, Mama?" (45). Before she has the time to come to terms with this inquiry and to think of an answer, a German man in the tour group accosts her with the words, "Wir haben übrigens bezahlt" ("By the way, we paid")—implying that she and her daughter joined the tour on the sly and had no right to stand there and listen to the guide's explanation. The juxtaposition of meticulous racial madness on the Nuremberg chart with the vigilant, self-righteous "law-and-order" mentality of the German tourist drives Petrowskaja to silent tears.

JAN HIMMELFARB

Many of the themes of Petrowskaja's book—the symbolism of stars and trains, the childhood in Soviet Ukraine, the inherited trauma of the Holocaust, and the dilemma of Jewish immigration to the land of the perpetrators—recur, in a much starker and more ostentatious manner, in Jan Himmelfarb's debut novel *Sterndeutung* (*Interpretation of Stars*, 2015), which is so far the newest contribution to the ever-growing corpus of Russian-German-Jewish immigrant fiction. Himmelfarb was born in Khar'kov, Ukraine, in 1985 and moved to Germany at age seven. His fictitious first-person narrator, Arthur Segal, is born in a moving, darkened railway car in October 1941 en route from Khar'kov to Stalingrad, as his mother and grandmother are fleeing eastward from the advancing German troops. In a touch of magic realism that seems borrowed from

Günther Grass's novel *The Tin Drum*, Segal remembers the exact circumstances of his birth. With the eyes of the newborn child, he sees other railway transports of the time "evacuating" German Jews to ghettos in the East, and later, as he is being evacuated from Stalingrad farther east to Tashkent, he sees trains ferreting Jews from all over Europe to Baltic execution sites and the extermination camps in Poland. The fact that the hero remembers his own birth on a moving train and has visions as a newborn of Jews being transported to their deaths via railway seems to him less fantastic than the actual events of the Nazi genocide, which the book proceeds to describe in gruesome detail, from the mass execution of the Khar'kov Jews to the gas chambers of Treblinka and Auschwitz.

These flashbacks to the Holocaust punctuate the flow of time during which the middle-aged narrator writes the story in the early 1990s, after he has arrived in Germany as a Jewish refugee and built a middle-class existence as a translator and used-car exporter. In many respects, he has done quite well. His daughter receives a stipend to study business management at a prestigious private university, which is named after its main financial benefactor, a wealthy German industrialist and, as it turns out, a former member of the Waffen-SS. At the daughter's graduation ceremony, the former SS man receives an honorary doctoral degree from the university. While the audience gives the benefactor a standing ovation, Segal remains seated and motionless. This rather impotent gesture of defiance is the extent of his protest, revealing that Segal remains trapped between his desire to somehow preserve his Jewish dignity and the pragmatic necessity to maintain his materially successful German lifestyle. The circumstances of his birth have forever marked him as a Jew. Looking back at his beginnings, he muses: "The first impression, as well as the second and all others, of light and trains and stars, were Jewish, and to be a Jewish infant, to be a Jew, meant exactly that—lack of light, trains, stars."[24]

CONCLUSION

With Petrowskaja's and Himmelfarb's books we have traveled an enormous distance from Wladimir Kaminer's persona of the happily integrated immigrant who depicts German society as a vibrant multicultural mix. One wonders whether Kaminer's success was boosted by the fact that he removed the guilt from the host society's hegemonic sense of superiority by impersonating a "subaltern"—and a Jew, no less!—who gladly glorifies the dominant culture. Kaminer's performance of the "cool" but harmless Russian, like Gorelik's persona of the female "immigrant overachiever" in her early novels, fit neatly into the utopian projection of the new Germany as a happy multicultural community. Vladimir Vertlib has challenged this perception by raising uncomfortable questions about German xenophobia and multicultural tokenism, which Olga Grjasnowa addressed in even more acerbic form. Gorelik's book *"But Your German Is Really Good!"* which came out in the same year as Grjasnowa's first novel, reads at times like a nonfictional elaboration of the issues raised by Grjasnowa. Katja Petrowskaja, with less polemic fanfare than Gorelik and Grjasnowa and much more historical depth and nuance, addresses the same question of uneasy belonging or nonbelonging triggered by the transnational migration of Russian Jews to Germany.

What does it mean to be a post-Soviet Russian-speaking Jew living in Germany and writing in German? Of course, for authors like Gorelik, Vertlib, Grjasnowa, or Himmelfarb, who acquired the German language in childhood or adolescence and speak it without an accent (or, in the case of Vertlib, with an Austrian accent), selecting German as the idiom of literary creativity was really the most natural choice. The situation is different for Wladimir Kaminer and Katja Petrowskaja, who learned German only at an adult age. Kaminer's thick Russian accent has become a proudly displayed trademark that boosts the appeal of his frequent oral performances. The challenges and opportunities of creating works of literature in a non-native language is not something that he spends much time mulling about. When asked by a Russian journalist what prompted him to write in German, his answer was: "Simply because nobody here understands Russian."[25] Petrowskaja's book, as we have seen, contains a built-in reflection about her ambivalent relationship to the "language of the enemy." Using the German language was "liberating" for her, as she explained in an interview with German broadcaster Deutsche Welle, because "when you write about this period [World War II] in Russian, you inevitably get trapped in a moral discussion about victory and willingness to sacrifice. Writing about the same events using German words means imagining a German counterpart. And in that way I was able to explain that the history of victim and perpetrator is passé for me. Those who continue in these roles inevitably get trapped in them, without understanding them."[26]

As far as their own identity is concerned, all of the writers under discussion here resist attempts by others to buttonhole them in a fixed ethnic category. When Wladimir Kaminer was asked by Deutsche Welle whether he sees himself as a Russian, a German, or a Jewish writer, his response was: "I understand that for others this is an important distinction. But personally I don't give a damn about it" ("mir selbst ist das schnurz").[27] Vladimir Vertlib has expressed his bemusement with critics and reviewers who refer to him as "a Russian living in Austria," a "Russian writer," "an Israeli living in Germany," a "Jewish-German writer of Russian descent," an "Austrian Russian," and even a "Hebrew author" (in spite of his minimal command of Hebrew).[28] In her book *"But Your German Is Really Good!,"* Lena Gorelik mocks journalists who want to know what percentage of her mentality is Russian, German, or Jewish,[29] while Katja Petrowskaja expresses resentment at being questioned about her Jewishness "in every second interview." As she puts it: "The shortest answer to the question who I am is my book, and it took me four-and-a-half years to formulate it."[30]

While all these authors embrace a composite identity that refuses to privilege one element over the other, there are nevertheless clear differences in their self-presentation and literary practice. Unlike Wladimir Kaminer, who has become "stuck" in his performance of a Russian ethnic routine that ultimately glorifies a hip new German multiculturalism, Lena Gorelik's attitude has evolved over the course of her career toward a more confrontational than conciliatory stance. This critical mind-set toward the German mainstream is also shared by Vladimir Vertlib, Olga Grjasnowa, Katja Petrowskaja, and Jan Himmelfarb, who have managed to use their "in-betweenness" as a springboard for linguistic and narrative creativity. While it seems safe to predict that Kaminer's future oeuvre will offer few surprises, one awaits Gorelik's, Vertlib's, Grjasnowa's, Petrowskaja's, and Himmelfarb's next books with curiosity.

NOTES

1. The exact number of "Russians" living in Germany is difficult to determine because of the heterogeneous nature of this population. Since the Russian-German *Spätaussiedler* (late re-migrants) are German citizens, they do not appear as a separate category on population statistics. The consensus among demographers is that immigrants from the former Soviet Union form today the largest foreign-born population group in Germany, with the Turks occupying the second place. I am indebted to Dr. Sonja Haug from the German Federal Office of Migration and Refugees for this information (e-mail to author, February 3, 2009).

2. Perhaps the only notable exception is the Russian-German author Eleonora Hummel, who published three novels (*Die Fische von Berlin*, 2005; *Die Venus im Fenster*, 2009; *In guten Händen, in einem schönen Land*, 2013) with Steidl Verlag in Göttingen.

3. For a survey of contemporary Russian immigrant fiction written in French, German, English, and Hebrew, see Adrian Wanner, *Out of Russia: Fictions of a New Translingual Diaspora* (Evanston, IL: Northwestern University Press, 2011).

4. This is by no means a complete list of recent Russian-German writers. Other authors not discussed in this chapter include Alina Bronsky (*Scherbenpark*, 2008; *Die schärfsten Gerichte der tatarischen Küche*, 2010; *Nenn mich einfach Superheld*, 2013), Marjana Gaponenko (*Annuschka Blume*, 2010; *Wer ist Martha?*, 2013), Olga Martynova (*Sogar Papageien überleben uns*, 2010; *Mörikes Schlüsselbein*, 2013), Julya Rabinovich (*Spaltkopf*, 2008; *Herznovelle*, 2011; *Die Erdfresserin*, 2012), and Nellja Veremej (*Berlin liegt im Osten*, 2013). Alina Bronsky's novels, translated by Tim Mohr, have come out with Europa editions, New York (*Broken Glass Park*, 2010; *The Hottest Dishes of the Tartar Cuisine*, 2011; *Just Call Me Superhero*, 2014).

5. Todd Samuel Presner, *Mobile Modernity: Germans, Jews, Trains* (New York: Columbia University Press, 2007), 15.

6. Wladimir Kaminer, *Russian Disco*, trans. Michael Hulse (London: Ebury Press, 2002). For a more detailed assessment of Kaminer's biography, public persona, and literary work, see Wanner, *Out of Russia*, 51–71.

7. Ivan Rebroff (1931–2008), born as Hans Rolf Rippert in Berlin-Spandau, became famous as a performer of Russian songs. With his beard, folkloric costumes, and fake accent, he mimicked a Russian persona to perfection.

8. Interestingly, the only negative comment posted on Amazon.de about *My White Nights* concerns the lone "ugly" German character in the book, an arrogant dentist who insists on pulling Anja's teeth without any apparent necessity. A reader objects to this episode because it allegedly leads to false generalizations about Germans and detracts from the lighthearted tone of the book. See "Vodka Lemon russisch oder deutsch," August 31, 2006, http://www.amazon.de/product-reviews/3453351061/ref=sr_1_1_cm_cr_acr_txt ?ie=UTF8&showViewpoints=1.

9. This episode inspired Vertlib's first book, the novella *Die Abschiebung* (*The Deportation*), published in 1995. Vertlib's second book, the autobiographical novel *Zwischenstationen* (*Intermediate Stations*, 1999), provides a fictionalized account of his wanderings between continents and languages. In the meantime, Vertlib has published six more books: *Das besondere Gedächtnis der Rosa Masur*, 2001; *Letzter Wunsch*, 2003; *Mein erster*

Mörder: Lebensgeschichten, 2006; *Am Morgen des zwölften Tages*, 2009; *Schimons Schweigen*, 2012; *Lucia Binar und die russische Seele*, 2015.

10. Vladimir Vertlib, *Letzter Wunsch: Roman* (Munich: Deutscher Taschenbuch Verlag, 2006), 231.

11. Vladimir Vertlib, *Spiegel im fremden Wort: Die Erfindung des Lebens als Literatur. Dresdner Chamisso-Poetikvorlesungen 2006* (Dresden: Thelem, 2007), 209.

12. Vladimir Vertlib, *Das besondere Gedächtnis der Rosa Masur: Roman* (Munich: Deutscher Taschenbuch Verlag, 2003), 227. Unless otherwise noted, all English translations from German and Russian are my own.

13. Vladimir Vertlib, *Zwischenstationen: Roman* (Munich: Deutscher Taschenbuch Verlag, 2005), 7.

14. An American edition of the novel, translated by Eva Bacon, appeared in January 2014 with Other Press, New York, under the title *All Russians Love Birch Trees*.

15. Olga Grjasnowa, *Der Russe ist einer, der Birken liebt* (Munich: Hanser Verlag, 2012), 57. Subsequent page references to this edition will be given directly in the text.

16. Interestingly, the male hero of Lena Gorelik's novel *Die Listensammlerin*, 2013, is a homosexual Soviet dissident. The persecution of homosexuals in the Soviet Union and increasingly in Putin's Russia makes them a quintessential abject "other."

17. See, for example, the story "Der türkische Kater" ("The Turkish Tomcat") in *Russendisko*.

18. Dirk Uffelmann, "Konzilianz und Asianismus: Paradoxe Strategien der jüngsten deutschsprachigen Literatur slavischer Migranten," *Zeitschrift für slavische Philologie* 62, no. 2 (2003): 305.

19. See Kanak Attak: About, accessed July 2, 2009, http://www.kanak-attak.de/ka/about/manif_deu.html.

20. Katja Petrowskaja, *Vielleicht Esther. Geschichten* (Berlin: Suhrkamp Verlag, 2014), 81. Subsequent page references to this edition will be given directly in the text.

21. Presner, *Mobile Modernity*, 15.

22. Petrowskaja's older brother Yohanan Petrovsky-Shtern, a prominent scholar of Jewish history at Northwestern University, reattached the "Shtern" to his last name.

23. Jens Mühling, "Lieber ganz fremd als halb," *Der Tagesspiegel*, March 8, 2014, http://www.tagesspiegel.de/kultur/ukraine-die-schriftstellerin-katja-petrowskaja-lieber-ganz-fremd-als-halb/9590042.html. Interestingly, the article presents Petrowskaja as a "Ukrainian writer."

24. Jan Himmelfarb, *Sterndeutung* (Munich: Beck, 2015), 269.

25. Maiia Kucherskaia, "Tragediia so strausami: Segodnia na znamenitom 'sinem divane' posidit Vladimir Kaminer," *Rossiiskaia gazeta*, October 8, 2004, http://www.rg.ru/2004/10/08/karminer.html.

26. Holger Heimann, "Language 'necessary struggle' for Bachmann winner" (English in the original), Deutsche Welle, July 9, 2013, http://dw.com/p/194AJ.

27. Klaudia Prevezanos, "Eine sehr skurrile Gemeinde," Deutsche Welle, February 10, 2003, http://dw.com/p/2Iof.

28. Vertlib, *Spiegel im fremden Wort*, 141–142.

29. Lena Gorelik, *"Sie können aber gut Deutsch!" Warum ich nicht mehr dankbar sein will, dass ich hier leben darf, und Toleranz nicht weiterhilft* (Munich: Pantheon, 2012), 11.

30. Mühling, "Lieber ganz fremd als halb."

CONTRIBUTORS

ELIZABETH BLAKE, Assistant Professor of Russian at Saint Louis University, focuses on issues relating to gender, ethnicity, exile, and political theologies in her various articles on nineteenth-century Russian and Polish literature, which include analyses of works by Fyodor Dostoevsky, Leo Tolstoy, and Bolesław Prus. Her monograph with Northwestern University Press, *Dostoevsky and the Catholic Underground* (2014), discusses the author's productive dialogue with writers such as Alexandre Dumas (père), Miguel de Cervantes, and Jean Racine as well as his critical evaluation of Polish and French Catholic revolutionaries, whom he encountered in Siberia and the West. Her current research projects include a historical examination of the Polish exile experience in Siberia (1848–1862) and an investigation of Catholic-Orthodox ecumenical dialogue in Eastern Europe in the 1870s.

GEORGE GASYNA (Ph.D., University of Toronto) was born in Łódź, Poland, and raised there and in Canada. He is Associate Professor in the Department of Slavic Languages and Literatures and the Program in Comparative and World Literature at the University of Illinois, where he also holds affiliate appointments in the Program in Jewish Culture and Society, the European Union Center, and the Russian, East European and Eurasian Center, and coordinates the Polish Studies Program. Professor Gasyna specializes in modern Polish literature, in particular twentieth- and twenty-first-century prose and drama. He also researches and teaches in the fields of continental modernism and the avant-garde, diasporic and migration studies, and Jewish-Polish relations. His articles have appeared in a number of journals, including *Slavic Review, Canadian Slavonic Papers,*

Polish Review, *Russian Literature*, and *Sarmatian Review*, as well as several anthologies on modern Polish writing and comparative literature. His book, *Polish, Hybrid, and Otherwise: Exilic Discourse in Joseph Conrad and Witold Gombrowicz*, was published in 2011 by Continuum/Bloomsbury. A new book project, on modern Polish borderland and provincial writing, titled *A Time for the Province*, is nearing completion.

CHIA YIN HSU, Associate Professor in the Department of History at Portland State University, has published several articles on Russian-Chinese interactions in relation to imperial Russian and early Soviet colonial and railroad policies. Her latest article is "The 'Color' of Money: The Ruble, Competing Currencies, and Conceptions of Citizenship in Manchuria and the Russian Far East, 1890s–1920s," in *Russian Review* (January 2014). She recently co-edited *The Cultural History of Money and Credit: A Global Perspective* and is currently working on a project on imperial Russian visions of urbanization at the Chinese and Russian frontier.

LESLIE PAGE MOCH (Ph.D., University of Michigan, 1979) is Professor of History at Michigan State University. Trained as a historian of France, she is one of the world's foremost historians of European migration. Her *Moving Europeans: Migration in Western Europe since 1650* (Indiana, 1992; rev. ed., 2003) remains a standard work in the field. She also has written *The Pariahs of Yesterday: Breton Migrants in Paris* (Duke University Press, 2012) and co-authored with Lewis Siegelbaum *Broad Is My Native Land: Repertoires and Regimes of Migration in Russia's Twentieth Century* (Cornell University Press, 2014).

HARRIET MURAV received her Ph.D. from Stanford University in comparative literature and is now Professor of Slavic Languages and Literatures and Comparative and World Literature at the University of Illinois at Urbana–Champaign and the editor of *Slavic Review*. She is the author of *Holy Foolishness: Dostoevsky's Novels and the Poetics of Cultural Critique* (Stanford University Press, 1992); *Russia's Legal Fictions* (University of Michigan Press, 1998), which was awarded the MLA 1999 Scaglione Prize for Studies in Slavic Languages and Literatures; *Identity Theft: The Jew in Imperial Russia and the Case of Avraam Uri Kovner* (Stanford University Press, 2003); and *Music from a Speeding Train: Jewish Literature in Post-Revolution Russia* (Stanford University Press, 2011), which was supported by a Guggenheim Fellowship. She is also the co-editor of *Photographing the Jewish Nation: Pictures from S. An-sky's Ethnographic Expedition* (Brandeis University Press, 2009), which was a finalist for the 2009 National Jewish Book Award. She is currently working on a translation of David

Bergelson's 1929 novel *Mides-hadin* (*Judgment*; with Sasha Senderovich), to be released with Northwestern University Press in 2017 and a new book project, *A Strange New World: Untimeliness, Futurity, and David Bergelson*.

JAN MUSEKAMP, Ph.D., is Adjunct Assistant Professor of Eastern European History at the European University Viadrina in Frankfurt (Oder), Germany. He also is a nonresident fellow with International and Area Studies at Washington University in St. Louis. His research interests include Central and Eastern European cultural history in the nineteenth and twentieth centuries, ethnic cleansing in twentieth-century Europe, cultural appropriation in European border regions, economic and cultural changes through the transport and communication innovations, and Central and Eastern European entangled history. His first book, *Zwischen Stettin und Szczecin: Metamorphosen einer Stadt von 1945 bis 2005 [From Stettin to Szczecin: Metamorphoses of a City, 1945–2005]*, (Wiesbaden: Harrassowitz Verlag, 2010), focuses on forced migrations and cultural appropriation in the Polish border city of Szczecin between 1945 and 2005. A second book, *A Cultural History of Transnational Mobility in East Central Europe: How the Royal Prussian Eastern Railroad Connected Paris to St. Petersburg and Kovno to New York*, is nearing completion.

LEWIS H. SIEGELBAUM is the Jack and Margaret Sweet Professor of History at Michigan State University. He has migrated from labor history to the history of consumption and material culture and from working on the Stalin era to the post-Stalin decades of Soviet history. Most recently, he plunged into the history of migration in twentieth-century Russia, and together with Leslie Page Moch wrote *Broad Is My Native Land: Repertoires and Regimes of Migration in Russia's Twentieth Century* (Cornell University Press, 2014). He has published *Stakhanovism and the Politics of Productivity in the USSR* (Cambridge University Press, 1988), *Soviet State and Society between Revolutions* (Cambridge University Press, 1994), and the award-winning *Cars for Comrades: The Life of the Soviet Automobile* (Cornell University Press, 2008; Russian edition, ROSSPEN, 2011). Among his edited volumes are *Stalinism as a Way of Life* (Yale University Press, 2000, co-edited with A. K. Sokolov), *Borders of Socialism* (Palgrave, 2006), and *The Socialist Car* (Cornell University Press, 2011). He is co-founder and editor with Jim von Geldern of the award-winning website Seventeen Moments in Soviet History (http://soviethistory.msu.edu).

KEELY STAUTER-HALSTED is Professor of History and Hejna Family Chair in the History of Poland at the University of Illinois at Chicago. Her teaching and research examine issues of identity, ethnicity, gender, and class in modern Poland. Professor Stauter-Halsted has published dozens of journal articles and book chapters in Polish and English on topics ranging from peasant nationalism to Polish-Jewish relations and gender history. Her first book, *The Nation in the Village: The Genesis of Rural National Identity in Austrian Poland* (Cornell University Press, 2001) was awarded the Orbis Prize for the best book in any aspect of Polish affairs. Her second monograph, *The Devil's Chain: Prostitution and Social Control in Partitioned Poland* was published with Cornell University Press in 2015. She also co-edited *Sexual Deviance and Social Control in Late Imperial Eastern Europe* with Nancy Wingfield in Journal of the History of Sexuality, 2011. Stauter-Halsted is currently researching on Polish return migration in the partitioned period.

NICOLE SVOBODNY is Senior Lecturer in International and Area Studies and Assistant Dean in the College of Arts and Sciences at Washington University in St. Louis. There she curates the Eurasian Studies concentration and teaches courses in Russian and comparative literature. Her research interests include modern Russian literature, life-writing, performance studies, and the interrelation of bodily experience with verbal expression. She co-edited the volume *Under the Sky of My Africa: Pushkin and Blackness* (Northwestern University Press, 2006). Her latest article, "'Tantsovshchik kak pisatel': Vatslav Nizhinskii i telesnost' iazyka," was published in *Novoe literaturnoe obozrenie* (October 2015). Currently she is working on a book-length project that explores Vaslav Nijinsky's engagement with language and literature as well as the treatment of Nijinsky's dancing in modernist literary works.

ANIKA WALKE, Ph.D., is Assistant Professor in the Department of History at Washington University in St. Louis. Anika was educated at the University of Oldenburg, Germany, and the State University of St. Petersburg, Russia, before she completed her doctorate at the University of California–Santa Cruz. Anika's research and teaching interests include World War II and Nazi genocide, migration, nationality policies, and oral history in the (former) Soviet Union and Europe. Her book, *Pioneers and Partisans: An Oral History of Nazi Genocide in Belorussia* (Oxford University Press, 2015), weaves together oral histories, video testimonies, and memoirs to show how the first generation of Soviet Jews experienced the Nazi genocide and how they remember it after the dissolution of the USSR in 1991. An ongoing research project looks at the long aftermath of the Nazi genocide in Belarus.

ADRIAN WANNER is Liberal Arts Research Professor of Slavic and Comparative Literature at the Pennsylvania State University. He is the author of *Baudelaire in Russia* (University Press of Florida, 1996), *Russian Minimalism: From the Prose Poem to the Anti-Story* (Northwestern University Press, 2003), and *Out of Russia: Fictions of a New Translingual Diaspora* (Northwestern University Press, 2011). In addition he has published six editions of Russian, Romanian, and Ukrainian poetry in his German verse translation. His most recent book, published in 2013, is a bilingual Russian-German edition of the poetry of Vladislav Khodasevich.

CHRISTOPHER J. WARD, Ph.D., serves as Professor of History at Clayton State University in metropolitan Atlanta, where he has taught since 2004. In 2010, Ward was named editor-in-chief of the journal *The Soviet and Post-Soviet Review*. Ward received his Ph.D. in Russian and Soviet history from the University of North Carolina at Chapel Hill in 2002. He is the author of a number of publications, most notably *Brezhnev's Folly: The Building of BAM and Late Soviet Socialism*, which was published by the University of Pittsburgh Press in 2009 and was reissued in paperback in 2010. Ward's articles have appeared in the scholarly journals *Global Crime* (United Kingdom), *Acta Slavica Iaponica* (Japan), *Problemy slavianovedeniia* (Russia), and *Canadian Slavonic Papers*.

ANNA WINESTEIN, Ph.D., is a historian of art and theater, independent curator, and cultural entrepreneur. She is Executive Director of the BR Cultural Partnership in Boston and previously served as Creative Director for the Hermitage Museum Foundation. Co-editor and co-author of *The Ballets Russes and the Art of Design* (Monacelli Press, 2009), she has also authored or contributed essays to numerous exhibition catalogs (her most recent essays are in *Dance and Fashion*, Yale University Press and MFIT, 2014; and *Revolutions in Russian Painting*, Bonnefanten Museum Maastricht 2013) and published articles in peer-reviewed journals and publication series. She has curated exhibitions at Sotheby's (Paris) and the Boston Public Library, among others, and consults with museums on film and other programming. She has been a cultural envoy for the US State Department and is a former Fulbright Scholar.

NATHANIEL D. WOOD is Associate Professor of History at the University of Kansas, where he teaches classes in modern European and East Central European history, urban history, and the cultural history of technology. He is the author of *Becoming Metropolitan: Urban Selfhood and the Making of Modern Cracow* (Northern Illinois University Press, 2010) and is presently working on a cultural history of bicycles, automobiles, and airplanes in the Polish lands before World War II.

INDEX

abjection, 287
Académie Colarossi, 143, 146, 151
Académie La Palette, 144
Académie Russe, 142, 158, 160
Académie Vitti, 143, 151
Afternoon of a Faun (Nijinsky choreography), 81–84, 85
Agamben, Giorgio, 293
agency, 6, 22–24, 100, 165, 166, 181, 265, 268
airports, 287
Akhmatova, Anna, 196, 204
Aleichem, Sholem, 272
Alexander II, 235, 236
Alexander III, 58, 159
Allied Forces, 16
All-Union Communist Party, 190
Alma-Ata (Kazakhstan), 198, 200, 204
Alvarado, Gonsalo, 224
ambivalence, 96
"Among Refugees" (Bergelson), 260, 263
Anatolia, 10
antisemitism, 9, 13, 172, 189, 199, 303, 304, 307, 308
Antokol'skii, Mark, 140
Apollon (journal), 147
apparatchiki (bureaucrats), 216
Armenians, 11
Art as Device (Shklovsky), 260, 264–266

artists, 22–23, 25; imperial pension holders, 140; Jewish, 142, 149, 156; post-Impressionists, 143; Russian Artistic Circle (RAC), 139–163; symbolists, 154
Athénée Saint-Germain, 150
Austin, J. L., 83, 104n16
Austria, 174–175
Austro-Hungarian Empire, 6, 9, 11
Auto magazine, 62, 66–68
automobiles, 21–22; chauffeurs, 67–68, 70, 115–116; as competition for railways, 74; limited to elites, 56–57, 66–67; Poland, 55–79; taxi services, 65–66
automobility, 4
automotive clubs, 67–68
avant-garde art, 92
aviation, 70–71
Awiata club and factory, 70

Babi Yar, 197
Baedeker and Murray guidebooks, 41
Baikal-Amur Mainline (BAM), 17, 23, 209–232; bribes, 224–225; failure to achieve internationalism, 227–228; foreigners on mainline, 217–218; propaganda campaign, 210, 212, 214, 220, 227–228; suspicion of foreigners, 226–227
Bakunin, Mikhail, 7, 243

Balkan Wars of 1912–1913, 10
ballet. *See* Nijinsky, Vaslav
Ballets Russes, 80
Balmont, Konstantin, 147, 152
Baltic republics, 16
Baltic Sea, 36
BAM–A Panorama of a Multinational Project, 220–221
BAMers, 210; chaperones, 213, 214; competitions, 214, 215; disenfranchisement, 223; lack of ideological dedication, 213, 215–217; language segregation, 222, 223–224; Soviet travelers abroad, 211–217; Warsaw Pact nations, 220–227. *See also* Baikal-Amur Mainline (BAM)
BAM–nachalo (BAM–The Beginning), 226
BAM Zone, 210, 218
ban, 293–296
bandits, 293–294
banishment, 7, 24
Baranov, I. G., 124–127
Bashkirtseva, Maria, 156
Belgium, 38, 42, 47
belonging, 9, 14, 19, 314, 317
Beniowski, Maurycy, 241
Benjamin, Walter, 261, 265
Benois, Alexandre, 155, 156–157
Benz, Carl Friedrich, 57–58
Bergelson, David, 24, 260–275; background, 262–263; Works: "Blindkeyt" ("Blindness"), 263; *Der toyber* (*The Deaf Man*), 260–261; *Mides-hadin* (*Judgment*), 261, 266, 267–270, 272; *Nokh alemen* (*The End of Everything*), 261; "Onheyb Kislev 1919" ("The Beginning of Kislev 1919"), 263; "Tsvishn emigrantn" ("Among Refugees"), 260, 263, 264
Berg, Nikolai, 247
Bergson, Henri, 261, 271
Berlin, 13, 260–275, 269, 294, 303
bicycle clubs, 68–69
bicycles, 21–22, 55–79; as commodities, 56, 59–60; democratizing force, 60, 61; health concerns, 73–74; international competitions, 71; limited to elites, 72; production, 71–72; velocipede as name for, 58
biopower, 293
Bleuler, Eugen, 92, 95, 96, 106n85
Blok, Alexander, 313
Bloom, Paul, 98
body: as machine, 261, 264–265, 271–273; prosthesis, 261, 265, 288; self-commodification, 269
Bogoliubov, Aleksei, 140, 143, 159
Bogusławski, Józef, 239–241, 246–250, 252–253
Bolsheviks, 91, 96, 262, 266, 272, 312
Borawski, Zygmunt, 68
borders, 2–3; closing, 3; eighteenth century, 6; literary analysis, 82–83; rivers, 17–18; sex trafficking across, 179–180
Borislavskii, N., 113
Borisov-Musatov, Viktor, 154
bourgeois domesticity, 121, 132n11
Brailovskaia, Rimma, 153
Brezhnev, Leonid, 219
Bristow, Edward, 180
broken men, 260
Brückner, Kristian, 221
Bułhakowa, Teresa, 251
bureaucracies, 6, 8–9, 12, 23, 170; BAM and, 212, 216, 218; evacuation and, 190, 196–197
Burt, Ramsay, 99
"But Your German Is Really Good!" (*"Sie können aber gut Deutsch!"*) (Gorelik), 304, 306, 317, 318
By a Thorny Path (*Ciernistym szlakiem*) (Tokarzewski), 250–251

Canadian Pacific steamer company, 173
canals, 38
capitalism, 267, 269
Caro, Leopold, 171
car ownership, 17
Carrière, Eugène, 148
Castro, Fidel, 214, 219
Catherine II, 251
Central Eastern Europe, 1–5, 36–37; as best, 282–289; as deficient, 280–282;

deglobalization, 49–50; facets of migration and mobility, 5–21
Chagall, Marc, 271
Chaplin, Charlie, 271, 272
chauffeurs, 67–68, 70
China, 37. *See also* Manchuria
Chinese: as objects of ethnographic study, 122–128; Russian tourist views of, 128–131
Chinese Eastern Railway (CER), 22, 108–136
Chinese religion, 127–128
Chinese workers, 118, 129–130
Chrapowiecki, Edward, 58
cinema, 261, 262
city, 260–275
city gates, 41
Civilian Evacuation Administration, 190
climate change, 97–98
collective farm *(kolkhoz)*, 192, 201, 202
colonialism, 22, 109–111
communication innovations, 36
Compagnie internationale des wagons-lits (International Sleeping Car Company), 47
Confederacy of Bar (Konfederacja Barska), 241, 251
Confession (Tolstoy), 86–93; dream coda, 87; "Eastern fable," 87–88, 89
connectivity, 25
Connelly, Mark, 176–177
consciousness, 9, 84–85, 98, 265, 267, 292, 313
Constructivism, Russian, 267
contagion of feeling, 93–94
Corbin, Alain, 175
Cormon, Fernand, 143
Cossack settlements, 244
costs of travel, 8–9
Côte d'Azur, 111, 132n23
Croatia, 20–21
Cuba, BAMers and, 213–214, 215, 218–220
Cuban Central Railway, 218
Cuban Comité Nacional de la Unión de Jóvenes Comunistas (UJC), 218–219
Cuban Revolution, 214, 219

cultural essences, dialectics of, 280–282
Curie, Marie, 152
Cvetkovski, Roland, 40
Cyklista magazine, 60, 64, 69, 72–73
Czaplicki, Henryk, 62, 63
Czapliński, Przemysław, 288
Czartoryski, Adam, 240, 241
Czechoslovakia, 16

Daimler, Gottlieb, 58
Daimler advertisements, 63, 75
Danube River, 17–18
Davidenko, Elizaveta, 143, 145–146, 147, 152
The Deaf Man (Der toyber) (Bergelson), 260–261
Dear Misha (Lieber Mischa) (Gorelik), 303, 305
De Dion-Bouton automotive company, 64
defamiliarization/estrangement *(ostranenie)*, 264–265, 271
deglobalization, 50
Deleuze, Gilles, 95–96, 106n79
Demchenko, Maria, 200
Denisov, Vassilii, 154
deportations, 13, 16
desire, education of, 121
Diaghilev, Sergei, 93, 103n11, 106n85, 155
Diary (Dziennik) (Gombrowicz), 279–282
The Diary of Vaslav Nijinsky (Nijinsky), 80–107; dance notation in original manuscript, 82, 86; "Eastern fable" in, 87–88, 89, 96; horizontal and vertical movement, 85–86; St. Moritz walks, 88–93; title and sections, 81, 86, 100, 103n6; Tolstoy's *Confession* and, 86–93; used in psychiatric reports, 100–101
Dix, Otto, 260
Di yidishe velt (The Jewish World) journal, 270–271
Dojczland (Stasiuk), 276–279, 282–289; insight and amnesia, 292–296; literary gastarbajter, 282–289; memory, contested, 289–292. *See also* Stasiuk, Andrzej
Dostoevsky, Fyodor, 237, 246, 248, 250, 251, 252

Druzhba (Friendship) trains, 211–212
Dubiecki, Maryan, 251
Dubson, Vadim, 190
Durov, Sergei, 249

East German Union of Free Youth (FDJ), 212
East Germany, BAMers and, 212–213
eau-forte, 144
École Russe des Hautes Études, 150, 157
Eile, Stanislaw, 239
Einfühlung, 93–94
Eisenstein, Sergei, 200
Eleventh World Festival of Youth and Students, 219
Emancipation of the Serfs (1861), 40
The Empathic Civilization (Rifkin), 98
empathy, 93–94, 98
England, 37
Esquina, José, 219
Esteja (Józefa ze Skórzewskich Kisielnicka), 61
Estonia, 20–21
ethnic discrimination, 10, 16–17
ethnography, 122–128
ethno-territorialists, 10, 16
European Neighborhood Policy, 20
European Union (EU), 20–21, 37, 277–278
evacuation, 23, 188–208; children, 193, 200; departures, 192–196; destinations, 198–202; documents required, 194, 196; elites, 199–200; groups targeted, 191–192; journeys, 196–198; requests, 193–195, *195*; returns, 202–204; Russian-nationality, 199; size of, 190–191, 207n44; sponsors, 193–195, 201
Evacuation Council (Soviet Union), 190, 200, 203
Evreiskoe schastie (Jewish Luck) (film), 272
Eydtkuhnen station (Prussia), 47, 48
Egyns (Our Own) journal, 263

F. A. Brockhaus printing house, 244
Fado (Stasiuk), 276, 278, 299n39
fascism, 267
Federation of Polish Cycling Associations, 71

"Feeling" (*chuvstvo*) (Nijinsky), 81, 85, 86, 89
feelings, 98–99; climate change, 97–98; communication of, 93–94
Festival of Anti-Imperialist Solidarity, Peace and Friendship, 219
Fichtenbaum (Heine), 313
"First Year of the Tenth Five-Year Plan: A Pacesetting Finish" competition, 214
forced labor, 15–16, 18, 217, 286
Forefathers' Eve (Dziady) (Mickiewicz), 239, 286
foreign labor, 15
fossil fuels, 97–98
Foucault, Michel, 96
fourteenth century, 37
France, 7, 17, 35–36, 38–40, 43; telegraphy, 47–48
Freiherr von Herberstein, Sigmund, 39
French Revolution, 7, 10, 38, 40
Freud, Sigmund, 261
Friendship Brigade (International Student Construction Brigade), 223–224
From the recollections of a cyclist (Ze wspomnienia cyklisty) (Prus), 62, 72
Fularki (resort), 111–112

Galicia, 168–169
Galician Automobile Club, 67
Galmakov, Iurii, 212–213
Gara de Nord train station (Bucharest), 285, 286, 289–290
Gastarbeiterliteratur (guest worker literature), 301
Gauguin, Paul, 143
Gawalewicz, Marian, 61
General Government, territory of, 16
generational differences, 25
genocide, 14–16, 19
German Empire, 6
German-Jewish relations, 302
Germany, 43; bicycles, 72; immigrants to, 301; philosemitism, 307; Polish knowledge of, 286–287; Polish migration to, 277–278; Russian immigration to, 301–302, 319n1; stagecoach system, 38. *See also Dojczland* (Stasiuk); Nazis

Germany Abolishes Itself (*Deutschland schafft sich ab*) (Sarrazin), 306
Gieysztor, Jakób, 249
gift, 314; welcoming, 283, 287, 296, 298n116
Giller, Agaton, 239–246, 257n41
globalization, 18, 37, 50
Gogol, Nikolai, 237–238, 103n6
The Gold Rush (Chaplin) (film), 271
Gol'shtein, Aleksandra, 143, 147–148, 149, 155, 157, 158, 160
Golubev, Viktor, 157–158
Gombrowicz, Witold, 279–282, 294
Gorelik, Lena, 302, 303–306, 309, 317, 318
Gorianchikov, Alexander, 238
Gosselin, Emilia, 252
grand tour, 37
Grass, Günther, 316
Great Britain, 43, 48; bicycling, 68, 73–74, 76
Great Patriotic War (World War II), 188–208
Greenblatt, Stephen, 94
Grjasnowa, Olga, 302, 308–311, 317
Grodzki, Stanisław, 64
Groza, Aleksander, 248
Guattari, Felix, 95–96, 106n79
guest worker (*Gastarbeiter*), 15, 282–289, 295–296
Guevara, Ernesto "Che," 214
Gunning, Tom, 271

Hamburg America steamship line (HA-PAG), 172
Hapsburg, House of, 6
Harbin, Manchuria, 109, 112
Havana to to Santiago de Cuba–Central Railway, 215, 218–220
Heine, Heinrich, 313
Herlihy, David, 72
hermeneutics of suspicion, 240
A Hero of Our Time (*Geroi nashego vremeni*) (Lermontov), 237
Herzen, Alexander, 7, 243
Himmelfarb, Jan, 302, 315–316
Hofmeister, Apolin, 247
Holocaust, 14, 16, 198–199, 289, 316
Hopkins, Antony G., 37

horses, 41, 42
Hôtel Lambert, 240, 241
House of the Dead (Dostoevsky), 238, 248, 250, 251, 254 See also *Notes From the House of the Dead*
humanitarian crisis, 2010s, 20
human rights, 10, 13
Hungarian Revolution, 236
Hungary, 13, 16, 18, 84, 213, 214, 215, 235
The Hunger Artist (Kafka), 269

Iakunchikova, Maria, 147
iams (post routes), 39
"I Am the Master of the Project" campaign, 215
Iaremich, Stepan, 152
Iastrebova, Lidiia, 119–122, 128–129
identity, 11, 12, 16, 17, 18, 19, 24, 36, 11,0, 115, 280, 282, 302–318
imagined community, 76, 79n69
immobility, 4, 99–101
Imperial Academy, 140–141, 142
industrialization, 12
information, movement of, 47–48
Injalbert, Jean-Antoine, 148
In Love with St. Petersburg: My Russian Journey (*Verliebt in Sankt Petersburg: Meine russische Reise*) (Gorelik), 305
inns, 41
intelligentsia, 191–192, 193
Intermediate Stations (*Zwischenstationen*) (Vertlib), 307–308
internal migration, 12–13; Soviet Union, 12–13
International Federation of Cycling, 71
international laborers, BAM line, 210, 211
international law, 16
Interpretation of Stars (*Sterndeutung*) (Himmelfarb), 315–316
inter-revolutionary epoch, 235–236
Into Flight: Stories of an exile (*W ucieczce: Opowiadania wygnańca*) (Tokarzewski), 251
intra-European movements, 18–19
Introduction to Non-Fascist Life (Foucault), 96
Iron Curtain, 17, 20

Iskusstvo (Art), 153
Itinerants, 141, 143
Ivan the Terrible, 200
Iwanowski, Eustachy Heleniusz, 246–248
Izvestiia OIMK, 123

Japan, 119, 124, 216, 229n28, 229n29
Jasieńczyk, Marjan, 62
Jews, 7, 9, 13, 269; artists, 142, 149, 156; evacuation, 192, 197–199; Russian, as German writers, 301–320; Soviet evacuees, 192, 193; travel agents, 169, 171, 172; tripartite identity in Germany, 302
Journey of a Prisoner (Podróż więźnia etapami do Syberyi w roku 1854) (Giller), 243–244
Judgment (Mides-hadin) (Bergelson), 261, 266, 267–270, 272
Jurbatov, Vladimir, 152
Juventud Rebelde (Rebellious Youth), 219

Kafka, Franz, 269
Kalinin, Mikhail, 201
Kamieński, Henryk, 244, 257n33, 308
Kaminer, Wladimir, 302–303, 307, 309–310, 316–317, 318
Kanak Attak, 310
Karamzin, Nikolai Mikhailovich, 35–36, 39, 40–41, 48
Kaschuba, Wolfgang, 49
Kharlamov, Aleksei, 158
Khotiantseva, Aleksandra, 153
Kiev Kultur-Lige, 263
Klaczko, Julian, 241
Kniazev, A. D., 222–223
Kniazev, A. N., 117
Kofman, Eleanore, 167
Kolchak, Alexander, 129
Komitet Centralny Narodowy (National Central Committee), 242–243
Komsomol'skaia pravda (Komsomol Truth) train, 222
Komsomol (USSR Young Communist League), 209–210, 211–212
Konarski, Szymon, 236, 244, 247
Königsberg (East Prussia), 46
Korzon, Tadeusz, 251

Kosygin, Aleksei, 196
Kozlovskii, B., 112–113, 130
Kracauer, Siegfried, 265, 267
Krasiński, Zygmunt, 239
Krenz, Egon, 212–213
Krogulec (the sparrow hawk, pseud. Antoni Orłowski), 64
Kruglikova, Elizaveta, 143–145, 145, 147, 151, 154, 157, 159–160
Kruglividenki, 145
Kuibyshev, evacuations, 195–196
Kurjer Warszawski (newspaper), 63, 64
Kuschel-Ausländer (cuddly foreigners), 310

landscape, 114, 132n23
langue, 91
Łasocki, Zygmunt, 172
Last Wish (Letzter Wunsch) (Vertlib), 307
Latin America, 169–170, 218–220
laughter, 261, 271
Law, 293
League of Nations' Commissariat for Refugees, 13–14
The Legal Indeterminacy of a Marriage (Die juristische Unschärfe einer Ehe) (Grjasnowa), 310–311
leisure, regime of access, 110–111
Leningrad, evacuations, 193–194
Lenin, Vladimir, 7
Leopold II, 47
Lermontov, Mikhail, 237, 313
Lerner, Daniel, 94
Letters of a Russian Traveler (Pis'ma russkogo puteshestvennika) (Karamzin), 35–36
Lewin, Moshe, 193
Liaodung Peninsula, 124
Libański, Edmund, 71
Lindig, Dieter, 220
linguistic adulteration, 128–129
Lista Wygnańców Polskich do roku 1860 (Giller), 243
List, Friedrich, 43, 49
Literature and Nationalism in Partitioned Poland (Eile), 239
Liverpool and Manchester Railway, 43
locomotions, 21–22
Lotnik i Automobilista magazine, 66, 69–71

INDEX

Louvre, 146
L Sz, Inż, 64–65
Lubomirski, Stanisław, 70
luftmentsh, 272
luggage regulations, 41

macadamized road (*Chaussee*), 39–41, 44
machine ensemble, 269
magic realism, 315–316
Magnitogorsk (Soviet Union), 12
mail coaches, 38
Maksimov, Sergei, 241, 246
Malczewski, Franciszek, 244, 245
Manchukuo regime, 119
Manchuria, 108–136; Russian concessionary, 109
Manley, Rebecca, 192, 203
manuscript culture, 237–240
maps, 43–45, 44, 45
Marie, Pierre, 150
"Martyre du Prieur Sierocinski" (manuscript), 241
massification, 266–267, 271
mass media, 94
The Mass Ornament (Kracauer), 267
Matveev, Boris, 159
Maybach, Wilhelm, 58
McKeown, Adam, 167
Mechnikov, Il'ia, 150
Mechnikova, Ol'ga, 143, 148
Melikhov, G. V., 118–119, 122, 129
Memoirs from a Sojourn in Siberia, 1860–1861 (*Pamiętniki z pobytu na Syberyi*) (Piotrowski), 240–242
memory, 119–120, 238–239, 243, 245, 249; contested, 289–292; insight and amnesia, 292–296; postmemory, 290, 299n47
mercantilist policies, 38
Meyerhold, Vsevolod, 261
Meyerowicz, John, 180
Mickiewicz, Adam, 239, 286
migration, 21–23; agents, 166, 168–170, 181–182; defined, 2–3; facets of, 5–21; female, trauma of, 173–181; forced, 7; "going to the Saxons," 286; imperial concerns, 167, 170, 186n27; missing persons reports, 174–176; self-abnegation, 277; social anxieties about, 164–165, 168–169; trials, 168–169, 172–173; urban setting and, 263–264; voluntary, 167, 169; Wadowice trial of 1889–1890, 172, 174
migration studies, 3
Migrationshintergrund (migration background), 310
Mikhalkov, Sergei, 200
Mikhoels, Solomon, 272
Milgroym (The Pomegranate) journal, 263
Militärmusik (*Military Music*) (Kaminer), 308
military use of transportation, 12, 39, 43, 74
Miłosz, Czesław, 280
Minority Treaties, 11–12
Mirecki, Aleksander, 248, 252
Mir Iskusstva (World of Art), 144, 147, 152, 153
Mobile Modernity (Presner), 311
mobility: defined, 2–3; developments in nineteenth century, 36–37; displacements, 95–97; facets of, 5–21; immobility, 4, 99–101; physical and psychic, 80–107; power relations, 3–4; psychic, 93–99; railroad networks and, 43; sensory enactment of, 84–85; social, 94; speech and silence, 82, 91; stillness in movement, 81–82; technology and, 262; vertical and horizontal movement, 85–86
mobility studies, 3
Moch, Leslie Page, 1–2
modernity, 49, 57, 76, 111, 302
modernization, 2, 6, 12, 14, 24, 94, 287–288. *See also* technology
Modern Times (Chaplin) (film), 271, 272
Monte Carlo Grand Prix, 76
Montparnasse Circle. *See* Russian Artistic Circle (RAC)
Morgen frayhayt (Morgen Freedom) journal, 263
Morozov, Savva, 158
Moscow: artists and, 144–147, 150–155; evacuees, 203
Moscow Metro, 13
Moscow School of Painting, Sculpture and Architecture (MSPSA), 142, 143
Moscow State Yiddish Theater, 268, 271

Mukonin, Vladimir, 218–219
Muslims, 10, 306
My prehistoric memoirs (*Mój pamiętnik przedhistoryczny*) (Korzon), 251
My White Nights (*Meine weißen Nächte*) (Gorelik), 303–305

Nabokov, Vladimir, 48–49, 280
Nagelmackers, Georges, 47
Napoleon, 39
Napoleonic Wars, 38–39
narrations, 21, 23–25; literary technology, 264–273; speed of, 265–266. See also Polish exiles to Siberia; technology; writers
narrative movement, 85–86
nationalist movements, 6, 7, 11, 171
national trauma, 238, 243, 245–246, 250, 254–255, 280
nation-states, 5, 10–12
Nazis, 14–16, 191, 199, 269, 285–286, 307; genocide, 14, 15, 16; Holocaust, 198–199, 289, 316; memory and, 289–292
New Economic Policy, 121
Nicholas I, 236
Nicholas II, 58, 157
Nijinska, Bronislava, 84
Nijinsky, Romola, 80, 83
Nijinsky, Vaslav, 22, 80–107; *Afternoon of a Faun*, 81–84, 85; dance notation system, 82, 84, 86, 104nn19, 24; displacements and, 95–97; ecology, concern for, 97–98; immobility, 99–101; institutionalization, 100–101; last performance (Suvretta House), 80–82; psychiatric diagnosis, 80–81; *Rite of Spring* (Nijinksy/Stravinsky), 83–84, 92–93, 97; St. Moritz writing, 86–93; stillness in movement, 82–83; vertical and horizontal movement in diary, 85–86; words as part of performance, 82
Nilus, E. Kh., 117–118
nonmigration, 4
Nord-Express, 47, 48–49
North America, 9, 43, 169, 301–302
nostalgia, 286

Notes From the House of the Dead (*Zapiski iz mertvogo doma*) (Dostoevsky), 237–238. See also *House of the Dead*
"Notes of a Madman" ("Zapiski sumasshedshego") (Gogol), 237–238, 103 n6
notes (*zapiski*), 237–238
Novoe Khudozhestvennoe Obshchestvo (New Artistic Society, NAS), 152
Nuremberg, 291, 299n34
Nuremberg Laws, 315

Ojczyzna (travel agency), 171–172
Olympics, 71
Omsk Affair, 241, 253–254, 258n54
On the Road to Babadag (Stasiuk), 276, 278
Opisanie zabajkalskiej krainy w Syberyi (*A description of the Zabaikal'sk region in Siberia*) (Giller), 244
OPOIAZ (*Obshchestvo izucheniia poeticheskogo iazyka*), 262
Orochi hunters, 124, 126
orphans, 193
Ostroumov, B. V., 112, 113
Other, 22, 289, 309–310, 314–315; ban, 293–296; Poles as, 278–279
Other Europe, 276
Ottoman Empire, 6, 7; Balkan Wars, 10

Pale of Settlement, 13
Paris: Montparnasse, 150–151; political émigrés, 143; Russian Artistic Circle (RAC), 13, 139–163; social unrest, 156
Paris Peace Treaty (1919), 11, 16
parole, 91
passports, 8, 12, 172, 294, 298n21
Patrice Lumumba University, 223–224
performance artists, 269
performative, 83, 88, 104nn16, 17
Perhaps Esther (*Vielleicht Esther*) (Petrowskaja), 311–314
Petrowskaja, Katja, 302, 311–315, 317, 318
Petruk, Iurii, 224
Petrushka (Nijinsky), 83
Piotrowski, Rufin, 239–240, 240–242
polaca (prostitute), 169

Poland, 15; bicycles and automobiles, 55–79; class issues, 67–68; dreams dashed or delayed, 68–76; dreams of the future, 57–66; EU accession, 277; Germany and, 276–289; infrastructure, lack of, 57; national trauma, 238, 243, 245–246, 250, 254–255, 280; sense of being behind, 56–57, 62, 63, 66

Poles: forced labor, 15, 18, 217, 286; Germans as hosts, 283; Germany, migration to, 277–278; as Other, 278–279. *See also* sex trafficking

Polish Automobile Club, 66, 67, 70

Polish exiles to Siberia, 235–259; Bogusławski, 239–241, 246–250, 252–253; documentary record, shaping, 253–254; Giller, 239–246, 257n41; locale, 243–245; national trauma, 238, 243, 245–246, 250, 254–255; Piotrowski, 240–242; Tokarzewski, 239–240, 246, 248–253, 257n44. *See also* writers

Polish-German relations, 286

Polish Touring Club, 67

political émigrés, Russian, 143, 149

politically motivated migration, 13

The Politics of the Avant-Garde (Williams), 261

Polska Akademia Umiejętności (Polish Academy of Learning), 247

Popkov, Petr, 196–197

Popov, V., 220

population exchange, 11

population transfer, 16–17

Port Arthur (Manchuria), 124–125

Positivists, 59

postal and carrier networks, 37–38, 40–42

postmemory, 290, 299n47

Potsdam Conference (1945), 16

power relations, 3–4

Presner, Todd Samuel, 302, 311

"primitives," 122–128

Prus, Bolesław, 55, 58–59, 62, 63, 72

Prussian-Russian border, 46

Prussia, stagecoach system, 38, 40–41

psychic mobility, 93–99

psychoanalysis, 95–96

Pugachev, Emelyan, 244

Pullman, George M., 47

Raczyński, Edward, 67

Raczyński, Karol, 67

railroad networks, 6, 8; between Antwerp and Cologne, 42; Chinese Eastern Railway (CER), 108–136; Chinese workers, 118; emergence of, 42–49; employees, 116–122; evacuations, 196–197; gauges, 45–46; Liverpool and Manchester Railway, 43; maps, 43–45, 44, 45; between Paris, Berlin, and St. Petersburg, 46–47; Siberian Railroad, 8, 108; St. Petersburg–Moscow, 45–46; Transsiberian Railroad, 47; between Warsaw and Vienna, 45, 46; World War I and, 12. *See also* Baikal-Amur Mainline (BAM); Havana to Santiago de Cuba–Central Railway; resorts (*kurorty*)

railroad stations, as city gates, 41

railway journey, 131; as metaphor, 302, 307–308, 311

railway workers, Soviet, 23, 209–232

Rebroff, Ivan, 303

"Recollections of a *Sybirak*: Memoirs of Józef Bogusławski" ("Wspomnienia Sybiraka: Pamiętniki Józefa Bogusławskiego"), 249, 250, 252

refugees, 10–11; crisis of 1930s, 14; Russian émigré-refugees, 118, 129; Russians in North Manchuria, 109, 118, 129. *See also* evacuation

regimes of migration, 189

regionalization, 25

relationships, 4, 5

relay stations, 38–39

Remembrances of bygone years (Wspomnienia polskich czasów dawnych i późniejszych) (Iwanowski), 247–248

remittances, 9–10

Renaissance, 37

Renaissance Self-Fashioning (Greenblatt), 94

Renier, Anicety, 247

repertoires of migration, 189
residential mobility, 3
resorts (*kurorty*), 108–136; appearance, location, and activities, 111–116; Chalantun, library at, 109; cultural life, 118–119, 120, 133n36; hunting, 115–116; "indigenous" primitive, 122–128; Japanese-run, 110; memoirists, 112–113, 124–128; nature and beauty, European norms, 113–116; photographic images, 111–112, 114; "rest homes" (*doma otdykha*), 111; restaurants, 117; Russian concessionary, 109; South Manchuria Railway, 110, 112; for workers, 110–111, 117; *zheleznodorozhniki* (railway workers), 116–122. *See also* railroad networks
Revolution of 1905, 161
Revolutionaries, 139, 149, 161, 235, 246, 262
Ricœur, Paul, 239
Rifkin, Jeremy, 98
Rilke, Rainer Maria, 313
Rite of Spring (Nijinksy/Stravinsky), 83–84, 92–93, 97
road conditions, 38–39, 72, 75–76
Röhr, Jan, 247
Rostocki, Aleksander, 64
Roux-Champion, Victor Joseph, 144
Rubezh (Borderlands) magazine, 114–116, 125, 126
Runei, Anni, 115
Russendisko (Kaminer), 302–303, 308, 317
Russian Artistic Circle (RAC), 139–163; charter document, 148–149, 155; context, 140–142; downturn, 156–160; location, 150–151; membership, 155–156; Moscow branch, 152–153; objectives and structure, 148–150; programs, 151–155; ringleaders, 142–148; St. Petersburg outpost, 146, 152
The Russian Australian (Iastrebova), 119–122, 128–129
Russian Civil War, 96, 109, 129, 262, 263
The Russian Debutante's Handbook (Shteyngart), 301–302
Russian Disco (*Russendisko*) (Kaminer), 302, 303, 308

Russian Emigration in China (Melikhov), 118–119
Russian émigrés in Manchuria. *See* resorts (*kurorty*)
Russian Empire, 6–7; Emancipation of the Serfs (1861), 40; events of 1905–1906, 142, 156–157; inland migration, 11; internal expansion, 7–8; October 1905 Manifesto, 157; postal systems, 39; railroads, 43–45; revolution of 1917, 12, 13; stagecoach systems, 39–40. *See also* Soviet Union
A Russian Is Someone Who Loves Birch Trees (*Der Russe ist einer, der Birken liebt*) (Grjasnowa), 308–309
Russianness: hierarchy of, 119, 129–130; nativization, 128–129
Russian Orthodox Church, 119
Russian Revolution (1917), 11, 12, 13, 22, 96, 109, 111, 142, 219, 261, 262, 264
Russian Soviet Federative Socialist Republic (RSFSR), 204
Russian State Archive of Social-Political History (RGASPI), 210
Ryback, Issachar Ber, 263, 269

Sabashnikova, Margarita, 147, 160
Salon d'Automne, 155
Salon du Champs de Mars, 154
Sandoz, Maurice, 81
Sarrazin, Thilo, 306
Sattelzeit (saddle time), 37
Sawicz, Franciszek, 247–248
Schenk, Benjamin, 41
Schivelbusch, Wolfgang, 50, 130, 269
schizophrenia, 81, 92, 95–96
Schizophrenia and Capitalism: The Anti-Oedipus (Deleuze and Guattari), 95–96, 106n79
Schlögel, Karl, 48
Ściegienny, Piotr, 236
Scriabin, Aleksander, 152
scriptible text (Barthes), 102
Seifert, Heiner, 220
self-abnegation, 277, 285
Self and Other, 49
self-marginalization, 277, 282, 285

self-Orientalization, 279
self-othering, 293–296
Sentimental Journey (Shklovsky), 262, 263–266
settler migrants, 17
seventeenth century, 39
Seven years of penal servitude (*Siedem lat Katorgi: Pamiętniki Szymona Tokarzewskiego 1846–1857*) (Tokarzewski), 246, 250–254
Severnaia pravda (Northern Truth), 221
sex trafficking, 23, 164–187; captivity narratives, 164–166; domestic prostitution and, 179–180; individual agency, 180–181; Lwów trial, Galicia, 168–169; migration fever and abuses, 169–173; migration literature, 165–167; moral panic, 164–165, 168–169; professional prostitutes, 175, 179–181; volunteerism and false promises, 177–179; wayward daughter stories, 175–177
Shaliapin, Fyodor, 152
Shcherbinin, Vladimir, 215–216
Shchukin, Ivan, 143, 157–158
Shevchenko, Aleksandr, 153
Shklovsky, Viktor, 24, 260–275; background, 262; Works: *Art as Device*, 260, 264–266; *Sentimental Journey*, 262, 263–266; *Theory of Prose*, 265; *Third Factory*, 272–273
Shteingol'ts, Abram Zakharovich, 201–202, 204
Shteyngart, Gary, 301–302
Siberia, 7, 191; BAMers in, 224; Nerchinsk region, 244, 251; Omsk prison, 241, 246, 248, 250; penal labor (*katorga*), 246; Polish exiles, 235–259; Zabaikal'sk region, 244–245
Siberian memoir ("Sybirski pamiętnik Józefa Bogusławskiego"), 246, 253
"Siberian mythopoesis," 239
Siberian Railroad, 8, 108
Sienkiewicz, Henryk, 60, 62, 71
Sierociński, Jan, 241, 242, 244–246, 248
Sino-Soviet Treaty, 118
sixteenth century, 37, 39
sleeping cars, 47

Ślewiński, Władysław, 143
Śliwowska, Wiktoria, 252
Slovaks, 10
social geography, 192
socialism, 17–18; BAMers and, 210–211, 218, 228; technology and, 261, 271–272
Socialist Revolutionaries, 262, 266
social mobility, 3, 94, 177–178
Société des Artistes Décorateurs, 154
Société Nationale des Beaux Arts, 154
Society for the Study of Manchuria, 122–124
Society of Itinerant Exhibitions, 141, 143
Society of Russian Artists in Paris (SRAP), 140, 150–151, 153, 155–159
Sokal, Emil, 55
sound qualities, 269–270
South Manchuria Railway (SMR), 110, 112, 124
sovereignty, 7, 10, 293
Soviet Union: educational institutions, 191–192; evacuation as migration, 188–208; evacuation of workers, 14; "fraternal circle of nations," 210–211, 214, 216, 218, 227–228; German invasion, 190; internal migration, 12–13; regimes of migration, 189; urban centers, migration to, 12. See also Russian Empire
space and time, conceptions of, 3, 37–42, 60–61
Special Administrative Region of the Three Eastern Provinces (SAR), 116
The Special Memory of Rosa Masur (*Das besondere Gedächtnis der Rosa Masur*) (Vertlib), 307
speed, 265–266
speed, age of, 56–57, 65, 76
Sport magazine, 69
stagecoach system, 36, 38–39; luggage regulations, 41; railroad networks and, 44–45
Stalin, Joseph, 191
Starley, John Kemp, 58
Stasiuk, Andrzej, 24, 276–300; as literary gastarbajter, 282–289, 295–296; self-marginalization, 278–279, 282; travel works, 278–279; as useful to

Stasiuk, Andrzej (*continued*)
  Germans, 283–284. See also *Dojczland* (Stasiuk)
State Armament Factory (Poland), 71
statelessness, 13–14, 118, 129
steam, age of, 41, 46
steamboats, 36, 47; sex trafficking and, 169, 172
Stoler, Ann, 121
stories, 312–313
St. Petersburg, 8, 36, 145–146, 152-153, 160, 262, 304–308
St. Petersburg–Moscow railroad, 45–46
Stravinsky, Igor, 81
Student Aviation Union, 71
students, movement of, 37
subalternity, 279, 289, 317
Sudbinin, Serafim, 158
Sue, Eugène, 252
Sushchevich, Valentin, 212, 214, 215, 218, 226–227
Świętochowski, Aleksander, 60–61
Sybiracy. See Polish exiles to Siberia
Szofer Polski (Polish chauffer) magazine, 68
Szokalski, Ksawery, 244–246, 248

Tales of Galicia (Stasiuk), 276
Tanaka, Kakuei, 216
Tarczyński, Jan, 64
Taskina, Elena, 127–128, 129
taxi services, 65–66
technology, 3; action by remote control, 267–268; body and, 260–275; literary, 264–273; prosthesis, 261, 265, 288; sound qualities, 269–270; speed, 265–266; visions of transportation and communication, 103. *See also* modernization
telegraphy, 47–48
Third Factory (Shklovsky), 272–273
The Three Sisters (Chekhov), 309
Tiller Girls, 267
time, 55, 272
timetables, 41
The Tin Drum (Grass), 316
Tokarzewski, Halina, 250–253, 254
Tokarzewski, Szymon, 239–240, 246, 248–253, 257n44
Tolstoy, Leo, 86–93; *Confession*, 86–93; *What Is Art?*, 93, 102; *Wise Thoughts for Every Day*, 101–102
Tomina, Tatiana, 220
trade networks, 20–21
trance, 101
transcontinental travel, 47
translingual Russophone émigrés, 302
transport revolution, 8, 21, 46
Transsiberian Railroad, 47
travel accounts, 35
travel times, 38, 40, 44, 47
Trynkowski, Jan, 250–251
Tseitlin, Abram, 192, 197, 204
Tsharni, Daniel, 261, 271, 272
Turgenev, Ivan, 140
Turkish-German literature, 301
Turks, 309–310
Tuszyński, Bogdan, 69, 71, 72–74
Tyszkiewicz, Stefan, 76

Uffelmann, Dirk, 279, 310
Ukraine, 19, 20
um/razum split, 90
Union des Femmes Peintres et Sculpteurs (Union for Women Painters and Sculptors), 142
Union of BAM Transport Workers, 215, 216
United Nations High Commissioner for Refugees (UNHCR), 13
United States, 8–9, 294
Urusov, Lev P., 150
US Holocaust Museum, 190
USSR Council of People's Commissars, 190
USSR Ministry of Transport Construction, 210

vacation destinations, French, 22
Verbitskii, Iurii, 213–214
Vertlib, Vladimir, 302, 306–308, 317, 318
Vesy (The Scales) magazine, 146, 147
veterans, 260
Vitiaz' (Champion) detachment, 222–223

Vologodskii, P. V., 129
Voloshin, Maksimilian, 144, 145, 146–147, 153, 160
Vorzeigeausländer (foreigner for show), 306
Vostochno-Sibirskaia Pravda (East Siberian Truth), 220

walking as performance, 83–85
The Wandering Jew (Le Juif errant) (Sue), 252
wanderlust, 46
Warsaw Pact nations, BAMers, 220–227
Warsaw Society of Cyclists, 58, 67, 69
Warthegau, 16
Wedding in Jerusalem (Hochzeit in Jerusalem) (Gorelik), 304, 305
Wenzlhuemer, Roland, 48
Westwood, John, 45–46
What Is Art? (Tolstoy), 93, 102
Whistler, George Washington, 45–46
whites, Russian, 109–110
Williams, Raymond, 261
winters, impact on travel, 36
Wise Thoughts for Every Day (Tolstoy), 101–102
women: artists, 22–23, 142–148, 155–156; bicyclists, 72–73; German immigrant authors, 303–306, 308–315; migration to North America, 9; shifting roles, 164–165; social mobility, 177–179; Soviet evacuation of, 191. *See also* sex trafficking

World War I, 10–12, 49–50, 80, 143; technology, 261
World War II, 12, 14–15, 17, 23, 311; memory and, 289–290
writers, 24–25; censorship and, 238–239; hybrid textual culture, 237; nineteenth-century manuscript culture, 237–240; Polish exiles, 235–259; Russian-Jewish-American immigrant fiction, 301–302; second language acquisition, 317–318. *See also* Polish exiles to Siberia
writing: mobility and, 81–107; performative, 83, 88, 104nn16, 17
Wydawnictwo Czarne publishing house, 283
Wysocki, Piotr, 241, 242, 244–246

Yiddish modernist culture, 262–263
Yugoslavia, 17, 20

Zaichek, Vladek, 220–221
Zapiski N. V. Berga o pol'skikh zagovorakh i vosstaniiakh, 1831–1862 (Berg), 247
zheleznodorozhniki (railway workers), 116–122
Zhukov, Nikolai Nikolaevich, 129
Żmichowska, Narcyza, 252
Zola, Émile, 61–62
Zolotoe Runo (The Golden Fleece) journal, 147
Zoo, or Letters Not about Love (Shklovsky), 260
Zvezdnyi (Starlit) trains, 211–212
Zweig, Stefan, 14

www.ingramcontent.com/pod-product-compliance
Lightning Source LLC
Chambersburg PA
CBHW070232240426
43673CB00044B/1767